ISBN 0692573674
EAN 978-0692573679 (q4m LLC)

©2015 Jeffry A. Borror / q4m LLC

Published by q4m LLC
6 Lounsbery Rd. Bedford Corners, New York, 10549, USA

The author and publisher of this book have used their best efforts in preparing this book, including development, research and testing of the examples given herein. The author and publisher make no warranty of any kind, expressed or implied with regard to the documentation or programs contained in this book.

2015 Printed in the United States of America

Cover Image: Hurricane Julio approaching Hawaii in 2014 taken by NASA from the international Space Station. Julio wisely steered clear of Pele.

q FOR MORTALS
VERSION 3

AN INTRODUCTION TO Q PROGRAMMING

Jeffry A. Borror
q4m LLC

Preface

This text represents a complete rewrite of *Q for Mortals*. Although the Table of Contents may look familiar, very little of the original text survived. This version targets all the features of q3.2, as well as correcting both errors of omission and commission in the original. All code snippets have been copied from the q3.2 console but they should work unchanged in q3.3. Please send corrections, additions and constructive suggestions to q4mortals@gmail.com.

A significant improvement in this version is that the author was learning q while writing the original, but he actually knows some q now. One thing that hasn't changed is the author's philosophy: You can only be young once but you can be immature your entire life.

Numerous people have been instrumental in shepherding this to print. First and foremost, the folks at First Derivatives and Kx. Of course, there would be no q gods or mortals without Arthur Whitney's brilliant invention of q and kdb+. Janet Lustgarten has been supportive of the effort from day one. Abby Gruen served as the midwife during the book's birth. Charles Skelton kept me honest. Simon Garland patiently answered my innumerable naive q questions. Brian Conlon and Victoria Shanks invited me to announce the book at Kx meetups.

Many colleagues suffered through early drafts of the text. My go-to proofreaders were Jose Cambronero, Kevin Ching, Simon Garland, Fermin Reig and Mike Rosenberg. They persevered through my horrendous typing and Word's inability to spell check the document—invariably insisting it was in French—over countless drafts. They also made valuable suggestions regarding content and presentation. To the others who are unnamed I am nonetheless grateful. All remaining errors are mine alone.

Thanks to Omar for patience and support as I spent weekends and vacations tethered to my MacBook. And thanks to Nuba and Devi for providing necessary distractions.

Table of Contents

xiv

0   Overview

0.0 The Evolution of Q

Arthur Whitney developed the q programming language and its database kdb+. Released by Kx Systems, Inc. in 2003, the primary design objectives of q are expressiveness, speed and efficiency. In these, it is beyond compare. The design tradeoff is a terseness that can be disconcerting to programmers coming from verbose traditional database programming environments—e.g., C++, Java, C# or Python—and a relational DBMS. Whereas the q programming gods revel in programs resembling an ASCII core dump, this manual is for the rest of us.

Q evolved from APL (A Programming Language), which was first invented as a mathematical notation by Kenneth Iverson at Harvard University in the 1950's. APL was introduced in the 1960s by IBM as a vector programming language, meaning that it processes a list of numbers in a single operation. It was successful in finance and other industries that required heavy number crunching.

The mitochondrial DNA of q traces from APL to A to A+ and to k. All were well suited to performing complex calculations quickly on vectors. What's new in q/kdb+ is that it processes large volumes of time series data very efficiently in the relational paradigm. Its syntax allows "select" expressions that are similar to SQL 92, and its collection of built-in functions provides a complete and powerful stored procedure language.

There is also some LISP in q's genes: the fundamental data construct of q is a list. Although the notation and terminology are different, symbols are drawn from their counterparts in Scheme.

The APL lineage of q also shows the influence of functional programming. In his 1977 Turing award lecture that introduced purely functional programming, Backus acknowledged inspiration from APL. While q is not purely functional, it is strongly functional in that even its basic data structures, list and dictionary, are viewed as mathematical mappings.

0.1 Philosophy

A proficient q developer thinks differently than in conventional programming environments such as C++, Java, C# or Python, henceforth referred to as "traditional programming." In order to get you into the correct mindset, we summarize some of the potential discontinuities for the q newbie—henceforth known as qbie.

Recall some of the data-related issues in traditional database programming:

In-memory representation—e.g., collections of objects—must be mapped to a different representation—i.e., tables—for persistence. It takes considerable effort to get the object-relational correspondence correct.

Objects must be mapped to another representation for transport, usually some binary or XML form that flattens reference chains.

Data manipulation—e.g., selection, grouping and aggregation—on large data sets is best done in stored procedures on the database server. Demanding numeric calculations are best done apart from the database on an application server.

Data transformation for GUI display is best done in a separate layer—e.g., to HTML5 and JavaScript in a browser.

Much of traditional programming design is spent getting the various representations correct, requiring many lines of code to marshal resources and synchronize the different representations. These are remarkably simple in q/kdb+.

Interpreted: Q is interpreted, not compiled. During execution, data and functions live in an in-memory workspace. Iterations of the development cycle tend to be quick because all run-time information needed to test and debug is immediately available in the workspace. Q programs are stored and executed as simple text files called scripts. The interpreter's (eval) and (parse) routines are exposed so that you can dynamically generate code in a controlled manner.

Types: Q is a dynamically typed language, in which type checking is mostly unobtrusive. Each variable has the type of its currently assigned value and type promotion is automatic for most numeric operations. Types are checked on operations to homogenous lists.

Evaluation Order: While q is entered left-to-right, expressions are evaluated right-to-left or, as the q gods prefer, left of right—meaning that a function is applied to the argument on its right. There is no operator precedence and function application can be written without brackets. Punctuation noise is significantly reduced.

Null and Infinity Values: In classical SQL, the value NULL represents missing data for a field of any type and takes no storage space. In q null values are typed and take the same space as non-nulls.   Numeric types also have infinity values. Infinite and null values can participate in arithmetic and other operations with (mostly) predictable results.

Integrated I/O: I/O is done through function handles that act as windows to the outside world. Once such a handle is initialized, passing a value to the handle is a write.

Table Oriented: Give up objects, ye who enter here. In contrast to traditional languages, you'll find no classes, objects, inheritance and virtual methods in q. Instead, q has tables as first class entities. The lack of objects is not as severe as might first appear. Objects are essentially glorified records (i.e., entities with named fields), which are modeled by q dictionaries. A table can be viewed as a list of record dictionaries.

Ordered Lists: Because classical SQL is the algebra of sets—which are unordered with no duplicates—row order and column order are not defined, making time series processing cumbersome and slow. In q, data structures are based on ordered lists, so time series maintain the order in which they are created. Moreover, simple lists occupy contiguous storage, so processing big data is fast. Very fast.

Column Oriented: SQL tables are organized as rows distributed across storage and operations apply to fields within a row. Q tables are column lists in contiguous storage and operations apply on entire columns.

In Memory Database: One can think of kdb+ as an in-memory database with persistent backing. Since data manipulation is performed with q, there is no separate stored procedure language. In fact, kdb+ comprises serialized q column lists written to the file system and then mapped into memory.

0.2 Mathematics Refresher

In order to understand q, it is important to have a clear grasp of the basic concepts and terminology of mathematical functions. In fact, the basic constructs of q can all be interpreted as function mappings. The following refresher is intended to help those who are rusty with mathematics.

0.2.1 Variables

In mathematics, a variable represents an unknown whose potential values can be drawn from a specified domain. The power of the concept is that a property or formula that can be demonstrated to hold for a variable is then known to hold for every particular value of its domain.

A variable has a symbolic representation—i.e., a name. The names of variables occur in syntactically well-formed expressions. In such a context, a variable is given meaning by substitution—i.e., all occurrences of the variable are replaced by a specific value. Once substitution is performed, the variable no longer is an unknown; it has the substituted value from that point onward. In the colloquial, a variable is substituted once in its lifetime.

Imperative programming languages, including q, abuse the concept of a variable. They use the term "variable" to mean a name associated with storage that can hold a value of a specific domain. This should be called an "assignable". The act of associating a name and a value, called *assignment*, is achieved by placing the value into the storage referenced by the name. Assignment is **not** substitution: the assignment can subsequently be changed and the variable will then have **that** value. Shared assignable variables are the source of great evil in concurrent and distributed computing.

0.2.2 Functions

In mathematics, a function associates a unique output value to each input value. The collection of all input values is the domain of the function and the collection from which the output values are chosen is the codomain (or range). A function is also called a map (or mapping) from its domain to its codomain.

The output value that a function f associates to an input value x is read "f of x" or "f at x" or "f on x" More verbosely, we apply (or evaluate) f at an argument to obtain the corresponding result. In mathematics and many programming languages, the output value of a function is represented with the function name to the left of its argument(s), which are enclosed in matched parentheses or brackets. Some functions can take multiple inputs, which are separated by commas or semicolons.

There are two basic ways to define a function: an algorithm or a graph. An algorithm is a sequence of operations on the input value(s) to arrive at the corresponding output value. For example, we define the squaring function, over the domain and codomain of real numbers, to assign as output value the input value times itself. Alternatively, you can define a function by explicitly listing its input-output associations. The collection of associated input-output pairs is the graph of the function.

As you will no doubt recall from many bucolic hours in high-school math class, a function defined by algorithm can be converted to a graph by feeding in input values, cranking out the associated outputs, and collecting the pairs into a table. In general, there is no explicit formula to calculate the values for an arbitrary input-output graph. If it is possible to define a function via a formula, this is usually the preferred way to specify it since it is compact, but there is no guarantee that the formula will be easy or quick to compute.

Here are the two forms for the squaring function over the domain of natural numbers 0 through 3, as you might recall them from school.

$f(x) = x^2$

I	O
0	0
1	1
2	4
3	9

When graphing a function, we normally think of the I/O table as a list of *(x,y)* pairs in the Cartesian plane.

```
(0, 0)
(1, 1)
(2, 4)
 ...
```

Alternately, we can view this as a pair of columns having positional correspondence.

```
0 |-> 0
1 |-> 1
2 |-> 4

  ...
```

This perspective will prove useful.

The number of inputs to a function is called its valence. Lower valences have their own terminology. A function of valence 1 (i.e., defined by a formula that has one parameter) is said to be monadic. For example, neg(x) takes a number and returns the result of reversing the sign. A function of valence 2 (i.e., two parameters) is said to be dyadic. For example, sum(x, y) takes two numbers and adds them to get the result. A function with no parameters is niladic. For example, a constant function with no parameters that returns 42.

Given functions *f* and *g* for which the codomain of *g* is the domain of *f*, the *composite*, denoted *f·g*, is the function obtained by chaining the output of *g* into *f*. That is, the composite assigns to an input *x* the output value *f(g(x))*. Observe the usual mathematical convention in which the order of the functions in the composite matches their order in the nested evaluation.

Pictorially, we can see that the composite chains the output of *g* into the input of *f*,

```
      g        f
x |-> g(x)|-> f(g(x))
```

The domain of the composite is the domain of *g* and its codomain is the codomain of *f*.

> **Convention**: In the body of this document, we shall use the term *map*, or *mapping*, as shorthand for "mathematical function" and will mean a q function when we write "function" without a modifier.

0.2.3 Natural Numbers

The natural numbers are the basis of computing. It is instructive to derive the natural numbers from the primitive notion of counting.

- Start with no items.
- For any number of counted items, we can count one more, called the *successor* of that number

We all did this on our fingers as children.

Mathematicians prefer symbols.

- Start with no items, written 0.
- For any number of counted items *n* we can count one more, called the *successor* of the number and written *s(n)*

Thus the natural numbers are built by iteration of counting "one more."

    0   s(n)   s(s(n))   s(s(s(n))) ...

Writing all those successors can be cumbersome so we give them symbolic names.

    0   1   2   3   ...

How do we guarantee that these are the **only** things in our collection? Without such assurance, a forger could add spurious items such as infinity or -1 and pass off the forged collection as the natural numbers.

0.2.4 Mathematical Induction and Recursion

The *principle of mathematical induction* says that the natural numbers comprise the minimal collection satisfying the following rules.

- The collection contains 0
- Whenever *n* is in the collection so is *s(n)*

For those who care, the formal expression of minimality is that given **any** collection satisfying these two properties, there is a unique map from our collection to that collection. The minimality requirement provides the guarantee that any collection satisfying these rules is essentially the same as our naturals—no more, no less.

Perhaps you are more familiar with the following equivalent way of stating the principle of mathematical induction: to prove that a property holds for all natural numbers, show that the collection of numbers for which it holds satisfies the above two rules.

Let's take stock. As defined above, a natural number has one of two forms:

- It is 0
- Or it is s(n) where n is a natural number previously defined.

Thus to define anything on all natural numbers, we must:

- Define it on 0
- For any natural number n on which it is defined, define it on s(n)

This is *inductive* definition. To define a function *f* on the natural numbers, we follow this prescription.

- Define the result of *f* at 0
- Assuming *f* is defined on a natural number n, define it on s(n)

An example of such a function is right in front of us: the successor s.

- s on 0 is s(0)
- s on n is s(n)

Now we look at a special case of this general inductive style of function definition with an added requirement (in bold).

- Define the value of *f* at 0
- Assuming *f* is defined on a natural number n, define it on s(n) **in terms of its value on n**.

A function defined in this manner is *recursive*. At first glance it seems that recursive definition might seriously limit the functions that we can define, but that is not the case.

0.2.5 Addition

What is addition? The key insight is that adding is merely counting "one mores"—i.e., counting applications of the successor *s*. Expressed inductively,

- Adding 0 applies *s* no times—i.e., returns the original number
- Provided we know how to add *n*, adding *s(n)* is one more application *of s*

Let's make addition so described into a recursive function. For an arbitrary natural number *m*, we define a recursive function *add_to_m(_)* that counts applications of the successor to *m*.

- *add_to_m* on 0 is *m*—i.e., apply *s* no times
- *add_to_m* on s(n) is s(*add_to_m(n)*)—i.e., apply *s* once more

Once you experience the Zen, you will see that we can **define** the customary notation for addition using *add_to_m*.

$$m+n \overset{\text{def}}{=} \text{add\_to\_m}(n)$$

It is an instructive exercise to prove the usual properties of addition. For example, show commutativity—which is not immediately obvious.

$$n+m \overset{?}{=} m+n$$

The proof uses mathematical induction (of course).

0.2.6 Recursion Restated

As a special case of addition, we observe that $n + 1$ is $s(n)$. Now we can restate the notion of recursive function definition in the more familiar form.

- Define f for the base case 0
- Express $f(n+1)$ in terms of $f(n)$

It is an interesting exercise left to the reader to prove that this is equivalent to the seemingly more powerful form:

- Define f for the base case 0
- Express $f(n+1)$ in terms of $f(0)$, …, $f(n)$

This is the form of recursive definition we shall assume in following chapters. We note that the second portion of this prescription—i.e., the inductive step—gives recursive functions their identifying characteristic. For a non-base input value, the function output involves applications of itself on "lesser" values. Consequently, evaluation involves unwrapping a nested series of such applications until the base case is reached.

0.2.7 Multiplication

Having defined addition recursively as counting how many times to apply the successor, we can do the same thing by counting how many times to apply addition. This is multiplication. In words,

- Multiplying by 0 performs no additions
- Provided we know how to multiply by n, multiplying by $s(n)$ is one more addition of n

We translate this into a recursive function *times_m*.

- *times_m* on 0 is the identity for addition-i.e., 0
- *times_m* on $n+1$ is $n+times\_m(n)$

Incidentally, the fact that multiplication counts how many times to add is why we call multiplication "times" in English and is how the "times" tables we all memorized in elementary school are derived. Again we **define** the customary notation for multiplication using *times_m*.

```
       def
  m*n  = times_m(n)
```

0.2.8 Exponentiation

Having defined multiplication recursively as counting how many times to apply addition, we repeat the same technique to define exponentiation. Namely, exponentiation counts how many times to apply multiplication. In words,

- Raising to the power 0 multiplies no times
- If we know how to raise to the power n, then raising to the power $s(n)$ is one more multiplication

We define the recursive function *m_power_of* as follows.

- *m_power_of* on 0 is the identity for multiplication—i.e., 1
- *m_power_of* on $n+1$ is *m*m_power_of(n)*

Again we **define** the customary notation in terms of the recursive *m_power_of*.

```
       def
  m^n  = m_power_of(n)
```

In summary, we have defined basic arithmetic using only recursion, 0 and "one more." The economy of induction is impressive.

0.2.9 Lists

Lists can also be defined inductively, starting with the empty list and the notion of adding one item to the list.

- The empty list, written (), is the list with no items
- Given a list L of items of some domain together with a value x of that domain, we obtain a new list by appending the value x to the end of the list, written L,x

The list constructed by successively appending $x_1, x_2, ..., x_n$ to the empty list is written

$$(x_1; x_2; ...; x_n)$$

Since lists are inductively defined, operations on lists can be defined recursively. For example, the *count* (i.e., length) of a list is defined as follows.

- The count of the empty list () is 0
- Given a list L of count n and an atom x, the count of L,x is 1+count L, which is 1+n

As an exercise you can extend the notion of appending a single value to appending one list to another and then prove—inductively of course—that for two lists L and M,

count(L,M) = count(L) + count(M)

0.2.10 Rationals and Reals

In everyday usage of mathematics, we implicitly identify things that aren't actually the same. Most common is identifying a natural number—e.g. 42—as a rational number or as a real number. But a natural number isn't actually a real number; it just plays one on TV.

Indeed, we have seen that natural numbers are obtained by counting "one more" starting from 0. Ignoring signs for the moment, a rational number is an equivalence class of formal quotients *a/b* of naturals, In plain speak, *a/b* and *c/d* are considered the same just when *ad = bc*. So 2/1 and 4/2 and 6/3, etc. are all considered to be the same. The naturals have a faithful embedding into the rationals in which *n* is mapped to *n*/1. This allows us to identify *n* with (the class of rationals equivalent to) *n*/1, but they are clearly different mathematical entities.

Similarly, a real number is (in the formulation most of us use) an infinite decimal—i.e., an infinite sequence of natural numbers representing place values in powers of 10. Long division converts a rational to its repeating decimal expansion, so there is an embedding of rationals into the reals, but *a/b* is manifestly **not** an infinite decimal.

The identification of naturals and rationals as reals is normally done without thinking. In fact, some argue vehemently that a natural number **is** a real number. It is not but it can be identified with one.

Another interesting fact of programming life is that normal data types can only represent an insignificant set of real numbers. Typically reals are represented by single or double precision floating point values.

12

Since these are limited to at most 16 decimal digits, they are clearly rationals, and a pretty limited set of rationals at that. Even "unlimited" decimal values are still rational, as any computer has finite storage. The way to represent a real properly is with a lazy sequence that presents digits "on demand."

The moral of the story is that we can normally go about our programming day without worrying about these distinctions. But there are situations where they matter.

1   Q Shock and Awe

The purpose of this chapter is to provide a whirlwind tour of some highpoints of q. We don't expect everyone to follow everything the first time through but we do expect that you will be impressed by the power and economy of q. The examples here should motivate careful reading of the following chapters. Once you complete the main text, come back to this chapter and you'll breeze through it.

1.1 Starting q

Your installation of q should have placed the q executable in $HOME/q (or $QHOME) on Unix-based systems, or in the q directory on the c: drive on Windows.

For Windows, start a q session by typing q on the command line; for Linux-based systems use rlwrap q so that you will have command line recall. You should see a new q session with the Kx Systems copyright notice followed by the q prompt indicated by a leading q) on the command line. This is the *q console*. Type 6*7 and press Enter or Return to see the result.

```
Arial42
q)□
```

Here the □ represents the cursor awaiting your next input.

> **Note**: In this document, sample q console sessions will always be displayed in fixed pitch font with shaded background. As a pedagogical device, in many q snippets we suppress the console response to an entered q expression, replacing it with an underscore. This means that you, the serious student, are expected to enter this expression into your own q session and see the result.
>
> ```
> q)"c"$0x57656c6c6c20646f6e6521
> _
> ```

You did do this, didn't you? This **is** a tutorial.

1.2 Variables

In q, as in most languages that allow mutable state, a "variable" should properly be called an "assignable". (See Mathematical

Refresher above for a discussion). Nevertheless, a *variable* in q is a name together with associated storage that holds whatever value has been most recently assigned to the variable. As a consolation, at least q does not misuse '=' for assignment, as do many languages; in q '=' actually means "test for equality."

Declaring a variable and assigning its value are done in a single step with the operator (:) which is called "amend" and is read "is assigned" or "gets." Here is how to create and assign variable a with integer value 42.

```
q)a:42
q)_
```

When you entered this in your q session, you noted that nothing is echoed to the console. In order to see that a has indeed been assigned, simply enter the variable.

```
q)a
42
```

A variable name must start with an alphabetic character, which can be followed by alpha, numeric or underscore.

Naming Style Recommendations

(1) Choose a name long enough to make the purpose of the entity evident, but no longer. The purpose of a name is to communicate to a reader of the code at another time—perhaps even you. Long names may not make code easier to read. For example, 'checkDisk' is clearer than 'cd' or 'chk' but is no less clear than 'checkDiskForFileConsistency'.

(2) Use verbs for function names; use nouns for data.

(3) Be consistent in your use of abbreviations. Be mindful that even "obvious" abbreviations may be opaque to readers whose native language is different than yours.

(4) Be consistent in your use of capitalization, such as initial caps, camel casing, etc. Pick a style and stick to it.

(5) Use contexts for name spacing functions.

(6) Do not use names such as 'int', 'float' or other words that have meaning in q. While not reserved, they carry special meaning when used as arguments for certain q operators.

(7) Accomplished q programmers avoid using the underscore character in q names. If you insist on using underscore in names, do not use it as the last character. Expressions

involving the built-in (_) operator and names with underscore will be difficult to read.

1.3 Whitespace

In general, q permits, but does not require, whitespace around operators, separators, brackets, braces, etc. You could also write the above expression as

```
a : 42
```

or,

```
a: 42
```

> **Tip:** Accomplished q programmers view whitespace around operators as training wheels on a bicycle.

Because the q gods prefer compact code, you will see programs with no superfluous whitespace...none, zilch, zip, nada. In order to help you get accustomed to this terseness, we use whitespace only in juxtaposition and after semicolon and comma separators. You should feel free to add whitespace for readability where it is permitted, but be consistent in its use or omission. We will point out where whitespace is required or forbidden.

1.4 The Q Console

The q console evaluates a q expression that you enter and echoes the result on the following line. An exception to this is the assignment operation—as noted above—that has a return value, even though the console does not echo it. You may wonder why. This is simply a q console design choice to avoid cluttering the display.

> **Note:** To obtain official console display of any q value, apply the built-in function (*show*) to it.
>
> ```
> q)show a:42
> 42
> ```

1.5 Comments

The forward-slash character '/' indicates the beginning of a comment. Actually, it instructs the interpreter to ignore everything from it to the end of the line.

> **Tip:** At least one whitespace character must separate '/' intended to begin a comment from any text to the left of it on a line.

In the following example, no definition of c is seen by the interpreter, so an error occurs.

```
q)b:1+a:42 / nothing here counts      c:6*7
q)c
'c
```

Notice the succinct (ahem) format of q errors: a single vertical quote (called "tick" in q-speak) followed by a terse error message. In this case, the error should be interpreted as "Error: c is not recognized."

The following generates an even more succinct error.

```
q)a:42/ intended to be a comment
'
```

> ***Coding Style Recommendation***:   The q gods have no need for explanatory error messages or comments since their q code is perfect and self-documenting. Even experienced mortals spend hours poring over cryptic q error messages such as the ones above. Moreover, many mortals eschew comments in misanthropic coding macho. Don't.

1.6 Assignment

A variable is not explicitly declared or typed. Instead, its assigned value determines the variable type. In our example, the expression to the right of the assignment is syntactically an integer value, so the name 'a' is associated with a value of type long integer. It is permissible to reassign a variable with a value of different type. Once this is done, the name will reflect the type of its newly assigned value. Much more about types in Chapter 2.

> **Important:** Dynamic typing combined with mutable variables is flexible but also dangerous. You can unintentionally change the type of a variable with a wayward assignment that might crash your program much later. Or you can inadvertently reuse a variable name and wipe out any data in the variable. An undetected typo can result in data being sent to a black hole. Be careful to enter variable names correctly.

Many traditional languages permit only a variable name to the left of an assignment. In q an assignment carries the value being assigned and can be used as part of a larger expression. So we find,

```
q)1+a:42
43
```

In the following example, the variable a is **not** referenced after it is assigned. Instead, the value of the assignment is propagated onward—i.e., to the left.

```
q)b:1+a:42
q)b
43
```

1.7 Order of Evaluation

The interpreter evaluates the above specification of b from right-to-left (more on this in Chapter 4). If it were verbose, the interpreter might say:

> The integer 42 is assigned to a variable named a, then the result of the assignment, namely 42, is added to the integer 1, then this result is assigned to a variable named b

Because the interpreter always evaluates expressions right-to-left, programmers can safely read q expressions left-to-right,

> The variable b gets the value of the integer 1 plus the value assigned to the variable a, which gets the integer 42

This is exactly as in mathematics where we would read $f(g(x))$ as "f of g of x" even though g is evaluated first and the result passed into f. We just dispense with the parentheses.

Recommendations on Assignment Style

- The ability to chain evaluation of expressions permits a single line of q code to perform the work of an entire verbose program. In general this is acceptable (even good) q style when not taken to the extreme with extremely long wrapped lines or nested sub expressions.
- Intra-line assignments, as above, can simplify code provided they are few and are referenced only within the line of creation.
- It is not bad form to make one assignment per line, provided you don't end up with one operation per line.
- Wannabe q gods carry terseness to the extreme, which quickly leads to write-only code.

1.8 Data Types 101

There are q data types to cover nearly all needs but a few basic types are used most frequently. In q3.0 and above, the basic integer type, called *long*, is a 64 bit signed integer. If you write a literal integer as in the snippets above, q creates a 64 bit signed integer value.

```
q)42
_
```

The basic floating point type in q is called *float*, often known as a "double" in many languages. This is an 8 byte value conforming to the IEEE floating point specification.

```
q)98.6
_
```

Arithmetic operations on integer and float values are pretty much as expected except for division, which is written as (%) since '/' has been preempted for comments (as well as other uses). Sorry, that's just the way it is. Also note that division **always** results in a float.

```
q)2+3
5
q)2.2*3.0
6.6
q)4-2
2
q)4%2
2f
```

Boolean values in q are stored in a single byte and are denoted as the binary values they really are with an explicit type suffix 'b'. One way to generate boolean values is to test for equality.

```
q)42=40+2
1b
q)42=43
```

The two most useful temporal types are *date* and *timespan*; both represent integral counts. Under the covers, a date is the number of days since the millennium, positive for post and negative for pre.

```
q)2000.01.01        / this is actually 0

q)2014.11.19        / this is actually 5436

q)1999.12.31        / this is actually -1
```

Similarly, a time value is represented by a timespan, which is a (long) integer count of the number of nanoseconds since midnight. It is denoted as,

```
q)12:00:00.000000000        / this is noon
```

One interesting and useful feature of q temporal values is that, as integral values under the covers, they naturally participate in arithmetic. For example, to advance a date five days add 5.

```
q)2000.01.01+5
```

Or to advance a time by one microsecond (i.e., 1000 nanoseconds) add 1000.

```
q)12:00:00.000000000+1000
```

Or to verify that temporal values are indeed their underlying values, test for equality.

```
q)2000.01.01=0

q)12:00:00.000000000=12*60*60*1000000000
```

The treatment of textual data in q is a bit complicated in order to provide optimum flexibility and performance. For now, we will focus on symbols, which derive from their namesake in Scheme and are akin to VARCHAR in SQL or strings in other languages. They are **not** what q calls strings!

Think of symbols as wannabe names: all q names are symbols but not all symbols are names. A symbol is atomic, meaning that it is viewed as an indivisible entity (although we shall see later how to expose the characters inside it).

Symbols are denoted by a leading back-quote (called "back tick" in q-speak) followed by characters. Symbols without embedded blanks or other special characters can be entered literally into the console.

```
q)`aapl
q)`jab
q)`thisisareallylongsymbol
```

Since symbols are atoms, any two can be tested for equality.

```
q)`aapl=`apl
```

1.9 Lists 101

The fundamental q data structure is a list, which is an ordered collection of items sequenced from left to right. The notation for a general list encloses items with '(' and ')' and uses ';' as separator. Spaces after the semi-colons are optional but can improve readability.

```
q)(1; 1.2; `one)
```

A few observations on lists.

- A list can contain items of different type; this usually requires wrapping the values in a variant type in other languages. That being said, it is best to avoid mixed types in lists, as their processing is slower than homogenous lists of atoms.
- Assuming you entered the above snippet, you have noticed that the console echoes the items of a general list one item per line.
- In contrast to most functional languages, lists need not be built up by "cons"-ing one item at a time, although they can be. Nor are they stored as singly-linked lists under the covers.

In the case of a homogenous list of atoms, called a *simple list*, q adopts a simplified format for both storage and display. The parentheses and semicolons are dropped. For example, a list of underlying numeric type separates its items with a space.

```
q)(1; 2; 3)
1 2 3
q)(1.2; 2.2; 3.3)
-
q)(2000.01.01; 2000.01.02; 2001.01.03)
-
```

A simple list of booleans is juxtaposed with no spaces and has a trailing `b` type indicator.

```
q)(1b; 0b; 1b)
101b
```

A simple list of symbols is displayed with no separating spaces.

```
q)(`one; `two; `three)
`one`two`three
```

Homogenous lists of atoms can be entered in either general or simplified form. Regardless of how they are created, q recognizes a list of homogenous atoms dynamically and coverts it to a simple list.

Next we explore some basic operations to construct and manipulate lists. The most fundamental is (til), which takes a non-negative integer *n* and returns the first *n* integers starting at 0 (*n* itself is **not** included in the result).

```
q)til 10
0 1 2 3 4 5 6 7 8 9
```

We obtain the first 10 integers starting at 1 by adding 1 to the previous result. Be mindful that q always evaluates expressions from right to left and that operations work on vectors whenever possible.

```
q)1+til 10
1 2 3 4 5 6 7 8 9 10
```

Similarly, we obtain the first 10 even numbers and the first ten odd numbers.

```
q)2*til 10
-
q)1+2*til 10
-
```

Finally, we obtain the first 10 even numbers starting at 42.

```
q)42+2*til 10
```

Another frequently used list primitive is join (,) that returns the list obtained by concatenating its right operand to its left operand.

```
q)1 2 3,4 5
1 2 3 4 5
q)1 2 3,100

q)0,1 2 3
```

To extract items from the front or back of a list, use the take operator (#). Positive argument means take from the front, negative from the back.

```
q)2#til 10
0 1
q)-2#til 10
```

Tip: Applying (#) always results in a list.

In particular, the idiom 0# returns an empty list of the same type as the first item in its argument. Using an atom argument is a succinct way to create a typed empty list of the type of the atom.

```
q)0#1 2 3
`long$()
q)0#0
`long$()
q)0#`
`symbol$()
```

Should you extract more items than there are in the list, (#) restarts at the beginning and continues extracting. It does this until the specified number of items is reached.

```
q)5#1 2 3
1 2 3 1 2
```

In particular, if you apply (#) to an atom, it will continue drawing that single atom until it has the specified number of copies. This is a succinct idiom to replicate an atom to a list of specified length.

```
q)5#42
42 42 42 42 42
```

As with atoms, a list can be assigned to a variable.

```
q)L:10 20 30
```

The items of a list can be accessed via indexing, which uses square brackets and is relative to 0.

```
q)L[0]
10
q)L[1]

q)L[2]

```

1.10 Functions 101

All built-in q operators are functions. The main differences between q's functions and the ones we mortals can write are:

- The built-ins are written and optimized in one of the underlying languages k or C.
- All q functions can be used with infix notation—i.e., as operators—whereas ours must be used in prefix form.

Functions in q correspond to "lambda expressions" or "anonymous functions" in other languages. This means that a function is a first class value just like a long or float value—i.e., it acquires a name only once it is assigned to a variable.

Conceptually, a q function is a sequence of steps that produces an output result from an input value. Since q is not purely functional, these rules can interact with the world by reaching outside the context of the function. Such actions are called *side effects* and should be carefully controlled.

Function definition is delimited by matching curly braces '{' and '}'. Immediately after the opening brace, the *formal parameters* are names enclosed in square brackets '[' and ']' and separated by semi-colons. These parameters presumably appear in the *body* of the function, which follows the formal parameters and is a succession of expressions sequenced by semi-colons.

Following is a simple function that returns the square of its input. On the next line we assign the same function to the variable sq. The whitespace is optional.

```
q){[x] x*x}
q)sq:{[x] x*x}
```

Here is a function that takes two input values and returns the sum of their squares.

```
q){[x;y] a:x*x; b:y*y; a+b}
q)pyth:{[x;y] a:x*x; b:y*y; a+b}
```

To apply a function to arguments, follow it (or its name, if it has been assigned to a variable) by a list of values enclosed in square brackets and separated by semi-colons. This causes the argument expression to be evaluated first, then the expressions in the body of the function to be evaluated sequentially by substituting each resulting argument for every occurrence of the corresponding formal parameter. Normally the value of the final expression is returned as the output value of the function.

Here are the previous functions applied to arguments.

```
q){[x] x*x}[5]
25
q)sq[5]

q){[x;y] a:x*x; b:y*y; a+b}[3;4]
25
q)pyth[3;4]
```

The variables a and b appearing in the body of the last function above are *local*—i.e., they are created and exist only for the duration of an application.

It is common in mathematics to use function parameters *x*, *y*, or *z*. If you are content with these names (in the belief that descriptive names provide no useful information to the poor soul reading your code), you can omit their declaration and q will understand that you mean the implicit parameters *x*, *y*, and *z* **in that order**.

```
q){x*x}[5]
25
q){a:x*x; b:y*y; a+b}[3;4]
25
```

This is about as pithy as it gets for function definition and application. Well, not quite. In q, as in most functional languages, we don't need no stinkin' brackets for application of a monadic function—i.e., with

26

one parameter. Simply separate the function from its argument by whitespace. This is called function *juxtaposition*.

```
q){x*x} 5

q)f:{x*x}
q)f 5
```

If you are new to functional programming this may take some getting used to, but the reduction of punctuation "noise" in your code is worth it.

1.11 Functions on Lists 101

Because q is a vector language, most of the built-in operators work on lists out of the box. In q-speak, such functions are *atomic*, meaning they recursively burrow into a complex data structure until arriving at atoms and then perform their operation. In particular, an atomic function operates on lists by application to the individual items. For example, plain addition adds an atom to a list, a list to an atom or two lists of the same length.

```
q)42+100 200 300
142 242 342
q)100 200 300+42

q)100 200 300+1 2 3
```

Perhaps surprisingly, this is also true of equality and comparison operators. (Recall the notation for simple boolean lists).

```
q)100=99 100 101
010b
q)100 100 100=100 101 102

q)100<99 100 101
```

Suppose that instead of adding things pair-wise, we want to add all the items across a list. The way this is done in functional languages is with *higher order functions*, or as they are called in q, *adverbs*. Regardless of the terminology, the idea is to take the operation of a function and produce a closely related function having the same "essence" but applied in a different manner.

You met the concept of higher-order functions in elementary calculus, perhaps without being properly introduced. The derivative and integral are actually higher order functions that take a function and produce a related function. Behind all the delta-epsilon mumbo-jumbo, the derivative of a given function is a function that represents the instantaneous behavior of the original. The (indefinite) integral is the anti-derivative—i.e., a function whose instantaneous behavior is that of the given function.

In the case of adding the values in a list, we need a higher-order function that takes addition and turns it into a function that works across the list. In functional programming this is called a *fold*; in q it is "over." The technique is to accumulate the result across the list recursively. (See Mathematical Refresher for more on recursion). Specifically, begin with an initial value in the accumulator and then sequentially add each list item into the previous value of the accumulator until the end the list. Upon completion, the accumulator holds the desired result.

If you are new to functional programming this may seem more complicated than just creating a *for* loop but that's only because you have been brainwashed to think that constructing a for loop is "real" programming. Watch how easy it is to do in q. In words, we tell q to start with the initial value of 0 in the accumulator and then modify (+) with the adverb (/) so that it adds across the list.

```
q)0 +/ 1 2 3 4 5
15
q)0 +/ 1+til 100
_
```

There is nothing special about built-in operator (+)—we can use any operator or even our own function.

```
q)0 {x+y}/ 1 2 3 4 5
_
q)0 {x+y}/ 1+til 100
_
```

In this situation we don't really need the flexibility to specify the initial value of the accumulator. It suffices to start with the first item of the list and proceed across the rest of the list. There is an even simpler form for this case.

```
q)(+/) 1 2 3 4 5
_
q)(+/) 1+til 100
_
```

If you are new to functional programming, you may think, "Big deal, I write *for* loops in my sleep." Granted. But the advantage of the higher-order function approach is that there is no chance of being off by one in the loop counter or accidentally running off the end of a data structure. More importantly, you can focus on *what* you want done without the irrelevant scaffolding of *how* to set up control structures. This is called *declarative programming*.

What else can we do with our newfound adverb? Change addition to multiplication for factorial.

```
q)(*/) 1+til 10
3628800
```

The fun isn't limited to arithmetic primitives. We introduce (|), which returns the larger of its operands and (&), which returns the smaller of its operands.

```
q)42|98
98
q)42&98
_
```

Use (|) or (&) with over and you have maximum or minimum.

```
q)(|/) 20 10 40 30
40
```

```
q)(&/) 20 10 40 30
_
```

Some applications of (/) are so common that they have their own names.

```
q)sum 1+til 10        / this is +/
55
q)prd 1+til 10        / this is */  -- note missing "o"
_
q)max 20 10 40 30     / this is |/
_
q)min 20 10 40 30     / this is &/
_
```

At this point the (/) pattern should be clear: it takes a given function and produces a new function that accumulates across the original list, producing a single result. In particular, (/) converts a dyadic function to a monadic *aggregate* function—i.e., one that collapses a list to an atom.

We record one more example of (/) for later reference. Recall from the previous section that applying the operator (#) to an atom produces a list of copies. Composing this with (*/) we get a multiplicative implementation of raising to a power without resorting to floating point exponential.

```
q)(*/) 2#1.4142135623730949
1.999999999999996
q)n:5
q)(*/) n#10
100000
```

The higher-order function sibling to over is *scan*, written (\). The process of scan is the same as that of over with one difference: instead of returning only the final result of the accumulation, it returns all intermediate values.

```
q)(+\) 1+til 10
1 3 6 10 15 21 28 36 45 55
q)(*\) 1+til 10

q)(|\) 20 10 40 30
20 20 40 40
q)(&\) 20 10 40 30

```

Scan converts a dyadic function to a monadic *uniform function*—i.e., one that returns a list of the same length as the input.

As with over, common applications of scan have their own names.

```
q)sums 1+til 10        / this is +\

q)prds 1+til 10        / this is *\    / note missing 'o'

q)maxs 20 10 40 30     / this is |\

q)mins 20 10 40 30     / this is &\

```

1.12 Example: Fibonacci Numbers

We define the Fibonacci numbers recursively.

- Base case: the initial sequence is the list 1 1
- Inductive step: given a list of Fibonacci numbers, the next value of the sequence appends the sum of its two last items.

We have the basic ingredients to express this in q. Start with the base case F0.

```
q)F0:1 1
q)-2#F0
_
q)sum -2#F0
_
q)F0,sum -2#F0
_
```

Notice that read from right-to-left, the last expression exactly restates the definition of the Fibonacci term: "take the last two elements of the sequence, sum them and append the result to the sequence." This is declarative programming—say "what" to do not "how" to implement it.

We abstract this expression into a function that appends the next item at an arbitrary point in the sequence.

```
q){x,sum -2#x}
_
```

Let's take it for a test drive on the first few terms.

```
q){x,sum -2#x}[1 1]
_
q){x,sum -2#x}[1 1 2]
_
```

Wouldn't it be nice if q had a higher-order function that applies a recursive function a specified number of times, starting with the base case? Conveniently, there is an overload of our friend (/) that does exactly this. Specify the base case and the number of times to iterate the recursion and it's done.

```
q)10 {x,sum -2#x}/ 1 1
1 1 2 3 5 8 13 21 34 55 89 144
```

1.13 Example: Newton's Method for n^{th} Roots

You may recall from elementary calculus the simple and powerful technique for computing roots of functions, called the Newton-Raphson method. (It actually bears little superficial resemblance to what Newton himself originally developed). The idea is to start with an initial guess that is not too far from the actual root. Then determine the tangent to the graph over that point and project the tangent line to the x-axis to obtain the next approximation. Repeat this process until the result converges within the desired tolerance.

We formulate this as a recursive algorithm for successive approximation.

- Base case: a reasonable initial value
- Inductive step: Given x_n, the n+1st approximation is: $x_n -$ $f(x_n) / f'(x_n)$

Let's use this procedure to compute the square root of 2. The function whose zero we need to find is $f(x) = x^2 - 2$. The formula for successive approximation involves the derivative of f, which is $f'(x) = 2*x$.

Given that we know that there is a square root of 2 between 1 and 2 due to the sign change of f, we start with 1.0 as the base case x0. Then the first approximation is,

```
q)x0-((x0*x0)-2)%2*x0
1.5
```

We abstract this expression to a function that computes the n+1st approximation in terms of xn

```
q){[xn] xn-((xn*xn)-2)%2*xn}
```

Now use it to run the first two iterations.

```
q){[xn] xn-((xn*xn)-2)%2*xn}[1.0]

q){[xn] xn-((xn*xn)-2)%2*xn}[1.5]
```

Observe in your console session that this looks promising for convergence to the correct answer.

Wouldn't it be nice of q had a higher-order function to apply a function recursively, starting at the base case, until the output converges? You won't be surprised that there is another overload of our friend over that does exactly this. Just specify the base case and q iterates until the result converges within the system comparison tolerance (as of this writing—Sep 2015—that tolerance is 10^{-14})

```
q){[xn] xn-((xn*xn)-2)%2*xn}/[1.5]
1.414214
```

To witness the convergence, do two things. First, set the floating point display to maximum.

```
q)\P 0            / note upper case P
```

> **Tip:** This displays all digits of the underlying binary representation, including the 17th digit, which is usually schmutz.

Second, switch the adverb from over to scan so that we can see the intermediate results.

```
q){[xn] xn-((xn*xn)-2)%2*xn}\[1.0]
_
```

As your console display shows, that is pretty fast convergence.

Why limit ourselves to the square root of 2? Abstracting the constant 2 into a parameter *c* in the function *f*, the successive approximation function becomes,

```
q){[c; xn] xn-((xn*xn)-c)%2*xn}
_
```

At this point we use a feature, related to *currying* in functional programming called *projection* in q, in which we only partially supply arguments to a function. The result is a function of the remaining, unspecified parameters. We indicate partial application by omitting the unspecified arguments. In our case, we specify the constant c as 2.0, leaving a monadic function of the remaining variable xn.

```
q){[c; xn] xn-((xn*xn)-c)%2*xn}[2.0;]
_
```

Since this is solely a function of xn, we can apply it recursively to the base case until it converges to obtain the same result as the original square root function.

```
q){[c; xn] xn-((xn*xn)-c)%2*xn}[2.0;]/[1.0]
_
```

But now we are free to choose any (reasonable) value for *c*. For example, to calculate the square root of 3.0.

```
q){[c; xn] xn-((xn*xn)-c)%2*xn}[3.0;]/[1.0]
_
```

Intoxicated with the power of function abstraction and recursion, why restrict ourselves to square roots? We abstract once more, turning the power into a parameter *p*. The new expression for the successive

33

approximation has a pth power in the numerator and an $p\text{-}1^{st}$ power in the denominator, but we already know how to calculate these.

```
q){[p; c; xn] xn-(((*/)p#xn)-c)%p*(*/)(p-1)#xn}_
```

Supplying *p* and *c* (only) leaves a function solely of xn, which we can once again iterate on the base case until convergence. We reproduce the previous case of the square root of 3.0; then we calculate the fifth root of 7.

```
q){[p; c; xn] xn-(((*/)p#xn)-c)%p*(*/)(p-1)#xn}[2; 3.0;]/[1.0]
q){[p; c; xn] xn-(((*/)p#xn)-c)%p*(*/)(p-1)#xn}[5; 7.0;]/[1.0]
_
```

It is amazing what can be done in a single line of code when you strip out unnecessary programming frou-frou. Perhaps this is intimidating to the qbie, but now that you have taken the blue pill, you will feel right as rain.

1.14 Example: FIFO Allocation

In the Finance industry, one needs to fill a sell order from a list of matching buys in a FIFO fashion. Although we state this scenario in terms of buys and sells, it applies equally to general FIFO allocation. We begin with the buys represented as a (time-ordered) list of floats, and a single float sell.

```
q)buys:2 1 4 3 5 4f
q)sell:12f
```

The objective is to draw successively from the buys until we have exactly filled the sell, then stop. In our case the result we are seeking is,

```
q)allocation
2 1 4 3 2 0
```

The insight is to realize that the cumulative sum of the allocations reaches the sell amount and then levels off: this is an equivalent statement of what it means to do FIFO allocation.

```
q)sums allocation
2 3 7 10 12 12
```

We realize that the cumulative sum of buys is the total amount available for allocation at each step.

```
q)sums buys
2 3 7 10 15 19f
```

To make this sequence level off at the sell amount, simply use (&).

```
q)sell&sums buys
2 3 7 10 12 12f
```

Now that we have the cumulative allocation amounts, we need to unwind this to get the step-wise allocations. This entails subtracting successive items in the allocations list.

Wouldn't it be nice if q had a built-in function that returned the successive differences of a numeric list? There is one (deltas) and—no surprise—it involves an adverb (called *each-previous*—more about that in Chapter 5).

```
q)deltas 1 2 3 4 5
1 1 1 1 1
q)deltas 10 15 20
_
```

Observe in your console display that (deltas) returns the initial item untouched. This is just what we need.

Returning to our example of FIFO allocation, we apply (deltas) to the cumulative allocation list and we're done.

```
q)deltas sell&sums buys
_
```

Look ma, no loops!

Now fasten your seatbelts as we switch on warp drive. In real-world FIFO allocation problems, we actually want to allocate buys FIFO not just to a single sell, but to a sequence of sells. You say, surely this must require a loop. Please don't call me Shirley. And no loopy code.

We take buys as before but now we have a list sells, which are to be allocated FIFO from buys.

```
q)buys:2 1 4 3 5 4f
q)sells:2 4 3 2
q)allocations
2 0 0 0 0
0 1 3 0 0
0 0 1 2 0
0 0 0 1 1 0
```

The idea is to extend the allocation of buys across multiple sells by considering both the cumulative amounts to be allocated as well as the cumulative amounts available for allocation.

```
q)sums[buys]
2 3 7 10 15 19f
q)sums[sells]
2 6 9 11
```

The insight is to cap the cumulative buys with each cumulative sell.

```
q)2&sums[buys]
2 2 2 2 2 2f
q)6&sums[buys]
2 3 6 6 6 6f
q)9&sums[buys]
2 3 7 9 9 9f
q)11&sums[buys]
2 3 7 10 11 11f
```

Contemplate this koan and you will realize that each line includes the allocations to all the buys preceding it. From this we can unwrap cumulatively along both the buy and sell axes to get the incremental allocations.

Our first task is to produce the above result as a list of lists.

```
2 2 2 2  2  2
2 3 6 6  6  6
2 3 7 9  9  9
2 3 7 10 11 11
```

Adverbs to the rescue! Our first task requires an adverb that applies a dyadic function and a given right operand to each item of a list on the left. That adverb is called *each left* and it has the funky notation (\:). We use it to accomplish in a single operation the four individual (&) operations above.

```
q)sums[sells] &\: sums[buys]
2 2 2 2  2  2
2 3 6 6  6  6
2 3 7 9  9  9
2 3 7 10 11 11
```

Now we apply (deltas) to unwind the allocation in the vertical direction.

```
q)deltas sums[sells]&\:sums[buys]
2 2 2 2 2 2
0 1 4 4 4 4
0 0 1 3 3 3
0 0 0 1 2 2
```

For the final step, we need to unwind the allocation across the rows.

The adverb we need is called (each). As a higher-order function, it applies a given function to each item of a list (hence its name). For a simple example, the following nested list has count 2, since it has two items. Using (count each) gives the count of each item in the list.

```
q)(1 2 3; 10 20)

q)count (1 2 3; 10 20)

q)count each (1 2 3; 10 20)
3 2
```

In the context of our allocation problem, we realize that (deltas each) is just the ticket to unwind the remaining cumulative allocation within each row.

```
q)deltas each deltas sums[sells] &\: sums[buys]
2 0 0 0 0 0
0 1 3 0 0 0
0 0 1 2 0 0
0 0 0 1 1 0
```

Voila! The solution to our allocation problem in a single line of q. The power of higher order functions (adverbs) is breathtaking.

1.15 Dictionaries and Tables 101

After lists, the second basic data structure of q is the *dictionary*, which models key-value association. A dictionary is constructed from two lists of the same length using the (!) operator. The left operand is the list of (presumably unique, though unenforced) *keys* and the right operand is the list of *values*. A dictionary is a first class value, just like an integer or list and can be assigned to a variable.

```
q)`a`b`c!10 20 30
a| 10
b| 20
c| 30
q)d:`a`b`c!10 20 30
```

Observe that dictionary console display looks like the I/O table of a mathematical mapping. No coincidence.

Given a key, we retrieve the associated value with the same square bracket notation as list indexing.

```
q)d[`a]
_
```

A useful class of dictionary has as keys a simple list of symbols and as values a list of lists of uniform length. We think of such a dictionary as a named collection of columns and call it a *column dictionary*.

```
q)`c1`c2!(10 20 30; 1.1 2.2 3.3)
c1| 10  20  30
c2| 1.1 2.2 3.3
q)dc:`c1`c2!(10 20 30; 1.1 2.2 3.3)
```

Retrieving by key yields the associated column, which is itself a list and so can be indexed.

```
q)dc[`c1]
10 20 30
q)dc[`c1][0]
10
q)dc[`c2][1]
_
```

Whenever such iterated indexing of nested entities arises in q, there is an equivalent syntactic form, called *indexing at depth*, to make things a bit more readable.

```
q)dc[`c1][0]
10
q)dc[`c1; 0]
10
q)dc[`c1; 1]
_
q)dc[`c1; 2]
_
```

Indexing at depth notation suggests thinking of dc as a two-dimensional entity; this is reasonable in view of its display above. Let's pursue this. Whenever an index is elided in q, the result is as if every legitimate value had been specified in the omitted index position. For a column dictionary, this yields the associated column when the second slot is omitted.

```
q)dc[`c1;]
10 20 30
q)dc[`c2;]
_
```

Things are more interesting when the index in the first slot is elided. The result is a dictionary comprising a section of the original columns in just the specified position.

```
q)dc[;0]
c1| 10
c2| 1.1
q)dc[;1]
_
q)dc[;2]
_
```

To summarize, we have an entity that retrieves columns in the first slot and section dictionaries in the second slot. The issue is that columns are conventionally accessed in the second slot of two-dimensional things. No problem. We apply the built-in operator (flip) (better called "transpose") to reverse the order of indexing. We still have the same column dictionary but slot retrieval is reversed: columns are accessed in the second slot and section dictionaries are retrieved from the first slot.

```
q)t:flip `c1`c2!(10 20 30; 1.1 2.2 3.3)
q)t[0; `c1]
10
q)t[1; `c1]
_
q)t[2; `c1]
_
q)t[0; `c2]
_
q)t[; `c1]
10 20 30
q)t[0;]
c1| 10
c2| 1.1
```

We emphasize that the data is still stored as a column dictionary under the covers; only the indexing slots are affected.

Observe that the console display of a flipped column dictionary is indeed the transpose of the column dictionary display and in fact looks like … a table.

```
q)flip `c1`c2!(10 20 30; 1.1 2.2 3.3)
c1 c2
------
10 1.1
20 2.2
30 3.3
```

A flipped column dictionary, called a *table*, is a first class entity in q.

In the table setting, the section dictionaries are called *records* of the table. They correspond to the rows of SQL tables. To see why, observe that the record at index 0 is effectively the horizontal slice of the table in "row" 0. Let's reexamine record retrieval, this time omitting the optional trailing semicolon from the elided second index.

```
q)t[0]
c1| 10
c2| 1.1
q)t[1]
_
q)t[2]
_
```

Looking at this syntactically, we might conclude that t is a list of record dictionaries. In fact it is, at least logically; physically a table is always stored as a collection of named columns.

Thus we have arrived at:

- A table is a flipped column dictionary.
- It is also a list of record dictionaries.

While we can always construct a table as a flipped column dictionary, there is a convenient syntax that puts the names together with the columns. The notation looks a bit odd at first but it will seem more reasonable when we encounter keyed tables later.

```
q)([] c1:10 20 30; c2:1.1 2.2 3.3)
c1 c2
------
10 1.1
20 2.2
30 3.3
```

A few notes.

- The square brackets are necessary to differentiate a table from a list
- The occurrence of ':' is **not** assignment. It is merely a syntactic marker separating the name from the column values
- The column names in table definition are **not** symbols, although they are converted to symbols under the covers.

1.16 q-sql 101

There are multiple ways to operate on tables. First, you can treat a table as the column dictionary that it is and perform basic dictionary operations on it. Qbies who are familiar with SQL may find it easier to use q's version of SQL-like syntax, called *q-sql*. In this section we explore basic q-sql features.

The fundamental q-sql operation is the select template, We say template because, unlike other q primitives, it is **not** evaluated right-to-left. Rather, it is syntactic sugar designed to mimic SQL SELECT. That said, we emphasize that although select does act like SQL SELECT in some respects, there is one fundamental difference. Whereas SQL SELECT operates on fields on a row-by-row basis, select performs vector operations on column lists. Insisting on thinking in rows with q tables will end in tears.

We construct a simple table for our examples.

```
q)t:([] c1:1000+til 6; c2:`a`b`c`a`b`a; c3:10*1+til 6)
q)t
```

The simplest form of select retrieves all the records and columns of the table by leaving unspecified which rows or columns—there is no need for the wildcard * of SQL. The 'select' and 'from' **must** occur together.

```
q)select from t
```

The next example shows how to specify which columns to return and optional names to associate with them.

```
q)select c1, val:2*c3 from t
```

We make several observations

- Result columns are separated by ',' and are sequenced left-to-right.
- Any q expressions inside select are evaluated right-to-left, as usual.
- As was the case with table definition syntax, instances of ':' are **not** assignment; rather, they are syntactic markers separating a column name to its left from the q expression to its right, which computes the column.
- Arbitrary q expressions can be used to produce result columns, provided all column lengths are the same.
- There are optional by and where phrases for grouping and constraints.

The next example demonstrates using the by phrase of select to perform grouping. The basic usage is similar to GROUP BY in SQL, in which the column expressions involve aggregate functions. All records having common values in the by column(s) are grouped together and then aggregation is performed within each group.

```
q)select count c1, sum c3 by c2 from t
c2| c1 c3
--| ------
a | 3  110
b | 2  70
c | 1  30
```

An advantage of q-sql by is that you can group on a computed column.

```
q)select count c2 by ovrund:c3<=40 from t
ovrund| c2
------| --
0     | 2
1     | 4
```

Closely related to select is the update template. It has the same syntax as select but semantically the names to the left of : are interpreted as columns to modify (or add, if not present). As with select, you can specify an optional where phrase, which limits the action to just those records satisfying specified constraint(s). Here is how to scale the c3 column of t just in the positions having c2 equal to `a.

```
q)update c3:10*c3 from t where c2=`a
c1    c2 c3
-----------
1000  a  100
1001  b  20
1002  c  30
1003  a  400
1004  b  50
1005  a  600
```

We emphasize that the operations in update are vector operations on columns, not row-by-row.

Not all of q-sql is included in the templates. For example, to sort a table ascending by column(s), use (xasc) with left operand the symbol column name(s) in major-to-minor order.

```
q)`c2 xasc t
```

1.17 Example: Trades Table

In this section we construct a toy trades table to demonstrate the power of q-sql.

A useful operator for constructing lists of test data is (?), which generates pseudo-random data. We can generate 10 numbers randomly selected, with replacement, from the first 20 integers starting at 0 (i.e., not including 20).

```
q)10?20                              / ymmv
4 13 9 2 7 0 17 14 9 18
q)10?20

q)10?20

```

We can similarly generate 10 random floats between 0.0 and 100.0 (not including 100.0).

```
q) 10?100.0

```

we can make 10 random selections from the items in a list

```
q)10?`aapl`ibm

```

Now to our trades table. Since a table is a collection of columns, we first build the columns. We apologize for using excessively short names so that things fit easily on the printed page.

First we construct a list of 1,000,000 random dates in the month of January 2015.

```
q)dts:2015.01.01+1000000?31
```

Next a list of 1,000,000 timespans.

```
q)tms:1000000?24:00:00.000000000
```

Next a list of 1,000,000 tickers chosen from AAPL, GOOG and IBM. It is customary to make these lower case symbols.

```
q)syms:1000000?`aapl`goog`ibm
```

Next a list of 1,000,000 volumes given as positive lots of 10.

```
q)vols:10*1+1000000?1000
```

As an initial cut, we construct a list of 1,000,000 prices in cents uniformly distributed within 10% of 100.0. We will adjust this later.

```
q)pxs:90.0+(1000000?2001)%100
```

Now collect these into a table and inspect the first 5 records. Remember, a table is a list of records so (#) applies.

```
q)trades:([] dt:dts; tm:tms; sym:syms; vol:vols; px:pxs)
q)5#trades
```

The first thing you observe in your console display is that the trades are not in temporal order. We fix this by sorting on time within date using (xasc).

```
q)trades:`dt`tm xasc trades
q)5#trades
```

Now we adjust the prices. At the time of this writing (Sep 2015) AAPL was trading around 100, so we leave it alone. But we adjust GOOG and IBM to their approximate trading ranges by scaling.

```
q)trades:update px:6*px from trades where sym=`goog
q)trades:update px:2*px from trades where sym=`ibm
q)5#trades
dt         tm                 sym  vol  px
-------------------------------------------------
2014.01.01 0D00:00:04.117137193 goog 6140 582.24
2014.01.01 0D00:00:06.227586418 ibm  7030 196.66
2014.01.01 0D00:00:07.611505687 ibm  7740 185.14
2014.01.01 0D00:00:11.415991187 goog 4130 605.34
2014.01.01 0D00:00:12.739158421 goog 8810 579.36
```

This looks a bit more like real trades. Let's perform some basic queries as sanity checks. Given that both price and volume are uniformly distributed, we expect their averages to approximate the mean. Using the built-in average function (avg) we see that they do.

```
q)select avg px, avg vol by sym from trades
```

Similarly, we expect the minimum and maximum price for each symbol to be the endpoints of the uniform range.

```
q)select min px, max px by sym from trades
```

Our first non-trivial query computes the 100 millisecond bucketed volume-weighted average price (VWAP). This uses the built-in dyadic function (xbar). The left operand of (xbar) is an interval width and the right operand is a list of numeric values. The effect of (xbar) is to shove each input to the left-hand end point of the interval of specified width in which it falls. For example,

```
q)5 xbar til 15
0 0 0 0 0 5 5 5 5 5 10 10 10 10 10
```

This is useful for grouping since it effectively buckets all the values within each interval to the left end-point of that interval. Recalling that a timespan is actually an integral count of nanoseconds since midnight, to compute 100 millisecond buckets we will use (xbar) with an interval of 100,000,000.

We also require (wavg), a dyadic function that computes the average of the numeric values in its right operand weighted by the values of its left operand.

```
q)1 2 3 wavg 50 60 70
_
```

Now we put things together in a single query. For convenience of display, we group by bucketed time within symbol.

```
q)select vwap:vol wavg px by sym,bkt:100000000 xbar tm from trades
_
```

That's all there is to it!

Our final query involves the maximum profit (or analogously, maximum drawdown) realizable over the trading period. To understand the concept, image that you have a DeLorean with flux capacitor and are able to travel into the future and record historical trade results. Upon returning to the present, you are given $1,000,000 to invest with the stipulation that you can make one buy and one sell for AAPL and you are not allowed to short the stock. As a good capitalist your goal is to maximize your profit.

Restating the problem, we wish to determine the optimum time to buy and sell for the largest (positive) difference in price, where the buy precedes the sell. We state the solution as a q koan, which you should contemplate until enlightenment.

```
q)select max px-mins px from trades where sym=`aapl
_
```

Two hints if Zen enlightenment is slow to dawn.

- Take the perspective of looking back from a potential optimum sell
- The optimum buy must happen at a cumulative local minimum; otherwise, you could back up to an earlier, lower price and make a larger profit.

1.18 File I/O 101

For this section we need to introduce the other q primitive text data type, called *char*. A single ASCII character is represented as that character in double quotes. Here are some examples.

```
q)"a"
q)" "
q)"_"
```

The char "a" is an atom but is **not** the same as its symbol cousin `a.

Things get sticky with a simple list of char. Enter such a list in general form and observe the simplified display echoed on the console.

```
q)("s";"t"; "r"; "i"; "n"; "g")
"string"
```

A simple list of char looks like a string from traditional languages and is even called a *string* in q. But this string is **not** an atom or even a first class entity in q; it is a list having count 6. And it should **not** be confused with its symbol cousin `string, which is an atom having count 1.

```
q)count "string"
q)count `string
```

With these preliminaries out of the way, we proceed to I/O. The way q handles I/O is Spartan. No instantiation of readers, writers, serializers and the like. We admit that the notation is funky, but you will grow to appreciate its conciseness just as a serious driver prefers a manual transmission.

File I/O begins with symbolic handles. A *symbolic file handle* is a symbol of a particular form that represents the name of a resource on the file system. The leading ':' distinguishes the symbol as a handle. For example,

```
`:path/filename
```

We use the following simple table in our demonstration.

```
q)t:([] c1:`a`b`c; c2:1.1 2.2 3.3)
q)t
_
```

Pick a destination to write your files. Because this tutorial is being, the examples here will use ,

```
/q4m/examples
```

You should replace this with your chosen directory in what follows.

To save the table t in a serialized binary data file, use the built-in function (set) with symbolic file handle as left operand and the source data as the right operand.

```
q)`:/q4m/examples/t set t
`:/q4m/examples/t
```

Observe that the console echoes the symbolic file handle in case of success. To read the stored data and deserialize it back into the session, use (get) with the symbolic file handle.

```
q)get `:/q4m/examples/t
_
```

Presto! It's out and back.

To write text data to a file we use one of the overloads of the infelicitously named (0:) operator. The key idea is that q considers a text file to correspond to a list of strings, one string per file record. We supply (0:) with a symbolic file handle as its left operand and a list of strings (i.e., a list of lists of char) in the right operand.

```
q)`:/q4m/life.txt 0: ("Meaning";"of";"life")
_
```

To read a text file as a list of strings, use (read0) with the symbolic handle.

```
q)read0 `:/q4m/examples/life.txt
```

And now, what everyone is waiting for: writing and reading csv files. Hold on to your hats, as this uses three different overloads of (0:). One to prepare the tables as text; the one we already met to write text files; and one to read formatted text files. Certainly a regrettable naming convention.

Preparing a table as csv text is simple; q handles the quoting and escaping of special characters. Apply (0:) with the defined constant csv as left operand and the table in the right operand.

```
q)csv 0: t
```

Your console display shows the table properly prepared as strings. Now compose this result with the previous overload of (0:) and write it out. As a check, we use (read0) to read back the text file.

```
q)`:/q4m/examples/t.csv 0: csv 0: t
q)read0 `:/q4m/examples/t.csv
```

Finally, we demonstrate the third overload of (0:) to parse the formatted csv file into the q session as a table. The right operand is a symbolic file handle. The left operand is a control list with two items. The first is a string of upper case characters indicating the types of each field within the text row.

The second item of the control list is the field separation character—in our case this is ','. This separator char should be enlisted if there are column headers in the first row of the file, as in our case. These headers are used as table column names. For our example we have,

```
q)("SF"; enlist ",") 0: `:/q4m/examples/t.csv
```

Here "S" and "F" indicate that there are two fields, having types symbol and float. The separator is an enlisted ','.

Yes, the naming and notation is obscure. But you have to admit that file I/O can't get much simpler.

48

1.19 Interprocess Communication101

For this section, you will need two open q sessions, best done on the same machine. We recommend that this machine be one that is not encumbered with enterprise security. Chose one session to be your "server" and open a port with the command \p (note lower case) followed by the port number. To verify that the port is open, execute the naked command \p and check that it echoes a 32-bit int of the port you opened.

```
q)\p 5042                    / on server
q)\p
5042i
```

The syntax of Interprocess Communication (IPC) is similar to that of File I/O. A *symbolic network handle* is a symbol of a particular form that identifies the name of a resource on the network. For our purposes, it suffices to consider a network handle of the simplest form.

```
`:localhost:5042
```

The leading ':' in the symbol identifies it as a symbolic handle. To the left of the second ':' is the name of the network resource—in this case, the machine on which the q session is running. To the right of ':' is a (presumably open) port on the destination machine that will be used for TCP/IP communication.

To open a connection, use a symbolic handle as argument to (hopen) and store the result in a variable, traditionally called h. Do that now in your "client" session after ensuring that the specified port is open in the "server" session.

```
q)h:hopen `:localhost:5042          / on client
```

The variable h is called an *open handle*. It holds a function for sending a request to the server and receiving the result of that request. Now we're ready to party.

There are three ways to send requests from the client to the server, only one of which is safe for production applications. For demonstration purpose (only), we show the simplest, which should only be used in development environments. When invoked with a string—i.e., a list of char—argument, the handle function h synchronously sends that string to the server, where it is executed, and any result is returned from the application of h.

```
q)h "6*7"              / on client
42
```

Clearly this isn't safe, as arbitrary text can be sent for nefarious purposes.

A safer way to make requests to the server is to invoke h with a list containing the name of a function that (presumably) exists on the server, followed by arguments to that function. When h is invoked with such a list argument, it (synchronously) causes the server to apply the named function to the transmitted arguments, and then returns any result from the server is its own output. This corresponds to call by name in traditional remote procedure call. It is safer since the server can inspect the symbolic function name and determine whether the requesting user is authorized to execute it

On your server process, create a simple function of two arguments.

```
q)f:{x*y}              / on server
```

On your client process, invoke h with a list containing the symbolic name of the remote function followed by its two arguments.

```
q)h (`f; 6; 7)         / on client
```

Observe that nothing is displayed on the server console since the function application there returns its result to the client. To close the connection with the server, flush buffers and free resources, apply (hclose) to the open handle.

```
q)hclose h        / on client
```

IPC doesn't get any easier.

1.20 Example: Asynchronous Callbacks

The IPC mechanism of q does not have callbacks built in but it is powerful enough that we can create callbacks ourselves. We assume that you have started separate client and server q sessions and have opened the connection from the client to the server, as in the previous section.

Heretofore, calls to the server were synchronous, meaning that at the point of the remote call, the client blocks until the requested work on the server completes and the result is returned. It is also possible to make the remote call asynchronous. In this case, the client does **not** block: the application of the open handle returns immediately.

In order to demonstrate this, we have to come clean about what is really in the open handle h. See for yourself by displaying the h from an open connection.

```
q)h:hopen `:localhost:5042
q)h
3i
```

Your result will probably not match this but it **will** be an integer. Yes, an open handle is just a positive 32-bit integer. When this (positive) integer is applied as a function, the call is synchronous. To make an asynchronous call, negate the value in h—i.e., neg h—and use this with function application syntax. Seriously.

Since nothing will be displayed in the client session, it helps to display progress on the server as the request is performed. Create the function echo in the server session.

```
q)echo:{show x}              / on server
```

Now make an asynchronous remote call to echo from the client.

```
q)(neg h) (`echo; 42)        / on client
```

Observe on your q consoles that the client application returns immediately with no result and that the server displays the progress message.

Now to callbacks. We begin by instrumenting a function rsvp on the server that, when invoked remotely, will call back to the client. It will receive two parameters: its own argument and the symbolic name of the client function to call.

```
q)rsvp:{[arg;cb] ..}         / on server
```

We initially invoke the server's (show) with the passed arg to indicate that we are hard at work on the transmitted data.

```
q)rsvp:{[arg;cb] show arg;}
```

Now for the big moment. To make the return call from the server to the client, we need the open handle of the connection for the remote call we are processing. This is conveniently placed in the q system variable .z.w ("who" called) for the duration of each remote call. We use it to make an **asynchronous** remote call (hence the neg) over the caller's handle, passing the provided callback name and our arduously computed result 43.

```
q)rsvp:{[arg;cb] show arg; (neg .z.w) (cb; 43);}
```

In the final step, we display another progress message on the server console indicating the remote call has completed. Since this function returns its actual result remotely, we end its body with ';' to ensure that it returns nothing locally.

```
q)rsvp:{[arg;cb] show arg; (neg .z.w) (cb; 43); show `done;}
```

We turn to the client side and create echo to serve as the function called back for this demonstration.

```
q)echo:{show x}              / on client
```

It remains to fire off the remote asynchronous call from the client. We pass the client open handle a list containing: the name of the remote function; the argument for the remote function; and the name of our own function to be called back during the remote computation. Be sure to do it asynchronously else you will get deadlocks.

```
q)(neg h) (`rsvp; 42; `echo)        / on client
```

Provided all went well, the server console will display:

```
q)42
`done
```

The client console should display:

```
q)(neg h) (`rsvp; 42; `echo)
q)43
```

And there you have it. Callbacks built from scratch in q using a few lines of code.

1.21 Websockets 101

In traditional web applications, the browser (as client) initiates requests and the server replies with the page or data requested using the http protocol. The web server does the serious data manipulation. In recent years, browsers and Javascript have evolved to levels of sophistication that permit quite powerful processing to be done safely on the client side—for example, input editing and display formatting. Indeed, you can use WebSockets to put a browser front end on traditional applications, replacing both the web server and proprietary GUI packages in one fell swoop (phrase used with its original meaning).

The key idea of WebSockets is that the client makes an initial http request to upgrade the protocol. Assuming the request is accepted, subsequent communication occurs over TCP/IP sockets protocol. In particular, once the WebSockets connection is made, either the client or server can initiate messaging.

We begin with a simple example that demonstrates how to connect a browser to a q process via WebSockets, request data and then display the result. We assume familiarity with basic html5 and Javascript. Enter the script below in a text editor and save it as `sample1.html` in a location accessible to your browser.

> **Note:** This script uses the `c.js` script for serialization and deserialization between q and javascript, which you can download from http://kx.com/q/c/c.js. For simplicity in this demo, we have placed a copy in the same directory as the `sample1.html` script so that it can be loaded with a (trivial) relative path. You should point this to the location of c.js in your q/kdb installation.

This script creates a minimal page with a field to display the result returned from the q server. After declaring some useful variables, we get to the interesting bits that create the WebSockets connection and handle the data from q. We create a WebSockets object and set its `binaryType` property to "arraybuffer", which is necessary for the exchange of q serialized data.

We wire the behavior of the connection object by attaching handler functions for WebSockets events. Most important are then onopen and `onmessage` events. When the connection is opened, we serialize a Javascript object containing a payload string and send it (asynchronously) to the q process; it will arrive there as a serialized dictionary. Conversely, when a serialized message is received from the q process, we deserialize it and invoke the `sayN` function on the content. The `sayN` function locates the display field on the page and copies its parameter there.

```
<!doctype html>
<html>
<head>
<script src="c.js"></script>
<script>
 var serverurl = "//localhost:5042/",
     c = connect(),
     ws;

  function connect() {
    if ("WebSocket" in window) {
      ws = new WebSocket("ws:" + serverurl);
      ws.binaryType="arraybuffer";
      ws.onopen=function(e){
        ws.send(serialize({ payload: "what is the meaning of life?" }));
      };
      ws.onclose=function(e){
      };
      ws.onmessage=function(e){
        sayN(deserialize(e.data));
      };
      ws.onerror=function(e) {window.alert("WS Error") };
    } else alert("WebSockets not supported on your browser.");
  }

    function sayN(n) {
        document.getElementById('answer').textContent = n;
    }
</script>
```

Now to the server side, where the q code is blissfully short. Start a fresh q session, open port 5042 and set the web socket handler .z.ws to a function that will be called on receipt of each message from the browser.

```
q)\p 5042
q).z.ws:{0N!-9!x; neg[.z.w] -8!42}
```

The handler first displays its parameter, which we do for demonstration only as we have no further use for it in this example. Then it serializes the answer using (-8!) and sends it back (asynchronously) to the browser. That's it!

Now point your browser to

    file:// sample1.html

and you should see the answer displayed in a font large enough to be seen from the international space station. Notice that there is no web server here other than q itself.

Now that we're warmed up, let's try a more interesting example. Here the browser will ask the q server to call out to the Yahoo Finance site and retrieve historical stock price and volume data for Apple. The browser will then use the publicly available High Charts package to display a spiffy stock history graph. In this example there will be a bit more Javascript and q, but it's tolerable. And again, no web server other than q.

First let's tackle the browser side. Save the following text file as ws101.html.

```
<!DOCTYPE HTML>
<html>
<head>
  <script src=
    "http://ajax.googleapis.com/ajax/libs/jquery/1.8.2/jquery.min.js">
  </script>
  <script src="http://code.highcharts.com/stock/highstock.js"></script>
  <script src=
    "http://code.highcharts.com/stock/modules/exporting.js"></script>
</head>
<body>
  <div id="container" style="height: 500px; min-width: 500px"></div>
</body>
<script src="c.js"></script>
<script>
  var serverurl = "//localhost:5042/",
      ws,
      c = connect(),
      ticker = "AAPL",
      startdt = "2008-01-01";

  function connect() {
    if ("WebSocket" in window) {
      ws=new WebSocket("ws:" + serverurl);
      ws.binaryType="arraybuffer";
      ws.onopen=function(e){
        toQ([ticker, startdt]);
      };
      ws.onclose=function(e){
      };
      ws.onmessage=function(e){
        return fromQ(e.data);
      };
      ws.onerror=function(e) {window.alert("WS Error") };
    } else alert("WebSockets not supported on your browser.");
  }

  function toQ(pl) {
    ws.send(serialize({ payload: pl }));
  }
  function fromQ(raw) {
    var data = deserialize(raw);
    return createChart(data);
  }
  function toUTC(x) {
    var y = new Date(x);
    y.setMinutes(y.getMinutes() + y.getTimezoneOffset());
    return y.getTime();
  }
  function createChart(data) {
    $('#container').highcharts('StockChart', {
      rangeSelector : {
        selected : 1
      },
      title : {
        text : ticker + ' Stock Price'
      },
      series : [{
        name : ticker,
        data : data.hist.map(function(x){return [toUTC(x.Date), x.Close]}),
        tooltip: {
```

```
            valueDecimals: 2
        }
    }]
    });
    }
</script>
</html>
```

We provide a concise description of the highlights, assuming familiarity with basic html5 and Javascript.

- Load external scripts from Google (for jquery) and High Charts (for the actual graphical display).
- Specify a simple html element to contain the actual graph.
- Load the local Kx file c.js for q serialization/deserialization.
- Create the connection by calling connect(), which assigns a handler for onopen that calls toQ with the data variables.
- Assign a handler to onmessage that passes the message to fromQ.
- Initialize the variables that specify the historical data we will request from Yahoo Finance.
- The toQ function wraps its parameter in a Javascript object, serializes it and (asynchronously) sends it to the q process where it will manifest as a serialized dictionary.
- The fromQ function deserializes a received q dictionary, which magically becomes a Javascript object, and passes it to the createChart function.
- The auxiliary function toUTC transforms q dates to a form suitable for High Stocks.
- The createChart function instantiates a High Stocks stock price graph and populates the appropriate properties. Note the use of map to iterate over the individual time series points; it is the functional programming equivalent of each in q. Also observe that we use the closing prices for the plot, as is customary.

> **Tip:** The alignment between Javascript objects and q dictionaries, along with built-in serialization/deserialization, makes data transfer between the browser and q effortless.

Now to the q server side, which has fewer lines of code that do much work. Save the following text file as ws101.q.

```
\p 5042

adjDate:{[dt] 0 -1 0i+`year`mm`dd$dt};        / 2015.01.01 -> 2015 0 1i

getHist:{[ticker; sdt; edt]
    tmpl:""\http://ichart.finance.yahoo.com/table.csv?s=",
        "%tick&d=%em&e=%ed&f=%ey&g=d&a=%sm&b=%sd&c=%sy\"";
```

```
  args:string ticker,raze adjDate each (sdt;edt);
  url:ssr/[tmpl; ("%tick";"%sy";"%sm";"%sd";"%ey";"%em";"%ed"); args];
  raw:system "wget  -q -O - ",url;
  t:("DFFFFJF"; enlist ",") 0: raw;
  Date xasc `Date`Open`High`Low`Close`Volume`AdjClose xcol t}

getData:{[ticker; sdt] select Date,Close from getHist[`$ticker;"D"$sdt;.z.D]}

.z.ws:{
  args:(-9!x) `payload;
  neg[.z.w] -8!(enlist `hist)!enlist .[getData; args; `err]}
```

Following is a description of the q code.

- Open port 5042
- Define the adjDate function that extracts a triple of ints comprising the year, month and day from a q date. Note the (weird) decrement of month, which is required by Yahoo Finance.
- Define the function getHist that does the real work.
- Create a string template for the url in which placeholders of the form "%*arg*" will be replaced with specific values.
- Run the start date and end date parameters through the date adjustment, stringify the results and concatenate onto the ticker string to form a list of actual argument strings for the url.
- Use the over operator (/) with ssr (string search and replace) and recursively replace each placeholder in the template with the corresponding stringified argument.
- Instruct the OS to make a wget web call to the fully specified Yahoo Finance url. This returns raw time series data as comma separated string records with column headers in the first row.
- Parse the text data into a table with the appropriate data types.
- Rename the columns suitably for user display, sort by date (just in case) and return the result.

The final entry in the q script sets the web sockets handler. Here is its behavior.

- Deserialize the passed Javascript object into a q dictionary and extract the payload field.
- Perform protected evaluation of the multi-variate getHist function on the passed arguments.
- Serialize the resulting time series table and **asynchronously** send it to the browser, where it appears as a serialized list of Javascript objects, one for each day.

To run this example, start a fresh q process and load the ws101.q script.

```
q) \l /pages/ws101.q
```

Now point your browser at

file:///pages/ws101.html

Wait a few seconds (depending on the speed of your internet connection) and—Voila!—you have a nifty graph of AAPL stock price.

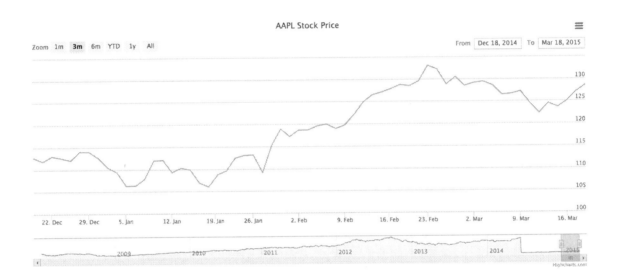

2   Basic Data Types: Atoms

2.0 Overview

All data is ultimately built from atoms. An *atom* is an irreducible value of a specific data type. The basic data types in q correspond mostly to those of traditional programming languages with additional date and time related types that facilitate time series.   The tables below summarize the basic data types, giving the corresponding types in SQL, Java and C#.   Other data types, including enumerations and functions, will be covered when they are discussed in later sections.

Q	SQL	Java	.Net
boolean	Boolean	Boolean	Boolean
guid		UUID	GUID
byte	Byte	Byte	Byte
short	Smallint	Short	Int16
Int	Int	Integer	Int32
long	Bigint	Long	Int64
Real	Real	Float	Single
float	Float	Double	Double
char	Char(1)	Character	Char
symbol	Varchar	String	(String)
date	Date	Date	
timestamp		Timestamp	DateTime
timespan		Timespan	TimeSpan
minute			
second			
time	Time	Time	TimeSpan

> **Tip:** The words under the q heading—boolean, short, int, etc.—are not reserved in q, so they are not displayed in a special font in this text. They do have special meaning when used as name arguments in some operators, so do not use them as names.

The next table collects the important information about q data types. We shall refer to this in subsequent sections.

Type	Size	Char Type	Num Type	Notation	Null Value
boolean	1	b	1	1b	0b
byte	1	X	4	0x26	0x00
short	2	H	5	42h	0Nh
int	4	I	6	42	0N
long	8	J	7	42j	0Nj
real	4	E	8	4.2e	0Ne
float	8	F	9	4.2	0n
char	1	C	10	"z"	" "
symbol	*	S	11	`zaphod	`
timestamp	8	P	12	2015.01.01T00:00:00.000000000	0Np
month	4	M	13	2006.07m	0Nm
date	4	D	14	2006.07.21	0Nd
(datetime)	4	Z	15	2006.07.21T09:13:39	0Nz
timespan	8	N	16	12:00:00.000000000	0Nn
minute	4	U	17	23:59	0Nu
second	4	V	18	23:59:59	0Nv
Time	4	T	19	09:01:02:042	0Nt
enumeration			20+	`sym$`kx	
table			98	([] c1:`a`b`c; c2:10 20 30)	
dictionary			99	`a`b`v!10 20 30	
function			100	{x}	
nil item			101	::	

2.1 Integer Data

Integer data types are ubiquitous in programming. There are three integer types in q.

2.1.1 long

In q versions 3.0 and later, the basic integer type is a signed eight-byte integer, called *long*. A literal is identified as a long by the fact that it contains only numeric digits, with an optional leading minus sign, and **no** decimal point. It may also have an optional trailing type indicator 'j' indicating it is a long and not another integer type. Here is a typical long integer value.

```
q)42
42
```

Observe that the type indicator 'j' is accepted but redundant.

```
q)42j
42
```

> **Important:** In q versions 2.8 and earlier the default integer type when no type indicator was given was the four byte int. Any 2.* long values given with 'j' will carry over to 3.* but if you intend a four byte value you must now explicitly include the type indicator 'i'.

2.1.2 short and int

The two smaller signed integer data types are *short* and *int*. The short type represents a two-byte signed integer and requires the trailing type indicator 'h'. For example,

```
q)-123h
-
```

Similarly, the int type represents a four-byte signed integer and requires the trailing type indicator 'i'.

```
q)1234567890i
-
```

> **_Important:_** Type promotion is performed automatically in arithmetic operations. However, for a homogenous list of atoms of "wide" type, should a narrower type be presented for update or append in place, the narrow type will not be automatically promoted and an error will result. This may be unintuitive in the context of other type promotion, but it will make sense for table columns.

2.2 Floating Point Data

Single and double precision floating point data types are supported. Double precision is more common.

2.2.1 float

The *float* type represents an IEEE standard eight-byte floating-point number, often called "double" in traditional languages. A float can hold (at least) 15 decimal digits of precision. It is denoted by optionally signed numeric digits with either a decimal point or an optional trailing type indicator 'f'. Observe that the console shortens the display of floats with no significant digits to the right of the decimal.

```
q)3.14159265

q)1f

q)1.0
```

A float can also be specified in scientific notation. Here the 'e' standards for "exponent"—i.e., a power of 10—and should not be confused with a type indicator. To the right of the 'e' is a two digit signed exponent. The '+' and leading 0 for a positive exponent are optional.

```
q)1.234e07

q)1.234e7

q)1.234e-7
1.234e-07
```

2.2.2 real

The real type represents a single precision, four-byte floating-point number and is denoted by numeric digits containing a decimal point and a trailing type indicator 'e'. Be mindful that this type is called 'float' in some languages. A real can hold at least 6 decimal digits of precision.

> **Note:** The real type is basically useless in finance since it does not provide enough precision for quantities expressed in currencies such as Yen. We recommend always using float.

The scientific notation of reals is awkward, given the presence of 'e' both for the exponent and the type indicator.

```
q)12.34e
_
q)1.234e7e
_
```

2.2.3 Floating Point Display

The q console display defaults to seven decimal digits of accuracy for float and real values by rounding the display in the seventh significant digit, even though more digits are stored.

```
q)f:1.23456789e-10
q)r:1.2345678e-10e
q)f
1.234568e-010
q)r
1.234568e+010e
```

You can change this by using the \P command (note upper case) to specify a display width up to 16 digits. If you issue \P 0 the console will display all 17 decimal digits of the underlying binary representation, although the last digit is unreliable.

```
q)f12:1.23456789012
q)f16:1.234567890123456
```

```
q)\P 12
q)f12
1.23456789012
q)f16
1.23456789012
```

```
q)\P 16
q)f12
1.23456789012
q)f16
1.234567890123456
```

```
q)\P 0
q)1%3
0.33333333333333331
```

2.3 Binary Data

Binary data can be represented as bit or byte values.

2.3.1 boolean

The *boolean* type uses one byte to store a bit and is denoted by the bit value with the trailing type indicator 'b'. There are **no** keywords for 'true' or 'false', nor are there separate logical operators for booleans.

```
q)0b
_
q)1b
_
```

Binary values are implicitly promoted to unsigned integers when participating in arithmetic expressions or comparisons. For example, the following yields an integer.

```
q)42+1b
_
```

The following yields a float.

```
q)3.1415+0b
_
```

> **Tip:** The ability of booleans to participate in arithmetic can be useful in eliminating conditionals.
>
> ```
> q)flag:1b
> q)base:100
> q)base+flag*42
> 142
> ```

2.3.2 byte

The *byte* type uses one byte to store an unsigned 16-bit value and is denoted by the **leading** type indicator '0x' followed by two hexadecimal digits. Upper or lower case can be used for the alpha hex digits but lower case is customary.

```
q)0x2a
```

```
q)0x2A
```

As with boolean, a byte participates in arithmetic via type promotion to signed int.

```
q)1+0x29
```

2.3.3 GUID

The *guid* type was introduced in q3.0. A GUID (globally unique identifier) is a 16-byte binary value that is unique across time and space (well, nearly so). It is ideally suited for locally generating a globally unique identifier without resorting to a central control mechanism—e.g., transaction ids. It can be used as a table key or in joins and is preferred to strings or symbols in such situations.

The guid type does not have a literal form since it is generated for you by a process that guarantees uniqueness. Applying (?) to the null guid value 0Ng generates a list of guids.

```
q)1?0Ng
,61f35174-90bc-a48a-d88f-e15e4a377ec8
q)2?0Ng

q)-1?0Ng

q)-2?0Ng

```

> *Tip:* The difference between using a positive integer vs. a negative integer to generate a list of GUIDs is that the positive case uses the same initial seed in each new q session whereas the negative case uses a random seed. The former is useful for reproducible results during testing but only the latter should be used in production; otherwise, your "GUIDs" will not be unique across q sessions.

You can import a guid generated elsewhere by parsing a string of 16 hex digits.

```
q)"G"$"61f35174-90bc-a48a-d88f-e15e4a377ec8"
```

You can also convert from a list of 16 bytes using an overload of (sv).

```
q)0x0 sv 16?0xff
```

> **Tip:** Unless these values have been constructed from a legitimate GUID creation process, there is no guarantee they will be unique.

The only operations available for guids are (~), (=), (<), (>) and (null).

2.4 Text Data

There are two atomic text types in q. They are more akin to the SQL types CHAR and VARCHAR than the character types of traditional languages.

2.4.1 char

A *char* holds an individual ASCII or 8-bit Unicode character that is stored in one byte. It corresponds to a SQL CHAR. It is denoted by a single character enclosed in double quotes.

```
q)"q"
```

Some keyboard characters—e.g., the double-quote—cannot be entered directly into a char since they have special meaning in the q console. As in C, special characters are escaped with a preceding back-slash '\'. The console display somewhat confusingly displays the escape, but the following are all actually single characters.

```
q)"\""              / double-quote
"\""
q)"\\"              / back-slash
q)"\n"              / newline
q)"\r"              / return
q)"\t"              / horizontal tab
```

Also as in C, you can escape any ASCII character by specifying its underlying numeric value as three octal digits.

```
q)"\142"
"b"
```

2.4.2 symbol

A symbol is an atom holding text. It is denoted by a leading back-quote, read "back tick" in q-speak.

```
q)`q

q)`zaphod
```

> **Important:** Symbols are used for names in q. All names are symbols but not all symbols are names.

A symbol is akin to a SQL VARCHAR, in that it can hold an arbitrary number of characters, but is different in that it is atomic. The char "q" and the symbol `kdb are both atomic entities. A symbol is irreducible, meaning that the individual characters that comprise it are **not** directly accessible.

A symbol is **not** a string. We shall see in Chapter 3 that there is an analogue of strings in q, namely a list of char. While a list of char is a kissing cousin to a symbol, we emphasize that a symbol is **not** a collection of char. The symbol `a and the char "a" are not the same, as we can see by asking q if they are identical.

```
q)`a~"a"
0b
```

> **Advanced**: A symbol can include arbitrary text, including text that cannot be directly entered from the console—e.g., embedded blanks and special characters such as back-tick. You can manufacture a symbol from any text by casting the corresponding list of char to a symbol. (You will need to escape special characters into the string.) See §6.1.5 for more on casting.
>
> ```
> q)`$"A symbol with blanks and `"
>  A symbol with blanks and `
> ```

2.5 Temporal Data

In the real world, time is measured in a system of units determined by calendars and clocks. A calendar measures multiples of days whereas a clock subdivides a day into smaller units. The notion of "telling time" associates a time to a number in the system of units provided by some choice of calendar and clock. We call such a value a *temporal type*.

Astronomers know that it is most convenient to put the calendar and clock together to have a single measure of time on all scales—i.e., UTC. In common practice, calendar and clock measurements can be made separately where the full scale is not needed.

Our system of calendars and clocks is a hodge-podge based on early astronomy. We measure days by counting rotations of the earth on its axis and years by counting revolutions of the Earth. Months evolved from lunar cycles tracking the changes in the phase of the moon.

Imposed on this is a sexigesimal counting system originated by the ancient Sumerians, who were evidently fond of 12. There were (almost) 360 days in a year and exactly 12 hours of daylight and darkness at equinox. There are 60 minutes in an hour. This was good enough for farmers and astronomers to predict sun and moon cycles 4000 years ago. Increased accuracy of clocks has forced us to adopt leap years, leap seconds and other adjustments to make things come out right. Social and legal customs result in differentiating days into various categories such as business days and holidays. Time zones attempt to make clock time correspond to sunlight and the legislative lunacy of daylight savings time shifts clocks with no actual benefit.

Computer systems have tried to map this mess into the ordered world of bits with varying levels of success. With the advent of nanosecond-based temporal types, time measurement in q is now logical and consistent in that all temporal values are integral counts. These counts are offsets from millennium and midnight, not some point in the 1970s when a system designer realized something had to be done about time.

Q handles time series and relational data in a consistent and efficient manner. It extends the basic SQL date and time data types to facilitate temporal operations, which are minimal in SQL and can be clumsy in traditional languages (e.g., Java's original date library and its time zones).

2.5.1 date

A *date* is stored as a four-byte signed integer and is denoted by *yyyy.mm.dd*, where *yyyy* represents the year, *mm* the month and *dd*

the day. The underlying value is the count of days from Jan 1, 2000—
positive for post-millennium and negative for pre.

```
q)2015.01.01

q)2000.01.01=0
1b
q)2000.01.02=1

q)1999.12.31=-1

```

Since real-world months and days begin at 1 (not zero), January is
`01`. Leading zeroes in months and days are required; their omission
causes an error.

```
q)2015.1.1
'2015.1.1
```

> **Tip:** The underlying day count can be obtained by casting.
>
> ```
> q)`int$2000.02.01
> 
> ```

2.5.2 Time Types

There are two versions of time, depending on the resolution required.
If milliseconds are sufficient, use the *time* type, which stores the count
of milliseconds from midnight in a 32-bit signed integer. It is denoted
by *hh:mm:ss.uuu* where *hh* represents hours on the 24-hour clock, *mm*
represents minutes, *ss* represents seconds, and *uuu* represents
milliseconds.

```
q)12:34:56.789

q)12:00:00.000=12*60*60*1000
1b
```

Leading zeroes are required in all constituents of a time value. The
underlying millisecond count can be obtained by casting to an int.

```
q)`int$12:00:00.000

```

If milliseconds are not sufficient, use the *timespan* type, which stores
the count of nanoseconds from midnight as a long integer.
It is denoted by *0Dhh:mm:ss.nnnnnnnnn* where *hh* represents hours on
the 24-hour clock, *mm* represents minutes, *ss* represents seconds, and
nnnnnnnnn represents nanoseconds. Observe that the leading '0D' is
optional.

```
q)12:34:56.123456789
0D12:34:56.123456789
q)12:34:56.123456            / microseconds become nanos
0D12:34:56.123456000
```

Leading zeroes in constituents are again required.

The underlying nanosecond count can be obtained by casting to a long.

```
q)`long$12:34:56.123456789
```

2.5.3 Date-Time Types

There are two date-time types. The first is deprecated and should not be used; we include it here in case you encounter it in older q code.

A *datetime* (deprecated) is the lexical combination of a date and a time, separated by 'T' as in the ISO standard format. A datetime value stores in a float the fractional day count from midnight Jan 1, 2000.

```
q)2000.01.01T12:00:00.000
```

```
q)2000.01.02T12:00:00.000=1.5
1b
```

The underlying fractional day count can be obtained by casting to float.

```
q)`float$2000.01.02T12:00:00.000
```

Extract the date and time portions from a datetime by casting.

```
q)`date$2000.01.02T12:00:00.000
```

```
q)`time$2000.01.02T12:00:00.000
```

> **Warning**: Do **not** use a datetime for a key or in a join since the underlying float value is fuzzy and may give unexpected results.

The preferred type is *timestamp*, which is the lexical combination of a date and a timespan, separated by 'D'. The underlying timestamp value is a long representing the count of nanoseconds since the millennium. Post-millennium is positive and pre- is negative.

```
q)2014.11.22D17:43:40.123456789
_
```

The underlying nanosecond count can be obtained by casting to long.

```
q)`long$2014.11.22D17:43:40.123456789
_
```

Extract the date and timespan constituents from a timestamp by casting.

```
q)`date$2014.11.22D17:43:40.123456789
_
```

```
q)`timespan$2014.11.22D17:43:40.123456789
_
```

> **Tip:** Use a timestamp instead of a datetime for a key column or in a join. Or separate into date and time columns.

2.5.4 month

The *month* type is stored as a 32-bit signed integer and is denoted by *yyyy.mm* with a trailing type indicator 'm'. A month value is the count of months since the beginning of the millennium. Post-milieu is positive and pre is negative.

```
q)2015.11m
_
```

```
q)2001.01m=12
1b
```

> **Tip:** Leaving off the type indicator 'm' yields a float. This is a common qbie error.
>
> ```
> q)2014.11                    / this is a float!
> 2014.11
> ```

The underlying month count can be obtained by casting to int.

```
q)`int$2015.01m
_
```

> **Tip:** Despite that fact that a month type counts months since the millennium and a date type counts days since the millennium, the first day of the month is equal to the month.

```
q)2015.07m=2015.07.01
1b
```

2.5.5 minute

The *minute* type is stored as a 32-bit signed integer and is denoted by *hh:mm*. A minute value counts the number of minutes from midnight.

```
q)12:30
```

```
q)12:00=12*60
1b
```

The underlying minute count can be obtained by casting to int.

```
q)`int$12:00
```

A minute equals its equivalent time and timestamp counterparts.

```
q)12:00=12:00:00.000
1b
q)12:00=12:00:00.000000000
```

2.5.6 second

The *second* type is stored as 32-bit signed integer and is denoted by *hh:mm:ss*. A second value counts the number of seconds from midnight.

```
q)23:59:59
```

```
q)23:59:59=-1+24*60*60
1b
```

The representation of the second type makes it look like an ordinary, time and it can function as that if you only need resolution to the second. However, a q time value is a count of milliseconds or nanoseconds from midnight, so the underlying values are different.

```
q)`int$12:34:56
45296i
q)`int$12:34:56.000
```

```
q)`long$12:34:56.000000000
```

Nevertheless, these values are equal in the eyes of q—as they should be, since they are merely representations in different units of the same position on a clock.

```
q)12:34:56=12:34:56.000
1b
q)12:34:56.000=12:34:56.000000000
```

2.5.7 Constituents and Dot Notation

The constituents of compound temporal types can be extracted using dot notation. For example, the field values of a date are named 'year', 'mm' and 'dd'; similarly for time and other temporal types.

```
q)dt.year
2014i
q)dt.mm

q)dt.dd


q)ti:12:34:56.789
q)ti.hh
12i
q)ti.mm

q)ti.ss

```

> **Important**: Unfortunately, at the time of this writing (Sep 2015) dot notation for extraction (still) does not work inside functions.

Thus we recommend avoiding dot notation altogether and using cast instead, as it always works for any meaningful temporal extraction or conversion. In addition to the individual field values, you can also extract higher-order constituents.

```
q)`dd$dt
1i
q)`mm$dt

q)`dd$dt

q)`month$dt
2014.01m
```

> **Tip:** To extract milliseconds or nanoseconds from a time type, cast to the underlying integer and mod the result by 1000 or 1000000000.
>
> ```
> q)(`int$12:34:56.789) mod 1000
> 789
> q)(`long$12:34:56.123456789) mod 1000000000
> _
> ```

2.6 Arithmetic Infinities and Nulls

Types whose underlying values are integer or floating point have special lexical forms representing values that lie outside the "normal" domain. We list the basic ones in the following table. The others are obtained by appending the appropriate type suffices.

Literal	Value
0w	Positive float infinity
-0w	Negative float infinity
0n	Null float ; NaN, or not a number
0W	Positive long infinity
-0W	Negative long infinity
0N	Null long

Observe the distinction between lower case `w` in the float literals and upper case `W` in the integer literals. The character 'w' was chosen for its resemblance to the infinity symbol. Seriously.

In q, division of numeric values always results in a float.
In mathematics, division of a positive value by 0 results in positive infinity and division of a negative value by zero results in negative infinity. So it is in q, with the funky symbols 0w and –0w for positive and negative float infinity respectively.

In mathematics, division of zero by zero is undefined. So it is in q, with 0n representing NaN—i.e., an undefined float. The float infinities perform exactly as they should in arithmetic and comparison operations, since they are required to do so by the IEEE spec.

The q philosophy is that any valid arithmetic expression will produce a result rather than a runtime error. Therefore, dividing by 0 produces a special float value rather than throwing an exception. You can perform a complex sequence of calculations without worrying about things blowing up in the middle or having to insert cumbersome exception trapping.

The integral infinities and nulls cannot be produced via division on normal integer values, since the result of division in q is always a float. Moreover, while integral nulls propagate as nulls should, the integral infinities do **not** perform as you would expect in arithmetic operations. The integral infinities **do** produce the correct results in comparisons; in fact, this is their rason d'etre.

```
q)42<0W
1b
q)-0W<42
_
```

To understand the integral nulls and infinities, realize that they are actually valid bit patterns for their corresponding types. Here are the long versions.

q	C Equivalent	Numeric
0N	MIN_INT	-9223372036854775808
-0W	MIN_INT+1	-9223372036854775807
0W	MAX_INT	+9223372036854775807

Consequently, ordering on integers is,

$$0N < -0W < \text{normal integer} < 0W$$

This explains some oddities.

```
q)9223372036854775806+1
0W
q)-0W-1
0N
q)-0W+1
-9223372036854775806
```

> **Tip:** The fact that q does not trap overflow explains the equally bizarre looking,
>
> ```
> q)0W+1
> 0N
> q)0W+2
> -0W
> q)0W+3
> -9223372036854775806
> ```

Implementing proper arithmetic on integer infinities would entail expensive tests in the arithmetic operators and an unacceptable slow-down for normal arithmetic.

2.7 Nulls

2.7.0 Overview of Nulls

The concept of a null value generally indicates missing data. This is an area in which q differs from both traditional programming languages and SQL.

In such languages as C++, Java and C#, the concept of a null value applies to complex entities (i.e., objects) that are allocated on the heap and accessed by pointer or reference. A null pointer corresponds to an unallocated entity, meaning that it has not been assigned the address of an initialized block of memory. (Tony Hoare, who introduced the concept of null pointer, calls it his "billion dollar mistake.") There is no concept of null for entities that are of value type. For those types that admit null, you test for null by asking if the value is equal to a special null marker.

The NULL value in SQL indicates that data is not present. The NULL value is distinct from any value that can actually be contained in a field and it does not have '=' semantics. That is, you do not test a field for null with = NULL. Instead, you ask if it IS NULL. Because NULL is a separate value, Boolean fields, for example, actually have three states: 0, 1 and NULL.

The q situation is more interesting. There are no references or pointers, so the notion of an unallocated entity does not arise. Most types have null values that are distinct from "normal" values and occupy the same amount of storage. Some types do not designate a distinct null value because there is no available bit pattern—i.e., for boolean, byte and char all underlying bit patterns are meaningfully employed. In this case, the value with no information content serves as a proxy for null.

The following table summarizes the way nulls are handled.

Type	Null
boolean*	0b
guid*	0Ng (00000000-0000-0000-0000-000000000000)
byte*	0x00
short	0Nh
Int	0N
long	0Nj
real	0Ne
float	0n
char*	" "
Sym	`
timestamp	0Np
month	0Nm
date	0Nd
datetime	0Nz
timespan	0Nn
minute	0Nu
second	0Nv
time	0Nt

2.7.1 Binary Nulls

The binary types have no null values. There is no room since every bit pattern is a legitimate value.

2.7.2 Numeric and Temporal Nulls

The numeric and temporal types have their own designated null values. Here the situation is similar to SQL, in that you can distinguish missing data from data whose underlying value is zero. In contrast, there is no universal null value and q nulls take the same space as non-nulls.

An advantage of the q approach is that the null values act like other values in expressions. The tradeoff is that you must use the correct null value in type-checked situations.

2.7.3 Text Nulls

Considering a symbol as variable length text justifies that the symbol null is the empty symbol, designated by a naked back-tick (`).

The null value for the char type is the blank character " ". As with binary data, you cannot distinguish between a missing char value and a blank value. Again, this is not seriously limiting in practice, but you should ensure that your application does not rely on this distinction.

Tip: The value "" is **not** a null char. It is an empty list of char.

2.7.4 Testing for Null

You could test for null using (=) but this requires a null literal of correct type. Because q is dynamically typed, this can result in problems if a variable changes type during program execution.

Always use the monadic (null) to test a value for null, as opposed to (=), as it provides a type-independent check. Also, you don't have to remember the funky null literals.

```
q)null 42

q)null `

q)null " "

q)null ""
```

3 Lists

3.0 Overview

All data structures in q are ultimately built from lists: a dictionary is a pair of lists; a table is a special dictionary; a keyed table is a pair of tables. Thus it is important to have a thorough grounding in lists.

All lists are equal but some lists are more equal than others. These are the lists of atoms of homogenous type, called *simple lists*—known in mathematics as vectors. They have optimum storage and performance characteristics.

While q's list operations are similar to those in other functional languages, lists are stored and processed quite differently.

- They are not stored as singly linked lists under the covers. Simple lists occupy contiguous storage and general lists are pointers in contiguous storage.
- Appending items to the end rather than "cons"-ing to the front.
- Efficient direct item access is available via indexing.
- A general list can hold items of different type without resorting to a union (sum) type

It may be instructive to think of q lists as dynamically allocated arrays.

3.1 Introduction to Lists

A list is an ordered collection. "A collection of what?" you ask. More precisely, a list is recursively defined as an ordered collection of atoms and other lists. We pay special attention to the case in which the list comprises atoms of uniform type.

3.1.1 List Definition and Assignment

A (*general*) *list* is an ordered collection of q data. The members of the collection are its *items*. The notation for a general list encloses its items within matching parentheses and separates them with semi-colons.

> **_Tip:_** Whitespace in list notation is optional. In what follows, we shall often insert optional whitespace after the semicolon separators for readability.

```
q)(1; 1.1; `1)

q)(1;2;3)

q)("a";"b";"c";"d")

q)(`Life;`the;`Universe;`and;`Everything)

q)(-10.0; 3.1415e; 1b; `abc; "z")

q)((1; 2; 3); (4; 5))

q)((1; 2; 3); (`1; "2"; 3); 4.4)

```

If you diligently entered each of these examples in your console, you have noticed that q does not always echo what you type. The initial and last three lists are *general* lists, meaning they are not homogenous atoms. This could mean atoms of mixed type, nested lists of uniform type, or atoms and nested lists of mixed type.

Items in a list are sequenced from left to right, providing an inherent order. The lists (1;2) and (2;1) are different. SQL is based on sets, which are inherently unordered. This distinction leads to some subtle differences between the semantics of queries on q tables versus the analogous SQL queries. The inherent ordering of lists makes large time series processing natural and fast in q, while it is cumbersome and slow in standard SQL due to the need to place things in order.

Lists can be assigned to variables exactly like atoms.

```
q)L1:(1;2;3)
q)L2:("z";"a";"p";"h";"o";"d")
q)L3:((1; 2; 3); (`1; "2"; 3); 4.4)
```

3.1.2 count

The number of items in a list is its *count*. You obtain the count of a list by asking for it with the monadic function (count).

```
q)count (1; 2; 3)
3
q)count L1
```

This is our first encounter with a q function (or operator), which we will learn about in Chapters 4 and 5. For now, we need only understand that (count) returns a long equal to the number of items in the list to its right.

> **Tip:** The maximum number of items for a list in q3.* is $2^{64}-1$. In q2.* it was 2 billion.

Observe that the count of an atom is 1 even though an atom is not a list.

```
q)count 42
1
q)count `zaphod
_
```

Other useful operations are provided by (first) and (last) that return the first and last item in a list, respectively.

```
q)first (1; 2; 3)
1
q)last (1; 2; 3)
3
```

3.2 Simple Lists

A list of atoms of a uniform type, called a *simple* list, corresponds to the mathematical notion of a *vector*. Such lists are treated specially in q. They have a simplified notation, take less storage and compute faster than general lists.

> **Tip:** You can always use general list notation, even for simple lists.

Whenever q recognizes that the items of a list are homogenous atoms, it dynamically converts to a simple list without asking for permission. It most cases, the storage and performance advantages justify the imposition. However, in some cases—such as deletion of an outlier item of non-uniform type—this can cause a programming headache because the list will no longer allow appends or updates with items that do not conform to the resulting uniform type.

3.2.1 Simple Integer Lists

The console display of a simple list of any numeric type omits the enclosing parentheses and replaces the separating semi-colons with (required) blanks. The following two expressions define the same list, as q verifies by testing for identity using (~).

```
q)(100;200;300)
q)100 200 300
q)100 200 300~(100; 200 ; 300)
1b
```

The console display of the first expression demonstrates the automatic conversion to simple lists previously mentioned.

Similar notation, with the addition of a single trailing type indicator, is used for simple lists of short and int.

```
q)(1h; 2h; 3h)
1 2 3h
q)(100i; 200i; 300i)
```

Tip: The trailing type indicator in the console display of a simple list applies to the entire list and not just the last item of the list; otherwise, the list would not be simple and would be displayed in general form.

```
q)(1; 2; 3h)
1
2
3h
```

3.2.2 Simple Floating Point Lists

Simple lists of float and real are notated the same as integral lists.

```
q)(123.4567; 9876.543; 99.0)
123.4567 9876.543 99
q)123.4567 9876.543 99
```

Observe that the q console suppresses the decimal point when displaying a float having zero(es) to the right of the decimal; but the value is not an integer. This notational efficiency for float display means that a list of floats having no decimal parts displays with a trailing 'f'.

```
q)1.0 2.0 3.0
1 2 3f
q)1 2 3f~1.0 2.0 3.0
```

Also observe that if you include what appears to be an integer in a list of float, q assumes that you are following its convention by merely omitting redundant data to the right of the decimal. That is, you get a list of float and not a general list.

```
q)1.1 2 3.3~1.1 2.0 3.3
_
```

3.2.3 Simple Binary Lists

The abbreviated notation for a simple list of boolean or byte data juxtaposes the individual data values together with **no** whitespace between. The 'b' type indicator for boolean trails the list.

```
q)(0b;1b;0b;1b;1b)
01011b
q)01011b
_
```

> **Tip:** A simple list of boolean atoms requires the same number of bytes to store as it has atoms. While the simplified notation is suggestive of a bit mask, multiple bits are not compressed to fit inside a single byte. The boolean list above uses 5 bytes of storage.

The '0x' indicator for a simple list of byte precedes the list.

```
q)(0x20;0xa1;0xff)
0x20a1ff
q)0x20a1ff~0x20;0xa1;0xff)
_
```

The display of a simple list of GUIDs is the same is that of integers—i.e., the values are separated by spaces.

```
q)3?0Ng
_
```

3.2.4 Simple Symbol Lists

The abbreviated notation for simple lists of symbols juxtaposes the individual atoms with no intervening whitespace.

```
q)(`Life;`the;`Universe;`and;`Everything)
`Life`the`Universe`and`Everything
q)`Life`the`Universe`and`Everything
_
```

Inserting spaces between symbol atoms causes an error.

```
q)`bad `news
'bad
```

3.2.5 Simple char Lists and Strings

The simplified notation for a list of char looks just like a string in most languages, with the juxtaposed sequence of characters enclosed in double quotes.

```
q)("s"; "t"; "r"; "i"; "n"; "g")
"string"
q)"string"
```

A simple list of char is actually called a *string*; however, it does not have the atomic semantics of a string in most languages. Since it is a list of char, **not** an atom, you cannot ask if two strings of different lengths are equal. You **can** ask if they are identical (as you can with any two q entities).

```
q)"string"="text"
'length
q)"string"~"text"
0b
```

3.2.6 Lists of Temporal Data

Since they are really integers, the abbreviated form for simple temporal lists separates items with a space.

```
q)(2000.01.01; 2001.01.01; 2002.01.01)

q)(00:00:00.000; 00:00:01.000; 00:00:02.000)
```

Specifying a list of mixed temporal types has a different behavior from that of a list of mixed numeric types. In this case, the list takes the type of the first item in the list; other items are widened or narrowed to match.

```
q)12:34 01:02:03
12:34:00 01:02:03
q)01:02:03 12:34
```

To force the type of a mixed list of temporal values, append a type specifier.

```
q)01:02:03 12:34 11:59:59.999u
01:02 12:34 11:59
```

3.3 Empty and Singleton Lists

Lists with one or zero items merit special consideration, especially since q's notation and display are not exactly intuitive.

3.3.1 The General Empty List

It is useful to have lists with no items. A pair of parentheses enclosing nothing (except optional whitespace) denotes the general empty list, which (annoyingly) has no console display.

```
q)()
q)
```

We shall see in §6.2 that it is possible to define an empty list with a specific type, so that only items of that type can be added to it.

Advanced: If you want to force the display of an empty list, use the q utility (-3!), which converts any q entity into a string suitable for display. Perhaps this utility should be called the "wizard of Oz" operator since it reveals what's behind the curtain.

```
q)L:()
q)L
q)-3!L
"()"
```

3.3.2 Singleton Lists

A *singleton* is a list containing a single item. As any postal clerk will tell you, an item in a box is not the same as an unboxed item. So an atom and a singleton containing that atom are different.

The syntax of a singleton presents a notational conundrum for q. We might expect to write the singleton list containing 42 as (42) but we cannot. The issue arises from q's use of parentheses both for list demarcation and for the usual mathematical grouping in expressions. The latter leads to the following sequence of arithmetic reductions.

$$(40+2) \rightarrow (42) \rightarrow 42$$

This forces (42) to be the **atom** 42.

Unfortunately, there is no way to type a singleton literal. Singletons are created by the function (enlist), which "boxes" its argument into a list with one item. Note that it manages to avoid the usual q predilection for aggressively short names.

```
q)enlist 42
,42
```

Observe that the console display of a singleton list uses the k form of enlist—i.e., monadic (,). Don't be fooled: we can't use this in q.

> **Tip:** A string with a single character cannot be written syntactically as "a"—this is a character atom. Use (enlist). This is a common error for qbies.
>
> ```
> q)"a"
> _
> q)enlist "a"
> _
> ```

A singleton need not contain an atom as its sole item; it can be any q entity.

```
q)enlist 1 2 3
1 2 3
```

```
q)enlist (10 20 30; `a`b`c)
10 20 30 a  b  c
```

Observe that the console display is not consistent with showing ',' and sometimes is downright confusing.

3.4 Indexing

A list is sequenced from left-to-right in the position of its items. The offset of an item from the beginning of the list is called its *index*. The initial item has index 0, the second item has index 1, etc. Thus a list of count *n* has items at indices 0 through *n* - 1.

> **Tip:** There is no item at index n. This is a common qbie mistake.

3.4.1 Index Notation

To access the item at index *i* in a list, follow the list immediately with [*i*]. This is called *item indexing*. For example,

```
q)(100; 200; 300)[0]
100
q)100 200 300[0]
100
q)L:100 200 300
q)L[0]
100
q)L[1]

q)L[3]                  / index out of bounds returns null value

q)L[2]

```

3.4.2 Indexed Assignment

Items in a list can also be assigned via item indexing. Thus,

```
q)L:1 2 3
q)L[1]:42
q)L
1 42 3
```

> **Important:** Index assignment into a simple list enforces strict type matching with no type promotion. Otherwise put, when you assign an item into a simple list, the type must match exactly—i.e., a narrower type is not widened.
>
> ```
> q)L:100 200 300
> q)L[1]:42h
> 'type
> ```

This may come as a surprise if you are accustomed to numeric values always being promoted in a dynamically typed language—e.g., q itself.

> **Tip:** Should you find exceptions to this in some releases of q3.*, do not count on them being there in future releases!

3.4.3 Indexing Domain

Providing an invalid data type for the index results in an error.

```
q)L:(-10.0; 3.1415e; 1b; `abc; "z")
q)L[1.0]
'type
```

In contrast, if you index outside the proper bounds of the list, the result is **not** an error. Instead you get a null value, indicating "missing data." Specifically, indexing outside the range of 0 to *(count L) – 1* yields a null of the type of the item at index 0. This is the most efficient thing to return in the case of a general list where there is no canonical item type.

```
q)L1:1 2 3 4
q)L1[4]
0N
q)L2:1.1 2.2 3.3
q)L2[-1]
0n
q)L3:(`1; 2; 3.3)
q)L3[0w]
```

> **Tip:** Pay special attention to the first example above that indexes the list at its count. Indexing one position past the end of the list is easy for qbies, especially if you're not accustomed to indexing relative to 0.

3.4.4 Empty Index and Null Item

An omitted index returns the entire list.

```
q)L:10 20 30 40
q)L[]
10 20 30 40
```

An omitted index is **not** the same as indexing with an empty list. The latter returns an empty list, so we use the (-3!) utility to reveal its display.

```
q)-3!L[()]
"()"
```

The syntactic form double-colon (::) denotes the nil item, which allows explicit notation or programmatic generation of an empty index.

```
q)L[::]
_
```

> **Advanced**: The type of the nil item does not match any other type in q. Consequently, inclusion of the nil item in a list forces the list to be general.
>
> ```
> q)L:(::; 1 ; 2 ; 3)
> q)type L
> 0h
> q)-3!L[0]
> "::"
> ```

This is one way to avoid a q nasty surprise when q would otherwise automatically convert a list to simple type. A simple case is when you reassign the only non-conforming item in the list.

```
q)L:(1; 2; 3; `a)
q)L[3]:4
q)L
1 2 3 4
q)L[3]:`a
'type
```

After the reassignment you can no longer assign `a back into the list in its original position. One way to avoid this is by placing :: in the list as a guard.

```
q)L:(::; 1 ; 2 ; 3; `a)
q)L[4]:4
q)L[4]:`a
q)
```

A drawback of this technique is that you must avoid passing :: on to expressions that use the actual data in the list.

3.4.5 Lists with Expressions

Any valid q expression can occur in list construction.

```
q)a:42
q)b:43
q)(a; b)
42 43
q)L1:1 2 3
q)L2:40 50
q)(L1; L2)
q)(count L1; sum L2)
```

> **Tip:** You cannot use the abbreviated notation of simple lists with variables.
>
> ```
> q)a:42
> q)b:43
> q)a b
> ': Bad file descriptor
> ```

The reason for this cryptic error message will be apparent when we deal with files later.

3.5 Combining Lists

3.5.1 Joining with (,)

We scoop the presentation on operators in the next chapter to describe the *join* operator (,). Its result is a new list in which (a copy of) the right operand is appended to the end of (a copy of) the left operand. Join accepts an atom in either argument—i.e., as if the corresponding singleton had been supplied.

```
q)1 2 3,4 5
1 2 3 4 5
q)1,2 3 4
1 2 3 4
q)1 2 3,4
1 2 3 4
```

Observe that if the arguments are not of uniform type, the result is a general list.

```
q)1 2 3,4.4 5.5
```

> **Tip:** To ensure that a q entity *x* becomes a list, use either (),x or x,(). This leaves a list unchanged but effectively enlists an atom. Such a seemingly trivial expression is actually useful and is our first example of a q idiom. You cannot use enlist x for the same purpose. Why not?

3.5.2 Merging with (^)

Another way to combine two lists of the same length is by coalescing them with (^). The result is given by the rule that the right item prevails over the corresponding left item except when the right item is null.

```
q)L1:10 0N 30
q)L2:100 200 0N
q)L1^L2
100 200 30
```

3.6 Lists as Maps

Thus far, we have considered a list as data—i.e., a static collection of its items. We can also view it as a mathematical mapping provided by item indexing. Specifically, a list provides a map whose domain is integers and whose codomain is the collection of its items (supplemented with a null value). The list map assigns the output value L[i] to the input value i.

    i |-> L[i]

Here are the I/O tables for some basic lists.

101 102 103 104

I	O
0	
	101
1	
	102
2	
	103
3	
	104

(`a; 123.45; 1b)

I	O
0	
	`a
1	
	123.45
2	
	1b

(1 2; 3 4)

I	O
0	
	1 2
1	
	3 4

The codomains of the first two examples are collection of atoms. The last example has a codomain comprised of lists.

A list not only acts like a map, it **is** a monadic map whose notation is the same as function application. This is a useful way of looking at things. We shall see in Chapter 4 that a nested list can be viewed as a multivalent map.

From the perspective of lists as maps, the fact that indexing outside the bounds of a list returns a null means the map is implicitly extended to the domain of all integers with null output value outside the list proper.

3.7 Nesting

Data complexity is built by using lists as items of lists.

3.7.1 Depth

Now that we're comfortable with simple lists, we return to general lists. *Nested* lists have item(s) that are themselves lists. The number of levels of nesting for a list is called its *depth*. Informally, the depth measures how much repeated indexing is necessary to arrive at only atoms. Atoms have depth 0 and simple lists have depth 1.

The notation of complex lists is reflected in nested parentheses. For pedagogical purposes, in this section only, we shall often use general notation to define even simple lists since the parentheses make things manifest. However, the console always displays lists in the most concise form.

Following is a list of depth 2 that has three items, the first two being atoms and the last a list. We also show its simplified notation.

```
q)L:(1;2;(100;200))
q)count L

q)L:(1;2;100 200)

q)count L
3
q)L[0]

q)L[1]

q)L[2]
100 200
```

3.7.2 Pictorial Representation

We present a pictorial representation that may help in visualizing levels of nesting. An atom is represented as a circle containing its value. A list is represented as a box containing its items. A general list is a box containing boxes and atoms.

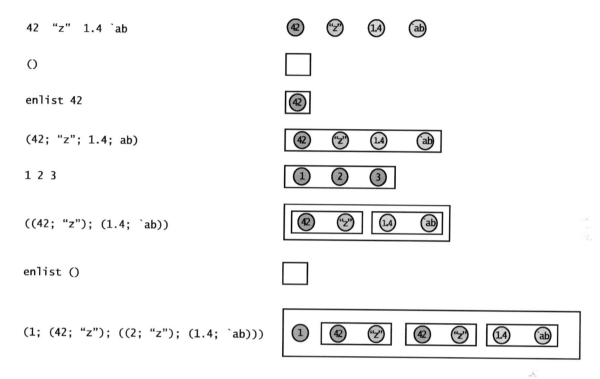

3.7.3 Examples

Following is a list of depth 2 with two elements, each of which is a simple list.

```
q)L2:((1;2;3);(`ab;`c))
q)count L2
2
```

Following is a list of depth 2 having three elements, two of which are general lists and one is an atom.

```
q)L3:((1; 2h; 3j); ("a"; `bc`de); 1.23)
q)count L3

q)L3[1]

q)count L3[1]

```

Following is a list of depth 2 having one item that is a simple list.

```
q)L4:enlist 1 2 3 4
q)count L4

q)count L4[0]

```

Following is a "rectangular" list that can be thought of as the 3x4 matrix its display resembles.

```
q)m:((11; 12; 13; 14); (21; 22; 23; 24); (31; 32; 33; 34))
q)m
11 12 13 14
21 22 23 24
31 32 33 34
q)m[0]

q)m[1]

q)m[1][0]
```

3.8 Iterated Indexing and Indexing at Depth

In the examples above, we saw that the display of nested lists suggests arrays from other languages. You can indeed think of them as "ragged" arrays, as long you are careful about the iterated indexing. Indexing at depth is an alternate notation that suggests nested lists can also be viewed as higher dimensional arrays.

3.8.1 Iterated Item Indexing

Retrieving an item in a nested list via a single index retrieves a top-most item.

```
q)L:(1; (100; 200; (1000; 2000; 3000; 4000)))
q)L[0]

q)L[1]
100
200
1000 2000 3000 4000
```

Interpreting list indexing as function application for positional retrieval, we can read the last line,

> Retrieve the item at index 1 from L

Since the result L[1] is itself a list, we can also retrieve its items via indexing. For example,

```
q)L[1][2]
1000 2000 3000 4000
```

Read this as,

> Retrieve the item at index 2 from the item at index 1 in L

We can once again index into this result.

```
q)L[1][2][0]
1000
```

Read this as,

> Retrieve the item at index 0 from the item at index 2
> in the item at index 1 in L

3.8.2 Indexing at Depth

There is an alternate notation for iterated indexing into a nested list. It is strictly syntactic sugar and amounts to the same thing under the covers. This notation is called *indexing at depth* and it looks exactly like application of a multi-valent function (which, in fact, it is). The previous retrieval can also be written as,

```
q)L[1;2;0]
```

From one point of view, indexing at depth simplifies the notation for retrieval of inner items from a nested list.

Tip: The semicolons in indexing at depth notation might make it appear that the collection of indices is a list. It is not, although we shall see later a way to perform indexing at depth in which the indices are a list. Also, don't confuse the semicolons with commas, which is a common qbie mistake.

Assignment via index at depth works but assignment does **not** work with iterated indexing.

```
q)L:(1; (100; 200; (1000 2000 3000 4000)))
q)L[1; 2; 0]: 999
q)L

q)L[1][2][0]:42
'assign
```

The last expression fails essentially because the intermediate retrievals are ephemeral—i.e., they not addressable entities.

To confirm that the notation for indexing at depth is reasonable, we return to our "matrix" example.

```
q)m:((11; 12; 13; 14); (21; 22; 23; 24); (31; 32; 33; 34))
q)m

q)m[0][0]
11
q)m[0; 0]
11
q)m[0; 1]

q)m[1; 2]

```

The indexing at depth notation suggests thinking of m as a multi-dimensional matrix, whereas repeated single indexing suggests thinking of it as an array of arrays. Chacun à son goût.

> **Advanced**: It is possible to create a (possibly ragged) array of a given number of rows or columns from a flat list using the reshape operator (#) by specifying 0N (missing data) for the number of rows or columns in the left operand.
>
> ```
> q)2 0N#til 10
> 0 1 2 3 4
> 5 6 7 8 9
>
> q)0N 3#til 10
> 0 1 2
> 3 4 5
> 6 7 8
> ,9
> ```

3.9 Indexing with Lists

As a vector language, q prefers to deal with lists whenever possible. To this end, there is no reason to restrict list retrieval to one item at a time.   Instead, we can ask for a list of items by passing a list of indices.

3.9.1 Retrieving Multiple Items

In this section, we begin to see the power of q as a vector language. We start with,

```
q)L:100 200 300 400
```

We know how to index single items of the list.

```
q)L[0]
100
q)L[2]
```

By extension, we can retrieve a list of multiple items via multiple indices. For simplicity we use simple list notation for the indices.

```
q)L[0 2]
100 300
```

The indices can be in any order, or even be duplicated and the corresponding items are retrieved. The shape of the output conforms to the input.

```
q)L[3 2 0 1]

q)L[0 2 0]
```

Here are some examples of indexing into literal lists.

```
q)01101011b[0 2 4]
011b
q)"beeblebrox"[0 7 8]
```

Tip: Using a list as an index demonstrates why getting the semi-colon separators right is essential when indexing at depth. Leaving them out or using commas effectively specifies multiple indices, and you will get a corresponding list of values from the top level.

3.9.2 Indexing via a Variable

When retrieving items via multiple indices, the indices can live in a variable.

```
q)L
100 200 300 400
q)I:0 2
q)L[I]
100 300
```

3.9.3 Indexing with Nested Lists

Observe that in our examples of list indexing, the result of index retrieval has the same shape as the index. If the index is an atom the result is an atom. When the index list was a simple list, the result was a list of the same count.

More generally, we can retrieve via an arbitrary collection of indices. The retrieved list has the same shape as the index list.

```
q)L:100 200 300 400
q)L[(0 1; 2 3)]
100 200
300 400
```

Do not confuse this with indexing at depth. In the present case all items are retrieved at the top level only

> **Advanced:** More precisely, the result of indexing via a list conforms to the index list. The notion of *conformability* of lists is defined recursively. All atoms conform. Two lists conform if they have the same number of items and each of their corresponding items conform. In plain language, two lists conform if they have the same shape.

3.9.4 Assignment with List Indexing

Recall that a list item can be (re)assigned via item indexing,

```
q)L:100 200 300 400
q)L[0]:100
q)L
_
```

Assignment via index extends to indexing via a simple list with the proviso that the index list and value list conform.

```
q)L[1 2 3]:2000 3000 4000
q)L
_
```

Assignment via a simple index list is processed in sequence—i.e., from left-to-right. Thus,

```
q)L[3 2 1]:999 888 777
```

is equivalent to,

```
q)L[3]:999
q)L[2]:888
q)L[1]:777
```

Consequently, in the case of a repeated item in the index list (not a swell idea), the right-most assignment prevails.

```
q)L:100 200 300 400
q)L[0 1 0 3]:1000 2000 3000 4000
q)L
_
```

You can assign a single value to multiple items in a list by using an atom for the assignment value. This is an example of a general phenomenon in q in which an atom is extended to conform to a list.

```
q)L:100 200 300 400
q)L[1 3]:999
q)L
_
```

3.9.5 Juxtaposition

Now that we're familiar with retrieving and assigning via an index list, we introduce a simplified notation that is common in functional programming. It is permissible to leave out the brackets and juxtapose the list and index with separating whitespace (usually just a blank). Some examples follow.

```
q)L:100 200 300 400
q)L[0]
100
q)L 0
100
q)L[2 1]
_
q)L 2 1
_
q)I:2 1
q)L I
_
q)L ::
_
```

| *Tip:* In the colloquial, "We don't need no stinkin' brackets!" |

Which notation you use is a matter of personal preference. In this tutorial, we initially use brackets, since this notation is probably most comfortable for qbies coming from traditional programming. Experienced q programmers often use juxtaposition since it reduces notational density, although brackets can eliminate some parentheses.

3.9.6 Find (?)

The find operator is (an overload of) dyadic (?) that returns the index of the first occurrence of the right operand in the left operand.

```
q)1001 1002 1003?1002
1
```

> **Tip:** Since find maps an item to its index, it is inverse to indexing—i.e., list positional retrieval thought of as a mapping.

If you try to find an item that is not in the list, the result is an integer equal to the count of the list.

```
q)1001 1002 1003?1004
3
```

One way to think of this result is that the position of an item that is not in the list is one past the end of the list, which is where it would be if you were to append it to the list.

Find is atomic in the right operand meaning that it extends to lists.

```
q)1001 1002 1003?1003 1001
_
```

3.10 Elided Indices

3.10.1 Eliding Indices for a Matrix

We return to the situation of indexing at depth for nested lists. For simplicity, we start with a rectangular list that displays as a matrix.

```
q)m:(1 2 3 4; 100 200 300 400; 1000 2000 3000 4000)
q)m
_
```

Analogy with traditional matrix notation suggests that we could retrieve a row or column from m by providing a "partial" index at depth. This indeed works because eliding an index in any slot is equivalent to specifying all legitimate indices for that slot.

```
q)m[1;]
100 200 300 400
m[;3]
4 400 4000
```

Observe that eliding the last index reduces to item indexing at the top level.

```
q)m[1;]~m[1]
```
—

> **Tip:** Because of this correspondence, it is permissible to drop the trailing semicolon. We recommend against this practice as it makes the purpose of code less evident.

The situation of eliding the first index is more interesting. It essentially retrieves a "column" as a slice through the top-level lists—i.e., a row.

3.10.2 Eliding Indices for Deeply Nested Lists

Let's tackle three levels of nesting. Here we can elide one or two indices in any slots.

```
q)L:((1 2 3;4 5 6 7);(`a`b`c`d;`z`y`x`;`0`1`2);("now";"is";"the"))
q)L
(1 2 3;4 5 6 7)
(`a`b`c`d;`z`y`x`;`0`1`2)
("now";"is";"the")

q)L[;1;]
4 5 6 7
`z`y`x`
"is"
q)L[;;2]
3 6
`c`x`2
"w e"
```

Interpret L[;1;] as,

> Retrieve all items at index 1 of each top level list

Interpret L[;;2] as,

> Retrieve the items at index 2 for each list at the second level

Observe that in L[;;2] the attempt to retrieve the item at index 2 of the string "is" was out of bounds and so resulted in the null value " ". This is the source of the blank in "w e" of the result.

As the final exam for this section, let's combine an elided index with indexing by lists to retrieve a cross-section of L. Try to predict the result before entering the expression into your console session.

```
q)L[0 2;;0 1]
```

Interpret this as,

> Retrieve the items at positions 0 and 1 from all columns in rows 0 and 2

Style Recommendation: In general, it is permissible to elide all trailing semicolons arising from elided indices. We consider this bad practice. Looking at the notation below, would you guess that the expression after the comment arose from that to the left of it? We didn't think so.

```
L[1;;]        / instead of L[1]
L[;1;]        / instead of L[;1]
```

3.11 Rectangular Lists and Matrices

3.11.1 Rectangular Lists

In this section, we further investigate matrix-like nested lists. A rectangular list is a list of lists all having the same count. This does not mean that a rectangular list is necessarily a traditional matrix, since there can be additional levels of nesting.

```
q)L:(1 2 3; (10 20; 100 200; 1000 2000))
q)L
1     2       3
10 20 100 200 1000 2000
```

A rectangular list can be transposed with (flip), meaning that the rows and columns are reflected across the diagonal. When (flip) is applied to a rectangular list, it physically transposes the data—i.e., it allocates new storage and copies the original data in column order.

```
q)L:(1 2 3; 10 20 30; 100 200 300)
q)L
1   2   3
10  20  30
100 200 300
q)flip L
1 10 100
2 20 200
3 30 300
```

This effectively reverses the first and second slots in indexing at depth.

```
q)L:(1 2 3; 10 20 30; 100 200 300)
q)M:flip L
q)L[1;2]
30
q)M[2;1]
30
```

3.11.2 Formal Definition of Matrices

Matrices are a special case of rectangular lists and are defined recursively. A matrix of dimension 0 is a scalar. A matrix of dimension 1 is a simple list—i.e., a vector. The count of a vector is usually called its length or dimension in mathematics. Some functional programming languages have tuples, which can be thought of as coordinates of fixed-dimension vectors with respect to a basis; q does not.

In q, vectors do not need to be of numeric type.

```
q)v1:1 2 3                               / vector of integers

q)v2:98.60 99.72 100.34 101.93          / float vector

q)v3:`so`long`and`thanks`for`all`the`fish   / symbol vector
```

For *n*>1, we define a *matrix of dimension n* as a list of matrices of dimension *n* - 1 all having the same size. Thus, a matrix of dimension 2 is a list of vectors, all having the same size. If all atoms in a matrix have the same type, we call this the *type* of the matrix.

3.11.3 Two and Three Dimensional Matrices

Let m be a two-dimensional matrix as defined in the previous section. The items of m are its *rows*. As we have already seen, the ith row of m can be obtained via item indexing as m[i]. Equivalently, we can use an elided index with indexing at depth to obtain the ith row as m[i;].

The console display of m in tabular form motivates defining the list m[;j] as the jth *column* of m. The notations m[i][j] and m[i;j] both retrieve the same item—namely, the item in row *i* and column *j*.

We make one final observation. Matrices are nested lists stored in row order. When the rows are simple, each occupies contiguous storage. This makes row retrieval very fast. On the other hand, columns must be picked out of the rows, so column operations are slower.

Advanced: By convention we consider a matrix to be a collection of rows. It would be equally valid to consider each vector as a column and a two dimensional array as a collection of columns. As we shall see in Chapter 8, a table is a collection of columns that are logically (not physically) transposed for ease of indexing. The constraints and calculations of q-sql operate on table column lists, so they are fast, especially when the columns are simple lists. In particular, a simple time series can be represented by two parallel lists, one holding temporal values and the other holding the associated values. Retrieving and manipulating the columns in vector operations is faster by orders of magnitude than performing the same operations in an RDBMS that stores data in rows with undefined order.

Higher dimensional matrices occur less frequently in q than in its ancestors. For completeness, here is an example of a three-dimensional 2x3x2 matrix—i.e., each of the two top-level items is a 3x2 matrix. Observe that the console display of mm is unenlightening.

```
q)mm:((1 2;3 4;5 6);(10 20;30 40;50 60))
q)mm

q)mm[0]

q)mm[1]
```

3.11.4 Matrix Flexibility

We have seen that although there is no separate construct for matrices in q, rectangular lists look and act like their mathematical matrix counterparts. However, they have features not available in simple mathematical notation or in most traditional languages. We have seen that a rectangular list can be viewed and manipulated both as a multi-dimensional array (i.e., indexing at depth) and as an array of arrays (repeated item indexing). In addition, we can extend individual item indexing with indexing via lists.

```
q)m:(1 2; 10 20; 100 200; 1000 2000)
q)m 0 2
```

3.12 Useful List Operations

In this section we demonstrate basic use cases for some list operations that are frequently used in following chapters.

3.12.1 til

The monadic (til) takes a non-negative integer *n* and returns a list of *n* consecutive natural numbers starting at 0. It is useful for constructing regular lists of integers.

```
q)til 10
0 1 2 3 4 5 6 7 8 9
q)1+til 10

q)2*til 10

q)1+2*til 10

q)-5+4*til 3
```

> **Tip:** If your code includes constructs of the form
>
>   *function* each til count …
>
> you are almost certainly writing loopy—i.e., non-vector—code, otherwise known as VBQ.

3.12.2 distinct

The monadic function (distinct) returns the unique items in its list argument, in order of first occurrence.

```
q)distinct 1 2 3 2 3 4 6 4 3 5 6
1 2 3 4 6 5
```

3.12.3 where

The basic form of (where) returns the indices of 1b in a boolean list—i.e., it reports where the ones are.

```
q)where 101010b
0 2 4
```

This is useful to operate at positions that are indentified by a predicate.

```
q)L:10 20 30 40 50
q)L[where L>20]:42
q)L
_
```

3.12.4 group

The monadic function (group) takes a list and returns a dictionary in which each distinct item of the argument is mapped to the indices of its occurrences, in order of occurence.

```
q)group "i miss mississippi"
i| 0 3 8 11 14 17
 | 1 6
m| 2 7
s| 4 5 9 10 12 13
p| 15 16
```

4 Operators

4.0 Operators and Verbs Are Functions

Purists call the q operators verbs. Reading the expression 2+3 right-to-left as "3 added to 2," the operand 3 is a noun (subject), the operator (+) is a verb and the operand 2 is a noun (object). They are really just built-in functions. We shall use all three terminologies—operator, function, and verb—interchangeably.

4.0.1 Function Notation

Operators are built-in functions used with in-fix notation. We examine functions in depth in Chapter 5, but cover some salient points here. There are two main differences between the functions we can write and built-in functions.

- Our functions must have alphanumeric names whereas q functions can have purely symbolic names.
- Our functions can only be used in prefix notation whereas q functions can be used prefix or infix.

Function application in q uses square brackets to enclose the arguments, and semicolons to separate multiple arguments. Thus the output value of a monadic function f for the input x is written f[x] We can omit the brackets for monadic application and write f x. Application of a dyadic function g on arguments x and y is written g[x;y] in prefix or x g y in infix.

An *atomic* function acts recursively on data structures. For example, applying it to a list is the same as applying it to each item in the listapter 5.

4.0.2 Primitives, Verbs and Functional Notation

The normal way of writing addition in mathematics and most programming languages uses an operator with infix notation—e.g., addition is written with a plus symbol between the two operands.

    2+3

In q, we can write addition this way and read it right-to-left as "add 3 to 2.".

```
q)2+3
```

A q dyadic function written with infix notation is also called a *verb*. This terminology arises from thinking of the operands as nouns that the functions act on. Although some purists are strict in using this terminology, we shall not be.

The *primitive operators* are built-in functions, including the basic arithmetic, relation and comparison operators. Some are represented by a single ASCII symbol such as '+', '-', '=', and '<'. Others use compound symbols, such as '<=', '>=', and '<>'. Still others have names such as 'not' or 'neg'.

An operator/verb can also be used with ordinary function notation. For example, we can also use (+) as a dyadic function that takes two numeric arguments and returns a numeric result. You probably wouldn't think twice at seeing sum[a;b] but you might blink at the following perfectly logical equivalent.

```
q)+[2;3]
```

Qbies will definitely need to get accustomed to,

```
q)=[2;3]
```

It is even possible to write a binary verb using a combination of infix and functional notation. This may look strange, even to initiates.

```
q)(2+)[3]
5
q)(2+)3
```

4.0.3 Extension of Atomic Functions

A fundamental feature of atomic functions is that their action extends automatically to the items in a list. Of course, if you want to combine two lists they must be of the same length.

108

```
q)neg 1 2 3
-1 -2 -3
q)1 2 3+10 20 30
11 22 33
q)1 2 3+10 20 30 40
'length
```

This applies to nested lists as well, provided they conform in shape for multivalent functions.

```
q)neg (1 2 3; 4 5)
-1 -2 -3
-4 -5
q)(1 2 3; 4 5)+(100 200 300; 400 500)
101 202 303
404 505
```

Another fundamental property of atomic operators is that they implicitly extend atom arguments to match lists.

```
q)100+1 2 3
101 102 103
q)1 2 3+100
_
```

Atom extension also applies with nested lists.

```
q)100+(1 2 3; 4 5)
101 102 103
104 105
q)(1 2 3; 4 5)+100
_
```

4.1 Operator Precedence

There is none.

4.1.1 Traditional Operator Precedence

Mathematical operators and most programming languages have a concept of operator precedence, which attempts to resolve ambiguities in the evaluation of arithmetic and logical operations in expressions. The arithmetic precedence rules were drummed into you in elementary school: multiplication and division are equal and come before addition and subtraction, etc. There are similar precedence rules for =, <, >, 'and' and 'or'.

4.1.2 Left-of-Right Evaluation

Although the traditional notion of operator precedence has the weight of incumbency (not to mention the imprecations of your fifth grade math teacher), it's time to throw the bum out. As mentioned in Chapter 1, q has no rules for operator precedence. Instead, it has one simple rule for evaluating any expression:

Expressions are evaluated left-**of**-right

which equates to

Expressions are evaluated right-**to**-left

Please review the Mathematics Refresher if the notion of left-of-right is new to you. The short version is that the composite $f(g(x))$, read "f of g of x" is evaluated by first substituting x into g and then substituting that result into f. Evaluating the inner function first actually becomes right-to-left. Thinking functionally makes "of" a paradigm not just a preposition.

The adoption of left-of-right evaluation frees q to treat expression evaluation simply and uniformly without redundant parentheses getting in the way. Infix or prefix notation can be used as suits the occasion. Left-of-right expression evaluation also means that there is no ambiguity in any expression—from the compiler's perspective if not yours. Parentheses can always be used to group terms and override the default evaluation order but there will be far fewer once you abandon old (bad) habits.

Tip: Arrange your expressions with the goal of placing parentheses and brackets on the endangered species list. Most are just programming noise unless you insist on writing Lisp.

4.1.3 The Gotcha of Left-of-Right Evaluation

Due to left-of-right evaluation, parentheses **are** needed to isolate the result of an expression that is the left operand of an infix operator. Let's take a closer look at this.

In any language you might have seen, the following expression evaluates to 10 but not in q. You can parenthesize or rearrange to get 10.

```
q)2*3+4
14
q)(2*3)+4
10
q)4+2*3
10
```

In some cases parentheses are simply unavoidable.

```
q)(2+3)*3+4
35
```

This is the one (and only) situation in which parentheses are necessary in q.

> If the left operand of an operator is an expression it **must** be parenthesized, otherwise the operator will bind to the right-most element of the expression.

> *Tip:* These parentheses on the left are often not needed in traditional programming and their omission in an overzealous extermination campaign is a common error for qbies. Please don't overreact by putting parentheses around all operands "to be safe." Spend five seconds and think about it. Eventually it will be second nature.

4.1.4 Rationale for No Operator Precedence

Operator precedence as normally encountered in programming languages is feeble. It requires all the components of an expression to be analyzed before anything can be evaluated. Moreover, it often results in the use of parentheses to override the very rules that are purportedly there to help.

Even more damning is that operator precedence forces complexity. Some programming languages (not q) allow user-written dyadic functions to be operators. This would entail the extension of precedence levels to cover user functions, even those as yet unborn. If you've worked in such a language, you eventually run out of precedence levels (and patience) and end up needing parentheses with operators of the same precedence!

4.2 Match (~)

The non-atomic dyadic match operator (~) applies to any two q entities, returning the boolean result 1b if they are identical and 0b otherwise. For two entities to match, they must have the same shape, the same type and the same value(s), but they may occupy separate storage locations. Colloquially, clones are considered identical in q.

This differs from the notion of identity in many traditional languages having pointers or objects. For example, in OO languages of C ancestry, objects are equal if and only if their underlying pointers address the same memory location. Identical twins are **not** equal. You must write your own method to determine if one object is a deep copy of another.

There are no restrictions as to the type or shape of the two operands for match. Try to predict each of the following results of match as you enter them into your console session.

```
q)42~40+2

q)42~42h

q)42f~42.0

q)42~`42

q)`42~"42"

q)4 2~2 4

q)42~(4 2;(1 0))

q)(4 2)~(4;2*1)

q)(())~enlist ()

q)(1; 2 3 4)~(1; (2; 3; 4))

q)(1 2;3 4)~(1;2 3 4)
```

Tip: While learning or debugging q (except for the q gods who write perfect q code every time), applying match can be an effective way to determine if you have what you intended. For example, qbies often trip over the following, thinking the latter is a singleton list.

```
q)42~(42)
1b
```

4.3 Equality and Relational Operators

It comes as a surprise to many who are new to vector programming that relational operators are atomic functions that return boolean values. Relational operations do not require the types of their operands to match, but they must be compatible.

4.3.1 Equality (=) and Disequality (<>)

The equality operator (=) differs from match (~) in that it is atomic in both operands, meaning it tests its operands atom-wise instead of in entirety. All atoms of numeric, temporal or char type are mutually compatible for equality, but symbols are compatible only with symbols.

Equality tests whether two compatible atoms represent the same value, without regard to type.

```
q)42=42i
1b
q)42=42.0
1b
q)42=0x42
1b
q)42="*"
1b
```

That last one may come as a surprise. It simply reflects that the underlying bit pattern of the ASCII char `*` is the same as the underlying bit pattern for the integer 42.

For temporal types the comparison is between the points on the calendar/clock rather than the underlying counts.

```
q)2000.01.01=2000.01.01D00:00:00.000000000
1b
q)2015.01.01<2015.02m
1b
q)12:00:00=12:00:00.000
1b
```

A symbol and a character are not compatible and an error results from the test,

```
q)`a="a"
'type
```

The not-equal primitive is (<>).

```
q)42<>0x42
0b
```

> **Tip:** The test "not equal" can also be achieved by applying (not) to the result of testing with (=). This what (<>) actually does.
>
> ```
> q)not 42=98.6
> 1b
> ```

When comparing floats, q uses multiplicative tolerance for non-zero values, which makes floating point arithmetic give reasonable results. At the time of this writing (Sep 2015) the tolerance is 10^{-14}.

```
q)r:1%3
q)r
0.3333333
q)2=r+r+r+r+r+r
1b
```

4.3.2 Not Zero (not)

The monadic, atomic operator (not) differs from its equivalent in some traditional languages. It returns a boolean result and has domain of all numeric, temporal and character types; it is not defined for symbols. The (not) operator generalizes the reversal of true and false bits to any entity having an underlying numeric value. It answers the Hamletonian question: to be, or not to be, zero.

The test against zero yields the expected results for boolean arguments.

```
q)not 0b

q)not 1b

```

The test against zero apples for any type with underlying numeric value.

```
q)not 0b

q)not 1b

q)not 42

q)not 0

q)not 0xff

q)not 98.6

```

For char values, (not) returns 0b except for the character representing the underlying value of 0.

```
q)not "*"

q)not " "

q)not "\000"

```

For temporal values, an underlying 0 corresponds to the stroke of midnight at the millennium for types including a date and simply midnight for time-only types.

```
q)not 2000.01.01
_
q)not 2014.01.01
_
q)not 2000.01.01T00:00:00.000000000
_
q)not 2000.01m
_
q)not 00:00:00
_
q)not 12:00:00.000000000
_
```

4.3.3 Order: <, <=, >, >=

Less than (<), greater than (>) less or equal (<=) and greater or equal (>=) are atomic and are defined for all compatible atom types. Numeric and char types are mutually compatible, but symbols are only compatible with symbols. As with equality, comparison for numeric and char types is based on underlying numeric value, independent of type.

```
q)4<42
_
q)4h>0x2a
_
q)-1.4142<99i
_
```

As with equality, the comparison for temporal types is between the points on the calendar/clock rather than the underlying counts.

```
q)2000.01.01<2000.01.01D00:00:00.000000001
1b
q)2015.01.01<2015.02m
_
q)12:00:01>12:00:00.000
_
```

For char atoms, comparing the underlying numeric value follows the ASCII collation sequence.

```
q)"A"<"Z"
q)"a"<"Z"
q)"A"<"0"
q)"?"<"?"
```

> **Tip:** To see the entire ASCII collation sequence in compact form, do this.
>
> ```
> q)16 16#"c"$til 256
> ```

Symbol comparison is based on lexicographic order.

```
q)`a<`b
q)`abc<`aba
```

Now that we are familiar with relational operations on atoms, let's examine their item-wise extensions to simple lists. Notice the simple boolean list returned.

```
q)2 1 3=1 2 3
q)10 20 30<=30 20 10
q)2=1 2 3
q)"zaphod"="Arthur"
q)`a`b`a`d=`ad`a`b
```

4.4 Basic Arithmetic: +, -, *, %

The arithmetic operators are atomic and come in dyadic and monadic flavors. We begin with the four operations of elementary arithmetic. Arithmetic operations are defined for all numeric and temporal types, and all numeric types are compatible.

Symbol	Name	Example
+	Plus	42+67
−	Minus	42.0-5.3456
*	Times	2h*3h
%	Divide	42%6

Arithmetic looks pretty much like other programming languages, except that division is represented by (%) since '/' is used to delimit comments. Simon Garland of KX points out that this is actually closer to ÷, division the way god meant it to be written.

```
q)2+3
_
q)a:6
q)b:7
q)b-a
_
q)a*b
_
q)4%2
2f
```

> **Tip:** The result of division is always a float.

The major learning adjustment in q arithmetic expressions is due to left-of-right evaluation and the absence of precedence.

```
q)6*3+4
42
```

Type promotion for arithmetic operators follows two rules:

- Binary types are promoted to int
- The result type of an operation is the narrowest type that will accommodate both operands.

Here are examples of binary data promotion. Note that arithmetic on booleans is **not** performed modulo 2.

```
q)1b+1b
2i
q)42*1b
42
q)5i*0x2a
210i
```

> **Important:** Overflow and underflow are not trapped on arithmetic operations on integer types.

```
q)9223372036854775806+4
-9223372036854775806
q)2*5223372036854775800
-8000000000000000016
q)-9223372036854775806-4
9223372036854775806
```

When a floating-point type occurs in an expression, the result is a float.

```
q)6+7.0
13f
q)1.0+1b
2f
q)6.0*7.0e
42f
```

> **Tip:** The symbols for arithmetic operators are **always** dyadic.

In particular, while '-' is used as a lexical marker to denote a negative number, there is no monadic function (-) to negate a numeric value. Its attempted use for such generates an error. Use the operator (*neg*) instead

```
q)42
42
q)-42
-42
q)a:42
q)-a              / error
'-
q)neg a
-42
```

Being atomic, arithmetic operators and their type promotion are performed atom-wise on lists.

```
q)1.0+10 20 30

q)10 20 30%1 2 3

q)100 200 300+1b

q)1+(100 200;1000 2000)

```

4.5 Maximum (|) and Minimum (&)

These atomic dyadic operators follow the same type promotion and compatibility rules as arithmetic operators. They are defined for all values with underlying numeric values but are not defined for symbols and GUIDs.

The maximum operator (|) returns the larger of its operands; this reduces to logical "or" for binary operands. The minimum operator (&) returns the smaller of its operands, which reduces to logical "and" for binary operands.

```
q)42|43

q)98.6&101.9
9
q)0b|1b

q)1b&0b

q)42|0x2b

q)"a"|"z"
"
q)`a|`z               / error

```

Being atomic they operate item-wise on lists.

```
q)2|0 1 2 3 4

q)11010101b&01100101b

q)"zaphod"|"arthur"

```

For readability of logical operations on binary data, (|) can also be written as (or) and (&) can be written as (and).

```
q)1b or 0b

q)1b and 0b

q)42 or 43

```

4.6 Amend (:)

An overload of (:) that is "assign in place."

4.6.1 Amend in C Language

We are familiar with the basic form of assignment.

```
q)a:42
```

Programmers from languages with C heritage are familiar with expressions such as,

```
    x += 2;          // C expression that assigns in place
```

This has the same effect as the following but can be more efficiently implemented at the machine instruction level.

```
x = x + 2;        // C expression
```

Reading the first statement succinctly as "add 2 to x in place" motivates the interpretation of the operation as "amend." To wit, the value assigned to x is amended by applying the operation + with the supplied operand 2.

4.6.2 Simple q Amend

Transliterating the above C expression to q yields the (+:) operation to amend a variable in place.

```
q)x:42
q)x+:1
q)x
_
```

There is nothing special about (+) here. Amend can be used with any symbolic operator having compatible signature.

```
q)a:43
q)a-:1
q)a
_
q)a&:21
q)a
_
```

> **Tip:** In spite of the linguistic dissonance, a q variable can be amended even if it has not been previously assigned.

In a fresh q session:

```
q)x
'x
q)x+:42
q)x
_
```

4.6.3 Amend with Lists

The capability to modify in place extends to lists and indexing.

```
q)L:100 200 300 400
q)L[1]+:99
q)L
```

```
q)L[1 3]-:1
q)L
```

```
q)L1:(1 2 3; 10 20 30)
q)L1[;2]+:100
q)L1
```

A very useful idiom is (, :) which appends to a list in place.

```
q)L:1 2 3
q)L,:4
q)L
```

```
q)L,:100 200
q)L
```

Tip: Amend does type promotion based on the operator it is combined with, except for (, :) which requires exact type match.

```
q)L:1.1 2 2 3.3
q)L[1]+:100
q)L,:100
'type
```

4.7 Exponential Primitives: sqrt, exp, log, xexp, xlog

4.7.1 sqrt

The atomic monadic (sqrt) has domain all numeric values and returns a float representing the square root of its input. It returns null when the square root is not defined.

```
q)sqrt 2
```

```
q)sqrt 42.4
```

```
q)sqrt 1b
```

```
q)sqrt -2
```

4.7.2 exp

The atomic monadic (exp) has domain all numeric values and returns a float representing the base *e* raised to the power of its input.

```
q)exp 1

q)exp 4.2

q)exp -12i

```

> **Tip:** Do not confuse the 'e' used in the display of base-10 scientific notation with the mathematical base of exponentials and natural logarithms.
>
> ```
> q)1e10          / this is one million
> 1e+10
> ```

4.7.3 log

The atomic monadic (log) has domain all numeric values and returns a float representing the natural logarithm of its input. It returns null when the logarithm is not defined.

```
q)log 1

q)log 42.0

q)log .0001

q)log -1

```

4.7.4 xexp

The atomic dyadic (xexp) has as domain all numeric values in both operands and returns a float representing the left operand raised to the power of the right operand. When the mathematical operation is undefined, the result is null.

```
q)2 xexp 5

q)-2 xexp .5

```

> **Tip:** We point out here, since it is our first encounter, a q naming convention. A monadic function—e.g., (exp)—sometimes has a dyadic version—(xexp)—with an `x` prepended to its name. In classic Arthurian fashion, the rationalization is that the additional parameter is `x`.

4.7.5 xlog

The atomic dyadic (xlog) has as domain all numeric values in both operands and returns a float representing the logarithm of the right operand with respect to the base of the left operand. When the mathematical operation is undefined the result is null.

```
q)2 xlog 32
5f
q)2 xlog -1
0n
```

4.8 More Numeric Primitives

4.8.1 Integer Division (div) and Modulus (mod)

The atomic dyadic (div) is atomic in both operands, which are numeric values. The result is the integer quotient of the left operand (*dividend*) by the (positive) right operand (*divisor*), which is equal to the result of normal division rounded **down** to the next lower integer. The operation returns null for non-positive divisor.

```
q)7 div 2
3
q)7 div 2.5
2
q)-7 div 2
-4
q)-7 div 2.5
-3
q)7 div -2
0N
q)3 4 5 div 2
1 2 2
q)7 div 2 3 4
3 2 1
q)3 4 5 div 2 3 4
1 1 1
```

The dyadic (mod) is atomic in both operands, which are numeric values. The result is the remainder of the integer quotient of the left operand (*dividend*) by the positive right operand (*divisor*). It is equal to

dividend − (*dividend* div *divisor*)

The result is null for non-positive divisor.

```
q)7 mod  2
1
q)7 mod 2.5
_
q)-7 mod  2
1
q)-7 mod 2.5
_
```

```
q)7 mod -2
_
q)3 4 5 mod 2
_
q)7 mod  2 3 4
_
q)3 4 5 mod 2 3 4
_
```

> **Tip:** Many languages use (%) for modulus, but it is division in q. This is a common mistake of qbies.

4.8.2 Sign (signum)

The atomic monadic (signum) has domain all numeric and temporal types and returns an int representing the sign of its input, where 1i represents positive, −1i represents negative and 0i represents a zero.

```
q)signum 42
1i
q)signum -42.0
_
q)signum 1b
_
q)signum 0
_
```

Temporal types are treated as their underlying offsets.

124

```
q)signum 1999.12.31
-
q)signum 12:00:00.000000000
-
```

4.8.3 reciprocal

The atomic monadic (reciprocal) has domain all numeric types and returns the float result of 1.0 divided by the input. It returns the appropriately signed infinity for the reciprocal of 0.

```
q)reciprocal 0.02380952
42.00001
q)reciprocal 0.0
0w
q)reciprocal -0.0
-0w
```

4.8.4 Floor and Ceiling

The atomic monadic (floor) has domain integer and floating point types and returns a long representing the largest integer that is less than or equal to its argument.

```
q)floor 4.2
4
q)floor 4
-
q) floor -4.2
-
```

> **Tip:** The (floor) operator can be used to truncate or round floating point values to a specific number of digits to the right of the decimal.
>
> ```
> q)x:4.242
> q)0.01*floor 100*x
> 4.24
> ```

Analogous to (floor), the atomic monadic (ceiling) has domain numeric types and returns the smallest long that is greater than or equal to its argument.

```
q)ceiling 4.2
5
q)ceiling 4
-
q)ceiling -4.2
-
```

> **Note:** For reasons known only to the q gods, (floor) and (ceiling) do not apply to short types.
>
> ```
> q)floor 4h
> 'type
> ```

4.8.5 Absolute Value (abs)

The atomic monadic (abs) has domain all integer and floating-point types. The result is the input when it is greater than or equal to zero and its negation otherwise. The result of (abs) has the same type as the argument except for binary types, which are type promoted to int.

```
q)abs 42

q)abs -42

q)abs 1b

```

4.9 Operations on Temporal Values

Because all q time values are integral offsets from canonical base points, properties and operations on temporal types are simple. For example, one value of a temporal type comes before another value of the same type just when the same is true of their underlying integer values. When dealing with temporal values of different types, q implicitly promotes to the wider type and then proceeds as just described.

Moreover, basic temporal arithmetic is integer arithmetic. The difference of two (absolute) temporal values of the same type is the span given by the difference of their underlying integer counts. Conversely, given a temporal value, adding an integer to it (i.e., to its underlying integer count) yields a temporal value of the same type.

Casting reveals the underlying integer count of any temporal value.

```
q)`int$1999.12.31
-1i
q)`int$2013.01m

q)`int$12:00:00.123

q)`long$12:00:00.123456789

```

> **Note:** There is no concept of time zone in q temporal values. Those of us who wrestled with Java's original time implementation are thankful.

4.9.1 Temporal Comparison

Comparison **within** a temporal type amounts to simple comparison of the underlying integral offsets.   Comparison **across** temporal types recognizes that the underlying values express different units and realizes them in common units.

For example, midnight on the second day of the millennium should be equal to the second day, but a naïve comparison of the underlying counts will not tell us.

```
q)2000.01.02=2000.01.02D00:00:00.000000000
1b
q)`int$2000.01.02
1i
q)`long$2000.01.02D02:00:00.000000000
93600000000000
```

Values of different types should be compared in the same units, which effectively amounts to converting to the most granular units. The cast operator has the logic for such conversions built-in.

```
q)`timestamp$2001.01.02
2001.01.02D00:00:00.000000000
```

To compare temporal values of different types, q converts to the most granular type and then does a straight comparison of the underlying values.

```
q)2000.01.01<2000.01.01D12:00:00.000000000
```

4.9.2 Temporal Arithmetic

In contrast to many traditional languages, expressions involving temporal types and numerical types that should make sense actually work as expected. For example, temporal values **are** their underlying offsets for equality and comparison testing against numeric values.

```
q)2000.01.01=0
1b
q)12:00:00=12*60*60

q)1999.12.31<0

```

Adding an integral value to a temporal value works because it is just added to the underlying offset.

```
q)2014.12.31+1
q)2015.01.01+til 31          / all days in January
q)12:00:00+1
```

Adding a temporal value to another causes it to be viewed as a span, as you would want.

```
q)12:00:00+01:00:00
```

One important case is adding a timespan to a date to yield a timestamp. There is actually some calculation under the covers to make this work.

```
q)2015.01.01+12:00:00.000000000
2015.01.01D12:00:00.000000000
```

The difference between two values of a temporal type that counts days is the int difference of their underlying day counts.

```
q)2001.01.01-2000.01.01
366i
q)2015.06m-2015.01m
```

The difference between two values of a type with time is the difference of the underlying offsets, expressed as the same type—i.e., as a span.

```
q)2015.01.01D00:00:00.000000000-2014.01.01D00:00:00.000000000
365D00:00:00.000000000
q)12:00:00-11:00:00
q)12:00-11:00
```

4.10 Operations on Infinities and Nulls

Here we summarize the various behaviors of nulls and infinities in one place.

The float infinities and nulls act in the mathematically correct fashion in numeric expressions and comparisons. Integer infinities act correctly in comparisons and act as their underlying (finite) values in other operations.

The bit patterns of the integral nulls and infinities are legitimate base-2 integral representations with the high-order bit being the sign.

Value	Bit Representation
0Wh	0111111111111111b
-0Wh	1000000000000001b
0Wi	01111111111111111111111111111111b
-0Wi	10000000000000000000000000000001b
0W	0111111111111111111111111111111111111111111111111111111111111111b
-0W	1000000000000000000000000000000000000000000000000000000000000001b

The same type promotion rules apply to a null as for a normal value of that type.

An infinity value equals or matches only itself. All nulls are equal (they represent missing data), but different type nulls do not match (type matters).

In contrast to some languages, such as C, separate instances of NaN are equal.

```
q)(0%0)=0%0
```

The (not) operator returns 0b for all infinities and nulls since they all fail the test of equality with 0.

```
q)not 0W
q)not -0W
q)not 0N
```

The (neg) operator reverses the sign of infinities but does nothing to nulls since sign is meaningless for missing data.

```
q)neg 0w
-
q)neg -0w

q)neg 0N
-
```

We saw previously that for any numeric type

> null < negative infinity < normal value < positive infinity

Nulls of different type, while equal, are not otherwise comparable—i.e., any relational comparison results in 0b.

Infinities of different type are ordered by their width. For positive infinities

> short < int < long < real < float

For negative infinities

> -float < -real < -long < -int < -short

Some examples follow. Try to predict the result before pressing Return.

```
q)42<0w
-
q)-0w<42.0
-
q)-0w<1901.01.01
-
q)-0w<0w
-
q)0w<0w
-
q)-0w<0w
-
q)-10000000<0N
-
q)0N<42i
-
q)0n<-0w
-
```

The null symbol is less than any other symbol

```
q)`a<`
-
```

The behavior of (|) and (&) with infinities and nulls follows from the rules for equality, comparison and type promotion mentioned already.

```
q)42|0w
q)-42&0N
q)0w|0n
q)-0w&0n
q)0n|0N
q)0Wi&0w
```

The last result obtains because int infinity is promoted to a long and its bit pattern corresponds to the maximal positive 32-but integer.

4.11 Alias (::)

Because q is strict, expressions are normally evaluated as soon as encountered by the interpreter. In particular, assignment with an expression on the right requires the expression to be evaluated before the result is assigned.

An *alias* is a variable that **is** an expression—i.e., it is **not** the result of expression evaluation but the expression itself. Otherwise put, an alias provides a way to defer evaluation of an expression.

Evaluation of an alias is *lazy*, meaning that it occurs only when necessary. More precisely, evaluation is *forced* when the variable is referenced, at which point a determination is made whether the expression needs to be (re)evaluated.

- If it is the first reference or if any variable in its associated expression has changed since the last evaluation, evaluation proceeds with the current values of all the variables in the expression. The result of the most recent evaluation is then stored internally and also returned. The stored result is said to be *memoized*.
- If no variables in the expression have changed since the previous evaluation, the memoized value is returned.

The alias variable is said to *depend* on any variables in its expression.

4.11.1 Creating an Alias with Double Colon

Double colon (::) used outside a function body defines the variable in the left operand as an alias of the expression in the right operand. When the alias is referenced, the underlying expression is (re)evaluated as described above. The following trivial example defines b as an alias for a, contrasted with c which is just assigned the value of a. Observe that the subsequently changed value of a is reflected in b but not in c.

```
q)a:42
q)b::a
q)c:a
q)a:43
q)b
43
q)c
42
```

Here is a more interesting alias.

```
q)w::(x*x)+y*y
q)x:3
q)y:4
q)w
25
q)y:5
q)w
34
```

The mysteriously named utility (0N!) is the identify function fortified with the side effect of displaying its input on the console.

It is a non-invasive way to inspect the inner workings of an in-flight evaluation.

```
q)w::(0N!x*x)+y*y
q)x:3
q)y:4
q)w
9
25
q)w
25
q)y:6
q)w
9
45
```

Observe that the first time w is referenced, the expression **is** evaluated, as indicated by the display of the value of x*x. On the next reference, the expression is **not** re-evaluated since none of the

132

variables it depends on have changed. After changing y, the last reference causes re-evaluation.

4.11.2 Alias vs. Function

A function also represents deferred evaluation. In the previous example, we could define,

```
q)fu:{(x*x)+y*y}
q)fu[3;4]
25
```

There are two key differences between an alias and the analogous function.

- To evaluate an expression wrapped in a function you explicitly provide the arguments and apply the function all in one step. With an alias you set the variables at any point in the program and the expression is evaluated when, and only when, the alias variable is referenced.
- The function does not memoize its result, so it recalculates on every application, even if the arguments do not change.

4.11.3 Dependencies

An alias variable *depends* on the entities in its associated expression. In our previous example w depends on x and y. A list of all dependencies is maintained in the system dictionary .z.b, which is also obtainable via the command \b.

```
q)w::(x*x)+y*y
q).z.b
x| w
y| w
```

Each key in .z.b is associated to all the entities that depend on it.

It is permissible to create an alias with another alias in its expression. This results in a chain of dependencies. The entire chain is resolved lazily upon reference.

```
q)u::w*w
q).z.b
x| w
y| w
w| u
q)x:3
q)y:4
q)u
_
```

Such a recursive definition leads to a hierarchy of dependencies, in which a variable depends not only on the variables in its own expression, but also any variables that its expression depends on, etc. You can easily build sophisticated dependency graphs this way.

> **Tip:** You can easily build unmaintainable code this way.

A dependency chain that would create a loop is detected and results in an error. Continuing the example above,

```
q)x::u
q)x
'loop
```

4.11.4 Views

Aliasing is commonly used to provide a database view by specifying a query as the expression.

```
q)t:([]c1:`a`b`c`a;c2:20 15 10 20;c3:99.5 99.45 99.42 99.4)
q)v::select sym:c1,px:c3 from t where c1=`a
q)v
sym px
--------
a    99.5
a    99.4
q)update c3:42.0 from `t where c1=`a
_
q)v
_
```

The table dependencies of a view are reflected in .z.b.

```
q).z.b
_
```

5 Dictionaries

5.0 Overview

A dictionary is a mapping defined by an explicit association between a key list and value list. The two lists must have the same count and the key list should be a unique collection. While general lists can be used to create a dictionary, many dictionaries involve simple lists of keys.

5.1 Dictionary Basics

A dictionary is an association between a list of keys and a list of values. Logically it can also be considered as key-value pairs but it is stored physically as a pair of lists.

5.1.1 Definition

A *dictionary*, sometimes called an *association*, is a mapping defined by positional correspondence between a domain **list** of *keys* and a codomain **list** of *values*. Dictionary creation uses the (!) operator—read "bang"—in contrast with the syntactic form for lists.

> *keys*!*values*

All dictionaries have type 99h.

Observe that the q console displays a dictionary as an I/O table.

```
q)10 20 30!1.1 2.2 3.3
10| 1.1
20| 2.2
30| 3.3
q) a`b`c!100 200 300
```

Neither the keys nor values need be simple lists but the keys should conform else odd things will happen during operations.

```
q)(`Arthur`Dent; `Zaphod`Beeblebrox; `Ford`Prefect)! 100 42 150
Arthur Dent      | 100
Zaphod Beeblebrox| 42
Ford   Prefect   | 150

q)1001 1002 1003!(`Arthur`Dent; `Zaphod`Beeblebrox; `Ford`Prefect)
```

A dictionary can be decomposed into its key and value lists using the primitives (key) and (value). The common number of keys or values is returned by (count).

```
q)d:`a`b`c!100 200 300
q)key d

q)value d

q)count d
```

Although q does not enforce uniqueness for keys (a historical accident) a dictionary does provide a unique output value for each input value. Indeed, only the first key occurrence is seen during lookup.

> **Advanced**: When you know that the keys are unique you can apply the `u# attrbite to the keys. This will effectively cause the dictionary to be a hash table with the attendant improvement in lookup speed over the default linear lookup.
>
> ```
> q)(`u#`a`b`c)!10 20 30
> ```

The order of the items in the key and value lists is significant, just as positional order is significant for lists. Although the I/O assignments and the associated mappings are equivalent regardless of order, differently ordered dictionaries are **not** identical.

```
q)(`a`b`c!10 20 30)~`a`c`b!10 30 20
0b
```

5.1.2 Empty and Singleton Dictionaries

You can create a general empty dictionary using empty key and value lists.

```
q)()!()
```

You can create a typed empty dictionary using typed empty key and value lists.

```
q)(`symbol$())!`float$()
```

> **Important:** Because both the keys and values are required to be lists, you must enlist atoms for a singleton dictionary.
>
> ```
> q)(enlist `x)!enlist 42
> x| 42
> ```

The following is **not** a singleton dictionary. This is a common mistake of qbies.

```
q)`x!42
`x!42i
```

For those who care, it is actually an enumerated value for a link column.

5.1.3 Lookup

To find the output value corresponding to an input key, we *look up* the key. Lookup uses the same notation as indexing into a list: brackets or juxtaposition.

```
q)d:`a`b`c!10 20 30
q)d[`a]
10
q)d `b
```

Similar to list indexing, lookup of a value not in the key list of a dictionary results in a null whose type is that of the initial item in the value list.

```
q)d[`x]
```

As with lists, key lookup in a dictionary is extended item-wise to a simple list of keys.

```
q)d[`a`c]

q)ks:`a`c
q)d ks
```

5.1.4 Reverse Lookup with Find (?)

Recall that the find operator (?) on a list returns the index of the first occurrence of the right operand.

```
q)10 20 30 10 40?10
0
```

Essentially it inverts the positional retrieval mapping. Extending this concept to dictionaries means reversing the key-to-value mapping of lookup. That is, (?) on a dictionary performs reverse lookup by mapping a value item to the first key associated to it.

```
q)d:`a`b`c`a!10 20 30 10
q)d?10
`a
```

The result of find on an argument not in the value list is a null whose type matches the initial item in the key list.

```
q)d:`a`b`c`a!10 20 30 10
q)d?40
`
```

5.1.5 Dictionary vs. List

It is possible to create a dictionary that seemingly behaves very much like an equivalent list by making the positional retrieval explicit.

```
q)L:10 20 30
q)d:0 1 2!10 20 30
q)L 0
10
q)d 0
10
q)L 1 2
20 30
q)d 1 2
20 30
d~L
_
```

The two are not the same. A major difference is that dictionaries can be extended via assignment and a list cannot.

> **Advanced**: This dictionary version of lists provides a compact and efficient representation of sparse lists.
>
> ```
> q)d1:0 100 500000!10 20 30
> q)d2:0 99 1000000!100 200 300
> q)d1+d2
> 0       | 110
> 100     | 20
> 500000  | 30
> 99      | 200
> 1000000 | 300
> ```

The implementation is left as an exercise for the reader.

5.1.6 Non-unique Keys and Values

As mentioned previously, non-unique keys are tolerated but lookup only sees the first occurrence.

```
q)ddup:`a`b`a`c!10 20 30 20
q)ddup[`a]
10
```

Reverse lookup works properly for non-unique keys but will only see the first non-unique value.

```
q)ddup?30
`a
q)ddup?20
`b
```

You can find all keys mapping to a given value as follows.

```
q)where 10=d
`a`d
```

5.1.7 Non-simple Keys and Values

Neither the key nor value lists of a dictionary are required to be atoms or uniform. Either can be nested lists.

```
q)d:(`a`b; `c`d`e; enlist `f)!10 20 30
q)d `f
30
q)d?20
`c`d`e
```

```
q)d:`a`b`c!(10 20; 30 40 50;  enlist 60)
q)d `b
30 40 50
q)d?30 40 50
`b
q)d?enlist 60
```

Be forewarned that an irregular key or value list—i.e., items do not conform—will confound lookup or reverse lookup, respectively.

```
q)dwhackey:(1 2; 3 4 5; 6; 7 8)!10 20 30 40   / atom 6 is whack
q)dwhackey 1 2
10
q)dwhackey 6
0N
q)dwhackval:10 20 30 40!(1 2; 3 4 5; 6; 7 8) / atom 6 is whack
q)dwhackval?3 4 5
20
q)dwhackval?6
_
```

The observed behavior is that lookup in either direction fails at the first
item of different shape.

5.2 Operations on Dictionaries

5.2.1 Amend and Upsert

As with lists, the items of a dictionary can be modified via assignment
to a key.

```
q)d:`a`b`c!10 20 30
q)d[`b]:42
q)d
_
```

In contrast to lists, dictionaries **can** be extended via assignment.

```
q)d:`a`b`c!10 20 30
q)d[`x]:42
q)d
_
```

Let's examine more closely this capability to modify or extend a
dictionary via key-value assignment. Given a dictionary d, a value k
that matches the type of the keys of d and a value v that matches the
type of the values of d, consider the assignment

        d[k]:v

It updates the existing key-value association when k is in key d, or
inserts (appends) a new key-value association when k is not in key d.

```
q)d:`a`b`c!10 20 30
q)d[`b]:42              / update
q)d[`x]:100             / insert
q)d
_
```

This update/insert behavior is called *upsert* semantics. Because tables
and keyed tables are dictionaries, upsert semantics pervade kdb+.

5.2.2 Extracting a Sub-Dictionary

Dictionary lookup on a key or a list of keys returns the associated values. It is possible to extract both keys and values using an overload of the take operator (#). The left operand is a **list** of keys, the right operand is the *source* dictionary and the result is a sub-dictionary for the specified keys. Viewed as a mapping, the result is the original restricted to the specified keys.

```
q)d:`a`b`c!10 20 30
q)d `a`c
_
q)`a`c#d
a| 10
c| 30
q)(enlist `c)#d
_
```

In the event of duplicate keys, only the first is extracted.

```
q)ddup:`a`b`a`c!10 20 30 20
q)`a`c#ddup
a| 10
c| 20
```

This operation works with non-simple keys.

```
q)dns:(`arthur`dent; `ford`prefect; `zaphod`beebelbrox)!100 150 42
q)(`arthur`dent; `zaphod`beebelbrox)#dns
arthur dent      | 100
zaphod beebelbrox| 42
```

5.2.3 Removing Entries

The adjoint operation to (#) is (_), which removes key-value pairs. Its syntax is the same—i.e., a list of keys as the left operand and a dictionary on the right—and it returns the dictionary obtained by removing the key-value pairs for the specified keys.

> **Note:** Whitespace is required to the left of (_) if the left operand is a variable since '_' is a valid terminal name character.

```
q)d:`a`b`c!10 20 30
q)`a`c _ d
b| 20
q)(enlist `b) _ d
_
```

Observe that all occurrences of a key are removed and that attempting to remove a key that does not exist has no effect.

141

```
q)d:`a`b`c`a!10 20 30 40
q
q)`a`c _ d

q)`x`a _ d

```

Removing all the entries in a dictionary leaves a dictionary with empty key and value lists of the appropriate types. The console will not display the empty dictionary but you can force the display with (-3!). In this case we get typed empty lists.

```
q)d:`a`b`c!10 20 30
q)`a`b`c _ d
q)-3!`a`b`c _ d
"(`symbol$())!`long$()"
```

The binary operator (cut) is the same as this overload of (_) on a dictionary.

```
q)`a`c cut d

```

There is another overload of (_) with a dictionary on the left and a **single** key on the right that deletes just that key, which is seldom used.

```
q)d _ `b
a| 10
c| 30
```

5.2.4 Basic Operations on Dictionaries

Because a dictionary is a map, it can be composed with another map to obtain a dictionary whose key-value association is the composite of the original and the new map. Another way to say this is that applying a function to a dictionary effectively applies it to the value list. Monadic functions are straightforward.

```
d:`a`b`c!10 20 30      composed with          neg

   `a   |→    10    |→    -10
   `b   |→    20    |→    -20
   `c   |→    30    |→    -30
```

```
q)d:`a`b`c!10 20 30
q)neg d
a| -10
b| -20
c| -30
```

And similarly for other monadic maps.

```
q)2*d

q)d=20

q)f:{x*x}
q)f d

```

When the domains of two dictionary maps are identical, performing a dyadic operation is also straightforward: do it value-with-value along the keys. For example, to add two dictionaries with a common list of keys, add their corresponding values.

```
q)d1:`a`b`c!1 2 3
q)d2:`a`b`c!10 20 30
q)d1+d2

```

What should happen when the domains lists are not identical? First, the domain of the resulting dictionary is the union of the domains—i.e., the union of the key lists. For items in the common domain—i.e., the intersection of the keys lists, we already know we should apply the operation value-with-value.

So the question becomes: what to do on non-common key items? The answer: Nothing! Since there really isn't anything to do where there is no matching key on the other side, simply carry the value to the result. In essence, this implies using the identity element for the operation in place of the missing value.

```
q)d1:`a`b`c!1 2 3
q)d2:`b`c`d!20 30 40
q)d1+d2
a| 1
b| 22
c| 33
d| 40
```

5.2.5 Join (,)

The join operator (,) merges two dictionaries. Clearly on disjoint keys the corresponding values should be carried over.

```
q)d1:`a`b`c!10 20 30
q)d2:`x`y!40 50
q)d1,d2
a| 10
b| 20
c| 30
x| 40
y| 50
```

On common keys, since q is right-to-left, the value of the right operand prevails over that of the left.

```
q)d1:`a`b`c!10 20 30
q)d2:`a`b`c!100 200 300
q)d1,d2
a| 100
b| 200
c| 300
```

Lo and behold, the entire right operand has been upserted into the left operand.

```
q)d1:`a`b`c!10 20 30
q)d2:`c`d!300 400
q)d1,d2
a| 10
b| 20
c| 300
d| 400
```

This is equivalent to each key-value association being upserted into the left

```
q)d1:`a`b`c!10 20 30
q)d1[`c]:300
q)d1[`d]:400
q)d1
_
```

Observe that join is not commutative: order matters.

```
q)d1:`a`b`c!10 20 30
q)d2:`c`d!300 400
q)d1,d2
_
q)d2,d1
_
```

5.2.6 Coalesce (^)

The coalesce operator is related to (,) in that it employs upsert semantics to merge two dictionaries. The difference is that right values prevail over left except for nulls in the right.

```
q)d1:`a`b`c!10 0N 30
q)d2:`b`c`d!200 0N 400
q)d1^d2
a| 10
b| 200
c| 30
d| 400
```

5.2.7 Arithmetic And Relational Operations

Following the general pattern, when an arithmetic operation is performed on dictionaries, the operation is performed on the common domain elements and the identity element implied elsewhere. Of course the value lists must have proper types for the operation.

```
q)d1:`a`b`c!10 20 30
q)d2:`b`c`d!200 300 400
q)d1+d2
a| 10
b| 220
c| 330
d| 400
```

For equality and comparison operations on dictionaries, the indicated operation is performed over the common keys. On disjoint keys, the appropriate null is effectively substituted for missing values. Due to all nulls being equal, a null value on a disjoint key will report 1b under equality test.

```
q)(`a`b`c!10 20 30)=`b`c`d!20 300 400
a| 0
b| 1
c| 0
d| 0
q)(`a`b`c!0N 20 30)=`b`c`d!20 300 0N
a| 1
b| 1
c| 0
d| 1
q)(`a`b`c!10 20 30)<`b`c`d!20 300 400
a| 0
b| 0
c| 1
d| 1
```

5.3 Column Dictionaries

Column dictionaries are the foundation for tables.

5.3.1 Definition and Terminology

A very useful type of dictionary maps a simple list of symbols to a rectangular list of lists.

```
q)`c1`c2!(`a`b`c; 10 20 30)
c1| a  b  c
c2| 10 20 30
```

Interpreting each symbol as a name and the corresponding list as a vector of column values, we call such a list a *column dictionary*. A general column dictionary has the form,

$$c_1 \ldots c_n! (v_1; \ldots ; v_n)$$

where each c_i is a symbol and the v_i are lists with common length (count). Such a dictionary associates the name c_i with the value list v_i.

The *type* of the column named by c_i is the type of its associated value list v_i. Often the v_i are all simple lists—i.e., each column is a vector of atoms of uniform type.

5.3.2 Simple Example

Let's make a column dictionary that holds the names of famous galactic travelers and their IQ scores.

```
q)travelers:`name`iq!(`Dent`Beeblebrox`Prefect;42 98 126)
q)travelers
name| Dent Beeblebrox Prefect
iq  | 42   98         126
```

In this dictionary, the values for the *name* column are,

```
q)travelers[`name]
`Dent`Beeblebrox`Prefect
```

Since this column is a list, we can index into it.

```
q)travelers[`name][1]
`Beeblebrox
q)travelers[`iq][2]
126
```

In general, whenever we encounter repeated indexing in q we can alternately write it as indexing at depth.

```
q)travelers[`name; 1]
`Beeblebrox
q)travelers[`iq; 2]
126
```

146

Thus `travelers` can be considered a two-dimensional entity indexed by name in the first slot.

5.3.3 General Case

For a general column dictionary defined as,

$$dc: c_1 \ldots c_n! (v_1; \ldots; v_n)$$

the ith element of column c_j is retrieved by,

$$dc[c_j][i]$$

Or equivalently,

$$dc[c_j;i]$$

The indexing at depth notation suggests thinking of the column dictionary as a two-dimensional data structure, indexed by column name and column position. Alternately, it is a positional map of two variables with symbolic name in the first parameter and column index in the second.

Specifying just an index in the second column is interesting. It essentially retrieves a "slice" of the original dictionary across that index. This slice is itself a dictionary. In our simple example of the previous section,

```
q)travelers[; 2]
name| `Prefect
iq  | 126
```

Let's summarize.

- A column dictionary can be viewed a two dimensional entity with retrieval by name in the first dimension and by position within column in the second.
- Specifying only a name retrieves the corresponding column, which can then be indexed by position.
- Specifying only a column index retrieves a slice dictionary that maps the names to the associated values across that column index.

This data structure has potential but there is a hitch: the indexing is backwards. That is, columns are retrieved in the first slot. Normally in two dimensional data structures, columns are retrieved in the second slot. We shall see shortly how to fix this.

5.3.4 Column Dictionary with a Single Column

Recall that every dictionary is constructed from a **list** of keys and a **list** of values. A column dictionary is further required to have a rectangular list of values—i.e., a list of lists of the same length.
Thus in order to make a column dictionary with a single column, we need to enlist the single key and enlist the single column list.

```
q)dc1:(enlist `c)!enlist 10 20 30
q)dc1
c| 10 20 30
```

> **Tip:** As noted previously, the following isn't even a valid dictionary, let alone a column dictionary.
>
> ```
> q)`c!1 2 3
> _
> ```

5.4 Flipping a Column Dictionary

No, this isn't what you do to a dictionary that cuts you off in traffic. Recall that a rectangular nested list can be transposed with the (flip) operator.

```
q)L:(10 20 30; 100 200 300)
q)L
10  20  30
100 200 300
q)flip L
10 100
20 200
30 300
```

A side effect of transposing the nested list data is that it reverses the slots for indexing at depth.

```
q)L:(10 20 30; 100 200 300)
q)M:flip L
q)L[0;0]
10
q)L[0;1]
20
q)L[0;2]
30
```

```
q)M[0;0]
10
q)M[1;0]
20
q)M[2;0]
30
```

Recall that applying (flip) to a nested list creates a copy of the original list in which the data has been reorganized. When a column dictionary is considered as a two-dimensional entity it is rectangular, since its column lists all have the same count. The console display shows this.

```
q)`c1`c2!(`a`b`c; 10 20 30)
c1| a  b  c
c2| 10 20 30
```

Thus it makes sense to transpose this rectangular data structure. Observe that the console display is exactly transposed.

```
q)dc:`c1`c2!(`a`b`c; 10 20 30)
q)dc
c1| a  b  c
c2| 10 20 30

q)t:flip dc
q)t
c1 c2
-----
a  10
b  20
c  30
```

We expect the transposed entity to have the slots reversed for indexing at depth.

```
q)dc[`c1; 0]
`a
q)dc[`c1; 1]
`b
q)dc[`c1; 2]
`c
q)t[0; `c1]
`a
q)t[1; `c1]
`b
q)t[2; `c1]
`c
```

Voila! We have fixed the indexing issue with our column dictionaries. Columns are now indexed in the second parameter. Let's translate the other aspects of the column dictionary retrieval into the transposed setting.

```
q)dc[`c1;]
`a`b`c
q)t[;`c1]
`a`b`c
```

```
q)dc[;0]
c1| `a
c2| 10
q)t[0;]
c1| `a
c2| 10
```

```
q)dc[`c2; 1]
20
q)t[1; `c2]
20
```

For the moment, forget the origin of t as a transposed column dictionary and examine it in isolation.

```
q)t[;`c1]
`a`b`c
q)t[0;]
c1| `a
c2| 10
q)t[1; `c2]
20
```

Let's look more closely at the section dictionaries that are now indexed in the first slot. Recall that we are permitted (although not encouraged) to omit trailing semi-colons for elided indices.

```
q)t[0]
c1| `a
c2| 10
q)t[1]
c1| `b
c2| 20
q)t[2]
c1| `c
c2| 30
```

If you were to meet such a beast out of context, you would say that it is a list of these funky section dictionaries.

We summarize our findings about the transpose of a column dictionary,

- It is a two-dimensional data structure that uses an integer index in the first slot and a column name symbol in the second slot.
- Specifying only an integer in the first slot retrieves a section dictionary across that index
- Specifying only a column name in the second slot retrieves that column.

- Specifying both an integer and a column name retrieves the "field" at that index in that column.
- It can be viewed as a list of section dictionaries.

We make two more observations about transposed column dictionaries. In general, if you transpose something twice, you get back the original.

```
q)dc~flip flip dc
1b
q)dc~flip t
1b
```

We restate this as:

- The flip of a transposed column dictionary is a (the original!) column dictionary

---

Important: Unlike the case of transposing rectangular lists, transposing a column dictionary does not physically re-arrange data.

A transposed column dictionary is stored in column order.

Instead, the result is a logical adjustment—meaning that the slots in indexing at depth are reversed.

6 *Functions*

6.0 Overview

In this chapter, we cover functions in depth. Before diving in, you may wish to review the Mathematics Refresher in Chapter 0 for the approach and terminology we adopt.

We describe various built-in functions along the way in this tutorial. Sometimes we shall use a built-in function with minimal explanation; simply look it up in Appendix A, which contains specifics and examples of nearly all the q built-in functions.

6.1 Function Specification

The notion of a function in q corresponds to a (mathematical) map that is specified by an algorithm. A *function* is a sequence of expressions to be evaluated, having optional input parameters and a return value. *Application* of a function is the process of evaluating the expressions in sequence, substituting actual arguments for any formal parameters. The result of the evaluation, should there be one, is the function's output value.

Because a q function can modify global variables, q is not a pure functional language. A mathematical function can never reach outside its own body and have side effects. You should minimize such behavior for code maintainability.

6.1.1 Function Definition

The syntax of function definition is a matching pair of braces '{' and '}' enclosing (optional) parameters followed by a sequence of expressions. In contrast to statically typed languages, the input parameters and the return value are not explicitly typed; in fact, they don't even need to be declared. Even the function name is optional.

Following is a full specification of a function that squares its input. In this case, the function simply returns the value of the (last) expression evaluated. We add optional whitespace after the parameter declaration for readability.

```
q){[x] x*x}
```

Apply this function by following it with an argument enclosed in square brackets. This causes the supplied argument to be substituted for all occurrences of the parameter x, the expression to be evaluated and the result returned as the output value.

```
q){[x] x*x}[3]
9
```

A function is a first class value—i.e., it is data just like a long or float. In particular, a function can be assigned to a variable, whereupon it acquires a name. This variable can be used in place of the function.

```
q)f:{[x] x*x}
q)f[3]
_
```

6.1.2 Function Notation and Terminology

The formal notation for function definition is,

$$\{[p_1; \ldots; p_n] \ e_1; \ldots; \ e_m\}$$

The optional p_1, ... , p_n are formal parameters. The expressions e_1, ... , e_m—which presumably involve the parameters—represent the steps of an algorithm that are evaluated in order. Note that while the expressions are sequenced left-to-right, an individual expression is always evaluated right-to-left.

For readability, in this text we shall normally insert optional whitespace after the square bracket that closes the parameter list, as well as after each semicolon separator. Other styles may differ.

> **Tip:** The semi-colons in the body are separators, not terminators. Do not place a semicolon after the last expression unless you deliberately want to suppress the return value.

In fact, (;) is an operator that evaluates its left operand and discards the result, then evaluates the right operand and returns that value. If you meditate on this, you will realize that this is precisely the behavior of the semi-colin separators in a function body.

```
q)a:2*3;6*7
42
q)a
6
```

The number of formal input parameters (implicit or explicit) is the function *valence*. Most common are *monadic* (valence 1) and *dyadic* (valence 2).

A *niladic* function in q is a function that has no meaningful input. This is similar to a function taking `void` in C. In functional programming this is represented as a function defined on a type called "unit" having a single value, often written (). In q it is written with an empty parameter declaration,

    f:{[] … }

and is applied with empty argument—i.e., f[]. In this case, the function either returns a constant or has *side effects*, meaning that it accesses resources outside its body.

```
q){[] 42}              / pure function returns constant 42

q){[] a*a}             / impure function: references global a
```

The maximum valence permitted as of this writing (Sep 2015) is 8; specifying more than eight parameters will cause an error. You can circumvent this restriction by encapsulating multiple parameters in a list or dictionary.

The output value of a function written in functional programming style is the value of the last expression in its body. This is the recommended style of writing q since it results in linear flow that is easy to follow and debug.

```
q){[x] x*x}

q){[x;y] a:x*x; b:y*y; r:a+b; r}
```

This convention can be supplanted by using a monadic overload of (:) that immediately terminates function evaluation and returns the value of the expression to its right. This style is discouraged.

```
q){[x] :x*x}                   / unnecessary use of :

q){[x] a:1; :x*x; b:3}         / dead code
```

> **Tip:** Q functions should be compact and modular: each function should perform a well-defined unit of work. Due to the power of q operators and built-in functions, many functions are one line. When a function exceeds 20 statements, you should look to refactor it.

> **Advanced**: When Arthur Whitney, the creator of q, says that q is not ambivalent, he doesn't mean that q is decisive. Rather, in contrast to k, q operators and built-in functions are **not** overloaded on valence, meaning that the same function does not have different behavior in a monadic and dyadic form. That said, q operators and built-in functions **are** overloaded on just about anything else, including the type, sign or rank of arguments—sometimes multiply so.

6.1.3 Function Application

The notation for function application parallels that of the formal parameters in its definition. The function is followed by square brackets enclosing arguments separated by semi-colons. Application causes the expressions in the function body to be evaluated in sequence, substituting the value of each argument for the corresponding formal parameter.

```
q){[x] x*x}[3]
9
q)f:{[x] x*x}
q)f[4]

q){[x;y] x+y}[3;4]
7
q)g:{[x;y] x+y}
q)g[3;4]

```

Function application in q is *strict*, meaning that expressions in arguments are evaluated **before** substitution is performed.

```
q)f:{[x] x*x}
q)f[0N!3+1]
4
16
```

The valence of a function is also called its rank. An application with too many arguments generates a 'rank error. This doesn't mean your code stinks, although it might.

```
q) {[x] x*x}[3;4]
'rank
```

Apply a niladic function with no arguments or with an arbitrary argument, which is ignored.

```
q)const42:{[] 42}
q)const42[]
_
q)const42[98.6]
_
```

6.1.4 Functions with No Return Value

Every q function has a return value but sometimes the value carries no meaningful information—i.e., it is used purely for side effects. For example, it may send off a message asynchronously without waiting for an acknowledgement of receipt or it may update a global table. To achieve the equivalent of a void return in C, make the expression after the last semi-colon in the function body empty.

```
q)fvoid:{[x] `a set x;}
q)fvoid 42
q)
```

In fact, the actual return value is the nil item :: that is a stand-in for void in this situation. Its display is suppressed in the q console but it can be revealed.

```
q)-3!fvoid 42
"::"
```

> *Tip:* A common error made by qbies is to use semi-colons in a function body as expression terminators rather than as separators. This effectively makes the function return nil since the last expression is empty.

6.1.5 We Don't Need No Stinkin' Brackets

There is an alternate notation for application of monadic functions (only) that dispenses with brackets. Simply separate the function from its argument with whitespace—customarily a single blank.

```
q){[x] 2*x} 42
84
q)f:{[x] x*x}
q)f 5
_
```

This convention for function application is called *juxtaposition* and is the norm in functional programming. While it may be jarring for newcomers, the decrease in superfluous punctuation—i.e., program noise—is worth the effort.

6.1.6 Application of a Name

When a function has been assigned to a global variable, it can be applied by name—i.e., use the symbol name of the variable in place of the variable itself.

```
q)f:{x*x}
q)f[5]

q)`f[5]
25
q)`f 5

q).my.name.space.f:{2*x}
q)`.my.name.space.f[5]
```

This works because a global variable is implemented as a symbolic-name/function pair in a dictionary. Referring to the variable is actually lookup by name. Consequently application by name does **not** work for local variables or q system variables.

> *Tip:* Do not confuse application using the function name with call-by-name in which parameters are passed by name.

6.1.7 Implicit Parameters

If, like mathematicians, you are satisfied with generic parameters *x*, *y* and *z*, you can omit the formal parameters and their brackets. Three implicit positional parameters x, y and z are automatically defined and available in a function's expressions when no parameters are explicitly declared. Thus, the following two specifications result in equivalent input-output relations.

```
{[x] x*x}

{x*x}
```

As do,

```
{[x;y] x+y}

{x+y}
```

> **_Important:_** When using implicit parameters, x is always substituted by the first actual argument, y the second and z the third.

The following function f only evaluates partially unless it is called with three parameters.

```
q)g:{x+z}              / likely meant x+y; requires 3 args in call

q)g[1;2]               / still waiting for 3rd arg-i.e., a projection
{x+z}[1;2]

q)g[1;2;3]             / 2nd arg is required but ignored
4
```

> **_Tip_**: Only use the names x, y and z for the first three parameters of a function, either explicit or implicit.

Any other use leads down the path to perdition.

```
q)evil:{[y;z;x] ...}              / don't do this!
```

6.1.8 Anonymous Functions and Lambda Expressions

Many traditional programming languages include the function name as part of its definition. A function without a name is then called an *anonymous* function. In functional programming, functions are all anonymous and are called *lambda expressions* or lambdas for short. All q functions are anonymous until assigned to a variable. Incidentally, the term lambda actually arose from a typesetting error in Church's early work on what became known as the lambda calculus.

An anonymous function can be useful as an in-line macro where it would otherwise be awkward to substitute. For example,

$$f\{[...] \; ...; \; \{...\}[...]; \; ...\}$$

It is arguably more readable to factor this out.

Another use for anonymous functions is a rudimentary form of dynamic dispatch, in which functions are placed in a collection (e.g., list, dictionary, table) and then selected dynamically (i.e., at runtime) rather than by an intrinsic name.

```
q)powers:({1}; {x}; {x*x}; {x*x*x})
...
q)selected:2
q)powers[selected]
{x*x}
```

6.1.9 The Identity Function (::)

When (::) is used with function application syntax, it is the identity function—i.e., it returns its input as output.

The naked identity function cannot be used with juxtaposition; it must be enclosed in parentheses.

```
q)::[42]

q)::[`a`b`c]

q):: 42                      / error

q)(::) 42
```

6.1.10 Functions Are Data

The q data entities we have met until now are atoms (of various types), lists and dictionaries. For those new to functional programming, it may come as a surprise that functions are also data. A function can be passed around just like a long or float—e.g., as an item in a list.

```
q(1; 98.6; {x*x})

q)f:{x*x}
q)(f; neg)

q)(f; neg)[0]

q)(f; neg)[1; 5]
```

A function can also be used as the input or output value of another function. For example, here is a function that expects a function and a value and applies the function to the value.

```
q)apply:{x y}
q)sq:{x*x}
q)apply[sq; 5]
```

A function that operates on other functions is called a *higher order function*. Higher order functions are a powerful concept from functional programming. The derivative and indefinite integral are higher-order functions in elementary calculus.

6.2 Call-by-Name

Ordinary function application in q uses call-by-value, meaning that arguments are reduced to values at the start of application. In the process, copies are made so that any original values are undisturbed. When the size of the input data is large, this copy may be prohibitive. In this case, there is an alternative method of application, *call-by-name*, in which names of (global) variables are passed instead of their values.

There is no special syntax for call-by-name in q. Instead, the function implementation simply expects a symbol containing the name of a variable and handles it appropriately. One example of a function that uses call by name is the built-in function (get), which returns the value of the global variable whose name is passed.

```
q)a:42
q) get `a
42
```

Another example is dyadic (set), which does the actual work of global assignment. It expects the name of a global variable and the value to be assigned.

```
q)`a set 43
`a
q)a
43
```

The result of any built-in call-by-name function application is the symbol that was passed as input. This enables call-by-name functions to be chained—i.e., composed.

> **Tip:** Do not confuse the return value of call-by-name with an error message. The former begins with a back-tick whereas the latter begins with tick.

6.3 Local and Global Variables

6.3.1 Defining Local and Global Variables

A variable that is assigned with (:) within a function body is called a *local* variable. For example, a is a local variable in the following function.

```
q)f:{a:42; a+x}
```

> **Tip:** As of this writing (Sep 2015), the maximum number of local variables permitted in a function is 24.

Some notes on local variables:

- A local variable exists only for the duration of an application. There is no notion of a static local variable that maintains its value across applications.
- A local variable is not visible outside its immediate scope of definition.
- A local variable cannot be used as an argument to a q function that uses call-by-name.
- A local variable is not visible within the body of a local function defined in the same scope. Otherwise put,

q does not have lexical scoping.

Here is a simple example demonstrating the lack of lexical scoping and its consequence. The function f defines a local variable a and a local function helper. In functional programming languages, the variable a is accessible throughout its scope of definition, which is the body of f. In particular, the variable a would be accessible within the body of helper.

```
q)f:{[p1] a:42; helper:{[p2] a*p2}; helper p1}
```

In q it is not. Nasty surprise!

```
q)f 5
{[p2] a*p2}
'a
```

Instead, you must declare an additional parameter in the local functions and pass the local variable as an argument. Projection provides a relatively clean way to do this.

```
q)f:{[p1] a:42; helper:{[a; p2] a*p2}[a;]; helper p1}
q)f 5
210
```

A variable assigned outside any function definition is called a *global* variable. Global variables are visible inside any function body.

```
q)b:7
q)f:{b*x}
q)f[6]
_
```

As of this writing (Sep 2015), the maximum number of global variables that can be referenced in a function is 32. If this is a problem, redesign your code. For example collect values in a list or dictionary and pass that; the dictionary essentially provides pass-by-name.

6.3.2 Assigning Global Variables within a Function

Although functional programming purists will cringe, you can assign a global within a function body. Some q programmers mistakenly use double colon (::), which works provided there is no local variable with the same name.

```
q)b:6
q)f:{b::7; x*b}
q)f[6]
42
q)b
7
```

> *Tip:* This usage of (::) is analogous to other forms of amend in place, such as (+:) or (,:), but using the assignment operator itself (:). This accounts for its somewhat unintuitive properties—it is not truly a global assignment operator.

If there is a local variable having the same name as the global you intend to assign, double-colon assigns the **local**, not the global.

```
q)b:6
q)f:{b:42; b::x; b}
q)f[98]
98
q)b
6
```

> **Tip:** We recommend against (::) for global assignment. Instead, use (set) which truly does global assignment and doesn't get hung up on a local-global name collision.

As we saw earlier, (set) uses call-by-name.

```
q)a:42
q)f:{a:98.6; `a set x}
q)f 43
`a
q)a
43
```

6.4 Projection

Projection means specifying only some of the parameters in function application, resulting in a function of the remaining parameters.

6.4.1 Function Projection

In some circumstances, a portion of the arguments to a multivalent function may be fixed while the remaining arguments vary. A common example is where a date is the last parameter and you apply the function for many dates keeping all other inputs fixed. In this situation, you can specify the fixed arguments and leave the others for later. This is called *projecting* the function onto the remaining arguments. Notationally, projection is a partial application in which some arguments are supplied and the others are omitted—i.e., nothing is in those slots.

For example, a homegrown dyadic function that adds its arguments can be projected onto the second parameter by providing just the first argument.

```
q)add:{x+y}
q)add[42;]
{x+y}[42;]
```

You can see from the console that q views the projection as a partial application that awaits its remaining argument(s). The projected function is a legitimate monadic function, which adds its input to the constant 42.

```
q)add[42;][3]
45
```

Since functions are first class, we can assign a projection to a variable and then apply it, none the wiser of its origin.

```
q)g:add[42;]
q)g[3]
_
```

Projection is related to *currying* in functional programming (named after Haskell Curry who did important early work on the theory of combinators). Both provide realizations of the mathematical observation that a function of two parameters is equivalent to a function of the first parameter that returns a function of the second parameter. This extends to multiple parameters as well. In q you simply project out successive parameters.

```
q)add3:{x+y+z}
q)add3[2][3][4]
9
```

Here we can view the result of add3 applied to 2 as a function that when applied to 3 returns a function that when applied to 4 yields add[2;3;4].

> **Style Recommendation:** We recommend that you do **not** omit trailing semi-colons in projections, as this can obscure the intent of code. For example, if you came upon the following while reading q code, how would you know that mystery is actually a dyadic function unless you saw the comment line?
>
> ```
> q)mystery:f[2]          / surprise! f is actually f:{x+y+z}
> ```

The brackets denoting a function projection are required, but the additional brackets in a monadic projection's application can be omitted using juxtaposition as with any function.

```
q){x+y}[42;][3]
_
q){x+y}[42;] 3
_
```

Choice of notation is a matter of coding style. Some coders have good style; many do not.

> ***Important:*** The function body in a projection is captured at the time it is first encountered by the interpreter.

Thus if the underlying function is subsequently changed, the projection is not.

```
q)f:{x-y}
q)g:f[42;]
q)g
{x-y}[42;]
q)g[6]

q)f:{x+y}
q)g

q)g[6]
```

6.4.2 Operator Projection

When used in infix form, a q operator can be projected by fixing its left operand (only). This requires parentheses. For example, the projection of (*) onto its right operand is,

```
q)(7*) 6
42
```

Due to the overloading of parentheses in q, an operator cannot be projected by fixing its right argument, since this would lead to notational ambiguity. For example, (-42) can only be the atom -42 and not a projection.

Nonetheless, every operator is a function, so you can project it in prefix form.

```
q)-[;42] 98
```

The whitespace is actually not necessary in juxtaposition here since the brackets make things unambiguous.

```
q)(7*)6

q)-[;42]98
```

Such notation is an acquired taste not shared by the author.

6.4.3 Multiple Projections

Functions having valence greater than two can be projected in multiple ways. For example, a function of valence three can be projected onto the second parameter by specifying the first and third. The result is a monadic function of the second parameter only.

```
q){x+y+z}[1;;3]
{x+y+z}[1;;3]
q){x+y+z}[1;;3] 2
6
```

We could arrive at the same result in two steps.

- *Step 1*: Project onto the second and third parameters by specifying just the first argument. This yields a dyadic function.

```
q){x+y+z}[1;;]
{x+y+z}[1;;]
q){x+y+z}[1;;][2;3]
_
```

- *Step two*: Project the resulting dyadic function onto its first parameter by providing only the second.

```
q){x+y+z}[1;;][;3]
{x+y+z}[1;;][;3]
q){x+y+z}[1;;][;3] 2
_
```

This is equivalent to projecting in the reverse order.

```
q){x+y+z}[;;3][1;]
{x+y+z}[;;3][1;]
q){x+y+z}[;;3][1;] 2
_
```

6.5 Everything Is a Map

Here we explore the deep relationship between q data structures and functions. While this section can be skipped on first reading, that would be like not eating your vegetables when you were a kid.

6.5.1 Similarity of Notation

You have no doubt noticed that the notation for list indexing, dictionary lookup and monadic function application are identical. Namely,

```
q)L:0 1 4 9 16 25 36
q)f:{x*x}
q)L[2]

q)L 2

q)f[2]

q)f 2

```

This is no accident. In Chapter 3 we saw that a list is a map defined by positional retrieval via item indexing. In Chapter 5 we saw that a dictionary is a map defined by key-value lookup. A function is a map defined by a sequence of expressions representing an algorithm for computing an output value from the input. The common notation is simply that of a map. It may take a little time to get accustomed to the Zen of q.

6.5.2 List of Indices, Keys and Arguments

Just as we can use a list of indices to retrieve items from a list, so can dictionary lookup retrieve a list of values corresponding to a list of keys. And a list of arguments to an atomic function yields a list of outputs. This justifies the common notation.

```
q)L:10 20 30 40 50
q)L[2 5]

q)I:2 5
q)L I

```

```
q)d:`a`b`c!10 20 30
q)ks:`a`c
d ks

```

```
q)f[2 5]

q)f I

```

In fact, these are all examples of composition of maps.

```
      I           L
0   |→    2    |→    4
1   |→    5    |→   25

     ks         d
0   |→   `a    |→   10
1   |→   `c    |→   30
```

168

$$
\begin{array}{ccccc}
 & \mathcal{I} & & f & \\
0 & |\rightarrow & 2 & |\rightarrow & 4 \\
1 & |\rightarrow & 5 & |\rightarrow & 25
\end{array}
$$

6.5.3 Indexing at Depth

Next we examine the correspondence between indexing at depth and multivalent function evaluation. Notationally, a nested list is a list of lists, but it can also be viewed functionally as multivariate position retrieval. The display of a nested list tells us how: go down then over.

```
q)a:(1 2 3; 100 200)
q)a
1 2 3
100 200
q)a[1;0]
100
```

The first index goes down and the second index goes over. A more deeply nested list is a positional map whose valence is one greater than the depth of nesting.

Similarly, a dictionary with complex values can also be viewed as a multivariate map.

```
q)d:`a`b!(1 2 3; 100 200)
q)d[`a;1]
2
```

In this case, the first parameter locates a key and the second goes into the value list.

6.5.4 Projection and Index Elision

You have no doubt noticed that the notations for function projection and elided indices in a list are identical. For example, an array is positional retrieval in which the first index is "down" and the second is "over." Thus eliding the first index indeed results in a list in which the remaining index is simply ordinary positional retrieval.

```
q)m:(10 20 30; 100 200 300)
q)m
10  20  30
100 200 300
q)m[1;2]
_
q)L:m[;2]
q)L
_
q)L[1]
_
```

6.5.5 Out of Bounds Index

Viewing a list as a map on an integer domain also motivates the behavior of item indexing in the case of an out of bounds index. In traditional languages, this would either result in some sort of uncaught error—the infamous indexing off the end of an array—or an exception.

By viewing a list as a function defined on a sub-domain of integers, it is reasonable to extend the domain of the function to all integers by assigning a null output value outside the proper domain. Here null means "missing value." As we have seen previously,

```
q)10 20 30 40[100]
0N
q)`a`b`c[-1]

q)(1.1; 1; `1)[3]
0n
```

The behavior for dictionaries is completely analogous.

```
q)d:`a`b`c!10 20 30
q)d[`x]
0N
```

6.6 Atomic Functions

The characterization of q as a vector language arises from the fact that most of the built-in operations are atomic. We examine the notion of atomic functions in more detail. The application of an atomic function is characterized by the fact that it recurses into an argument's structure until it gets to atoms and then applies there. It does this without explicit loops or other control flow constructs.

6.6.1 Monadic Atomic Functions and "map"

Atomic behavior is easiest to see with a monadic function.

170

```
q)neg 10
-10

q)neg 10 20 30
-10 -20 -30

q)neg (10 20 30; 40 50)
-10 -20 -30
-40 -50

q)neg `a`b`c!10 20 30
a| -10
b| -20
c| -30

q)neg `a`b`c!(10 20; 30 40 50; 60)
a| -10 -20
b| -30 -40 -50
c| -60
```

A consequence of this behavior is that the result of a monadic atomic function always has the same shape as its argument—i.e., the output conforms to the input.

A special case of this is that applying an atomic function to a list is the same as applying it to each item in the list, which is sometimes described as "atomic functions extend automatically to lists." Similar functionality is achieved with "foreach" in traditional languages and the higher-order function "map" in functional languages.

6.6.2 Dyadic Atomic Functions and zip

Atomic behavior is more interesting for dyadic functions. A dyadic function can be atomic in either or both arguments. The first case can be thought of as a monadic atomic function if you fix the non-atomic argument—i.e. project the function. For example, find (?) is atomic in only its second argument since it consumes the entire first argument in its search.

```
q)10 20 30?10
0
q)10 20 30?10 20 30 40 50
0 1 2 3 3
q)(enlist 10)?10
0
q)10 20?10
0
q)10 20 30 40 50?10
0
```

The arithmetic, comparison and relation operators are all atomic in both operands. This leads to four cases for application:

- atom with atom
- atom with list
- list with atom
- list with list

In the last case, the two list operands must have the same length.

```
q)1+10
11
q)1+10 20 30
11 21 31
q)1 2 3+10
11 12 13
q)1 2 3+10 20 30
11 22 33
```

Similar behavior is achieved with "zip" in traditional and functional programming.

6.6.3 Creating Atomic Functions

Brief meditation reveals that the composition of atomic functions is atomic. Hence, the guaranteed way to build your own atomic functions is to compose built-in atomic functions. First monadic.

```
q)f:{(x*x)+(2*x)-1}
q)f 0
-1
q)f til 10
-1 2 7 14 23 34 47 62 79 98
```

Now dyadic.

```
q)pyth:{sqrt (x*x)+y*y}
q)pyth[1; 1]
1.414214
q)pyth[1; 1 2 3]
1.414214 2.236068 3.162278
q)pyth[1 2 3; 1 2 3]
1.414214 2.828427 4.242641
```

You might ask how to get this behavior with a function that is not atomic. Timely question.

6.7 Adverbs

Adverbs are higher-order functions that modify the behavior of functions for application on lists. The terminology derives from thinking of q operators as verbs. Proficiency in the use of adverbs is one skill that separates q pretenders from q contenders.

Not every function is atomic, but we may still want to apply it to individual items of a data structure without loopy code. Adverbs to the rescue.

6.7.1 Monadic each

We have seen that an atomic function automatically applies to the atoms in a nested list.

```
q)neg (1 2 3; 4 5)
-1 -2 -3
-4 -5
```

Clearly a function that aggregates a list into an atom cannot be atomic since it collapses the list structure. In particular, aggregate functions operate only at the top level of a nested list.

```
q)count 10 20 30
3
q)count (10 20 30; 40 50)
2
```

Suppose instead that we want to count each of the two items in our nested list. This is precisely what the (each) adverb does. It modifies a monadic function so that it applies to each item in a list rather than to the list as a whole. When used infix, (each) follows the function after (required) whitespace.

```
q)count each (10 20 30; 40 50)
3 2
```

The nature of (each) as a higher-order function is more clearly revealed in its equivalent prefix form. This may look odd at first, but it shows that (each) takes a function and modifies its behavior by applying to each item in a list.

```
q)each[count] (10 20 30; 40 50)
3 2
```

We could say informally that (each) makes a non-atomic function act atomically...at least at one level. For deeply nested lists, you need to iterate (each) to apply a function at deeper levels.

```
q)(count each) each ((1 2 3; 3 4); (100 200; 300 400 500))
3 2
2 3
q)each[each[count]] ((1 2 3; 3 4); (100 200; 300 400 500))
```

The effect of iterated (each) is perhaps most clearly observed when applied to a matrix, where successive higher-order applications cause the original function to be applied on another axis.

```
q)count (1 2 3; 10 20 30)

q)count each (1 2 3; 10 20 30)

q)(count each) each  (1 2 3; 10 20 30)
```

You can use (each) with any monadic function, although it is redundant on atomic functions.

```
q)reverse "live"
"evil"
q)reverse ("life"; "the"; "universe"; "and"; "everything")

q)reverse each ("life"; "the"; "universe"; "and"; "everything")

q)neg each (1 2 3; 4 5)
```

It often arises that you want to convert a vector of length n to an n x 1 matrix. You can do that with (enlist each) but (flip enlist) executes faster for large lists.

```
q)enlist each 1001 1002 1004 1003
1001
1002
1004
1003
q)flip enlist 1001 1002 1004 1003
```

6.7.2 each-both (')

An atomic operator automatically applies to corresponding pairs of items when applied to lists of the same length.

```
q)1 2 3+10 20 30
11 22 33
```

The dyadic join operator (,) is not atomic since it consumes (copies of) both of its operands in their entirety when it concatenates.

```
q)"abc","de"
"abcde"
```

Suppose we want to join list items pair-wise. For example,

```
q)("abc"; "uv") ?????? ("de"; "xyz")
"abcde"
"uvxyz"
```

The adverb each-both (') modifies a dyadic function (operator, verb) to apply pairwise to corresponding list items. Conventionally no whitespace should be between (') and the function it modifies but this does not generate an error. In some programming languages, each-both is called "zip".

```
q)("abc"; "uv"),'("de"; "xyz")
"abcde"
"uvxyz"
```

There is no effect when the arguments are atoms.

```
q)3,'4
3 4
```

A function modified by each-both has the usual properties of atomic dyadic functions. For example, you get a length error if arguments don't line up.

```
q)("abc"; "uv"),'("de"; "xyz"; "uhoh")
'length
```

The modified function also extends an atom to match a list. You will see this idiom often. For example,

```
q)1,'10 20 30
1 10
1 20
1 30
q)1 2 3,'10

q)2#'("abcde"; "fgh"; "ijklm")
"ab"
"fg"
"ij"
```

If you are so inclined, you can use a function modified by each-both in prefix form. This is not common but can simplify things in functional form of queries (see §9.12).

```
q),'[("abc"; "uv"); ("de"; "xyz")]
_
```

The idiom (, ') works fine for making a list of pairs from two simple lists but does not always work as expected with general lists. For example it loses the enlisting of the singleton in the following.

```
q)L1:(enlist `a; `b)
q)L2:1 2
q)L1,'L2
`a 1
`b 2
```

A reliable way to make a list of pairs from a pair of lists is:

```
q)flip (L1; L2)
  `a 1
, `b 2
```

> **Advanced:** A nice example of (,') arises when both operands are tables. Since a table is a list of records, it is possible to apply (,') to tables with the same number of rows. The record dictionaries in each row are upserted, resulting in a sideways join of the tables.
> ```
> q)t1:([] c1:1 2 3)
> q)t2:([] c2:`a`b`c)
>
> q)t1,'t2
> c1 c2
> -----
> 1  a
> 2  b
> 3  c
> ```

6.7.3 each-left (\:)

An atomic operator extends an atom in the right operand to match a list on the left.

```
q)1 2 3+10
_
```

The each-left adverb (\:) modifies a dyadic function so that it applies the second argument with each item of the first argument—for example, to append a string to each string in a list. We insert unnecessary whitespace around the modified function in the following example to make it more readable.

176

```
q)("abc"; "de"; enlist "f") ,\: ">"
"abc>"
"de>"
"f>"
```

Traditionally there is no space between the adverb and the function it modifies but this causes no error.

6.7.4 each-right (/:)

An atomic operator extends an atom in the left operand to match a list on the right.

```
q)10+1 2 3
```
_

The each-right adverb (/:) modifies a dyadic function so that it applies the first argument to each item of the second argument. For example, to prepend a string to each string in a list. Again we surround the modified function with unnecessary whitespace for readability.

```
q)"</" ,/: ("abc"; "de"; enlist "f")
```
_

Composing the last two examples makes data xml-ey (say it aloud) without loops.

```
q)"</",/:("abc"; "de"; enlist "f"),\:">"
```
_

6.7.5 Cross Product

A cross (Cartesian) product of two lists pairs each item on the left with each item on the right. If we compose join with each-right and each-left, we are almost there, except that there is an extra level of nesting, which we eliminate with the built-in (raze).

```
q)1 2 3,/:\:10 20
1 10 1 20
2 10 2 20
3 10 3 20
```

```
q)raze 1 2 3,/:\:10 20
1 10
1 20
2 10
2 20
3 10
3 20
```

The built-in operator (`cross`) computes this cross product.

```
q)1 2 3 cross 10 20
_
```

Observe that we could alternatively compose each-left with each-right and would arrive at the transpose of the previous result.

```
q)raze 1 2 3,\:/:10 20
1 10
2 10
3 10
1 20
2 20
3 20
```

6.7.6 Over (/) for Accumulation

The over adverb (/) is a higher order function that provides the principle mechanism for recursion in q. In its simplest form it modifies a dyadic function to accumulate results over a list.

Suppose we want to add the first 10 natural numbers starting at 1. In imperative programming this requires control flow: initialize a result variable, establish a loop counter and then loop while adding into the result until the counter reaches the end of the list. In functional programming, simply declare that you want to accumulate starting with an initial value of the accumulator. No counters, no tests, no loop. You say "what" to do rather than "how" to do it.

Let's see this in q. For readability, we have included optional whitespace.

```
q)0 +/ 1 2 3 4 5 6 7 8 9 10
55
```

In this expression, we apply a compound operator formed from (+) modified by over (/).

> **Important:** There can be no whitespace between the function and '/', due to '/' also being used to begin a comment.

The initial accumulator value is the left operand and the list to accumulate over is the right operand. Under the covers, each item of the list is progressively added into the accumulator, moving across the list until the end is reached. The final accumulated value is returned. In our example, 1 is added into the initial accumulator value of 0 to get 1; then 2 is added to this value to get 3; and so on until the end of the list. Just like old-fashioned imperative code, except you never see it. Here is an instrumented form of accumulating sum. It uses the (0N!) operator to display the accumulator x paired with the next input y before returning their sum.

```
q)addi:{0N!(x;y); x+y}
q)0 addi/ 1 2 3 4 5
0 1
1 2
3 3
6 4
10 5
15
```

Observe that as a higher-order function (/) takes a dyadic function and returns a related dyadic function. The operands of the modified function are no longer symmetric—i.e., the left operand is the initial accumulator value and the right operand is the list to be accumulated.

> **Tip:** In functional programming languages over is called fold or reduce. Along with (each) this completes the famous map-reduce paradigm.

Often the generality of specifying the initial value of the accumulator is unnecessary. In our summation example, we could initialize the accumulator with the first list item and then accumulate the remaining items. The syntax for this form encloses the modified function in parentheses and omits the initial accumulator.

```
q)(+/) 1 2 3 4 5 6 7 8 9 10
55
```

Another way to think of this is by representing the list in general form.

(1; 2; 3; 4; 5; 6; 7; 8; 9; 10)

Then (+/) effectively replaces the semi-colons with '+', associated to the left.

A few notes about the alternate form of over.

- The parentheses are mandatory
- The modified function in this form is monadic
- This construct is actually k and not q. Don't tell anyone you are writing k.

Both the monadic and dyadic forms can be written in prefix.

179

```
q)+/[0; 1 2 3 4 5 6 7 8 9 10]

q)+/[1 2 3 4 5 6 7 8 9 10]

```

The basic over pattern is powerful. Use various dyadic functions to obtain common aggregate operations.

```
q)(*/) 1 2 3 4 5 6 7 8 9 10          / product
3628800
q)(|/) 7 8 4 3 10 2 1 9 5 6          / maximum
10
q)(&/) 7 8 4 3 10 2 1 9 5 6          / minimum
1
```

Common aggregates are given their own names in q.

(+/)	sum
(*/)	prd
(|/)	max
(&/)	min

> **Note**: Anyone with information about the location of the missing 'o' in (prd) please notify Kx.

The edge cases when the above aggregates are applied to empty lists are completely determined by the appropriate invariants. For example, for (|/) the following must hold for the join of any numeric lists L1 and L2.

$$max[L1,L2] = max[L1]|max[L2]$$

After a moment of meditation we realize that choosing either L1 or L2 to be an empty list of numeric type forces,

```
q)(|/) `long$()
-0w
q)(|/) `float$()
-0w
```

> **Advanced**: For those who know about such things, the above equation says that (|/) is a morphism from the free monoid of lists with concatenation (,) to the monoid of naturals with (|). The edge case says the morphism preserves the identity.

Other edge cases are analogous.

```
q)(&/) `long$()
0w
q)(+/) `long$()
q)(*/) `long$()
q)(,/) ()
```

Applying (,/) across a list concatenates the items, effectively eliminating the top level of nesting. If there is only one level of nesting, this flattens a list of lists to a plain list. The function (,/) goes by the descriptive name (raze).

```
q)(,/) ((1 2 3; 4 5); (100 200; 300 400 500))
1 2 3
4 5
100 200
300 400 500
q)raze ((1 2 3; 4 5); (100 200; 300 400 500))
```

> **Advanced**: For those who know about monads, lists compromise a monad. In Haskell-speak, (each) serves as fmap, (enlist) as return and (,/) as join.

You can use your own function with either form of over. The modified function can even be used infix, even though your original function cannot.

```
q)f:{2*x+y}
q)100 f/ 1 2 3 4 5 6 7 8 9 10
q)(f/) 1 2 3 4 5 6 7 8 9 10
```

6.7.7 More Over: Iteration

The next pattern of recursion we investigate is a another declarative equivalent of loopy code. In this version of (/), the left operand is a natural number indicating how many times to perform the iteration and the right operand is the initial value.

Let's compute the nth Fibonacci number—see §1.1.12 for a more detailed derivation of fib. Again the modified function can be used infix or prefix.

```
q)fib:{x,sum -2#x}
q)10 fib/ 1 1
1 1 2 3 5 8 13 21 34 55 89 144
q)fib/[10; 1 1]
```

Yet another version of (/) runs the recursion until convergence, or until a loop is detected. Our example uses a simple form of Newton-Raphson—see §1.1.13 for a detailed exposition for n^{th} roots. In this section we illustrate a variation of the square root in which we use a numerical approximation for the derivative. The approximation is the slope of the secant through points an epsilon to the left and right of x. This works provided we make epsilon sufficiently small because the derivative is defined as the slope of the tangent, which is the limit of the slope of the secant as epsilon approaches 0. Recall that in order to compute the square root of 2, we find the zero of {-2+x*x}.

```
q)f:{-2+x*x}
q)secant:{[f;x;e] (f[x+e]-f x-e)%2*e}
q){x-f[x]%secant[f; x; 1e-6]}/[1.5]
1.414214
```

How does q determine convergence? At each step the result is compared to that of the previous step. If the two agree within equality tolerance (10^{-14} at the time of this writing—Sep 2015) the algorithm is considered to have converged and the recursion is complete; otherwise it continues.

Mathematically, it is possible to generate an infinite loop with Newton-Raphson. To wit, we select the function $x^3 - 2x + 2$ and choose the initial value 0, which causes the algorithm to go into a cycle.

```
q)newtcycle:{[xn] xn-((xn*xn*xn)+(-2*xn)+2)%-2+3*xn*xn}
q)newtcycle/[0.0]
1f
```

How did q detect the cycle and stop the iteration? At each step it compares the result with the initial value. If they match, a cycle has occurred and the recursion is halted; otherwise it continues. Note that we mean "match" literally as in the (~) operator.

> **Tip:** If the values are equal but of different type, no cycle is detected and the loop will continue. In our example, providing a non-float initial value will cause an infinite loop. You will have to kill your console session if you enter the following.
>
> ```
> q)newtcycle/[0]          / oops
> ```

The final overload of (/) is equivalent to a "while" loop in imperative programming. It provides a declarative way to specify a test to end the iteration. Thinking functionally, we provide a predicate function that is applied to the result at each step. The iteration continues as long as the predicate result is 1b and stops otherwise. For example, we stop the computation of the Fibonacci sequence once it exceeds 1000 as follows.

```
q)fib:{x,sum -2#x}
q)fib/[{1000>last x}; 1 1]
1 1 2 3 5 8 13 21 34 55 89 144 233 377 610 987 1597
```

6.7.8 Scan (\)

The scan adverb (\) is a higher-order function that behaves just like (/) except that it returns all the intermediate accumulations instead of just the final one. Whereas over produces an aggregate function that collapses a list, scan produces a function whose output has the same number of items as its input—i.e., a *uniform* function. Informally, scan is a "running" version of over.

We omit optional whitespace in the following so that you can get accustomed to reading "real q."

```
q)0+\1 2 3 4 5 6 7 8 9 10
1 3 6 10 15 21 28 36 45 55
q)(*\)1 2 3 4 5 6 7 8 9 10

q)(|\)7 8 4 3 10 2 1 9 5 6

q)(&\)7 8 4 3 10 2 1 9 5 6

q)100 f\1 2 3 4 5 6 7 8 9 10

q)(f\)1 2 3 4 5 6 7 8 9 10
```

All the variations of over are also available with scan. Switching to scan can be useful to see intermediate results of an accumulation. For example, we can see how fast Newton-Raphson converges to the square root by setting the float display to unlimited precision and running scan.

```
q)newtsqrt\[1.0]
q)\P 0
q)newtsqrt\[1.0]
1 1.5 1.4166666666666667 1.4142156862745099 1.4142135623746899
 1.4142135623730951
```

6.7.9 each-previous (':)

The adverb each-previous (':) provides a declarative way to perform a dyadic operation on each item of a list with its predecessor.

> **Tip:** During traversal of the list, the current item is the left operand and the previous item is the right operand.

Since the initial item of the list does not have a predecessor, we must provide one in the left operand of the modified operator. One choice is the initial item of the source list. For example, to calculate the deltas of a list of prices.

```
q)100 -': 100 99 101 102 101
0 -1 2 1 -1
```

As with the other adverbs, there is a monadic form of each-previous (technically, it is k). It may come as a surprise that the monadic form does **not** choose the initial item of the input list as the initial predecessor. Rather, it returns the initial item of the input on (-) and (%).

```
q)(-':)100 99 101 102 101
100 -1 2 1 -1
q)deltas 100 99 101 102 101
100 -1 2 1 -1

q)(%':)100 99 101 102 101
100 0.98999999999999999 1.0202020202020201 1.0099009900990099
0.99019607843137258
q)ratios 100 99 101 102 101
_
```

The motivation is that the initial predecessor is implicitly chosen as the identity for the dyadic function (assuming such exists). This has the advantage of preserving desirable invariants.

```
q)sums deltas 100 99 101 102 101
100 99 101 102 101
q)deltas sums 100 99 101 102 101
_
```

On the other hand, if you are looking for anomalies in absolute differences—e.g., price changes—you will get a nasty surprise.

```
q)deltas 100 99 101 102 101
100 -1 2 1 -1
```

It is easy enough to make our own version for this case.

```
q)deltas0:{first[x] -': x}
q)deltas0 100 99 101 102 101
0 -1 2 1 -1
```

A powerful idiom with each-previous uses match (~) to test if successive items are identical. It is actually more useful to know where they do not match; the latter is built in as (differ).

```
q)(~':) 1 1 1 2 2 3 4 5 5 5 6 6
011010001101b
q)not (~':) 1 1 1 2 2 3 4 5 5 5 6 6
100101110010b
q)differ 1 1 1 2 2 3 4 5 5 5 6 6
_
```

Observe that the 1b values in the result of differ are the start points for runs of identical items, so (where) yields their indices. Then use (cut) to split them out.

```
q)L:1 1 1 2 2 3 4 5 5 5 6 6
q)where differ L
0 3 5 6 7 10
q)(where differ L) cut L
1 1 1
2 2
,3
,4
5 5 5
6 6
```

Now let's do some q.

```
q)runs:(where differ L) cut L        / store runs
q)ct:count each runs                 / store count of each run
q)runs where ct=max ct               / find the runs of maximum length
1 1 1
5 5 5
```

While some q coders don't like the style, we point out that the above can be written in a single line of q using intra-line assignments.

```
q)runs where ct=max ct:count each runs:(where differ L) cut L
_
```

Using comparison and the correct initial value, we can also use the above technique to find runs of increasing or decreasing values.

```
q)L:9 8 7 11 10 12 13
q)(where -0W>':L) cut L
9 8 7
11 10
,12
,13
q)(where 0W<':L) cut L
,9
,8
7 11
10 12 13
```

This is the raison d'être for integer infinities.

6.8 General Application

We have seen that the syntactic forms of list indexing, key lookup and function application can use either square brackets or juxtaposition.

```
q)L:(1 2;3 4 5; enlist 6)
q)L[0]
1
q)L 1

q)L[0 2]

q)L[1][2]

q)L[1; 2]

```

```
q)d:`a`b`c!(1 2; 3 4 5; enlist 6)
q)d[`a]
1 2
q) d `a

q)d[`a`c]

q)d[`a][1]

q)d[`a; 1]

```

```
q)f:{x*x}
q)f[0]

q)f 1

q)f[0 2]

q)g:{x+y}
q)g[1][2]

q)g[1;2]
)
```

It turns out that both forms are syntactic sugar for how q actually treats application. You won't be surprised that application is actually a higher-order function that takes a function and value(s) and evaluates the function at the value(s). Thorough understanding of the general application is another test that separates the q pretenders from the contenders. The simpler forms of general application are usually written infix and are traditionally considered to be verbs.

6.8.1 Verb @

Basic application comprises retrieving a list item by index, looking up a dictionary value by key, or evaluating a monadic function. These are all instances of application of a univalent mathematical mapping. These are to be distinguished from indexing at depth, which is discussed in the next section.

The higher-order function (@) is the true form of basic application in q. It applies a monadic mapping to an argument. As with all built-in functions, it can be written infix or prefix.

```
q)10 20 30 40@1
20
q)L:10 20 30 40
q)L@1
_
q)@[L; 1]
_
q)count@L
_
q)@[count; L]
_
q){x*x}@L
_
```

```
q)d:`a`b`c!10 20 30
q)d@`a
_
q)@[d;`b]
_
```

Applying a niladic function with (@) is best done using the nil argument :: but any argument suffices since it is ignored.

```
q)f:{6*7}
q)f[]
_
q)@[f; ::]
_
q)f@(::)
_
q)f@43
42
```

For contrast with vector application in the next section, we collect previously discussed facts about ordinary application with a non-atom argument.

- For lists, dictionaries and atomic functions, (@) application yields an output that conforms to the shape of the input.
- An aggregate function collapses the top level of nesting from the input.
- A uniform function has output the same length as an input list.

Advanced: The function (@) also applies to tables and keyed tables since they are lists and dictionaries, respectively. Since a table is a list of records, using (@) retrieves records; for dictionaries and keyed tables it looks up keys.

```
q)t:([]c1:1 2 3; c2:`a`b`c)
q)t@1
c1| 2
c2| b
```

```
q)d:`a`b`c!10 20 30
q)d@`b
_
```

```
q)kt:([k:`a`b`c] v:1.1 2.2 3.3)
q)kt@`c
v| 3.3
```

6.8.2 Verb Dot (.)

Indexing a list at depth, retrieving a nested value from a dictionary and evaluating a function with multiple parameters are all instances of applying a multivariate mapping. The higher-order function (.) is the true form of multi-variate application in q. It applies a multivariate mapping to multiple arguments and can be written infix or prefix.

Note: The right argument of (.) must be a list.

Tip: Separate verb (.) from its operands by whitespace if they are names or literal constants, as proximity to dots used in name spacing and in decimal numbers can lead to confusion.

Here we show various forms of indexing at depth rewritten with (.).

```
q)L:(10 20 30; 40 50)
q)L[1][0]
40
q)L[1; 0]

q)L . 1 0

```

```
q)d:`a`b`c!(10 20 30; 40 50; enlist 60)
q)d[`b][0]
40
q)d[`b; 0]

q)d . (`b; 0)

```

```
q)g:{x+y}
q)g[1; 2]

q)g . 1 2

```

Observe that verb dot effectively allows us to apply a multivariate function to a list of arguments instead of multiple individual arguments. Mathematically, this means that we are thinking of the function as defined on a vector instead of its individual components.

Dot application provides function application syntax that is conveniently independent of the valence of the function. This is useful for situations in which a function and its arguments are generated dynamically—e.g., dynamic dispatch—and the valence cannot be known in advance.

```
q)g:{x+y}
q)f:g
q)f . 1 2

q)h:{x+y+z}
q)f:h
q)f . 1 2 3

```

You can apply a monadic function with (.). The insight is that a function of a scalar is inter-convertible with a function of a singleton vector. This is realized in q if you enlist the argument and use (.) for application.

```
q)f:{x*x}
q)f@5

q)f . enlist 5

q)f . enlist 1 2 3
1 4 9
```

> ***Advanced***: We conclude that (.) can apply a function of any valence and that (@) is actually unnecessary. Most q programmers do use (@) where applicable (pun intended).

To denote an elided index with (.) application, use the nil item.

```
q)m:(1 2 3;4 5 6)
q)m[0;]

q)m . (0; ::)

q)m . (::; 1)

```

Evaluating a niladic function with (.) should properly use the enlisted nil item, although any enlisted value will suffice since it is ignored.

```
q)f:{6*7}
q)f . enlist (::)

q)f . enlist 42

```

> ***Advanced:*** Let's climb the philosophical mountain. All data structures in q are composed from lists and dictionaries. Because q views both lists and dictionaries as mathematical mappings, retrieval from each is function application. Retrieval from un-nested lists and dictionaries is monadic application with (@). Retrieval from nested entities is multivariate application with (.). In light of the previous observation that a monadic function can be viewed as a function on a singleton vector, the function (.) provides a mechanism for retrieval from an arbitrary data structure. Gazing out from the summit, we see that all application is actually (.).

Following are some examples of complex data structures and indexing at depth. See if you can predict them before entering at the console. (They make good q test questions)

```
q)L:10 20 30
q)L . enlist 1

```

```
q)m:(10 20 30; 100 200 300)
q)m . 0 1

```

```
q)ds:(`a`b`c!10 20 30; `x`y!100 200)
q)ds . (0; `b)

```

```
q)mix:(10 20 30; `a`b`c!(1; 2; (300 400)))
q)mix . (1; `c; 1)
```

```
q)dc:`c1`c2!(1 2 3; `a`b`c)
q)dc . (`c2; 1)
```

```
q)t:([]c1:1 2 3;c2:`a`b`c)
q)t . (1; `c2)
```

And for keyed tables (see §8.4).

```
q)kt:([k:`a`b`c] v:1.1 2.2 3.3)
q)kt . `b`v
```

> **Tip:** Note that indexing at depth fails for accessing items inside a nested column.
>
> ```
> q)t:([] c1:`a`b`c; c2:(1 2; 100 200 400; enlist 1000))
> q)t . (1; `c2)
> 100 200 400
> q)t . (1; `c2; 1)
> 'rank
> ```

6.8.3 General Form of Verb Application

The uses of (@) and (.) seen heretofore are actually special cases of more general higher-order functions of greater valence. Since these must be written prefix, we begin by writing some simple examples of verb application from the previous section into prefix form. We use lists for simplicity but other data structures are also applicable.

```
q)L:10 20 30 40 50
q)@[L; 1]
20
q)@[L; 0 2]
10 30
```

```
q)m:(10 20 30; 100 200 300)
q).[m; 0 2]
30
```

Each application above can be viewed as **retrieval** from the data structure along a subdomain of its definition. From this perspective, the general forms to come will apply an **arbitrary operation** along a subdomain. Otherwise said, they modify a substructure **within** the original structure. This is a very powerful technique that is not present in traditional programming languages.

6.8.4 General Apply (@) with Monadic Functions

We restate the (@) retrieval examples from the previous section.

```
q)L:10 20 30 40 50
q)@[L; 1]
20
q)@[L; 0 2]
10 30
```

Now instead of simply retrieving along the subdomain, we supply a function to be **applied** along the subdomain.

```
q)@[L; 1; neg]
10 -20 30 40 50
q)@[L; 0 2; neg]
-10 20 -30 40 50
```

Effectively we reach inside (a copy of) the list, apply (neg) along the specified subdomain, and return the modified list. Contrast this with normal application on the subdomain, which returns only the modified items.

```
q)neg L@0 1
-10 -20
```

The significance of enhanced application is that it returns the entire modified list, which allows the result to be chained (i.e., composed) into further operations. If you don't think this is a big deal, think again.

The syntax for general application of a monadic atomic function on a list is,

```
@[L;I;f]
```

where L is the list and I is a collection of indices into L. Viewing L as a mapping, I is a top-level subdomain of L. In fact, this form generalizes to any data structure viewed as a mapping. For example, given a dictionary and a list of keys,

```
q)d:`a`b`c!10 20 30
q)ks:`a`c
q)@[d; ks; neg]
a| -10
b| 20
c| -30
```

> **_Important:_** For compound data structures such as nested lists, tables and keyed tables, application of (@) occurs along a subdomain at the top level. We'll see how to reach down into data structure in the next section.
>
> ```
> q)m:(10 20 30; 100 200 300; 1000 2000 3000)
> q)@[m; 0 2; neg]
> -10    -20   -30
> 100    200   300
> -1000 -2000 -3000
> ```

All the examples we have shown thus far work against copies of the input data structure. It is also possible to modify the original data structure in place. Although q does not have references, general application provides pass-by-name with the name being a symbol. We demonstrate with a simple example. In the first application, the original L is unchanged; in the second it is modified.

```
q)L:10 20 30 40
q)@[L; 0; neg]
-10 20 30 40
q)L
10 20 30 40
```

```
q)@[`L; 0 ; neg]
 L
q)L
-10 20 30 40
```

Observe that the result of an application of pass-by-name is the passed symbolic name. This allows chaining of function applications that modify in place.

6.8.5 General Apply (@) with Dyadic Functions

In the previous section we saw how to apply a **monadic** function within the top level of a data structure. In the same way, we can apply a dyadic atomic function using (@) by providing the function together with an operand to apply along the subdomain. Clearly the shape of the supplied operand must conform to the specified subdomain. The exception is applying with an atom, in which case the latter is automatically extended to match the subdomain.

```
q)L:10 20 30 40
q)@[L; 0 1; +; 100 200]
110 220 30 40
q)@[L; 0 1; +; 100]
_
```

```
q)d:`a`b`c!10 20 30
q)@[d; `a`b; +; 100 200]
a| 110
b| 220
c| 30
q)@[d; `a`b; +; 100]
```

The general form of functional (@) for a dyadic atomic function is,

```
@[L; I; g; v]
```

The notation is suggestive of lists, but L can be any data structure, viewed as a mapping. Here I is a top-level subdomain of L; g is a dyadic function; and v is an atom or list conforming to I.

We contrast application along a subdomain with normal application on the extracted substructure.

```
q)L:10 20 30 40
q)@[L; 0 1; +; 100 200]
110 220 30 40
q)100 200+L@0 1
110 220
```

As in the monadic case, application of (@) along a subdomain of compound data structures (e.g., nested lists, tables and keyed tables) occurs at the top Level.

```
q)m:(10 20 30; 100 200 300; 1000 2000 3000)
q)@[m; 0 2; +; 1 2]
11   21   31
100  200  300
1002 2002 3002
```

> **Tip:** A useful case of dyadic application uses the assignment operator (:) to modify values along the subdomain.
>
> ```
> q)L:10 20 30 40
> q)@[L; 0 2; :; 42 43]
> 42 20 43 40
> ```

As in the monadic case, to apply to the original in place, instead of to a copy, use pass-by-name.

```
q)L:10 20 30 40
q)@[`L; 0 2; :; 42 43]
`L
q)L
42 20 43 40
```

6.8.6 General Apply (.) for Monadic Functions

We have seen that general (@) applies a function on a vector along the top level of a data structure. Now consider indexing at depth.

> **Tip:** Although the construct is valid at any depth, there is a case to be made for not going beyond depth two in q (i.e., data normalization with tables).

We begin by restating simple examples of indexing at depth in prefix notation, using moderately nested lists and dictionaries for simplicity.

```
q)m:(10 20 30; 100 200 300)
q).[m; 0 1]
20
```

```
q)d:`a`b`c!(10 20 30; 40 50; enlist 60)
q).[d; (`a; 1)]
20
```

In contrast with (@), the vector argument of (.) reaches down into the data structure and picks out a single point in the domain. Here we target that point with a monadic function.

```
q).[m; 0 1; neg]
10 -20 30
100 200 300
```

```
q).[d; (`a; 1); neg]
a| 10 -20 30
b| 40 50
c| ,60
```

As before, these applications work against a copy of the data. To modify the original in place, (.) supports pass-by-name.

```
q).[m; 0 1; neg]
q)m
```

```
q).[`m; 0 1; neg]
`m
q)m
```

```
q).[d; (`a; 1); neg]
```

```
q)d
```

```
q).[`d; (`a; 1); neg]
 d
q)d
```

We previously saw that to elide an index in (.) retrieval, we place the nil item (::) in that slot. The same holds for general application, where it means apply the function along **all** indices at that level.

```
q).[m; (0; ::); neg]
-10 -20 -30
100 200 300
```

```
q)d:`a`b`c!(100 200 300; 400 500; enlist 600)
q).[d; (`a; ::); neg]
a| -100 -200 -300
b| 400 500
c| ,600
```

```
q).[d; (::; 0); neg]
a| -100 200 300
b| -400 500
c| ,-600
```

The general form of (.) for monadic functions is,

```
.[L; I; f]
```

Here L is a data structure, I is an in-depth subdomain of L and f is a monadic atomic function.

6.8.7 General Apply (.) for Dyadic Functions

By now you can predict how general application (.) with a dyadic function works. The form of functional (.) for a dyadic function is,

```
.[L; I; g; v]
```

Here L is a data structure, I is an in-depth subdomain of L, g is a dyadic function and v is an atom (for g atomic) or a vector that conforms to I. To apply in place use pass-by-name.

```
q)m:(10 20 30; 100 200 300)
q).[m; 0 1; +; 1]
10  21  30
100 200 300
q).[m; (::; 1); +; 1 2]
10  21  30

q)m

q).[`m; (::; 1); +; 1]

q)m

q).[`m; (::; 1); :; 42]
 m
q)m

```

```
q)d:`a`b`c!(100 200 300; 400 500; enlist 600)
q).[d; (`a; 1); +; 1]

q).[d; (`a; ::); +; 1]

q).[d; (::; 0); +; 1]

q)d

q).[`d; (::; 0); :; 42]

q)d

```

7   *Transforming Data*

7.1 Types

Casting is a way to convert a value of one type to a compatible type. Sometimes the conversion is exact; other times information is lost. Enumeration and parsing in q also fit into the cast pattern.

7.1.1 Basic DataTypes

A type can be specified in three equivalent ways: a char, a short and a symbol.   For convenience, we repeat the data types table from Chapter 1.

type	type symbol	type char	type num

boolean	boolean	B	
			1h
guid	`guid	G	2h
byte	`byte	X	
			4h
short	`short	H	
			5h
int	`int	I	
			6h
long	`long	J	7h
real	`real	E	
			8h
float	`float	F	
			9h
char	`char	C	
			10h
symbol	`	S	
			11h
timestamp	`timestamp	P	12h
month	`month	M	
			13h
date	`date	D	
			14h
datetime	`datetime	Z	
			15h
timespan	`timespan	N	
			16h
minute	`minute	U	
			17h
second	`second	V	
			18h
time	`time	T	
			19h

7.1.2 The (type) Operator

The non-atomic monadic function (type) can be applied to any entity in q to return its data type expressed as a short. It is a "feature" of q that the data type of an atom is negative whereas the type of a simple list is positive.

```
q)type 42
-7h
q)type 10 20 30
7h
q)type 98.6
-9h
q)type 1.1 2.2 3.3
_
```

```
q)type `a
-11h
q)type `a`b`c

q)type "z"
-10h
q)type "abc"
_
```

Observe that infinities and nulls have their respective types.

```
q)type 0w
-7h
q)type 0N
_
q)type -0w
-9h
q)type 0n
_
q)type `
-11h
```

The type of any general list is 0.

```
q)type (42h; 42i; 42j)
0h
q)type (1 2 3; 10 20 30)
_
q)type ()
_
```

The type of any dictionary, including a keyed table, is 99h.

```
q)type (`a`b`c!10 20 30
99h
q)type ([k:`a`b`c] v:10 20 30)
_
```

The type of any table is 98h.

```
q)type ([] c1:`a`b`c; c2:10 20 30)
98h
```

7.1.3 Type of a Variable

Since q is a dynamically typed language, a variable has the type of the value currently assigned to it. Unlike statically typed languages, there is no predeclaration of type.

```
q)a:42
q)type a
-7h
q)a:"abc"
q)type a
10h
```

In more detail, the variable a above is an association between the name `a and its assigned value. Since this is the first time that the variable is assigned, the q interpreter creates an entry for the key `a in its dictionary of global variables and associates it with the value 42.

```
q)get `.
a| 42
```

On the subsequent assignment, there is already an entry for the key `a in the dictionary, so the value "abc" is upserted.

```
q)get `.
a| "abc"
```

The type of a variable **is** the type of the value associated with the variable's name.

Global variables are stored in ordinary q dictionaries with special names. For example, the symbol `. is the name of the default global dictionary. Start a fresh q session and observe the life of this dictionary using (value).

```
q)value `.
q)a:42
q)value `.
a| 42
q)f:{x*x}
q)value `.
a| 42
f| {x*x}
..
```

> **Note:** Since q internally uses the same dictionary structures available to us, it has been said (crassly) that q eats its own dog food.

7.2 Cast

Casting renders an underlying value of one type into another compatible type. For example, a short integer has a natural interpretation as a long integer. In the Mathematical Refresher we discussed the implicit identifications of naturals with their rational counterparts and rationals with their repeating decimal real counterparts. These identifications are actually examples of casting, since the numeric values representing the different types are the same in essence.

Since q is dynamically typed, casting occurs at run-time using the dyadic operator ($), which is atomic in both operands. The right operand is the source value and the left operand specifies the target type. There are three ways to specify the target type, indicated by the first three columns of the type table at the beginning of this chapter.

- A (positive) numeric short type value

- A char type value
- A type name symbol

7.2.1 Casts that Widen

In these examples, no information is lost in the cast, as the target type is wider than the source type. Here are examples using the short type specification in the target.

```
q)7h$42i          / int to long
42
q)6h$42           / long to int
42i
q)9h$42           / long to float
42f
```

It is arguably more readable to use the type char. Here are the same examples recast (ouch) to use the type char.

```
q)"j"$42i
42
q)"i"$42
42i
q)"f"$42
42f
```

It is arguably most readable to use the symbolic type name.

```
q)`int$42

q)`long$42i

q)`float$42

```

7.2.2 Casts across Disparate Types

It may come as a surprise that q allows casting between superficially disparate types. When the underlying values are the same, the types are essentially just different representation formats, so why not allow a cast? We use the symbolic names in the following examples; the other formats work equally well.

The underlying value of a char is its position in the ASCII collation sequence, so we can cast char to and from integers, provided the integer is less than 256.

```
q)`char$42
"*"
q)`long$"\n"
```

The underlying value of a date is its count of days from the millennium, so we can cast to and from an int.

```
q)`date$0
2000.01.01
q)`int$2001.01.01 / millennium occurred on leap year
```

The underlying value of a timespan is its count of nanoseconds from midnight, so we can cast it to and from long.

```
q)`long$12:00:00.0000000000
43200000000000
q)`timespan$0
```

7.2.3 Casts that Narrow

Some casts lose information. This includes the usual suspects of float to integer and wider integers to narrower ones.

```
q)`long$12.345
12
q)`short$123456789
32767h
```

Cast any numeric to a boolean using the C philosophy that zero is 0b and anything else is 1b.

```
q)`boolean$0
0b
q)`boolean$0.0
0b
q)`boolean$123
1b
q)`boolean$-12.345
1b
```

We can also extract constituents from complex types.

```
q)`date$2015.01.02D10:20:30.123456789
2015.01.02
q)`year$2015.01.02
2015i
q)`month$2015.01.02
2015.01m
q)`mm$2015.01.02
1i
q)`dd$2015.01.02
2i
```

```
q)`hh$10:20:30.123456789
10i
q)`minute$10:20:30.123456789
10:20
q)`uu$10:20:30.123456789
20i
q)`second$10:20:30.123456789
10:20:30
q)`ss$10:20:30.123456789
30i
```

> **Tip:** This is to be preferred over dot notation since the latter does not work inside functions.

7.2.4 Casting Integral Infinities

When integral infinities are cast to integers of wider type, they **are** their underlying bit patterns, reinterpreted. Since these bit patterns are legitimate values for the wider type, the cast results in a finite value.

```
q)`int$0Wh
32767i
q)`int$-0Wh
-32767i
q)`long$0Wi
2147483647
q)`long$-0Wi
-2147483647
```

7.2.5 Coercing Types

Casting can be used to coerce type-safe assignment. Recall that assignment into a simple list must strictly match the type.

```
q)L:10 20 30 40
q)L[1]:42h
'type
q)L,:43h
'type
```

This situation can arise when the list and the assignment value are created dynamically. Coerce the type by casting it to that of the target, provided of course that the cast is legitimate.

```
q)L[1]:(type L)$42h
q)L,:(type L)$43h
q)L
_
```

> **Tip:** The type of a simple list is positive to make this construct work.

7.2.6 Cast is Atomic

Cast is atomic in the right operand.

```
q)"i"$10 20 30
10 20 30i
q)`float$(42j; 42i; 42j)
42 42 42f
```

Cast is atomic in the left operand.

```
q)`short`int`long$42
42h
42i
42
q)"ijf"$98.6
99i
99
98.6
```

Cast is atomic in both operands simultaneously.

```
q)"ijf"$10 20 30
10i
20
30f
```

7.3 Data to and from Text

Recall that a q string is a simple list of char. All grown-up programming languages have a mechanism for translating literal text into values and vice versa. It isn't strictly correct to say that converting a value to a string and parsing a string are casts since the value is only implicit in the text, but the operations are closely related and use the same operator in q.

7.3.1 Data to Strings

The function (string) can be applied to any q entity to produce a text representation suitable for console display or storage in a file. Here are the key features of (string).

- The result is always a list of char, never a single char. Thus you will see singleton char lists from single digits.
- The result contains no q type indicators or other decorations. In general, the result is the most compact representation of the input, which may not actually be convertible (i.e., parsed) back to the original value.
- Applying (string) to an actual string (i.e., list of char) probably will not give you what you want.

Following are some examples.

```
q)string 42
"42"
q)string 4
,"4"
q)string 42i
"42"

q)a:2.0
q)string a
,"2"

q)f:{x*x}
q)string f
"{x*x}"
```

The (string) function is clearly not atomic—for example, it takes the atom 42 to the list "42". However, it is pseudo-atomic, in that it recurses into its argument and applies to the individual atoms. As such, the result conforms to the input, which explains its behavior on strings.

```
q)string 1 2 3
,"1"
,"2"
,"3"
q)string "string"
,"s"
,"t"
,"r"
,"i"
,"n"
,"g"
q)string (1 2 3; 10 20 30)
,"1"  ,"2"  ,"3"
"10" "20" "30"
```

> ***Tip:*** Use (`string`) to convert a list (or column) of symbols to strings.
>
> ```
> q)string `Life`the`Universe`and`Everything
> _
> ```

7.3.2 Creating Symbols from Strings

Casting from a string (i.e., a list of char) to a symbol is a foolproof way to create symbols. It is the **only** way to create symbols with embedded blanks or other special characters that cannot be entered into a literal symbol. To cast a char or a string to a symbol, use (`` `$``).

```
q)`$"abc"
`abc
q
q)`$"Hello World"
_
```

> ***Tip:*** Do not use `` `symbol$`` for this as it generates an error. This is a common qbie mistake.

You can include any characters in a symbol this way but you may need to escape them into the string.

```
q)`$"Zaphod \"Z\""
`Zaphod "Z"
q)`$"Zaphod \n"
`Zaphod
```

> ***Note***: The source string is left and right trimmed during the cast. The author knows no workaround to force leading or trailing blanks into a symbol. Why would you want them there, anyway?

```
q)string `$"   abc   "
"abc"
```

The monadic (`` `$``) is atomic and will thus convert an entire list (or column) of strings to symbols.

```
q)`$("Life";"the";"Universe";"and";"Everything")
`Life`the`Universe`and`Everything
```

7.3.3 Parsing Data from Strings

The (`$`) operator is overloaded to parse strings into data of any type exactly as the q interpreter does. This overload is invoked by using an **uppercase** type char as the target left operand and a string in the right operand. If the specified parse cannot be performed, a null of the target type is returned—i.e., missing or bad data—instead of an exception.

```
q)"J"$"42"
42
q)"F"$"42"
42f
q)"F"$"42.0"
42f
q)"I"$"42.0"
0Ni
q)"I"$" "
0Ni
```

Date parsing is flexible with respect to the format of the date..

```
q)"D"$"12.31.2014"
2014.12.31
q)"D"$"12-31-2014"

q)"D"$"12/31/2014"

q)"D"$"12/1/2014"

q)"D"$"2014/12/31"

```

To create a function from a string, use the built-in (value), which **is** the q interpreter or (parse), which is the parse step of the interpreter.

```
q)value "{x*x}"
{x*x}
q)parse "{x*x}"
```

7.4 Creating Typed Empty Lists

The general empty list has type 0 since it has no items and therefore affords no canonical way to determine a type.

```
q)type ()
0h
```

An issue arises when appending an item in place to a general empty list, Namely, if that item is an atom, the resulting singleton list is now a simple list of the type of the atom.

```
q)L:()
q)type L
0h
q)L,:42
q)type L
7h
```

Should this list be a column in a table, this can be problematic. For example, suppose you intend the column to be a list of floats but the first row appended to the table happens to have a long in the field for this column. Then the errant field is accepted, the type of the column is set to long, and all subsequent appends of float raise a 'type error.

```
q)c1:()
q)c1,:42
q)c1,:98.6
'type
```

To avoid this, cast the empty list using the name of the desired type, which makes it an empty simple list of that type. Now only atoms of the specified type can be appended in place.

```
q)c1:`float$()
q)c1,:42
'type
q)c1:98.6
q)c1
_
```

Notice that an operation that yields a simple list retains the type on an empty result.

```
q)0#10 20 30
_
```

This yields a succinct idiom to create typed empty lists.

```
q)0#0
`long$()
q)0#0.0
)
q)0#`
_
```

Important: There is no way in q to type nested empty lists.

7.5 Enumerations

We have seen that the dyadic cast operator ($) transforms its right operand into a conforming entity of the type specified by the left operand. In the basic cast form, the left operand can be a char type abbreviation, a type short, or a symbol type name. In this section, casting is extended to user-defined target domains, providing a functional version of enumerated types.

7.5.1 Traditional Enumerations

To begin, recall that in traditional languages, an enumerated type is a way of associating a series of names with a corresponding set of integral values. Often the sequence of numbers is consecutive and begins with 0. The association is usually given a name and represents a new type.

A traditional enumerated type serves multiple purposes.

- It allows a descriptive name to be used instead of an arbitrary number—e.g., 'red', 'green', `blue' instead of 0, 1 and 2.
- It enables type checking to ensure that only permissible values are supplied—e.g., choosing a color name from a list instead of remembering its number is less prone to error.
- It provides namespacing, meaning the same name can be reused in different domains without fear of confusion—e.g., color.blue and note.blue (the flatted fifth).

There is also a subtler, more powerful use of enumerations: normalizing data.

7.5.2 Data Normalization

Broadly speaking, data normalization seeks to eliminate duplication, retaining only the minimum required data. In the archetypal example, suppose you know that you will have a list of text entries taken from a fixed and reasonably short set of values—e.g., stock exchange ticker symbols. Storing a long list of such strings verbatim presents two problems.

- Values of variable length complicate storage management and make retrieval inefficient.
- There is potentially much duplication of data arising from repeated values. This is hard to keep in sync when values change.

Let's see how an enumeration solves both problems. The key ingredients are a (presumably repetitive) list v of symbols drawn from a unique list of symbols u. As in the case of ticker symbols, it may be that we know the list u in advance.

```
q)u:`g`aapl`msft`ibm
q)v:1000000?u
q)v
`g`g`msft`aapl`msft`aapl`msft`ibm`msft`aapl`g`ibm`aapl`msft`msft`aapl`g
..
```

Or it may be that we are given v and need to determine u.

```
q)v
`jha`jha`fna`fed`fna`fna`jha`jha`jgc`pkh`pkh`pkh`fna`fed`jha`cpi`pkh`pk
h`igb
q)u:distinct v
q)u
`jha`fna`fed`jgc`pkh`cpi`igb`hln`mjh`ooj
```

In any case, we have a list of symbols v drawn from a unique list u.

Consider a new list k that represents the position in u of each item of v. This can be generated by our old friend the find operator (?).

```
q)u:`g`aapl`msft`ibm
q)v:1000000?u
q)k:u?v
q)k
2 1 1 3 3 1 0 0 0 3 0 2 2 1 2 3 1 0 1 1 2 1 2 0 2 1 1 0 1 1 3 0..
```

The key observation is that u and k together carry precisely the same information as v; indeed, they can be used to reconstitute it.

```
q)u[k]
`msft`aapl`aapl`ibm`ibm`aapl`g`g`g`ibm`g`msft`msft`aapl`msft`ibm`aapl..
q)v~u[k]
1b
```

After a bit of Zen, you will recognize that u and k exactly constitute a traditional enumeration discussed above. Indeed, u is the list of names, while the associated values are (implicitly) the indices of the items in u. Every symbol in v can be replaced by the corresponding index in k—exactly what a traditional compiler does for an enumeration.

Why would we want to do this trade? Easy-peasy-lemon-squeezy: speed and compactness. First, v is a list of variable length text, which is time-consuming to search, whereas k is a uniform list of integers, which is very fast to traverse. Moreover, u and k normalize the data of v. In general, v will have many repetitions of each symbol, but u stores each symbol once. Reading and writing the index list k from/to disk is a block operation that will be very fast.

Advanced: Extra credit for recognizing that in terms of maps, v is the composite map u · k. For all you category theorists, we have factored

---

> the map of the non-unique list v through the unique list u via the index map k. Mathematically,
>
> $$v = u \cdot k$$

Let's examine the storage requirements for a list of symbols in more detail. Say that the count of u is a and the maximum width of the text inside the symbols in u is b. For a list v of variable count x, the amount of storage required is potentially

$b*x$

For the indexed form, the storage is known to be,

$a*b+4*x$

which represents the fixed amount of storage for u plus the variable amount of storage for the simple integer list k. If a is small and b is even moderately large, the factorization is significantly smaller.

This can be seen by comparing the sizes of v, u and k in a slightly modified version of our example.

```
v:`ccccccc`bbbbbbb`aaaaaaa`ccccccc`ccccccc`bbbbbbb
u:distinct v
u
`ccccccc`bbbbbbb`aaaaaaa

k:u?v
k
0 1 2 0 0 1
```

Now imagine v and k to be much longer.

7.5.3 Enumerating Symbols

The process of converting a list of symbols to the equivalent list of indices described in the previous section is called *enumeration* in q. It uses (yet another overload of) ($) with the name of the variable holding the unique symbols as the left operand and a list of symbols drawn from that domain on the right.

Under the covers, ($) does the indexing operation in the previous section and then replaces each symbol with its index. Fortunately, you don't have to see how the sausage is made—i.e., q hides all this from you and displays the enumerated symbols in their reconstituted form with the name of the unique domain as an annotation. Continuing the example of the previous section:

```
q)`u$v
`u$`msft`aapl`aapl`ibm`ibm`aapl`g`g`g`ibm`g`msft`msft`aapl`msft..
```

You can recover the underlying integer values (i.e., k above) by casting to an integer.

```
q)ev:`u$v
q)`int$ev
2 1 1 3 3 1 0 0 0 3 0 2 2 1 2 3 1 0 1 1 2 1 2 0 2 1 1 0 1 1 3 ..
```

Let's summarize. The basic form of an enumerated symbol is,

   `u$v

where u is a simple list of unique symbols and v is either an atom appearing in u or a (possibly nested) list of such. We call u the *domain* of the enumeration and the projection (`u$) is *enumeration over u*. Under the covers, applying the enumeration (`u$) to a vector v produces the index list k as above.

Important: For this style of enumeration, all potential values must be in the list u; otherwise you will get a 'cast error when trying to enumerate.

```
q)u:`a`b`c
q)`u$`d
'cast
```

We shall see in §7.5.7 an alternate approach when the full extent of u is not known in advance.

When working with tables in kdb, by convention all symbol columns in all tables are enumerated over a common domain sym. You will hear this referred to as the *sym list* or the *sym file*, depending on where it resides.

Important: Although integers are 64-bit in q3+, for reasons known to the q gods, enumerations are 32-bit.

7.5.4 Using Enumerated Symbols

We continue with the example of the previous section, renamed to use the standard sym domain.

```
q)sym:`g`aapl`msft`ibm
q)v:1000000?sym
q)ev:`sym$v
```

The enumerated ev can be substituted for the original v in nearly all situations.

```
q)v[3]
`aapl
q)ev[3]
`u$`aapl

q)v[3]:`ibm
q)ev[3]:`ibm

q)v=`ibm
000100010010011101000010010100000000100100000001000000001100001001011..
q)ev=`ibm

q)where v=`aapl
4 5 19 20 21 31 33 34 41 42 43 49 58 59 61 74 81 83 90 94 95 98 114..
q)where ev=`aapl
4 5 19 20 21 31 33 34 41 42 43 49 58 59 61 74 81 83 90 94 95 98 114..
000100010010011101000010010100000000100100000001000000001100001001011..

q)v?`aapl
4
q)ev?`aapl
4

q)v in `ibm`aapl
000111010010010011101011110010100010110100101110001010000001111011001011..
q)ev in `ibm`aapl
000111010010010011101011110010100010110100101110001010000001111011001011..
```

While the enumerated version is item-wise equal to the original, the entities are not identical.

```
q)all v=ev
1b
q)v~ev
0b
```

This is because the types matter with (~).

7.5.5 Type of Enumerations

Each enumeration is assigned a new numeric data type, beginning with 20h. Starting with q version 3.2, the type 20h is reserved for the conventional enumeration domain sym, whether you use it or not (you should). The types of other enumerations you create will begin with 21h and proceed sequentially. The convention of negative type for atoms and positive type for simple lists still holds. In a fresh q session we see the following.

```
q)sym1:`g`aapl`msft`ibm
q)type `sym1$1000000?sym1
21h

q)sym2:`a`b`c
q)type `sym2$`c
-22h
```

In contrast, the sym domain has type 20h even if created after another enumeration. Continuing in the previous session,

```
q)sym:`b`c`a
q)type `sym$100?sym
20h
```

Enumerations with different domains are distinct, even when all the constituents are the same.

```
q)sym1:`c`b`a
q)sym2:`c`b`a
q)ev1:`sym1$`a`b`a`c`a
q)ev2:`sym2$`a`b`a`c`a

q)ev1=ev2
11111b
q)ev1~ev2
0b
```

7.5.6 Updating an Enumerated List

The normalization provided by an enumeration reduces updating all occurrences of a given value to a single operation. This can have significant performance implications for large lists with many repetitions. Continuing with our example above, suppose the list u contains the items in a stock index and we wish to change one of the constituents. A single update to u suffices.

```
q)sym:`g`aapl`msft`ibm
q)ev:`sym$`g`g`msft`ibm`aapl`aapl`msft`ibm`msft`g`ibm`g..
q)sym[0]:`twit
q)sym
`twit`aapl`msft`ibm
q)ev
`sym$`twit`twit`msft`ibm`aapl`aapl`msft`ibm`msft`twit`ibm`twit..
```

In contrast, to make the equivalent update to v requires changing **every** occurrence.

```
q)v
`g`g`msft`ibm`aapl`aapl`msft`ibm`msft`g`ibm`g…
q)@[v; where v=`g; :; `twit]
```

216

> **Important:** Be extremely cautious about modifying the sym list manually (better not to do it at all). Should you corrupt the sym list, your entire database will be scrambled! Make a persistent copy/backup before modifying the list, else update your CV after.

7.5.7 Dynamically Appending to an Enumeration Domain

One situation in which an enumeration is more complicated than working with the denormalized data is when you want to add a new value. Continuing with the example above, appending a new item to an ordinary list of symbols is a single operation. We saw in §7.5.4 this is not the case when the new value is not in the enumeration domain.

```
q)sym:`g`aapl`msft`ibm
q)v:1000000?sym
q)ev:`sym$v
q)v,:`twtr
q)ev,:`twtr
'cast
```

The new value **must** first be added to the unique list.

```
q)sym,:`twtr
q)ev,:`twtr
```

In practice, to use ($) with dynamically generated values, you must test to see if the value you intend to append is already in the enumeration domain and, if not, append it there first. Fortunately, q has anticipated this situation.

If you cannot know the full extent of the enumeration domain in advance, you can use (yet another overload of) (?) to create the domain on the fly. The syntax of (?) is the same as the enumeration overload of ($)—i.e., the **name** of a (unique) list of symbols as left operand and a source symbol or list of symbols as right operand.

This application of (?) has the side effect of first checking to see if the source symbols are in the domain named by the left operand, and appends any that aren't. In any case, it returns the enumerated version of the source just like ($).

You can build the enumeration domain from scratch.

217

```
q)sym:()
q)`sym$`g
'cast
q)`sym?`g
 sym$`g
q)sym
,`g
q)`sym?`ibm`aapl
 sym$`ibm`aapl
q)sym
`g`ibm`aapl
q)`sym?`g`msft
 sym$`g`msft
q)sym
`g`ibm`aapl`msft
```

Our previous example now works, with (?) in place of ($).

```
q)ev,:`u?`twtr
```

7.5.8 Resolving an Enumeration

An enumerated symbol can be substituted for its equivalent symbol value in most expressions. However, there are some situations in which you need non-enumerated values. One case is converting from one enumeration domain to another, which happens when copying from one kdb+ database to another or in merging two databases.

Given an enumerated symbol, or a list of such, you can recover the un-enumerated value(s) by applying the built-in (value). In our on-going example,

```
q)sym:`g`aapl`msft`ibm
q)v:1000000?sym
q)ev:`sym$v

q)value ev
`aapl`g`msft`msft`ibm`msft`msft`msft`msft`msft`g`ibm`ibm`ibm..
q)v~value ev
1b
```

This is another overload of (value), the function that is essentially the q interpreter.

8 Tables

8.0 Overview

Tables are first class entities in q, meaning they are data structures that live in memory just like lists or dictionaries.   A q table is essentially a collection of named columns implemented as a dictionary. Consequently, q tables are column-oriented, in contrast to the row-oriented tables in relational databases.   Moreover, since lists are ordered, so are columns, in contrast to SQL where the order of rows is undefined. The fact that q tables comprise ordered column lists makes kdb+ very efficient at storing, retrieving and manipulating sequential data. One important example is time series data.

Kdb+ handles relational and time series data in the unified environment of q tables.   There is no separate data definition language, no separate stored procedure language and no need to map internal representations to a separate form for persistence.   Just q tables, expressions and functions.

Tables are built from dictionaries, so it behooves the cursory reader to review Chapter 5 before proceeding.

8.1 Table Definition

8.1.1 Review of Table as Column Dictionary

We summarize our findings on column dictionaries from §5.4.   We began with a rectangular collection of named column lists.

```
q)dc:`name`iq!(`Dent`Beeblebrox`Prefect;98 42 126)
q)dc[`iq;]
98 42 126
q)dc[;2]
name| `Prefect
iq  | 126
q)dc[`iq; 2]
126
```

Transpose it with (flip) to get a table.

219

```
q)t:flip `name`iq!(`Dent`Beeblebrox`Prefect;98 42 126)
q)t[;`iq]
98 42 126
q)t[2;]
name| `Prefect
iq  | 126
q)t[2;`iq]
126
```

We repeat our findings about a table defined this way.

- It is a two dimensional data structure that uses an integer index in the first slot and a symbol column name in the second slot.
- Specifying only an integer in the first slot retrieves a section dictionary across that index—i.e., a record.
- Specifying only a column name in the second slot retrieves that column.
- Specifying both an integer and a column name retrieves the "field" at that row in that column.
- A table is logically a list of section dictionaries.
- The **only** effect of flipping the column dictionary is to reverse the order of its indices; no data is rearranged under the covers.

All tables have type 98h.

```
q)type t
98h
```

The proper way to extract a table column is by eliding the row index. For table columns (only), you can omit the leading semi-colon in the syntax.

```
q)t[;`iq]

q)t[`iq]

q)t[`name`iq]
Dent Beeblebrox Prefect
98   42        126
```

Since it is possible to retrieve values from a dictionary using dot notation, this is also true for tables.

```
q)t.name

```

> **Tip:** Unfortunately dot notation doesn't work inside functions so we recommend not using it at all.

8.1.2 Table Display

Observe that the row and column display of a table is indeed the transpose of the dictionary display. This reflects the transposed indices, even though the internal data layout is the same.

```
q)dc
name| Dent Beeblebrox Prefect
iq  | 98   42         126

q)t
name       iq
-------------
Dent       98
Beeblebrox 42
Prefect    126
```

8.1.3 Table Definition Syntax

Constructing a table by flipping a column dictionary is useful when you need to build the table on the fly. There is an alternate syntax to define tables that makes things a bit more readable.

$$([]\ c_1:L_1;\ \ldots;\ c_n:L_n)$$

Here c_i is a symbol representing a column name and L_i is the corresponding list of column values. The L_i are lists of equal count, but can be atoms as long as at least one is a list. The brackets will contain key columns for keyed tables—explained in §8.3.3—but are empty for tables. For readability, in this tutorial we shall often include optional whitespace after the closing square bracket and to the right of semicolon separators.

The colons in table definition syntax are **not** assignment. They are part of the syntactic sugar and serve as markers separating column names from column values.

> **Tip:** Do not omit the square brackets in table definition syntax. The interpreter will not complain and you will end up with a list, rather than a table, and the colons will be assignment.

Here is how to define our favorite table using table definition syntax, which is arguably simpler.

```
q)t:([] name:`Dent`Beeblebrox`Prefect; iq:98 42 126)
q)t~flip `name`iq!(`Dent`Beeblebrox`Prefect;98 42 126)
1b
```

The value lists in table definition syntax can originate from variables, which is useful for programmatic table definition. In this case the column names are the variable names.

```
q)c1:`Dent`Beeblebrox`Prefect
q)c2:98 42 126
q)([] c1; c2)
```

This example shows that if you don't explicitly specify column names, q will create them on a best effort basis. In this example, it used the variable names. It will also try to make duplicate column names unique by appending a numeric suffix.

Any valid q expression can appear to the right of the semi-colon in table definition syntax; it is evaluated as part of the table construction. You must ensure that the resulting column lists all have the same length.

```
q)([] c1:1+til 5; c2:5#42)
```

Provided you specify at least one column as a list, atoms will be extended to match.

```
q)([] c1:`a`b`c; c2:42; c3:98.6)
c1 c2 c3
--------
a  42 98.6
b  42 98.6
c  42 98.6
```

Using an atom in this way might appear to assign a default value. It does not.

> **Tip:** You cannot define a single row table using all atoms. You must enlist at least one of the atoms.
>
> ```
> q)([] c1:`a; c2:100)
> 'rank
> q)([] enlist `a; c2:100)
> ```

If you create a table as the flip of a column dictionary, item-wise extension is performed when the column dictionary is flipped into a table.

```
q)`c1`c2`c3!(`a`b`c;42;1.1)
c1| `a`b`c
c2| 42
c3| 1.1

q)flip `c1`c2`c3!(`a`b`c;42;1.1)
c1 c2 c3
---------
a  42 1.1
b  42 1.1
c  42 1.1
```

8.1.4 Table Metadata

The column names of a table can be retrieved as a list of symbols with (cols).

```
q)cols t
```

The function (meta) applied to a table retrieves its metadata. The result is a keyed table (see §8.4.1) with one record for each column in the original table.

- The key column c of the result contains the column names.
- The column t contains a symbol denoting the type char of the column.
- The column f contains the domains of any foreign key or link columns.
- The column a contains any attributes associated with the column.

```
q)meta t
c    | t f a
-----| -----
name | s
iq   | j
```

When (meta) displays an **upper** case type char for a column, this indicates that column is a *compound* list in which all fields are simple lists of the indicated type. Such tables arise, for example, when you group without aggregating in a query. Here is one created manually. Observe the upper case 'J' in the t column for column c2.

```
q)meta ([] c1:1 2 3; c2:(1 2; enlist 3; 4 5 6))
c | t f a
--| -----
c1| j
c2| J
```

> **Advanced**: When (meta) is applied to a partitioned table that has been mapped into memory, it only examines the most recent partition. Thus it makes the implicit assumption that the partition slice schemas are consistent across the partitions. In the event that the partition slices are not consistent, (meta) blithely reports the schema found in the most recent partition. In order to determine the offending partition, you will have to run (meta) on each of the partition slices and determine the outliers. This is relevant because the .Q utilities will **not** prevent you from writing an inconsistent partition slice and you may discover the error later.

The function (tables) takes a symbolic namespace (see §12.1) and returns a sorted symbol list of the names of tables in that context. For example, we list all tables in the root context for a fresh q session.

```
q)t2:([] c1:1 2 3; c2:(1 2; enlist 3; 4 5 6))
q)t:([] name:`Dent`Beeblebrox`Prefect; iq:98 42 126)
q)tables `.
`t`t2
```

Alternatively, the command (\a) provides the same result. If no argument is provided, it returns the result for the current context.

8.1.5 Records

Since a table is logically a list of dictionary records, (count) returns the number of records. In our example,

```
q)count t
_
```

Now let's inspect the sequence of records.

```
q)t
name       iq
--------------
Dent        98
Beeblebrox 42
Prefect    126

q)t[0]
name| `Dent
iq  | 98
q)t[1]
name| Beeblebrox
iq  | 98
```

Since a record dictionary slices across the table display horizontally, this motivates calling the value portion of the record dictionary a table *row*. The record associates column names with the values in a physical row. To retrieve the naked values of a row—i.e., without the column names—simply apply (value) to the record dictionary.

```
q)value t[1]
`Beeblebrox
42
```

8.1.6 Flipped Column Dictionary vs. List of Records

Is a table a flipped column dictionary or a list of records? Logically it is both, but physically it is stored as a column dictionary. In fact, q dynamically recognizes a conforming list of dictionaries that could be formed into a table and reorganizes the data into columnar form automatically. It doesn't ask for permission or seek forgiveness.

To verify this, we first create a list of non-conforming dictionaries that differ in the *italicized* key names. As expected it has type 0.

```
q)type (`name`iq!(`Dent;98); `nome`iq!(`Beeblebrox;42))
0h
```

Once we make the names agree so that the records conform, (type) tells us that q has indeed converted the list to a table.

```
q)type (`name`iq!(`Dent;98); `name`iq!(`Beeblebrox;42))
98h
```

This is no mere illusion. The data have been reorganized into columns.

Tip: Here is a useful special case of this phenomenon. Start with a simple dictionary and enlist it to create a singleton. What is this?

```
q)enlist `a`b!10 20
```

It is a table because it is a singleton list of records that conform.

You might think that you don't want q to do this automatic reorganization, but you would be wrong. In general, column retrieval and manipulation will be significantly faster than operations on a list of dictionaries, especially if the columns are simple—i.e., the column values are stored contiguously.

A downside of tables being stored as columns is that row deletion is an expensive operation because all the column lists must be compressed to close the resulting gap. The best way to deal with this in large tables is not to do it. Instead of deleting a row, use a separate column that holds a flag indicating whether the row has been deleted and then exclude the "deleted" rows. Then compress this column to save space since it will be sparse.

8.2 Empty Tables and Schema

We saw in the previous section that a table can be defined and populated in one step using table syntax.

```
q)t:([] name:`Dent`Beeblebrox`Prefect; iq:98 42 126)
```

Fully listing columns with literals is usually done only with smaller tables—e.g., lookup tables. Large tables are usually created programmatically from computed data or data read from files or received over the wire.

In these circumstances, it is useful to create an empty table initially and then populate it later by appending in place. You could do this with general empty lists.

```
q)([] name:(); iq:())
```

All columns here are lists of general type, so data of any type can be appended in the first record. Should the first item being appended to an empty column be an atom (a common case), the column becomes a singleton list with that atom—i.e., a simple list of that type. As with all simple lists, type checking will thereafter be enforced for all inserts and updates to that column. Consequently all subsequent appends must match the initial one.

This situation is fine provided you are guaranteed that all data will match the initial record. Unfortunately, real world data can be highly unpredictable. Should the first record be bad, type checking will reject all subsequent good data.

Recommendation: It is good practice to specify the types of all columns in an empty table. In the table definition, cast an empty list to the appropriate type.

```
q)([] name:`symbol$(); iq:`int$())
```

226

A shorter, and arguably less obvious technique is the following.

```
q)([] name:0#`; iq:0#0)

q)([] name:0#`; iq:0#0)~ ([] name:`symbol$(); iq:`int$())
1b
```

Whichever form you use, it ensures that only data of the appropriate type can be appended.

8.3 Basic select and update

We shall cover q-sql in depth in Chapter 9, but we provide an introduction here in order to extract and display data in our examples. We use the following sample table in this section.

```
q)t:([] name:`Dent`Beeblebrox`Prefect; iq:98 42 126)
```

8.3.1 Syntax of select

The basic select is a template that takes the form,

```
select [cols] from table
```

where *table* is either a table or a keyed table and *cols* is a comma separated list of columns. This expression results in a list of **all** records for the specified columns. This corresponds to the SQL statement,

```
SELECT * FROM table
```

In q you do not write the wildcards when you want all columns in the table; simply omit the columns and you get them all.

This basic select syntax may seem comfortably familiar from SQL, but it should seem odd to the qbie who is just getting accustomed to parsing expressions right-to-left. Neither 'select' nor 'from' represent functions that can stand alone. There are many options for the basic select template whose elements appear between the 'select' and 'from' or after the *table* element.

8.3.2 Displaying the Result

The result of (select) is always a table. You may think of it as a list of (conforming) records but it is actually constructed as a column dictionary.

```
q)select from t
name       iq
-------------
Dent       42
Beeblebrox 98
Prefect    126
```

8.3.3 Selecting Columns

To select specific columns, list them comma-separated in left-to-right order between 'select' and 'from'. You can optionally provide column names using the same colon format as table definition syntax.

```
q)select name from t
name
----------
Dent
Beeblebrox
Prefect
q)select c1:name, c2:iq from t
_
```

8.3.4 Basic update

The syntax of (update) is the same as (select), but named columns represent replacement by the values to the right of the colon. In our example,

```
q)update iq:iq%100 from t
_
```

8.4 Primary Keys and Keyed Tables

In SQL, one can declare one or more column(s) of a table as a primary key. This means that the values in the column(s) are unique over the domain of the rows, making it possible to identify and retrieve a row via its key value. These two features motivate how q implements a keyed table.

228

8.4.1 Keyed Table

We begin with a simple key—i.e., the key is a single column of simple type. The approach is to place the key column in a separate table parallel to a table containing the remaining columns to obtain a table of keys and a table of values. Since a table is logically a list of records, this is the same as a list of key records and list of value records. We establish a positional correspondence between these lists via a dictionary mapping.

A *keyed table* is a dictionary mapping a table of key records to a table of value records. This represents a mapping from each row in a table of (presumably unique) keys to a corresponding row in a table of values—i.e., a positional correspondence of key rows to value rows. Using dictionary lookup on a key (record) retrieves the corresponding value record in the remaining columns. This is just what a primary key should do. Note that the key mapping assumes that the key records and value records are in corresponding order.

> ***Important:*** A keyed table is **not** a table—it is a dictionary and so has type 99h.

Keys should be unique but (sadly) this is not enforced. As we have already noted, dictionary creation does not enforce key uniqueness. A value row associated with a duplicate key is not accessible via key lookup, but it can be retrieved via a select on the key column.

8.4.2 Simple Example

Let's see how this works for our previous example. We begin with a flipped column dictionary to make things explicit.

```
q)v:flip `name`iq!(`Dent`Beeblebrox`Prefect;98 42 126)
```

Now say we want to add a key column eid containing employee identifiers. We begin by placing the identifiers in a separate table. Recall from §5.3.4 that we must enlist both the column name and the value list for single column table.

```
q)k:flip (enlist `eid)!enlist 1001 1002 1003
```

Now establish the association between the two tables.

```
q)kt:k!v
```

229

Voilà! The console display of a keyed table is the combination of dictionary display and table display. It lists the key column(s) on the left, separated by a vertical bar from the value columns on the right.

```
q)kt
eid | name       iq
----| -------------
1001| Dent        98
1002| Beeblebrox  42
1003| Prefect    126
```

8.4.3 Keyed Table Definition Syntax

Fundamentalists insist on constructing a keyed table as a dictionary of flipped dictionaries, but most folks prefer to use table definition syntax.

> **Note:** Due to space limitations on the printed page we cannot fit our keyed table examples on a single line, so we wrap the lines, with column alignment for readability. You cannot enter such a multiline statement into the q console, but you can place it in a script. If you are following this tutorial line by line, you can copy/paste the individual lines onto a single line in the q console.

Here is the fundamental form of our keyed table.

```
q)kt:(flip (enlist `eid)!enlist 1001 1002 1003)!
      flip `name`iq!(`Dent`Beeblebrox`Prefect;98 42 126)
```

It is arguably simpler to use table definition syntax. This is a generalization of (plain) table definition in which key column(s) are placed between the square brackets and the value columns are after the square brackets.

```
q)kt:([eid:1001 1002 1003]
       name:`Dent`Beeblebrox`Prefect; iq:98 42 126)
```

> **Note:** Placing key column(s) inside the square brackets is consistent with the notation for a (regular) table since a regular table has no keys.

To define an empty keyed table, use empty key and value columns.

```
q)ktempty:([eid:()] name:(); iq:())
```

As with regular tables, empty columns should be typed with either of the following constructs to ensure data integrity.

```
q)ktempty:([eid:`int$()] `symbol$name:(); iq:`int$())
```

```
q)ktempty:([eid:0#0] name:0#`; iq:0#0)
```

8.4.4 Accessing Records of a Keyed Table

Since a keyed table is a dictionary mapping, it provides access to records in the value table via key lookup. Remember that the records in the key table and value table are section dictionaries.

```
q)kt[(enlist `eid)!enlist 1002]
name| `Beeblebrox
iq  | 42
```

Yikes! This is a cumbersome way to retrieve by key.

Fortunately, you can abbreviate the full dictionary specification of a key record to its key value. Our example reduces to,

```
q)kt[1002]
name| `Beeblebrox
iq  | 42
```

Now we can lookup the value for an individual column.

```
q)kt[1002][`iq]
42
```

Or we can use the equivalent index at depth notation.

```
q)kt[1002;`iq]
42
```

After the customary moment of q Zen, we realize that the net effect of "placing a key on a table" is to convert indexing of the rows from row number to key value.

8.4.5 Retrieving Multiple Records

We have seen how to lookup a single record in a keyed table by key value.

```
q)kt[1001]
name| `Dent
iq  | 98
q)kt 1001
_
```

You might think it is possible to retrieve multiple records from a keyed table via a simple list of keys. You would be wrong.

```
q)kt[1001 1002]
`length
```

> **Tip:** This works for a compound key—i.e., a multi-column key—just not for a single column key.

To lookup multiple key values in a keyed table, we could use one of the following constructs to generate a list of enlisted keys.

```
q)kt[(enlist 1001;enlist 1002)]
name       iq
-------------
Dent       98
Beeblebrox 42

q)kt[flip enlist 1001 1002]
_
```

This is still pretty cumbersome, so back to the drawing board. Since we are supposed to provide a list of key records for lookup, we can simply create an anonymous table whose records are precisely the form we need.

```
q)kt ([] eid:1001 1002)
_
```

Now that's slick!

With such a nifty way to create a list of key records in hand, we recall from §5.2.2 that a sub-dictionary can be extracted using a list of keys as the left operand of (#). Applying this to our keyed table,

```
q)([] eid:1001 1002)#kt
eid | name       iq
----| -------------
1001| Dent       98
1002| Beeblebrox 42
```

The Zen of keyed tables...no select statement required.

8.4.6 Reverse Lookup

Because a keyed table is a dictionary, it is possible to perform reverse lookup from value records to key records. Let's show an example having a single value column.

```
q)kts:([eid:1001 1002 1003] name:`Dent`Beeblebrox`Prefect)
q)kts
```

As in the case of key lookup, we can use an anonymous table with a list of value records.

```
q)kts?([] name:`Prefect`Dent)
```

8.4.7 Components of a Keyed Table

Since a keyed table is a dictionary mapping the table of keys to the table of values, the functions (key) and (value) extract the constituents.

```
q)key kt
```

```
q)value kt
```

The function (keys) returns a list of symbolic key column name(s).

```
q)keys kt
```

Observe that (cols) retrieves all column names of the keyed table— i.e., from both the key and value tables.

```
q)cols kt
```

8.4.8 Tables vs. Keyed Tables

It is possible to convert dynamically between a regular table having a column of potential key values and the corresponding keyed table using dyadic primitive (xkey). The right operand is the source table/keyed table and the left operand is a symbol (or list of symbols) with the column name(s) to be used as the key.

```
q)t:([] eid:1001 1002 1003;
       name:`Dent`Beeblebrox`Prefect; iq:98 42 126)

q)`eid xkey t
eid | name       iq
----| -------------
1001| Dent         98
1002| Beeblebrox   42
1003| Prefect     126
```

Conversely, to convert a keyed table to a regular table, use (xkey) with an empty general list as the left operand.

```
q)kt:([eid:1001 1002 1003]
       name:`Dent`Beeblebrox`Prefect; iq:98 42 126)
q)kt

q)() xkey kt
eid  name       iq
------------------
1001 Dent         98
1002 Beeblebrox   42
1003 Prefect     126
```

You can also use an overload of (!) to key/unkey tables. The left operand is a non-negative integer that specifies the number of left-most columns to include in the key, where 0 indicates none—i.e., no keys. With t and kt as above,

```
q)1!t

q)0!kt

```

> **Tip:** While these forms are terse, the first makes your code less obvious since the new key column(s) are only implicit.

The table/keyed table conversions above (in both forms) work on copies and do not affect the original table. Use call-by-name to modify the original.

```
q)`eid xkey `t
`t
q)t

q)() xkey `kt
`kt
q)kt

```

If (xkey) is applied with a column that does not contain unique values, the result is not a error but rather a keyed table that does not have a true primary key.

```
q)t:([] eid:1001 1002 1003 1001;
        name:`Dent`Beeblebrox`Prefect`Dup )
q)ktdup:`eid xkey t
q)ktdup
eid | name
----| ----------
1001| Dent
1002| Beeblebrox
1003| Prefect
1001| Dup
```

Duplicate key values are not accessible via key lookup.

```
q)ktdup 1001
name| Dent
```

They are accessible via select.

```
q)select from ktdup where eid=1001
eid | name
----| ----
1001| Dent
1001| Dup
```

8.4.9 Compound Primary Key

The q implementation of a keyed table as a dictionary mapping between a pair of tables carries over unchanged to compound keys. Recall that a compound key in SQL is a collection of multiple columns that together provide a unique value for each row. A compound key in q is simply a table association k!v in which k has multiple columns. Presumably each record in the key table has a unique combination of field values, but this is **not** checked.

Here is our galactic travelers table redone to replace the employee id with a compound key comprising last and first names.

```
q)ktc:([lname:`Dent`Beeblebrox`Prefect;
        fname:`Arthur`Zaphod`Ford];
        iq:98 42 126)
```

Observe that the console displays a compound keyed table with the key columns on the left of the vertical bar and the value columns to the right.

```
q)ktc
lname      fname | iq
-----------------| ---
Dent       Arthur| 98
Beeblebrox Zaphod| 42
Prefect    Ford | 126
```

Here is lookup by a compound key record,

```
q)ktc[`lname`fname!`Beeblebrox`Zaphod]
_
```

As with a simple key, we can abbreviate a full key record to the key value for key lookup.

```
q)ktc[`Dent`Arthur]
_
```

The empty keyed table can be typed using table definition syntax with either of the following,

```
q)ktc:([lname:`symbol$();fname:`symbol$()] iq:`int$())
q)ktc:([lname:0#`;fname:0#`] iq:0#0)
```

For the fundamentalists, here is the same compound keyed table built from its constituent column dictionaries.

```
q)ktc:(flip `lname`fname!
       (`Dent`Beeblebrox`Prefect;`Arthur`Zaphod`Ford))!
       flip (enlist `iq)!enlist 98 42 126
```

Most will agree that the table definition syntax is simpler.

8.4.10 Retrieving Records with a Compound Primary Key

Unlike a simple key, we can lookup multiple value records with a list of compound keys.

```
q)ktc (`Dent`Arthur;`Prefect`Ford)
_
```

Of course the nifty construct with an anonymous table works with compound keys too.

```
q)ktc ([] lname:`Dent`Prefect; fname:`Arthur`Ford)
_
```

As does the use of (#) to retrieve a sub keyed table from a list of keys.

```
q)K:([] lname:`Dent`Prefect; fname:`Arthur`Ford)
q)K#ktc
lname    fname | iq
---------------| ---
Dent     Arthur| 98
Prefect  Ford  | 126
```

8.4.11 Extracting Column Data

In this section we use the following example tables. The first has a simple key of long and the second a compound key of symbols.

```
q)kts:([k:101 102 103] v1:`a`b`c; v2:1.1 2.2 3.3)
q)kts

q)ktc:([k1:`a`b`c;k2:`x`y`z] v1:`a`b`c; v2:1.1 2.2 3.3)
q_ktc
```

In the previous section we saw how to retrieve **all** the value columns using an anonymous table of keys.

```
q)kts[([] k:101 103)]

q)ktc[([] k1:`a`c;k2:`x`z)]
```

Often we need to extract the naked column data from some value columns. No problem for the fundamentalist. Since the result of the lookup is a sub-table of the value table, we can index into it to get the column list(s).

```
q)kts[([] k:101 103)][`v1]
 a`c
q)ktc[([] k1:`a`c;k2:`x`z)][`v1`v2]
```

And we can simplify using indexing at depth.

```
q)kts[([] k:101 103); `v1]

q)ktc[([] k1:`a`c;k2:`x`z); `v1`v2]
```

8.5 Foreign Keys and Virtual Columns

A foreign key in SQL is a column in one table whose values are members of a primary key column in another table. Foreign keys are the mechanism for establishing relations between tables.

An important feature of a foreign key is that the RDBMS enforces referential integrity, meaning that values in the foreign key column are **required** to be in the related primary key column. Before you can insert a row having a foreign key field value that is not there, you must first ensure there is a row with that primary key in the related table.

8.5.1 Definition of Foreign Key

A foreign key in q should provide a relation with referential integrity (in one direction, at least). Can we implement this with a construct we already know in q? The setting is a collection of record items in a column list that are drawn from the (supposedly) unique record items in another column list. Sound familiar? It is precisely the situation of an enumeration!

A *foreign key* is one or more table columns whose values are defined as an enumeration over the key column(s) of a keyed table. As in the case of symbol enumeration (`` `sym$ ``), the enumeration restricts foreign key values to be in the list of primary key values.

8.5.2 Example of Simple Foreign Key

We return to the galactic travelers keyed table.

```
q)kt:([eid:1001 1002 1003]
       name:`Dent`Beeblebrox`Prefect; iq:98 42 126)
```

Suppose we have a table with the detail records of the results of repeated IQ tests of the travelers.

```
([] eid:1003 1001 1002 1001 1002 1001; sc:126 36 92 39 98 42)
```

This table has no restriction on `eid` other than it be a long. To ensure that only `eid` values for actual travelers can be entered, we make the `eid` column in this table a foreign key related to the `eid` column in kt. This is done by enumerating over the name of the keyed table—i.e., `` `kt$ ``.

Tip: When q sees the name of a keyed table in an enumeration domain it knows to use the list of key records.

Here is the enumeration of the column in isolation.

238

```
q)`kt$1002 1001 1001 1003 1002 1003
```

As in the case of symbol enumeration, q looks up the index of each foreign key value in the list of key records and, under the covers, replaces the field value with that index. Also as with symbols, the enumeration is displayed in reconstituted form instead of as the underlying indices. To see the underlying indices, cast to an integer.

```
q)`long$`kt$1002 1001 1001 1003 1002 1003
1 0 0 2 1 2
```

As always, the enumeration can be substituted for the original in normal operations.

```
q)1003=`kt$1002 1001 1003 1002 1003
000101b
```

And now, the moment of truth. Does the enumeration provide referential integrity?

```
q)`kt$1004
'cast
```

It does. Attempting to enumerate a value that is not in the primary key column causes an error.

We put this together with table definition syntax to define a details table with a foreign key over kt.

```
q)tdetails:([] eid:`kt$1003 1001 1002 1001 1002 1001;
           sc:126 36 92 39 98 42)
```

Observe that a foreign key is denoted by the name of the target keyed table in the f column in the output of (meta).

```
q)meta tdetails
c  | t f  a
---| ------
eid| j kt
sc | j
```

The built-in function (fkeys) applied to a table (or keyed table) returns a dictionary in which each foreign key column name is mapped to its primary key table name.

```
q)fkeys tdetails
eid| kt
```

8.5.3 Resolving a Foreign Key

When you wish to resolve a foreign key—i.e., get the actual values instead of enumerated values—apply (value) to the enumerated column.

```
q)meta update value eid from tdetails
c  | t f a
---| -----
eid| j
sc | j
```

Observe that there is no longer an entry in the f column.

8.5.4 Foreign Keys and Relations

In SQL, a join is used to splice back together data that has been normalized via relations. The splice is done along a foreign key that establishes a relation to the primary key. In the result, columns from both tables are available using dot notation.

The same effect is achieved in q using foreign keys but you don't need to perform the join explicitly. The notation is similar, but the operation is different enough to warrant close attention.

Let tf be a table having a foreign key column f enumerated over a keyed table kt. All columns in kt are available via dot notation in a (select) expression whose *from* domain is tf. To access a column c in kt, use the notation f.c in the (select) expression. This column takes the name c by default in the result.

In our galactic travelers example, we can access columns in kt via a (select) on tdetails. Here is a query that retrieves a "foreign" column in addition to one from tdetails.

```
q)select eid.name, sc from tdetails
name       sc
-------------
Prefect    126
Dent       36
Beeblebrox 92
Dent       39
Beeblebrox 98
Dent       42
```

There is an implicit left join between tdetails and kt here.

> ***Tip:*** The implicit join with dot notation is powerful and convenient when your tables are in normal form and there are multiple foreign key relations. For example, a query could retrieve,
>
> ```
> select name.street.city.zip.country from residents where …
> ```
>
> in a single select with no explicit joins.

8.6 Working with Tables and Keyed Tables

In this section, we use the galactic travelers tables.

```
q)t:([] name:`Dent`Beeblebrox`Prefect; iq:98 42 126)
q)kt:([eid:1001 1002 1003] name:`Dent`Beeblebrox`Prefect;
    iq:98 42 126)
```

8.6.1 Appending Records

The fundamental way to append a record to a table is to view the table as a list of records and join with (,:). Note that the fields in the record do not need to be in column order.

```
q)t,:`name`iq!(`W; 26)
q)t,:`iq`name!(200; `Albert)
q)t
_
```

You can also append naked row values with (,:) but the fields **must** be in column order.

```
q)t,:(`H; 142)
_
q)t,:(97; `J)
'type
q)t
_
```

8.6.2 First and Last Records

Because a table is logically a list of records, the functions (first) and (last) retrieve the initial and final records, respectively.

```
q)first t
name| `Dent
iq  | 98
q)last t
_
```

A keyed table is a dictionary so functions apply to the value table.

```
q)first kt
name| `Dent
iq  | 98
q)last kt
_
```

Because tables and keyed tables are ordered, these functions can be used for aggregation in queries without any need of the SQL clause ORDER BY—provided your table was created in order.

You can retrieve the first or last *n* records of a table or keyed table using the take operator (#). Why does this work? Tables are lists and keyed tables are dictionaries and (#) works on both. Since (#) always returns a list and the extracted records conform, q recognizes the result of (#) as a table or keyed table with the same schema as the input.

```
q)2#t
_
q)-3#kt
_
```

Also see §9.3.2.4 for another way to achieve this result using select[n].

8.6.3 Find

The find operator (?) used with a table returns the index of a record—i.e., its row number.

```
q)t?`name`iq!(`Dent;98)
0
```

As usual, the record can be abbreviated to a row list provided the fields have the right type and order.

```
q)t?(`Dent;98)
_
```

Since find is atomic in the right operand, you can determine multiple row indices.

```
q)t?((`Dent;98);(`Prefect;126))
_
```

Since a keyed table is a dictionary, find (?) performs a reverse lookup of a value record/row and returns the first associated key record.

```
q)kt?`name`iq!(`Dent;98)
eid| 1001
q)kt?(`Dent;98)
_
```

As with key lookup, a single column must have enlisted values, or you can use the anonymous table construct.

```
q)t1:([] eid:1001 1002 1003)
q)t1?enlist each 1001 1002
0 1
q)t1?([] eid:1001 1002)
_
```

8.6.4 Union with (,)

The join operator (,) is defined for tables and keyed tables since they both comprise lists of records. It is essentially the same as UNION in SQL.

You can use (,) to append a record to (a copy of) a table, but no type checking will be performed.

```
q)t,`name`iq!(`Slaartibartfast; `123)
name            iq
------------------
Dent            98
Beeblebrox      42
Prefect         126
Slaartibartfast `123
```

> **Tip:** Using a row with (,) will not yield a table. Instead you get a general list.
>
> ```
> q)t,(`Slaartibartfast; 110)
> `name`iq!(`Dent;98)
> `name`iq!(`Beeblebrox;42)
> `name`iq!(`Prefect;126)
> `Slaartibartfast
> 110
> ```

Tables having **exactly** the same (meta) result can be joined to form a table. Since a table is a list of records, the result is obtained by appending the records of the right operand to those of the left.

```
q)t,([] name:1#`w; iq:1#26)
_
q)t,t
_
```

Two tables with the same columns in different order can not be joined because the order of columns is significant in q.

```
q)t,([] iq:1#42; name:`w)
'mismatch
```

Two keyed tables with the same (meta) result can be joined with (,). Because a keyed table is a dictionary whose keys and values are record lists, the operation has upsert semantics. Keys in the right operand that are not in the left operand are treated as append (i.e., insert), whereas the right operand acts as an update on common key values. In other words, the right operand is upserted into the left.

```
q)kt,([eid:1003 1004] name:`Prefect`w; iq:150 26)
eid | name       iq
----| --------------
1001| Dent        98
1002| Beeblebrox 42
1003| Prefect    150
1004| w           26
```

8.6.5 Coalesce (^)

Coalesce (^) can be used to merge two keyed tables having the same columns. Its behavior derives from its behavior on dictionaries. For a common key value and a common column, the value of the column in the right keyed table prevails over that of column in the left keyed table, except where the right column is null, in which case the left column value survives. On non-common keys the individual values carry thru.

The behavior of (^) is the same as (,) when there are no nulls in a column in the right table.

```
q)([k:`a`b`c] v:10 0N 30)^([k:`a`b`c] v:100 200 0N)
k| v
-| ---
a| 100
b| 200
c| 30

q)([k:`a`b`c`x] v:10 0N 30 40)^([k:`a`b`c`y]; v:100 200 0N 0N)
_
```

The performance of (^) is slower than that of (,) since fields of the right operand must be checked for null.

8.6.6 Column Join

Two tables with the same number of records can be joined sideways with join-each (,') to create a *column join* in which the columns are aligned in parallel

```
q)([] c1:`a`b`c),'([] c2:100 200 300)
c1 c2
------
a  100
b  200
c  300
```

When the column lists of the tables are not disjoint, the operation on the common columns has upsert semantics because each record is a dictionary.

```
q)([] c1:`a`b`c; c2:1 2 3),'([] c2:100 200 300)
c1 c2
------
a  100
b  200
c  300
```

A sideways join on keyed tables requires that the key records conform, meaning that the key columns must have identical meta. The columns from the right operand are aligned along common keys and appended elsewhere.

```
q)([k:1 2 3] v1:10 20 30),'([k:3 4 5] v2:1000 2000 3000)
k| v1 v2
-| -------
1| 10
2| 20
3| 30 1000
4|    2000
5|    3000
```

8.7 Complex Column Data

8.7.1 Simple Example

There is no restriction on the column lists of a table other than they are rectangular. In practice, simple lists are preferable because they are faster, more storage efficient and are easier to process. There are situations in which it may be convenient to use nested column lists, although far less often than most q programmers seem to think. In general, it is more efficient to flatten columns and then use joins or grouping to create structure on the way out. For those who simply must have nested column structure, we provide examples here.

Suppose we want to keep track of a pair of daily observations, say a low temperature and a high temperature in Hawaii. The normal form stores the low and high values in separate columns with flat lists for rows and columns.

```
q)tf:([] d:2015.01.01 2015.01.02; l:67.9 72.8; h:82.1 88.4)
q)tf 0

q)tf `l

q)tf `h

```

Alternatively, we can store pairs in a single column, resulting in nested lists for records and columns.

```
q)tp:([] d:2015.01.01 2015.01.02; lh:(67.9 82.10; 72.8 88.4))
q)tp 0
d | 2015.01.01
lh| 67.9 82.1
q)tp `lh
67.9 82.1
72.8 88.4
```

This example can easily be generalized to the situation of n-tuples. For example, we could store the daily values of a yield curve. Further, the fields can have different length or even different type, although the latter is strongly discouraged as it will not be possible to persist them in kdb.

8.7.2 Operations on Compound Column Data

The case of a nested column in which all items are simple lists of the same type is handled specially in kdb. We call this a *compound* column. There is no requirement that the simple lists all have the same length.

As an example, say we want to analyze the weekly gross revenues for movies and we don't care about the titles (we don't have room to display them here). Since there will be a different number of movies in release each week, the number of observations in each field will vary. An oversimplified time series that fits within the margins looks like the following in which the gross revenues are in millions.

```
tm:([] wk:2015.01.01 2015.01.08;
       rv:(38.92 67.34; 16.99 5.14 128.23 31.69))

q)tm
wk         rv
------------------------------------
2015.01.01 38.92 67.34
2015.01.08 16.99 5.14 128.23 31.69
```

Storing complex values in a single column in a table enables sophisticated operations to be performed in a single expression, provided you remember:

Nested columns mean adverbs. Lots of adverbs.

Using our movie data, we can produce the sorted, the average and high gross for each week in one expression.

```
q)select wk, srt:desc each rv, avgr:avg each rv,
       hi:max each rv from tm
wk         srt                        avgr    hi
-------------------------------------------------
2015.01.01 67.34 38.92                53.13   67.34
2015.01.08 128.23 31.69 16.99 5.14 45.5125 128.23
```

While sorts and aggregates such as MAX and AVG are standard SQL, think of how you'd produce the sorted sub list and the aggregates together. In your favorite traditional programming environment, you'll soon discover that you need a sordid list of rows and a loop to unravel it.

Now let's compute the drops between the ranked revenue numbers within each week. No loop required in q.

```
q)select wk, drp:neg 1_'deltas each desc each rv  from tm
wk         drp
-----------------------------
2015.01.01 ,28.42
2015.01.08 96.54 14.7 11.85
```

8.7.3 Compound Foreign Key

A nested column is how to make a foreign key on a compound primary key. We recast the galactic travelers to make a keyed table with common key of last and first name.

```
q)ktc:([lname: `Dent`Beeblebrox`Prefect;
       fname:`Arthur`Zaphod`Ford]; iq:98 42 126)
```

We create a details table with a foreign key over ktc by placing the names in the foreign key column.

```
q)tdetails:([] name:`ktc$(`Beeblebrox`Zaphod;
                        `Prefect`Ford;`Beeblebrox`Zaphod);
          sc:36 126 42)
```

The columns of ktc are available as virtual columns from tdetails.

```
q)select name.lname, name.iq, sc from tdetails
lname        iq  sc
--------------------
Beeblebrox  42   36
Prefect     126 126
Beeblebrox  42   42
```

When defining the schema of a table with a compound key column, specify the foreign key as a cast of an empty list.

```
q)([] name:`ktc$();sc:`long$())
```
_

When the foreign key comprises multiple types you also cast the general list with the foreign table in its schema.

```
q)ktc:([k1:1 2 3; k2:2001.01.01 2001.01.02 2001.01.03]
       v: 1. 2. 3.)

q)tfc([] fk:`ktc$(); s:`symbol$())
q)tfc,:(`ktc$(1; 2001.01.01); `a)
q)tfc,:(`ktc$(1; 2015.01.01); `a)
'cast
```

The failure of the cast in the second append is correct; it is enforced referential integrity.

8.8 Attributes

Attributes are metadata that you attach to lists of special forms. They are also used on a dictionary domain or a table column to speed retrieval for some operations. The q interpreter can make certain optimizations based on the structure of the list implied by the attribute.

Attributes (other than `g#) are descriptive rather than prescriptive. By this we mean that by applying an attribute you are asserting that the list has a special form, which q will check. It does **not** instruct q to (re)make the list into the special form; that is your job. A list operation that respects the form specified by the attribute leaves the attribute intact (other than `p#), while an operation that breaks the form results in the attribute being removed in the result.

The syntax for applying an attribute is (yet) another overload of (#), whose left operand is a symbol specifying the attribute and whose right operand is the target list.

> **Note:** The attribute is applied to the target list in place, not on a copy.

Kx says not to expect significant benefit from an attribute for less than a million items. This is why attributes are not automatically applied in mundane situations. You should test your use case to see whether applying an attribute provides performance benefit. Do not just apply attributes blindly, as they consume resources.

8.8.1 Sorted (`s#)

Applying the sorted attribute (`s#) to a simple list indicates that the items of the list are sorted in ascending order; there is no way to indicate a descending sort. When a list has the sorted attribute, linear search is replaced with binary search, which makes certain operations faster—for example find (?), equality (=), (in) and (within).

When an attribute is successfully applied to a list, it becomes part of the list and is displayed on the q console. Observe that q checks to see that the list is actually sorted when th attribute is applied.

```
q)`s#1 2 4 8
`s#1 2 4 8
q)`s#2 1 3 4
's-fail
```

The sort function (asc) automatically applies the sorted attribute to its result but (til) does not.

```
q)asc 2 1 8 4
`s#1 2 4 8
q)til 5
0 1 2 3 4
```

When a list with an attribute is amended with (,:) the result is checked to see that the attribute is preserved; if not, it is removed.

```
q)L:`s#1 2 3 4 5
q)L,:6
q)L
_
q)L,:0
q)L
_
```

One place to apply the sorted attribute is on the date or time column of a simple time series.

```
q)t:([] ti:`s#00:00:00 00:00:01 00:00:03; v:98 98 100.)
q)meta t
c | t f a
--| -----
ti| v   s
v | f
```

Applying the sorted attribute to a table unintuitively applies the parted attribute (see next section) to the first column.

```
q)meta `s#([] ti:00:00:00 00:00:01 00:00:03; v:98 98 100.)
c | t f a
--| -----
ti| v   p
v | f
```

Applying the sorted attribute to a dictionary applies the attribute to the key list. Lookup is faster because binary search is used. A side effect of the way binary search is implemented is that the mapping given by the dictionary is now a step function, meaning that values between successive key values are "filled in."

```
q)d:`s#10 20 30 40 50!`a`b`c`d`e
q)key d
`s#10 20 30 40 50
q)d 10
`a
q)d 12
`a
q)d 15
_
q)d 20
`b
```

Since a keyed table is a dictionary of tables, applying the sorted attribute to a keyed table applies to the table of keys that, in turn, applies to the initial key column.

250

```
q)meta `s#([k:1 2 3 4] v:`d`c`b`a)
c| t f a
-| -----
k| j   s
v| s
```

8.8.2 Unique (`u#)

Applying the unique attribute (`u#) to a list indicates that the items of the list are distinct. Knowing that the elements of a list are unique makes (distinct) the identity function and shortens some operations—i.e., if an operation has found one of what you're looking for, it's done.

> **Note:** Applying (`u#) essentially causes q to create a hash table, which uses storage and adds overhead. It is best to apply the attribute after the list has been created, if possible. If you have a column that will always have unique values and your large table does not change often, you can get a significant performance speedup with (`u#).

Observe that uniqueness is checked. Don't take the error message personally.

```
q)`u#2 1 4 8
`u#2 1 4 8
q)`u#2 1 4 8 2
'u-fail
```

An amend that does not preserve uniqueness causes the attribute to be lost.

```
q)L:`u#2 1 4 8
q)L,:3
q)L

q)L,:2
q)L
2 1 4 8 3 2
```

The unique attribute can be applied to the domain of a dictionary, a column of a table, or the key column of a keyed table. It cannot be applied to a dictionary, a table or a keyed table directly.

8.8.3 Parted (`p#)

The parted attribute (`p#) indicates that all common occurrences of any value in a list are adjacent. Viewing the list as a map, the parted attribute says that its graph is a step function with distinct steps. The parted attribute can be applied to a simple list of any type whose underlying value is integral—e.g., the integer types, dates, times, timestamps, timespans. You can also apply parted on a list of enumerated symbols since the underlying index values are integral.

> **Note:** The parted attribute causes q to create an underlying structure that keeps track of the steps. Because the attribute is not preserved under most operations you should apply it only after the list is fully created. One exception is that when two lists have (`p#) and their values are disjoint, the attribute will be preserved when the lists are joined with (,).

Here is a simple example of a parted list. Notice that the items are neither sorted nor unique.

```
q)`p#2 2 2 1 1 4 4 4 4 3 3
`p#2 2 2 1 1 4 4 4 4 3 3
```

Notice that the rather nasty error does not say 'p-fail; rather it contains a 'u-fail error.

```
q)`p#2 2 2 1 1 4 4 4 4 3 3 2
k){$[3=x;(`#y;`u#y i;(i:&~=':y),#y);(y;`u#!r;+\0,#:'x;,/x:. r:=y)]}
'u-fail
#
`u
2 1 4 3 2
q.o))
```

With the exception in the note above, the parted attribute is **not** preserved under any operation on the list, even if the operation preserves the property.

```
q)L:`p#1 1 2 3 3
q)L
_
q)L,:3
q)L
1 1 2 3 3 3
```

Historical time series databases for ticker symbols are usually sorted by time within symbol with the parted attribute applied to the (enumerated) symbol column. This makes queries by ticker fast and guarantees that results for a given symbol are returned in time order.

8.8.4 Grouped (`g#)

The grouped attribute (`g#) differs from other attributes in that it can be applied to any list. It causes q to create and maintain an index—

essentially a hash table. Grouped can be applied to a list when no other assumptions about its structure can be made.

For example,

```
q)`g#1 2 3 2 3 4 3 4 5 2 3 4 5 4 3 5 6

q)L:`g#100?100
q)L

q)L,:1 1 1 1
q)L

```

The grouped attribute is maintained as operations are performed on the list, which can cause significant processing overhead in addition to the storage required. Best to apply it after the entire list has been created, if possible.

Applying the grouped attribute to a table column roughly corresponds to placing an index on a column in an RDBMS. As of this writing (Sep 2015), in q3.2 the maximum number of grouped attributes that can be placed on a single table is unlimited.

8.8.5 Remove Attribute (`#)

The operations (`#) removes any attribute that may currently be applied. For example,

```
q)L:`s#til 10
q)L

q)`#L

```

9 Queries: q-sql

9.0 Overview

We call the collection of functions for manipulating tables *q-sql*, since many of them resemble their SQL counterparts in form or function. The usual suspects such as insert, select, update, are present, as well as functionality that is not available in traditional SQL. But appearances can be deceiving: there are some significant differences in the syntax and behavior.

The first important difference is that a q table has ordered rows and columns. This is particularly useful when dealing with the situation where records arrive in time order. Appending them to a table ensures that they enter—and stay—in order. Subsequent select operations always retrieve the records in order without any need for sorting.

A second difference is that a q table is stored physically as a collection of column lists. This means that operations on column data are vector operations. Moreover, for simple column lists, atomic, aggregate and uniform functions applied to columns are especially simple and fast since they reduce to direct memory addressing.

A third difference is that q-sql provides upsert semantics. Recall that upsert semantics on a dictionary mean that when a key-value pair is applied with (,) and the key is present, the value is updated; otherwise the pair is inserted. In the context of tables and keyed tables, which are both dictionaries, this has far-reaching consequences for many common operations, including joins. Upsert semantics permeate q-sql.

In this chapter, we cover the important features of q-sql, beginning with simple examples for each. Eventually more complex examples are introduced.

Some examples are based on the sp.q script included in the q installation files. Tables in the script are,

```
q)meta s
c     | t f a
------| -----
s     | s
name  | s
status| j
city  | s
```

```
q)meta p
c     | t f a
------| -----
p     | s
name  | s
color | s
weight| j
city  | s
```

```
q)meta sp
c  | t f a
---| -----
s  | s s
p  | s p
qty| j
```

You should load and display these tables in your console session now.

9.1 Inserting Records

There are multiple ways to insert—i.e., append—records in q.

> **Tip:** The (upsert) functon is superior to (insert) and is to be preferred. We include (insert) for nostalgia only.

9.1.0 Append Using Amend

Since a table is (logically) a list of records, it is possible to append records in place using (,:). Type checking on field values is performed.

```
q)t:([] name:`symbol$(); iq:`int$())
q)t,:`name`iq!(`Beelbrox; 42)
q)t,:`name`iq!(`Dent; 98.0)
'type
```

Amend can also be used with a row of naked field values provided the fields align exactly with the target columns.

```
q)t,:(`Prefect; 126)
```

Applying amend to a table repeatedly with the same argument results in duplicate records.

256

```
q)t,:(`Prefect; 126)
q)t,:(`Prefect; 126)
q)t
_
```

You can use amend to append to a keyed table using the full record form, but you will quickly see why no one does this.

```
q)kt:([eid:`long$()] name:`symbol$(); iq:`long$())
q)kt,:(enlist (enlist `eid)!enlist 1001)!enlist `name`iq!(`Beeblebrox;
42)
```

It is much easier to use naked field values, provided they align exactly with both the key and value columns.

```
q)kt,:(1002; `Dent; 98)
q)kt
_
```

Amend has upsert semantics on keyed tables, so repeated operation on the same key will retain only the last values.

```
q)kt,:(1002; `Dent; 101)
q)kt
_
```

9.1.1 Basic insert

Those who prefer the familiarity of SQL can append records to an existing global table using the dyadic function (insert) whose left operand is a symbol containing the name of a **global** table (*target*) and whose right argument is a record, or list of records, conforming to the target. The result is a list of integers representing the row number(s) of the appended record(s).

> ***Important:*** Since (insert) essentially reduces to amend in place, fields are type checked.
>
> - If the target column is simple, the type must match exactly.
> - If the target column is an untyped empty list, the result will take the type of the field in the initial (insert).

For a regular—i.e., non-keyed—table, the effect of (insert) is to append a new record with the specified field values. Let's use our simple example.

```
q)t:([] name:`Dent`Beeblebrox`Prefect; iq:42 98 126)
```

Here is how to insert a single record or the equivalent row list.

```
q)`t insert (`name`iq)!(`Slartibartfast; 134)
,3
q)`t insert (`Marvin; 150)
,4
q)t
```

Repeatedly applying (insert) to a table with the same argument results in duplicate records.

```
q)`t insert (`Marvin; 150)

q)`t insert (`Marvin; 150)

q)
```

Since a list of conforming records is a table, inserting a list of records is the same as inserting a table. Observe that use of (3#) to truncate the table.

```
q)t:3#t
q)`t insert (`name`iq!(`Slartibartfast; 134); (`name`iq!(`Marvin;
200)))

q)t

q)t:3#t
q)`t insert ([] name:`Slartibartfast`Marvin; iq:134 200)

```

You can also use (insert) in prefix form, possibly with the table name projected. For example, the previous insert can be written as,

```
q)insert[`t; (`Slartibartfast; 134)]

q)insert[`t;] (`Slartibartfast; 134)

```

9.1.2 Bulk Columnar Insert

We have seen that it is possible to insert a naked list of row values instead of the full record dictionary. We have also seen that it is possible to bulk insert a list of conforming records, which is just a table with the same schema as the target.

It is also possible to bulk insert naked field values but there is a twist. To bulk insert naked field values, you provide a list of **columns** not a list of rows.

258

```
q)t:([] name:`Dent`Beeblebrox; iq:98 42)
q)`t insert ((`Prefect; 126); (`Marvin; 200))
`type
q)`t insert (`Prefect`Marvin; 126 200)
8 9
```

After a brief q Zen meditation, you will realize that this is consistent with the previous bulk insert of a table, since a table is a collection of columns. From this perspective, we should view the insertion of a single naked row more correctly as a trivial list of column atoms.

9.1.3 Insert into Empty Tables

Inserting into a table that has been initialized with empty lists of general type causes the result table to take the type of the first record inserted. In particular, an atomic field in the inserted record results in a simple column with its type.

```
q)t:([] name:(); iq:())
q)`t insert (`Dent;98)
,0
q)meta t
c    | t f a
-----| -----
name | s
iq   | j
```

This is fine as long as all the types in the initial record are correct. Should any field have an unintended type, subsequent records of the correct type will all be rejected.

```
q)t:([] name:(); iq:())
q)`t insert (`Dent;98.0)
,0
q)`t insert (`Beeblebrox; 42)
`type
```

> **Recommendation**: It is good practice to type all columns in an empty table. This will ensure that incorrect types are rejected and correct ones accepted.
>
> ```
> q)t:([] name:`symbol$(); iq:`int$())
> q)`t insert (`Dent;98.0)
> `type
> q)`t insert (`Beeblebrox; 42)
> ,0
> ```

It is also possible to insert a **list** of conforming records (i.e., a table) into a table that does not exist. This is the same as assigning the table to a variable of the specified name.

```
q)tnew
'tnew
q)`tnew insert enlist `c1`c2!(`a; 10)

q)tnew
_
```

9.1.4 Insert and Foreign Keys

When inserting data into a table that has foreign key(s), the values destined for the foreign key column(s) are checked to ensure that they appear in the primary key column(s) pointed to by the foreign key(s). This is referential integrity (well, half of it).

Returning to our previous foreign key example.

```
q)kt:([eid:1001 1002 1003]
       name:`Dent`Beeblebrox`Prefect; iq:98 42 126)

q)tdetails:([] eid:`kt$1003 1002 1001 1002 1001;
           sc:126 36 92 39 98)
```

The first insert in the following succeeds but the second fails when trying to enumerate the foreign key value 1042 that does not appear in kt.

```
q)`tdetails insert (1002;42)
,5
q)`tdetails insert (1042;150)
'cast
```

Recall that enumeration is a form of cast.

9.1.5 Insert into Keyed Tables

You can use (insert) to append data to a keyed table, but this probably does not have the desired semantics. Specifically, you can insert into a keyed table only if the key value is **not** already in the table. For this and other reasons, (upsert) should normally be preferred over (insert).

Since a keyed table is a dictionary, to use (insert) we should properly provide a dictionary entry comprising a key record and a value record.

```
q)kt:([eid:1001 1002] name:`Dent`Beeblebrox; iq:98 42)
q)`kt insert (enlist ((enlist `eid)!enlist 1003))!enlist `name`iq!(`w;
21)
,2
```

Yikes! Nobody does this. Instead, you provide a list of raw field values with the proviso that they align exactly across the key and value columns.

```
q)`kt insert (1005; `Marvin; 200)
,3
`t insert (1004;`Slartibartfast;158)
,2
```

Repeating the last insert now fails because the key value 1004 already exists.

```
q)`kt insert (1004; `Marvin; 200)
'insert
```

> **Tip:** The records in the keyed table are stored in insert order rather than key order.
>
> ```
> q)kt
> ```
> _

9.2 upsert

The upsert template is like (insert), only better. Except for the last sub-section on keyed tables, all the examples in the previous section all work the same for upsert.

9.2.1 Upsert Replacing insert

Here we repeat some examples from the previous section to demonstrate that upsert can (and should) be used in place of (insert) for appending rows to a table.

```
q)t:([] name:`Dent`Beeblebrox`Prefect; iq:42 98 126)
q)`t upsert (`name`iq)!(`Slartibartfast; 134)
`t
q)`t upsert (`Marvin; 150)
_
q)`t upsert ([] name:`Slartibartfast`Marvin; iq:134 200)
_
q)t:3#t
q)upsert[`t; (`Slartibartfast; 134)]
_
```

> **Tip:** To bulk upsert naked field values, use rows instead of columns.
>
> ```
> q)t upsert ((`Prefect; 126); (`Marvin; 200))
> ```

9.2.2 Upsert by Name

A limitation of (insert) is that it uses pass-by-name, so it can only operate against global tables. In contrast, upsert supports both pass-by-name and pass-by-value. Thus it can be used with anonymous or local tables.

```
q)([] c1:`a`b; c2:10 20) upsert (`c; 30)
c1 c2
-----
a  10
b  20
c  30
```

```
q)f:{t:([] c1:`a`b; c2:10 20); t upsert x}
q)f (`c; 30)
c1 c2
-----
a  10
b  20
c  308.2
```

9.2.3 Upsert on Keyed Tables

We have seen that (insert) has undesirable semantics on keyed tables—i.e., it rejects "duplicate" keys. What we really want is, well, upsert semantics.

```
q)`kt upsert (1001; `Beeblebrox; 42)

q)`kt upsert (1001; `Beeblebrox; 43)

q)kt
eid | name        iq
----| -------------
1001| Beeblebrox 43
```

This is the second reason to use upsert instead of (insert).

9.2.4 Upsert on Persisted Tables

You can use (upsert) to append records to serialized and splayed tables. Simply pass the handle of the file or splayed directory as the name of the table. This is the final strike against (insert), since it cannot do this

We serialize a table and then append a row to it.

```
q)`:/q4m/tser set ([] c1:`a`b; c2:1.1 2.2)
`:/q4m/tser upsert (`c; 3.3)
`:/q4m/tser
q)get `:/q4m/tser
_
```

> **Tip:** Upserting to a serialized table reads the entire table into memory, updates it and writes out the result.

Next we splay a table and then append a row to it. Observe that we ensure that all symbols are enumerated, as required for splayed tables.

```
q)`:/q4m/tsplay/ set ([] c1:`sym?`a`b; c2:1.1 2.2)
`:/q4m/tsplay/
q)`:/q4m/tsplay upsert (`sym?`c; 3.3)
`:/q4m/tsplay
q)select from tsplay
_
```

Upserting to a splayed table does **not** read the persisted image into memory; rather, it appends to the ends of the column files. This allows incremental creation of large splayed (or partitioned) tables by upserting chunks that comfortably fit into memory. See §11.3 for more details on splayed tables.

> **Tip:** Upserting to a table in either form will destroy any attributes on table columns. You will have to reapply them.

9.3 The select Template

In this section we investigate the general form of select, which like all q-sql templates, has required and optional elements. The template elements contain phrases that are expressions (presumably) involving column values of a specified table. The template is converted by the interpreter into a functional form and is applied against the table to produce a result table. While the syntax and behavior of select resemble the analogous SQL statement, the underlying mechanics are quite different.

> **Important:** The result of select is always a table.

We examine each of the constituents of select in detail. We introduce the concepts with illustrative examples using trivial tables so that the basic mechanics are not obscured by large or complex data.

9.3.1 Syntax

The select template has the following form, where elements enclosed in matching angle brackets (<...>) are optional.

$$\text{select } <p_s> <\text{by } p_b> \text{ from } t_{exp} <\text{where } p_w>$$

The *select* and *from* keywords are required; omission or mistyping either results in an error. The table expression t_{exp}, which is any q expression whose value is a table or keyed table, is also required. The remaining elements p_s, p_b and p_w are optional. They are called the *select*, the *by* and the *where* phrases, respectively.

> **Tip:** If where is present and t_{exp} is itself a select expression, the inner expression should be enclosed in parentheses to avoid confusion in the binding of the where phrase.

Each phrase in the select template is a comma-separated list of subphrases. A *subphrase* is an arbitrary q expression (presumably) involving columns of t_{exp} or columns of another table accessed via foreign key. The evaluation of sub phrases within a phrase is sequenced left-to-right by the commas, but each sub phrase expression is evaluated right-to-left, like any q expression.

> **Important:** The commas separating the sub phrases are separators, so it is not necessary to enclose a sub phrase in parentheses unless the expression contains the join operator (,). Any expression containing the operator (,) within any template phrase must be enclosed in parentheses or it will be interpreted as the separator. Forgetting this is both easy and painful.

The order of evaluation of the (select) template is:

1. from expression $\qquad t_{exp}$
2. where phrase $\qquad p_w$
3. by phrase $\qquad p_b$
4. select phrase $\qquad p_s$

9.3.2 The select Phrase

We begin our examples with the select phrase because it is the easiest. We shall use the following table for our examples.

```
q)t:([] c1:`a`b`c; c2:10 20 30; c3:1.1 2.2 3.3)
```

The select phrase specifies the columns in the result table, one per sub phrase. If the select phrase p_s is absent, all columns are returned. There is no need for the * wildcard of SQL.

```
q)select from t

q)t~select from t
1b
```

To specify result columns, list them separated by commas. Whitespace after commas is optional but some think it improves readability, especially for complicated queries.

```
q)select c1, c3 from t

```

9.3.2.1 Result Column Names

To specify names for the result columns, place the name followed by colon before the subphrase.

```
q)select c1, res:2*c2 from t
c1 res
------
a  20
b  40
c  60
```

Notes:

- The colon used to specify a name is **not** assignment; it is simply part of the syntax of the template.

- Just as with the use of colon in a variable assignment, the column name is part of the syntactic sugar. It is not a symbol and **cannot** be parameterized. Use functional form if you need this—see §9.12.

- Unlike in SQL, columns in the select phrase do not actually exist until the final result table is returned. Thus a computed column **cannot** be used in other column expressions.

If you do not provide a name for a computed column, q determines one.

- Normally the name is taken from the left-most term in the column expression.
- When q cannot determine a name it uses 'x'.

- If q's chosen name duplicates a previously determined column name, it will suffix it with '1', '2', etc. to make it unique. Recall that columns are sequenced from left to right.

```
q)select c1, c1, 2*c2, c2+c3, string c3 from t
c1 c11 x   c2   c3
------------------
a  a   20 11.1 "1.1"
b  b   40 22.2 "2.2"
c  c   60 33.3 "3.3"
```

9.3.2.2 The Virtual Column i

A virtual column i represents the offset of each record in the table—i.e., i is the row number. It is implicitly available in the select phrase.

```
q)select i, c1 from t
x c1
----
0 a
1 b
2 c
```

Observe that select does not carry the name i into the result.

> **Tip:** You can name the result column ix to avoid confusion with the always-present virtual column i.
>
> ```
> q)select ix:i, c1 from t
> ```

9.3.2.3 select distinct

The special form (select distinct) returns only unique records in the result—i.e., it eliminates duplicates.

```
q)select distinct from ([] c1:`a`b`a; c2:10 20 10)
c1 c2
-----
a  10
b  20
```

9.3.2.4 select[]

You can return the first or last *n* records in a select by using function parameter syntax after 'select'. A positive integer parameter returns the first records, a negative parameter the last.

```
q)select[2] from s where city<>`athens
s | name  status city
--| ------------------
s1| smith 20     london
s2| jones 10     paris
```

```
q)select[-1] from s where city<>`athens
s | name  status city
--| ------------------
s4| clark 20     london
```

We could achieve the same result using (#) after the select (i.e., to its left).

```
q)2#select from s where city<>`athens
```

```
q)-1#select from s where city<>`athens
```

The difference is that the (#) construct requires computing the entire result set and then keeping only the desired rows, whereas select[n] only extracts the desired number of rows. The latter will be faster and consume less memory for large tables.

This syntax is extended to select[n m] where m is the starting row number and n is the number of rows.

```
q)select[1 2] from s where city<>`athens
```

One final extension of the syntax specifies a sorting criterion inside the brackets. For ascending sort, place '<' before a column name and for descending sort use '>'.

```
q)select[>name] from s where city<>`athens
```

```
q)select[<city] from s where city<>`athens
```

You can combine the two syntax extensions by separating them with a semicolon.

```
q)select[2; >name] from s where city<>`athens
```

> ***Tip:*** The items inside the brackets must be in this order.

9.3.2.5 Select on Nested Columns

You can use select on tables with nested columns but things become more complicated. The rule of thumb is that you will need adverbs...lots of adverbs.

Let's take a simple example.

```
q)show tnest:([] c1:`a`b`c; c2:(10 20 30; enlist 40; 50 60))
c1 c2
----------
a  10 20 30
b  ,40
c  50 60
```

What can we do with this table? We **cannot** apply an aggregate or uniform operation straight to c2 since the fields do not conform.

```
q)select avg c2 from tnest
'length
```

We **can** apply an aggregate or uniform function to each field of c2 in tnest.

```
q)select avg each c2 from tnest
_
```

Similarly we can use each-both to compute a weighted average using two columns.

```
q)update c3:(1.1 2.2 3.3; enlist 4.4; 5.5 6.6) from `tnest
`tnest
q)select wtavg:c2 wavg' c3 from tnest
_
```

9.3.3 Filtering with where

The where phrase controls which records of the input table are actually used in the query. The effect of the where phrase is to include only the records that meet its criteria.

9.3.3.1 Basic where

The action generalizes the built-in (where) function on lists (See §3.12.3). Recall that a table is logically a list of records.

```
q)t:([] c1:`a`b`c; c2:10 20 30; c3:1.1 2.2 3.3)
q)t where t[`c2]>15
c1 c2 c3
--------
b  20 2.2
c  30 3.3
q)select from t where c2>15
_
```

In fact, you can provide a boolean list to where.

```
q)select from t where 011b
_
```

9.3.3.2 The Virtual Column i in where

The virtual column i is useful for paginating a table. Use (within), which returns a Boolean indicating whether the left operand is in the closed interval specified in the right operand, to determine the bounds of the page.

```
q)tbig:100#t
q)select from tbig where i within 50 99
_
```

To use this construct with non-literal values as the endpoints, you **must** use general list notation, since simple list notation cannot be used with variables.

```
q)s:50
q)e:99
q)select from tbig where i within (s;e)
_
```

9.3.3.3 Multiple where Subphrases

Each where subphrase is a predicate expression that produces a boolean result vector corresponding to records passing or failing a criterion. The **logical** effect of multiple subphrases is to join them with "and". Note that the parentheses are necessary in the second query.

```
q)r1:select from t where c2>15,c3<3.0
q)r2:select from t where (c2>15)&c3<3.0
q)r1~r2
1b
```

However, since the where sub phrases are sequenced from left-to-right, their order affects the actual processing. As each subphrase is applied, only the records it passes are tested in the next subphrase. The net effect is a progressively narrowed sublist of rows to consider.

269

There is often an optimal order that significantly narrows in the first one or few subphrases, which in turn reduces the amount of processing.

> **Important:** Place the most limiting where subphrase first, followed by others in decreasing strictness.

Consider the following table comprising a million observations of two variables a and b taken every millisecond starting at midnight. On the author's laptop, the version of the query that narrows the time interval first executes in under a millisecond whereas the one specifying the variable name first takes 15 milliseconds.

```
q)t:([] c1:00:00:00.000+til 1000000;c2:1000000?`a`b;c3:1000000?100.)
q)\t select from t where c1 within 00:00:01.000 00:00:01.999, c2=`a
0
q)\t select from t where c2=`a, c1 within 00:00:01.000 00:00:01.999
15
```

9.3.3.4 Nested Columns in where

Nested columns generally require adverbs, and the where phrase is no different. A common mistake made by qbies is, when trying to find a specific string in a column of strings, they forget that strings are not first class in q.

```
q)t:([] f:1.1 2.2 3.3; s:("abc";enlist "d";"ef"))
q)select from t where s="ef"
'length
=
q)select from t where s~"ef"
f s
---
q)select from t where s~\:"ef"
f   s
--------
3.3 "ef"
```

The first query is in error because it tests atomic equality between a simple list and a nested list. The second query does not achieve the desired result because it asks if the entire column matches the specified string. The final query works because it tests the specified string for match against each string in the column.

> **Tip:** For matching strings, the (like) operator is more efficient. See
> §A.44 for a detailed description but we only need the special case that
> asks if two strings match exactly—i.e., no wildcards. The fact that
> (like) is pseudo-atomic in the left operand makes it suited for
> comparing against a column. It is actually faster than the above
> expression with (~\:) for large lists.
>
> ```
> q)select from t where s like "ef"
> _
> ```

9.3.3.5 fby in where

A common use case in a query is to filter on groups. For example, in
the following example using the table p from the distribution samples,
we wish to include only the records having the maximum weight in
their respective cities. We could start with a correlated sub query.

```
q)select max weight by city from p
city  | weight
------| ------
london| 19
paris | 17
rome  | 17
```

But you run into the issue of what to do with the other fields in the sub
query. Do without aggregation, which loses the information of where
the maximum occurs?

```
q)select name, color, max weight by city from p
city  | name              color          weight
------| --------------------------------------------
london| `nut`screw`cog `red`red`red 19
paris | `bolt`cam          `green`blue 17
rome  | ,`screw            ,`blue      17
```

Or do you apply other aggregates that will pick values that are
uncorrelated with the original?

```
q)select first name, first color, max weight by city from p
city  | name  color weight
------| ------------------
london| nut   red   19
paris | bolt  green 17
rome  | screw blue  17
```

In SQL you would use HAVING, but q is having none of that. Instead
use (fby) in the where phrase—see §9.3.3.5. Since it returns the
value of the aggregate across each group, you simply compare the
target column to the (fby) result to get a boolean vector with 1b at
precisely the records whose fields match the aggregate on the group.

Used in a where phrase, (fby) takes the form

$$(f_{agg}; expr_{col}) \text{ fby } c$$

The left operand is a two-item list comprising an aggregate function f_{agg} and a column expression $expr_{col}$ on which the function will be applied. The right operand c is the column to be grouped.

In our example,

```
q)select from p where weight=(max;weight) fby city
p | name  color weight city
--| ----------------------
p2| bolt  green 17     paris
p3| screw blue  17     rome
p6| cog   red   19     london
```

Now we include another where phrase for the desired result.

```
q)select from p where weight=(max;weight) fby city,color=`blue
p | name  color weight city
--| --------------------
p3| screw blue  17     rome
```

To group on multiple columns, encapsulate them in an anonymous table in the right operand of (fby).

```
q)t:([]sym:`IBM`IBM`MSFT`IBM`MSFT;
      ex:`N`O`N`N`N;time:12:10:00 12:30:00 12:45:00 12:50:00 13:30:00;
      price:82.1 81.95 23.45 82.05 23.40)
q)select from t where price=(max;price) fby ([]sym;ex)
sym  ex time     price
----------------------
IBM  N  12:10:00 82.1
IBM  O  12:30:00 81.95
MSFT N  12:45:00 23.45
```

9.3.4 Grouping and Aggregation

In contrast to SQL, where grouping and aggregation are performed together, in q-sql they are independent. In this section we use the tables defined in the sp.q script included in the distribution.

```
q)p
p | name  color weight city
--| ----------------------
p1| nut   red    12     london
p2| bolt  green  17     paris
p3| screw blue   17     rome
p4| screw red    14     london
p5| cam   blue   12     paris
p6| cog   red    19     london
```

```
q)s
s | name  status city
--| ------------------
s1| smith 20     london
s2| jones 10     paris
s3| blake 30     paris
s4| clark 20     london
s5| adams 30     athens
```

```
q)sp
s  p  qty
---------
s1 p1 300
s1 p2 200
s1 p3 400
s1 p4 200
s4 p5 100
s1 p6 100
s2 p1 300
s2 p2 400
s3 p2 200
s4 p2 200
s4 p4 300
s1 p5 400
```

9.3.4.1 Aggregation without Grouping

When an aggregate function is applied against a column of simple type in the select phrase, the result is an atom. If all columns in the select phrase are computed with aggregation and there is no grouping, the result will be a table with a single row—e.g., a summary or rollup. While q has many built-in aggregates, you can also define and use your own.

Here we calculate the total and mean order quantity using the built-in aggregates (sum) and (avg).

```
q)select total:sum qty, mean:avg qty from sp
total mean
-------------
3100  258.3333
```

9.3.4.2 Grouping without Aggregation

The *by* phrase groups rows having common values in specified column(s), much like GROUP BY in SQL. The result of a query including a by phrase is a keyed table whose key column(s) are those in the by phrase. This is well-defined because the grouping along like values ensures uniqueness of the keys.

The action of the by phrase is a generalization of the built-in function (group) on lists (See §3.12.14). A query that groups without aggregation results in nested columns. One way to think of this is that each group of values is folded into a single field in the result.

```
q)t:([] c1:`a`b`a`b`c; c2:10 20 30 40 50)
q)t[`c2] group t[`c1]
a| 10 30
b| 20 40
c| ,50
q)select c2 by c1 from t
c1| c2
--| -----
a | 10 30
b | 20 40
c | ,50
```

> ***Tip:*** Grouping without aggregation is the most common way qbies unintentionally create nested columns. Nested columns are slower, more cumbersome to use (they require a heavy dose of adverbs) and are usually unnecessary. And you can't just cast a nested column to a simple one; you must apply an aggregate or some other operation that flattens a list.

Observe that (ungroup) can be used to reverse the nested result of grouping without aggregation. It is not quite an inverse since it returns the original records ordered on the by column(s).

```
q)ungroup select c2 by c1 from t
c1 c2
-----
a  10
a  30
b  20
b  40
c  50
```

There are use cases that group on specified column(s) and want **all** the remaining columns to be nested in the result. For this use (xgroup), which takes the symbolic column name(s) to be grouped as left operand and a table as right operand. The result is a keyed table that is that same as listing all the non-grouped columns in the equivalent select.

Using the distribution example,

```
q)`p xgroup sp
p | s                    qty
--| ------------------------------------------
p1| `s$`s1`s2            300 300
p2| `s$`s1`s2`s3`s4 200 400 200 200
p3| `s$, `s1             ,400
p4| `s$`s1`s4            200 300
p5| `s$`s4`s1            100 400
p6| `s$, `s1             ,100
```

Again (ungroup) is an inverse up to record order.

```
q)ungroup `p xgroup sp
_
```

9.3.4.3 Grouping with Aggregation

Normally you will group using by together with aggregation in the select phrase. The effect is to aggregate along the groups, collapsing each group of rows into a single record. The result is a keyed table whose key columns are the grouped column(s).

```
q)select sum c2 by c1 from t
c1| c2
--| --
a | 40
b | 60
c | 50
```

To group on multiple columns, specify multiple by subphrases, which results in a compound key in the result.

```
q)t:([] desk:`a`b`a`b`a`b; acct:`1`2`3`4`1`4; pnl:1.1 -2.2 3.3 4.4 5.5 -.5)
q)select ct:count desk, sum pnl by desk,acct from t
desk acct| ct pnl
---------| -------
a    1   | 2  6.6
a    3   | 1  3.3
b    2   | 1  -2.2
b    4   | 2  3.9
```

> **Tip:** In contrast to SQL, every column in the by phrase is automatically included in the key column(s) of the result and should not be duplicated in the select phrase.

A by subphrase can be a q expression, meaning that you can group on computed columns. This is very powerful and is not present in SQL. Following is a useful example that averages the observations of our time series in 100 millisecond buckets.

```
q)t:([] c1:00:00:00.000+til 1000000;c2:1000000?`a`b;c3:1000000?100.)
q)select avg c3 by 100 xbar c1, c2 from t
c1            c2| c3
---------------| --------
00:00:00.000 a | 49.44874
00:00:00.000 b | 54.21254
00:00:00.100 a | 45.59306
00:00:00.100 b | 40.59436
```

> **Tip:** In an unexpected special case of implicit grouping with aggregation, specifying a by phrase together with empty select phrase is equivalent to applying (last) to all columns. A moment's thought reveals this is quite useful for financial time series, where you often want the most recent value of a group.

```
q)t:([] desk:`a`b`a`b`a`b; acct:`1`2`3`4`1`4; pnl:1.1 -2.2 3.3 4.4 5.5
-.5)
q)select by desk from t
desk| acct pnl
----| ---------
a   | 1    5.5
b   | 4    -0.5
```

9.4 The exec Template

The syntax of the exec template is identical to that of select.

$$\text{exec } <p_s> \ <\text{by } p_b> \text{ from } t_{exp} \ <\text{where } p_w>$$

Whereas select always returns a table, the result type of exec depends on the number of columns in its select phrase. One column yields a list; more than one column yields a dictionary.

When more than one column is specified the select phrase, the result is a dictionary mapping column names to the column lists produced. The essential difference from select is that the column lists do not have to be rectangular—i.e., they are not required to have the same length—and the resulting dictionary is not flipped into a table. For example, the following query fails with select because the proposed column dictionary is not rectangular but it succeeds with exec.

```
q)t:([] name:`a`b`c`d`e; state:`NY`FL`OH`NY`HI)
q)select name, distinct state from t
'length
q)exec name, distinct state from t
name | `a`b`c`d`e
state| `NY`FL`OH`HI
```

A common use of exec is when there is only one column in the aggregate phrase and no by phrase. The result is the computed column list devoid of other structure—i.e., not a dictionary or table. This is useful to extract a column dynamically. With t as above,

```
q)select name from t
name
----
a
b
c
d
e
q)exec name from t
`a`b`c`d`e
```

When using exec to extract a single column of a table, you can place constraints on other columns.

```
q)exec name from t where state in `NY`HI
`a`d`e
```

9.5 The update Template

9.5.1 Basic update

The update template has identical syntax to select.

$$\text{update } <p_u> \ <\text{by } p_b> \text{ from } t_{exp} \ <\text{where } p_w>$$

The semantic difference is that colons in the update phrase p_u identify modified or new columns instead of simply assigning column names. If the left of a colon is a column that exists in the table, that column is updated with the result of the expression to the right of the colon. If the left of a colon is not a column in the table, a new column of that name with the result of the expression is added to the end of the column list. The original table is not affected.

```
q)t:([] c1:`a`b`c; c2:10 20 30)
q)update c1:`x`y`z from t
c1 c2
-----
x  10
y  20
z  30
q)t

q)update c3:`x`y`z from t
c1 c2 c3
--------
a  10 x
b  20 y
c  30 z
q)t

```

The implicit naming conventions are the same as in select so you can
omit the name and colon for existing columns in many cases. With t
as above,

```
q)(update c2:c2+100 from t)~update c2+100 from t
1b
```

In the examples above, the table was passed by value and so the
original was not modified. To modify the table in place, pass it by
name.

```
q)t:([] c1:`a`b`c; c2:10 20 30)
q)update c1:`x`y`z from `t

q)t

q)update c3:`x`y`z from `t

q)t

```

Qbies coming from DDL may not immediately appreciate how useful it
is that update can add new columns dynamically. For example, you
can add a "constant" column by taking advantage of the fact that
scalars are extended to match vectors. This is **not** a default value for
the column in subsequent records.

```
q)t:([] c1:`a`b`c; c2:10 20 30)
q)update c3:42 from t

```

Often you will apply update with a where phrase that limits the scope
of the modification.

```
q)t:([] c1:`a`b`c; c2:10 20 30)
q)update c2:c2+100 from t where c1<>`a
c1 c2
------
a  10
b  120
c  130
```

> ***Tip:*** The actions in the where phrase and the update phrase are vector operations on entire column lists. This is the Zen of update.

If you add a new column in update with a where phrase, the fields in the non-selected rows will have the null value of the appropriate type.

```
q)update c3:1b from t where c2>15
c1 c2 c3
--------
a  10 0
b  20 1
c  30 1
```

You can use any q expression to the right of the colon providing the size and type match the targeted location.

```
q)update c2:42 43  from t where c2>15
'length
q)update c2:42 43 44  from t where c2>15
'length
q)update c2:42.0 43  from t where c2>15
'type
```

9.5.2 update-by

When the by phrase is present, the update operation is performed along groups. This is most useful with aggregate and uniform functions. For an aggregate function, the entire group gets the value of the aggregation on the group.

```
q)update avg weight by city from p
p | name   color weight city
--| -------------------------
p1| nut    red   15     london
p2| bolt   green 14.5   paris
p3| screw  blue  17     rome
p4| screw  red   15     london
p5| cam    blue  14.5   paris
p6| cog    red   15     london
```

A uniform function is applied along the group in place. This can be used to compute cumulative volume of orders, for example.

```
q)update cumqty:sums qty by s from sp
```

9.6 The delete Template

The final template, delete, allows either rows or columns to be deleted. Its syntax is a simplified form of select, with the restriction that either p_{cols} or p_w can be present but not both.

$$delete <p_{cols}> \text{ from } t_{exp} <where \ p_w>$$

If p_{cols} is present as a comma-separated list of columns, the result is t_{exp} with the specified columns removed. If p_w is present, the result is t_{exp} after records meeting the criteria of p_w are removed. Someone always asks, can you delete rows and column simultaneously? But the rest of us meditating on the Zen of q realize this makes no sense.

When the table is passed by value, the operation is on a copy. When the table is passed by name, the operation is in place. Deleting from a copy,

```
q)t:([] c1:`a`b`c; c2:10 20 30)
q)delete c1 from t

q)delete from t where c2>15

q)t

```

To delete in place,

```
q)delete from `t where c2=30

q)delete c2 from `t

q)t

```

> **Tip:** When you want to select all but a few columns, it is easier to delete the ones you don't want than list all the ones you do.
>
> ```
> q)t:([] c1:1 2; c2:`a`b; c3:1.1 2.2; c4:2015.01.01 2015.01.02)
> q)(select c1, c2, c4 from t)~delete c3 from t
> 1b
> ```

9.7 Sorting

Recall that tables and keyed tables comprise lists of records and therefore have an inherent order. A table or keyed table can be reordered by sorting on any column(s). In contrast to SQL, there is no equivalent to ORDER BY in the select template. Instead, built-in functions that sort tables are applied after select.

9.7.1 xasc

The dyadic (xasc) takes a scalar, or list of, symbolic column name(s) as its left operand and a table or table name as its right operand. It returns the records of the table sorted ascending on the specified column(s). The sort column list is specified in major-to-minor sort order.

To work on a copy pass by value.

```
q)t:([] c1:`a`b`c`a; c2:20 10 40 30)
q)`c2 xasc t
c1 c2
-----
b  10
a  20
a  30
c  40
```

```
q)`c1`c2 xasc t
c1 c2
-----
a  20
a  30
b  10
c  40
q)t
_
```

```
q)t
c1 c2
-----
20 z
10 y
30 x
20 a
```

To sort in place pass by name.

```
q)`c1`c2 xasc `t
_
q)t
_
```

9.7.2 xdesc

The dyadic (xdesc) behaves exactly as (xasc), except that the sort is performed in descending order.

```
q)t:([] c1:`a`b`c`a; c2:20 10 40 30)
q)`c1`c2 xdesc t
c1 c2
-----
c  40
b  10
a  30
a  20
```

9.7.3 Mixed Sort

We point out that (xasc) and (xdesc) are stable sorts, meaning that the order of two records having the same sort key value is preserved in the result. This makes it possible to compose ascending and descending sort to obtain mixed sorts. For example, to sort c2 descending within c1 ascending in t above,

```
q)`c1 xasc `c2 xdesc t
_
```

9.8 Renaming and Rearranging Columns

Since a table is the flip of a column dictionary, its columns are both named and ordered. There are built-in primitives to rename and reorder columns. Their names are unfortunately chosen and their usage may seem awkward at first since they focus on the left-most columns. Nonetheless, they work well in practice.

We use the following table in this section.

```
q)t:([] c1:`a`b`c; c2:10 20 30; c3:1.1 2.2 3.3)
```

9.8.1 xcol

The dyadic (xcol) takes a scalar, or list of, symbolic column name(s) as its left operand (*names*) and a table or keyed table (*source*) as its right operand. The columns in *names* must appear in *source*. The result is a table obtained by renaming the left-most columns of source according to *names*.

```
q)`new1`new2 xcol t
_
q)t
_
```

There is no pass-by-name version of (xcol). To modify the source reassign it.

> **Tip:** You can use constructs such as the following to rename isolated columns if your table has many columns and the targeted columns area not left-most.
>
> ```
> q)@[cols[t];  where cols[t]=`c2;  :;  `new2] xcol t
> q)@[cols[t];  where cols[t] in `c1`c3;  :;  `new1`new3] xcol t
> ```

9.8.2 xcols

Now you will see what we mean about the unfortunate naming convention. The dyadic (xcols) takes a scalar, or list of, symbolic column name(s) as its left argument (*names*) and a table (*source*) as its right argument. The output is the result of reordering the columns in *names* so that those in *names* occur at the beginning—i.e., left-most in the display. Columns not specified in *names* are left in original order at the end—i.e., right-most.

Notes:
- The *source* operand can **not** be a keyed table.
- There is no pass-by-name version of (xcols). To modify the source you must reassign it.

For example,

```
q)`c3 xcols t
q)`c3`c2 xcols t
q)t
```

9.9 Joins

The essence of relational database design is normalizing data using relations and keys and then reassembling with joins. Normalization eliminates duplicate data, which takes up space and is hard to keep consistent. Joins restore the original flat rectangular form that makes data easy to work with (there's a reason spreadsheets are so popular). Simple use cases include a master-detail relation or a lookup table.

In SQL the relational structure with primary and foreign keys is static, It must be defined in a separate language (DDL) before the data can be used. Foreign key/primary key relations must be pre-established in order for joins to take place.

In q, tables are first-class entities in the language. You can define tables and relations statically, but it is easy to create them dynamically. It is even possible to join tables that could have a relation but don't.

A join sews back together along a foreign key/primary linkage data that has been factored into normal form. A join can be classified as inner or outer. An *inner join* pairs **only** records in both operands having matching keys. A *left outer join* includes **all** records in the left operand, pairing them with records having matching key in the right operand, should such exist. A *right outer join* reverses left and right in this description.

In q there are built-in inner and left outer joins; if you need a right join, reverse the operands. There is no operator for a full outer join but you can construct one; be careful what you wish for with large tables.

Joins can also be classified by how key matching is determined. Most joins are *equijoins*, meaning that the keys must be equal. In q there are also non-equijoins, called "as of" joins, in which a key is tested for less than or equal against keys in another table.

9.9.1 Implicit Join

Given a primary key table *m* with key column(s) *k* and a table *d* with a foreign key linking to *k*, a left join can be expressed in various SQL notations. For example,

```
m LEFT JOIN d ON m.k = d.k
```

A SELECT statement for this join refers to columns in the join by using dot notation based on the constituent tables.

```
SELECT d.col_d, m.col_m FROM m LEFT JOIN d WHERE m.k = d.k
```

As we saw in Chapter 8, a foreign key in q is accomplished with an enumeration over the key column(s) of a keyed table. A left join is implicit in the following query on the detail table.

```
select col_d, k.col_m from d
```

For example, in the sp.q distribution script, the table sp has foreign keys to both s and p. We can extract columns from the left join with s by issuing a query against sp and using dot notation on the foreign key to get columns in s.

```
q)select sname:s.name, qty from sp
_
```

This generalizes to the situation where d has multiple foreign keys. For example, in the sp.q distribution script, we can select records from the join of sp, s and p from a query against sp.

```
q)select sname:s.name, pname:p.name, qty from sp
_
```

Implicit joins extend to the situation in which the targeted keyed table itself has a foreign key to another keyed table.

```
q)emaster:([eid:1001 1002 1003 1004 1005]
currency: `gbp`eur`eur`gbp`eur)
q)update eid: `emaster$1001 1002 1005 1004 1003 from `s
q)select s.name, qty, s.eid.currency from sp
_
```

9.9.2 Ad hoc Left Join (lj)

To create an ad hoc left outer join between tables that **could** have a foreign key relationship, use the dyadic (lj). When the foreign key exists, that linkage is used; otherwise, the linkage is constructed dynamically. The join is 2-3 times faster if the foreign key already exists.

> *Tip:* If you intend to perform the join more than a few times, it pays to create the foreign key up front.

The right operand is a keyed table (*target*) and the left operand is a table or keyed table (*source*) having either a foreign key to target or column(s) that match the key column(s) of target in name and type. The result is all the records and columns of *source* augmented with the records and columns of *target* along matching keys. For those records in *source* having no matching key, the augmented columns contain null values.

In the following example we see all the records of t in the result, with null values in the kt column(s) where there is no matching key.

```
q)t:([] k:1 2 3 4; c:10 20 30 40)
q)kt:([k:2 3 4 5]; v:200 300 400 500)
q)t lj kt
k c  v
--------
1 10
2 20 200
3 30 300
4 40 400
```

Observe that when the source table has a foreign key, an ad hoc left join is equivalent to listing all columns from both tables in an implicit join.

```
q)kt:([k:1 2 3 4 5]; v1:10 20 30 40 50; v2:1.1 2.2 3.3 4.4 5.5)
q)tf:([] k:`kt$1 2 3 4; c:10 20 30 40)
q)(tf lj kt)~select k,c,k.v1,k.v2 from tf
1b
```

> **Important:** When the tables source and target have duplicate non-key columns, the operation has upsert semantics.

That is, the values in the right operand (target) columns prevail over those in the left operand (source). This is different from SQL where the result contains both columns with suffixes to ensure unique names.

```
q)t:([] k:1 2 3 4; v:10 20 30 40)
q)kt:([k:2 3 4 5]; v:200 300 400 500)
q)t lj kt
k v
-----
1 10
2 200
3 300
4 400
```

You can also use (lj) with a left operand keyed table.

```
q)kt1:([k:1 2 3 4]; v:10 ON 30 40)
q)kt:([k:2 3 4 5]; v:200 300 400 500)
q)kt1 lj kt
_
```

9.9.3 Column Lookup

You can perform a column lookup against a keyed table within a query without using a join. The insight is that a keyed table is a dictionary whose key list comprises its key records, so it will perform the lookup provided we put the column in an anonymous table conforming to those key records—see §8.4.5. Here we demonstrate the case where the lookup column names do not natively match the key columns, so we rename columns to match in the anonymous table.

```
q)t:([] k:1 2 3 4; c:10 20 30 40)
q)kt:([k1:2 3 4 5]; v:2.2 3.3 4.4 5.5)
q)select c, v:kt[([] k:k1); `v] from t
c  v
------
10
20 2.2
30 3.3
40 4.4
```

Especially for a single column, this is simpler (and more impressive to your colleagues) than the equivalent join.

```
q)select c,v from t lj `k xkey select k:k1,v from kt
c  v
------
10
20 2.2
30 3.3
40 4.4
```

Here is an example using compound keys and column renaming to match the lookup table.

```
q)t:([] f:`rocky`bullwinkle; l:`squirrel`moose; c:10 20)
q)kt:([fn:`rocky`bullwinkle`fearless; ln:`squirrel`moose`leader]
      v:1.1 2.2 3.3)
q)select c, v:kt[([] fn:f; ln:l); `v] from t
c  v
------
10 1.1
20 2.2
```

9.9.4 Ad Hoc Inner Join (ij)

Given a primary key table *m* with key column(s) *k* and a table *d* with a foreign key linking to *k*, an inner join can be expressed in various SQL notations,

m,d WHERE m.k = d.k

m INNER JOIN d ON m.k = d.k

A SELECT statement for this join refers to columns in the join by using dot notation based on the constituent tables.

SELECT d.col$_d$, m.col$_m$ FROM m,d WHERE m.k = d.k

The dyadic inner join operator (ij) performs an inner join between two tables that **could** have a foreign key relationship.

287

> *Tip:* The same performance observations hold as for (lj).

As with (lj), the right operand is a keyed table (*target*) and the left operand is a table or keyed table (*source*) having column(s) that are either foreign key(s) over *target* or exactly match the key column(s) of *target* in name and type. The matching is done via the foreign key or by common column name(s) between *source* and the key column(s) of *target* if there is no foreign key relationship. The result contains the columns from source and target joined along common keys.

The following example shows that (ij) returns just those records with matching keys in both tables.

```
q)t:([] k:1 2 3 4; c:10 20 30 40)
q)kt:([k:2 3 4 5]; v:2.2 3.3 4.4 5.5)
q)t ij kt
k c  v
--------
2 20 2.2
3 30 3.3
4 40 4.4
```

As with (lj), upsert semantics holds for duplicate columns.

```
q)t:([] k:1 2 3 4; v:10 20 30 40)
q)kt:([k:2 3 4 5]; v:200 300 400 500)
q)t ij kt
k v
-----
2 200
3 300
4 400
```

You can also use (ij) with a left operand keyed table.

```
q)kt1:([k:1 2 3 4]; v:10 0N 30 40)
q)kt:([k:2 3 4 5]; v:200 300 400 500)
q)kt1 ij kt
```

9.9.5 Equijoin (ej)

The triadic equijoin operator (ej) corresponds to a SQL inner join between tables in the second and third parameters along specified column names in the first parameter. The right operand does not have to be a keyed table. Unlike (ij), **all** matching records in the right table appear in the result. As with any join, upsert semantics holds on duplicate columns.

```
q)t1:([] k:1 2 3 4; c:10 20 30 40)
q)t2:([] k:2 2 3 4 5; c:200 222 300 400 500; v:2.2 22.22 3.3 4.4 5.5)

q)t1 ij `k xkey t2
k c   v
---------
2 200 2.2
3 300 3.3
4 400 4.4
```

```
q)ej[`k;t1;t2]
k c   v
-----------
2 200 2.2
2 222 22.22
3 300 3.3
4 400 4.4
```

9.9.6 Plus Join (pj)

Plus join (pj) is a left join that replaces upsert semantics for duplicate column names with addition. This is useful when you have two tables with identical schemas having all non-key columns numeric. For example, you have an organizational hierarchy and you want to rollup numeric results.

The operands of (pj) are the same as for (lj) with the additional requirement that all non-key columns are numeric. The semantics are that duplicate columns are added along matching keys and missing or null values are treated as zero.

For example,

```
q)t:([] k:`a`b`c;  a:100 200 300; b:10. 20. 30.; c:1 2 3)
q)kt:([k:`a`b] a:10 20; b:1.1 2.2)
q)t pj kt
k a   b    c
------------
a 110 11.1 1
b 220 22.2 2
c 300 30   3
```

Observe that this is the same as,

```
q)kt1:([k:`a`b`c] a:10 20 0; b:1.1 2.2 0.0; c:0 0 0)
q)t pj kt1
k a   b    c
------------
a 110 11.1 1
b 220 22.2 2
c 300 30   3
```

9.9.7 Union Join

The equivalent of an ordinary SQL union on tables with matching schemas is simply (,). Indeed, it joins two lists of compatible records.

```
q)t1:([] c1:`a`b; c2:1 2)
q)t2:([] c1:`c`d; c2:3 4)
q)t1,t2
c1 c2
-----
a  1
b  2
c  3
d  4
```

Union join (uj) is more powerful in that it vertically combines **any** two tables, or keyed tables. The records of the right operand are appended to those of the left operand in the following manner. The result table is widened with new columns of the same name and type for the columns of the right operand that do not appear in the left operand. The initial records in the result come from the left operand and have nulls in the new columns. Records from the right operand have their field values under the appropriate columns. An example is worth a thousand words.

```
q)t1:([] c1:`a`b`c; c2: 10 20 30)
q)t2:([] c1:`x`y; c3:8.8 9.9)
q)t1 uj t2
c1 c2 c3
--------
a  10
b  20
c  30
x     8.8
y     9.9
```

Continuing the previous example, you can use (uj/) to combine a list of disparate tables.

```
q)t3:([] c1:`e`f`g; c2:50 60 70; c3:5.5 6.6 7.7)
q)(uj/) (t1; t2; t3)
```

You can also apply (uj) to keyed tables, where upsert semantics hold on both rows and columns.

```
q)kt1:([k:1 2 3] v1:`a`b`c; v2:10 20 30)
q)kt2:([k:3 4] v2:300 400; v3:3.3 4.4)
q)kt1 uj kt2
k| v1 v2  v3
-| ----------
1| a  10
2| b  20
3| c  300 3.3
4|     400 4.4
```

> **Tip:** The operation of (uj) is expensive so it should only be used when necessary; in particular, when the tables conform, use (,) or (raze). Be especially cautious when low latency is paramount.

9.9.8 As-of Joins

As-of joins are so-named because they most often join tables along time columns to obtain a value in one table that is current as of a time in another table. As-of joins are non-equijoins that match on less-than-or-equal. They are not restricted to time values.

The fundamental as-of join is the triadic function (aj). It joins tables along common columns using most recent values. The syntax of (aj) is,

$$aj[\ `c_1 \ldots \ `c_n; t_1; t_2]$$

where $`c_1 \ldots \ `c_n$ is a simple list of symbol column names common to t_1 and t_2, which are the tables to be joined. There is no requirement for any of the join columns to be keys but the join will be faster on keys. The columns of both tables are brought into the result.

The semantics of (aj) are as follows. The match on all specified columns **except the last** is by equals. Assuming the records are sequenced by c_n in both tables, for a given c_n value in t_1, the match picks the greatest c_n in t_2 less than or equal to the given value in t_1. Specifically, if the c_n columns are sequenced temporal values, for each c_n value in t_1 the match picks the t_2 row whose c_n value is in effect "as of" the time in t_1.

The canonical example for (aj) is matching trades with quotes. To know if a trade represents best execution, you want to compare the trade price to the current quote—i.e., the most recent quote up to and including the time of the trade. When matching the trades and quotes, you clearly want an equi-join and the date and symbol and a non-equijoin on the time.

```
q)show t:([] ti:10:01:01 10:01:03 10:01:04;
           sym:`msft`ibm`ge;
           qty:100 200 150)
ti       sym  qty
-----------------
10:01:01 msft 100
10:01:03 ibm  200
10:01:04 ge   150
```

```
q)show q:([] ti:10:01:00 10:01:01 10:01:01 10:01:02;
           sym:`ibm`msft`msft`ibm;
           px:100 99 101 98)
ti       sym  px
-----------------
10:01:00 ibm  100
10:01:01 msft 99
10:01:01 msft 101
10:01:02 ibm  98
```

```
q)aj[`sym`ti;t;q]
ti       sym  qty px
--------------------
10:01:01 msft 100 101
10:01:03 ibm  200 98
10:01:04 ge   150
```

It is worth stepping through this example in detail. We begin with the first record in t. We look for the quote records matching `msft as of the trade time 10:01:01. There are two such records, both stamped 10:01:01 but the last one has price 101, which is reflected in the result. Next we look for the last quote record for `ibm as of 10:01.02, which is the quote record stamped 10:00:02 with price 98. Finally there are no quote records matching `ge at 10:01:04.

If you want the time of the matching quote in the result instead of the time of the trade, use (aj0).

```
q)aj0[`sym`ti;t;q]
ti       sym  qty px
--------------------
10:01:01 msft 100 101
10:01:02 ibm  200 98
10:01:04 ge   150
```

The simpler function (asof) performs the same match as (aj) but with a table against a single record. The result picks out the remaining columns in the matched row of the table.

```
q)t:([] ti:10:01:01 10:01:03 10:01:04;
        sym:`msft`ibm`ge;
        qty:100 200 150;
        px:45 160 55)
q)t
_
q)t asof `sym`ti!(`ibm;10:01:03)
qty| 200
px | 160
```

A list of such dictionary records conforms—i.e., is a table—and (asof) matches against each record.

```
q)t asof ([] sym:`msft`ibm; ti:10:01:01 10:01:03)
qty px
-------
100 45
200 160
```

Asof joins are also useful with non-numeric data. Suppose we have a table containing a history of state changes—e.g., employee promotions. An asof join will determine the state "as of" any point in time.

```
q)promotions:([] name:`nuba`devi`nuba`devi`nuba;
               dt:2000.01.01 2005.02.14 2010.02.01 2012.08.12
2015.11.01;
               title:`associate`analyst`director`cfo`retired)
q)promotions asof `name`dt!(`nuba; 2009.07.04)
title| associate
q)promotions asof `name`dt!(`devi; 2015.12.01)
_
q)events:([] name:`nuba`devi; dt: 2009.07.04 2015.12.01)
q)aj[`name`dt; events; promotions]
_
```

9.9.9 Window Join

Window joins are a generalization of as-of joins and are specifically geared for analyzing the relationship between trades and quotes in Finance. The idea is that you want to investigate the behavior of quotes in a neighborhood of each trade. For example, to determine how well a trade was executed, you need to examine the range of bid and ask prices that were prevalent around the trade time.

Writing such a query manually would be cumbersome. Instead, q provides the built-in window join (wj) that computes on an interval around each trade. Specifying the set up takes a bit of work but then all the hard work is done for you.

So that things fit on the page, we use a simple example involving trades for one ticker symbol `aapl and times that are in seconds. The

293

general case is essentially the same. First we create the trades and quotes tables; note that they are required to be unkeyed.

```
q)show t:([]sym:3#`aapl;time:09:30:01 09:30:04 09:30:08;price:100 103
101)
_
```

```
q)show q:([] sym:8#`aapl;
           time:09:30:01+(til 5),7 8 9;
           ask:101 103 103 104 104 103 102 100;
           bid:98 99 102 103 103 100 100 99)
_
```

We construct fixed-width windows of 2 seconds before and one second after each trade time. (There is no requirement that the windows be of uniform width.)

```
q)w:-2 1+\:t `time
q)w
_
```

For readability we place the names of the sym and time columns in a variable.

```
q)c:`sym`time
```

The actual form for (wj) is:

```
wj[w;c;t;(q;(f0;c0);(f1;c1))]
```

Here w is a list of windows, c is the list of sym and time column names, t is the trades table. The final parameter is a list with the quotes table and a pair of lists, each with an aggregate function and a column name.

To see all the values in each window, pass the identity function (::) in place of the aggregates. The result is similar to grouping without aggregate in a query and is helpful to see what is happening within each window.

```
q)wj[w;c;t;(q;(::;`ask);(::;`bid))]
sym  time     price ask             bid
----------------------------------------------
aapl 09:30:01 100   101 103         98 99
aapl 09:30:04 103   103 103 104 104 99 102 103 103
aapl 09:30:08 101   104 103 102     103 100 100
```

Now we apply (wj) with actual aggregates for the maximum ask and minimum bid over each window. Here you see the results of the aggregate functions run within each window.

294

```
q)wj[w;c;t;(q;(max;`ask);(min;`bid))]
sym  time      price ask bid
----------------------------------
aapl 09:30:01 100   103 98
aapl 09:30:04 101   104 99
aapl 09:30:08 105   108 104
```

As opposed to the aggregates being run over only the quote values within each window, you can also include the quotes that are current at the beginning of the window. This matters if there is no quote precisely at the beginning time of the window. For this case use (wj1), whose syntax is identical to (wj).

```
q)wj1[w;c;t;(q;(::;`ask);(::;`bid))]
sym  time      price ask             bid
-----------------------------------------------------------
aapl 09:30:01 100   101 103            98 99
aapl 09:30:04 101   103 103 104 104 99 102 103 103
aapl 09:30:08 105   107 108 107 108 104 106 106 107
```

9.10 Parameterized Queries

Relational databases have stored procedures, which are database programs incorporating SQL statements. The programming languages are not part of the SQL standard. They vary significantly across vendors but are generally third-generation imperative languages.

This situation forces a programmer to make a choice: learn a proprietary language to place functionality close to the data, or extract the data into an application server to perform calculations. Various multi-tier architectures have evolved to address this problem, but they increase system cost and complexity.

This separation is obviated in kdb+, since q is the stored procedure language and it has the power and performance to process big data. Any q function that operates on a table is effectively a stored procedure. Function parameters can be used to supply specific values for queries.

In particular, the select, exec, update and delete templates can be invoked within a function with parameters to yield a *parameterized query*.

> **Important:** Parameterized queries with templates have restrictions:
>
> - A column cannot be passed as a parameter since columns are part of the syntactic sugar of the template. They only become symbols under the covers.
> - Multiple parameters cannot be implicit—i.e., they must be declared explicitly. Although this seems to work for a single parameter, we recommend making **all** parameters explicit.

We follow our own advice in the following examples.

```
q)t:([] c1:`a`b`c; c2:10 20 30; c3:1.1 2.2 3.3)
q)select from t where c2>15
```

```
q)proc:{[sc] select from t where c2>sc}
q)proc 15
```

```
q)proc2:{[nms;sc] select from t where c1 in nms, c2>sc}
q)proc2[`a`c; 15]
```

You **can** pass a table as a parameter to a template, either by value of by name.

```
q)t:([] c1:`a`b`c; c2:10 20 30; c3:1.1 2.2 3.3)
q)proc3:{[t;nms;delta] update c2+delta from t where c1 in nms}
q)proc3[t;`a`c;100]
```

```
q)t
```

```
q)proc3[`t;`a`c;100]
```

```
q)t
```

> **Tip:** There is no need to restrict stored procs in q to the templates. Any expression that operates on tables can serve.
>
> ```
> q)t:([] c1:`a`b`c; c2:10 20 30; c3:1.1 2.2 3.3)
> q)procf:{[cs] cs#t}
> q)procf `c1`c2
> ```

You can effectively parameterize column names in two ways, only one of which is good practice. First, you can mimic a common technique from SQL in which the query is created dynamically: build the query text in a string and then invoke the interpreter programmatically using (value). This is comparatively slow. Worse, it exposes your application to injection attacks, since any q expression that appears inside the text will be executed.

The preferred method is to use the functional form for queries—see §9.12—which is fast and secure. In functional form, all columns are referred to by symbolic name, so columns names can be passed as symbols. In fact, **any** component of a query can be passed as an argument in functional form.

9.11 Views

A SQL view is effectively a query expression whose result set can be used like a table. Views are useful for encapsulating data—e.g., hiding columns, or simplifying complex queries.

A q-sql *view* is a named table expression created as an alias with the double-colon operator (::). It is common to use the templates in views but this is not a limitation.

In the following example, contrast u, which is a q variable that is assigned the result of a query, to the view (alias) v that is the query expression itself.

```
q)t:([] c1:`a`b`c; c2:10 20 30)
q)u:select from t where c2>15
q)v::select from t where c2>15
q)u

q)v

q)update c2:15 from `t where c1=`b
 t
q)u
c1 c2

q)v
c1 c2
-----
c  30
```

Observe that when the underlying table changed, u did not change but the next reference to v does reflect the update.

To find the underlying query of a view, or any alias, apply the function (view) to the symbol alias name.

```
q)view `v
"select from t where c2>15"

q)a:42
q)b::a
q)view `b
```

To list all the views in a namespace, use the function (views) with the context name. For example, to list the views in the root,

```
q)views `.
`b`v
```

9.12 Functional Forms

In the experience of the author, functional form is the most difficult q topic for most qbies. Among the reasons for this are:

- The high level of abstraction and generalization
- There is nothing like it in SQL or other programming languages
- In vintage Arthurian fashion, information density is maximized

Full disclosure: functional form is difficult. Along with adverbs and generalized application, it completes the Big Three aspects of q that separate q pretenders from contenders. Fortunately there is a cheat that can be helpful in most situations.

The function (parse) can be applied to a string containing a template query to produce a parse tree whose items (nearly) work in the equivalent functional form. A complication is that the operators are displayed in k form instead of q.

> *Tip:* The constraint portion of the result of (parse) applied to a string containing a q-sql query template generally has an extra level of (enlist) that should be removed for the corresponding functional form. The console display of the parse tree shows the k form of (enlist)—i.e., `,'—so you will actually see `,,'.

The functional forms of the four templates select, exec, update and delete are powerful because they allow all constituents to be parameterized. They can be used for any query but are especially handy for queries that are generated or completed programmatically. The q interpreter parses the syntactic sugar of the templates into their equivalent functional forms, so there is no performance difference.

> *Tip:* We recommend writing table operations in fundamental or template form unless you anticipate needing to parameterize column names. The folks who assume your code will thank you.

There are two functional forms, one for select and exec, the other for update and delete. The types of the arguments passed determine the overload. The forms are,

```
?[t;c;b;a]          / select and exec

![t;c;b;a]          / update and delete
```

where
- t is a table or the name of a table
- a is a dictionary of aggregates
- b is a dictionary of groupbys or a flag controlling other aspects of the query
- c is a list of constraints.

The expressions in a, b and c can involve columns of t and also any variables that are in scope. The rules for expression interpretation are:

- Columns are always represented by their symbolic names
- Consequently, any literal symbols, or lists of symbols, appearing in the expressions must be distinguished. This is done by enlisting them. Really.

We warned you this wasn't going to be easy.

We shall use the following sample tables in our examples.

```
q)t:([] c1:`a`b`a`c`a`b`c; c2:10*1+til 7; c3:1.1*1+til 7)
q)ft:{([] c1:`a`b`a`c`a`b`c; c2:10*1+til 7; c3:1.1*1+til 7)}
```

9.12.1 Functional select

We begin with the functional form corresponding to the simplest select query, which uses (yet another) overload of (?).

```
q)select from t

q)?[t; (); 0b; ()]

q)?[t; (); 0b; ()]~select from t
1b
```

In this degenerate functional form,

- The constraint parameter is the empty list

- The by parameter is the special value 0b indicating there is no grouping in a select query
- The aggregate parameter takes the special value of the general empty list, indicating there is no aggregate phrase

Observe that we can pass the table by name and we can also parameterize the table by substituting any q expression that returns a table or keyed table.

```
q)?[`t; (); 0b; ()]
q)?[ft[]; (); 0b; ()]
```

Now we add a constraint—i.e., a where phrase. The constraint parameter must be a **list** of q parse trees, one item for each sub phrase in the where phrase. The parse tree for each sub phrase can be obtained by converting the expression fully to prefix form and then transforming each function into a list with it followed by all its arguments. Remember, columns names become symbols and literal symbols get enlisted.

```
q)select from t where c2>35,c1 in `b`c
q)?[t; ((>;`c2;35); (in;`c1;enlist `b`c)); 0b; ()]
```

Next we demonstrate aggregation without grouping. The aggregate parameter is dictionary whose keys are column names and whose value list is a list of parse trees, one for each sub phrase of the aggregate phrase. Again, column names are symbols and literal symbols get enlisted.

> **Tip:** While q will assign default columns names in the templates, you must explicitly provide all columns names in functional form.
>
> ```
> q)select max c2, c2 wavg c3 from t
> q)?[t; (); 0b; `maxc2`wtavg!((max;`c2); (wavg;`c2;`c3))]
> ```

Next we demonstrate grouping without aggregation. As with the aggregate parameter, we construct a dictionary with column names and parse trees of the by sub phrases. In this particular example, we demonstrate how to handle the case of grouping on a single column. Recall that a singleton dictionary requires the key and value to be enlisted—this enlist is separate from enlisting literal symbols in functional form.

```
q)select c2 by c1 from t
q)?[t; (); (enlist `c1)!enlist `c1; ()]
```

Finally we put the pieces together. We find code to be more readable if you separately construct the three parameters as variables and pass these in to the functional form.

```
q)select max c2, c2 wavg c3 by c1 from t where c2>35,c1 in `b`c
q)c:((>;`c2;35); (in;`c1;enlist `b`c))
q)b:(enlist `c1)!enlist `c1
q)a:`maxc2`wtavg!((max;`c2); (wavg;`c2;`c3))
q)?[t;c;b;a]
```

Now that wasn't so bad, was it? OK, maybe it was.

Next we show the functional form for the special case (select distinct). In this case set the *by* parameter to 1b.

```
q)t:([] c1:`a`b`a`c`b`c; c2:1 1 1 2 2 2; c3:10 20 30 40 50 60)
q)select distinct c1,c2 from t
q)?[t; (); 1b; `c1`c2!`c1`c2]
```

The extended form (select[n]) adds a fifth parameter to the functional form.

```
q)t:([] c1:`a`b`c; c2:10 20 30)
q)select[2] from t
q)?[t;();0b;();2]
```

The extended form (select[>c_i]) adds two additional parameters to the functional form. The first is the initial value for the comparison and the second is a list with the k form—seriously!—of the comparison operator for the sort along with the column name for the sort.

```
q)t:([] c1:`a`b`c`a; c2:10 20 30 40)
q)select[>c1] c1,c2 from t
q)?[t;();0b; `c1`c2!`c1`c2; 0w; (>:;`c1)]
```

9.12.2 Functional exec

The functional form for exec is nearly identical to that of select. Slight variations in the parameters indicate which is intended. Since the constraint parameter carries over unchanged, we omit its discussion in this section.

The functional form for exec on a single result column depends on whether you want a list or dictionary to be returned. Assuming there is no grouping, use the empty list for the *by* parameter. For a list result, specify the aggregate as a parse tree; for a dictionary result, specify a dictionary mapping the result name to its parse tree.

```
q)t:([] c1:`a`b`c`a; c2:10 20 30 40; c3:1.1 2.2 3.3 4.4)
q)exec distinct c1 from t

q)?[t; (); (); (distinct; `c1)]

q)exec c1:distinct c1 from t

q)?[t; (); (); (enlist `c1)!enlist (distinct; `c1)]
```

For exec on multiple columns without grouping, specify the *by* parameter as the general empty list and the aggregate parameter as a dictionary mapping column names to a list of parse trees.

```
q)exec distinct c1, c2 from t

q)?[t; (); (); `c1`c2!((distinct; `c1); `c2)]
```

To group on a single column, specify its symbol name in the *by* parameter.

```
q)exec c2 by c1 from t

q)?[t; (); `c1; `c2]
```

More complex grouping in an exec seems to revert to the equivalent select.

302

9.12.3 Functional update

The syntax of functional form of update is identical to that of select except that (!) is used in place of (?). In the following examples you will need to keep track of the different uses of enlist:

- making a list of parse trees from a single parse expression
- creating singleton dictionaries
- distinguishing literal symbols from column names.

```
q)t:([] c1:`a`b`c`a`b; c2:10 20 30 40 50)
q)update c2:100 from t where c1=`a

q)c:enlist (=;`c1;enlist `a)
q)b:0b
q)a:(enlist `c2)!enlist 100
q)![t;c;b;a]


q)update c2:sums c2 by c1 from t
c1 c2
-----
a  10
b  20
c  30
a  50
b  70
q)![`t; (); 0b; (enlist `c2)!enlist(sums;`c2)]

q)t

```

Observe that we switched to passing by name in the last functional query.

9.12.4 Functional delete

The syntax of functional delete is a simplified form of functional update.

```
![t;c;0b;a]
```

where t is a table, or the name of a table, c is a list of parse trees for where sub phrases and a is a **list** of column names. Either c or a, but not both, must be present. If c is present, it specifies which rows are to be deleted. If a is present it is a list of symbol column names to be deleted. In the latter case you must specify c as an empty list of symbols.

As before, distinguish the various uses of (enlist) in the examples.

```
q)t:([] c1:`a`b`c`a`b; c2:10 20 30 40 50)
q)delete from t where c1=`b

q)![t;enlist (=;`c1;enlist `b);0b;`symbol$()]


q)delete c2 from t

q)![`t;();0b;enlist `c2]
`t
q)t

```

Again observe that we switched to call by name in the last query.

9.13 Examples

At this point we know enough about tables to do some damage. You should go back and (re)read *Q Shock and Awe*. It will now be straightforward.

9.13.1 The trades Table

We shall demonstrate further examples in this section based on the trades table created there. Here we encapsulate the steps in a function so that it can be run for an arbitrary list of tickers and an arbitrary number of rows. On the author's two-year-old MacBook Pro, it takes a few seconds to create a table with 10,000,000 rows.

```
q)mktrades:{[tickers; sz]
  dt:2015.01.01+sz?31;
  tm:sz?24:00:00.000;
  sym:sz?tickers;
  qty:10*1+sz?1000;
  px:90.0+(sz?2001)%100;
  t:([] dt; tm; sym; qty; px);
  t:`dt`tm xasc t;
  t:update px:6*px from t where sym=`goog;
  t:update px:2*px from t where sym=`ibm;
  t}
q)trades:mktrades[`aapl`goog`ibm; 10000000]
```

9.13.2 The instrument Table

The instr table is a static keyed table containing basic information about the companies whose financial instruments (stocks in our case) are traded. Its schema has fields for the stock symbol, the name of the company and the industry classification of the company.

```
q)insr:([sym:`symbol$()] name:`symbol$(); industry:`symbol$())
```

We populate `instr` using (upsert).

```
q)`instr upsert (`ibm; `$"International Business Machines"; `$"Computer
Services")
`instr
q)`instr upsert (`msft; `$"Microsoft"; `$"Software")
`instr
q)`instr upsert (`goog; `$"Google"; `$"Search")
`instr
q)`instr upsert (`aapl; `$"Apple"; `$"Electronics")
`instr

q)instr
_
```

Now we make `sym` a foreign key to `trades`.

```
q)update `instr$sym from `trades
`trades
q)meta trades
c  | t f      a
---| ---------
dt | d        s
tm | t
sym| s instr
qty| j
px | f
```

9.13.3 Basic Queries

Here we demonstrate basic operations against the `trades` and `instrument` tables.

We can count the total number of trades in several ways. The last version causes q to do the most work and should be avoided. Observe that q does not carry the name of its own virtual column `i` to the result of `select`.

```
q)count trades
_
q)exec count i from trades
10000000
q)select count i from trades
x
-------
10000000
q)
q)count select from trades
10000000
```

Let's count the number of trades for an individual symbol.

> **Tip:** For splayed and partitioned tables, only the `select` expression works.
>
> ```
> q)exec count i from trades where sym=`ibm
>
> q)select count i from trades where sym=`ibm
>
> ```

We can count the number of trades across all symbols. The second version unkeys the result.

```
q)select count i by sym from trades
sym | x
----| -------
aapl| 3333498
goog| 3330409
ibm | 3336093
```

```
q)() xkey select count i by sym from trades

```

We find one day's trades for aapl.

```
q)select from trades where dt=2015.01.15,sym=`aapl

```

We find all lunch hour trades for goog. Note that (`within`) includes both endpoints. Also recall that you must use general list notation if the endpoints are variables.

```
q)select from trades where sym=`goog, tm within 12:00:00 13:00:00

```

```
q)noon:12:00:00
q)thirteen00:13:00:00
q)select from trades where sym=`goog, tm within (noon;thirteen00)

```

We find the maximum daily price for aapl. Due to our uniform distribution, it is statistically constant.

```
q)select maxpx:max px by dt from trades where sym=`aapl
dt        | maxpx
----------| -----
2015.01.01| 110
2015.01.02| 110
2015.01.03| 110
2015.01.04| 110
..
```

We find the minimum and maximum trade price over the trading range for each symbol by company name. We point out that this is actually grouping on a computed column since the foreign key is resolved to the `instrument` table via an implicit join.

```
q)select lo:min px, hi:max px by sym.name from trades
name                        | lo   hi
----------------------------| -------
Apple                       | 90   110
Google                      | 540  660
International Business Machines| 180  220
```

We find the total and average trade volume for specific symbols. Due to our simplistic construction, the volumes are statistically the same.

```
q)select totq:sum qty, avgq:avg qty by sym
   from trades where sym in `ibm`goog
sym | totq        avgq
----| -------------------
goog| 16670706340 5005.603
ibm | 16702382420 5006.57
```

We find the high, low and close over one minute intervals for Google.

```
q)select hi:max px,lo:min px,open:first px, close:last px by
dt,tm.minute
   from trades where sym=`goog
dt         minute| hi     lo     open   close
-----------------| --------------------------
2015.01.01 00:00 | 658.98 540.72 610.98 561.66
2015.01.01 00:01 | 659.4  542.82 594.24 595.86
2015.01.01 00:02 | 652.5  540    625.26 583.5
..
```

We demonstrate how to use our own functions in queries. Suppose we define a funky average that weights items by their position. Notice that we use intra-line assignment to avoid counting x three times.

```
q)favg:{(sum x*1+til ctx)%ctx*ctx:count x}
```

Then we can apply (favg) just as we did the built-in q function (avg).

```
q)select favgpx:favg px by sym from trades
sym | favgpx
----| --------
aapl| 49.99748
goog| 300.0155
ibm | 100.0009
```

9.13.4 Meaty Queries

In this section, we demonstrate more interesting q-sql examples against the `trades` table.

We find volume weighted average price by day and for 100 millisecond buckets for aapl. Note that latter takes a few seconds for 100,000,000 trades on the author's laptop.

```
q)select vwap:qty wavg px by dt from trades where sym=`ibm
dt        | vwap
----------| --------
2015.01.01| 200.064
2015.01.02| 200.0207
2015.01.03| 200.0109
..
```

```
q)select vwap:qty wavg px by dt,100 xbar tm  from trades where sym=`ibm
dt         tm           | vwap
-----------------------| ------
2015.01.01 00:00:00.700| 194.8
2015.01.01 00:00:01.300| 200.96
2015.01.01 00:00:03.900| 215.34
..
```

We use (fby) to select records attaining the maximum price each day for each sym.

```
q)select from trades where px=(max;px) fby sym
dt         tm           sym  qty  px
-------------------------------------
2015.01.01 00:20:05.835 goog 9750 660
2015.01.01 00:33:19.125 goog 3150 660
2015.01.01 00:42:13.379 goog 8790 660
2015.01.01 00:42:58.623 aapl 6090 110
..
```

We use (favg) from the previous section to demonstrate that user functions can appear in any phrase of the query.

```
q)select from trades where px<2*(favg;px) fby sym
dt         tm           sym  qty  px
-------------------------------------
2015.01.01 00:00:00.448 goog 6940 540.18
2015.01.01 00:00:00.602 aapl 540  94.63
2015.01.01 00:00:00.754 ibm  3100 194.8
..
```

We find the average daily volume and price for all instruments and store the result for following example.

```
q)show atrades:select avgqty:avg qty, avgpx:avg px by sym, dt from
trades
sym  dt         | avgqty   avgpx
---------------| ----------------
aapl 2015.01.01| 4997.978 99.99409
aapl 2015.01.02| 5006.318 100.0012
aapl 2015.01.03| 5002.49  100.0019
aapl 2015.01.04| 5012.752 99.97018
..
```

We find the days when the average price went up. Note that create our own (deltas0) to return 0 for the initial item since the behavior of the built-in (deltas) doesn't work well for this purpose. Observe that the nested result columns scroll off the page.

```
q)deltas0:{first[x] -': x}
q)select dt, avgpx by sym from atrades where 0<deltas0 avgpx
sym | dt
----|  ------------------------------------------------------------
    -
aapl| 2015.01.02 2015.01.03 2015.01.05 2015.01.07 2015.01.08
2015.01.10..
goog| 2015.01.01 2015.01.02 2015.01.03 2015.01.05 2015.01.07
2015.01.00..
ibm | 2015.01.05 2015.01.07 2015.01.08 2015.01.10 2015.01.11
2015.01.13..
```

To compact the display, take only the first few field values.

```
q)select 2#dt, 2#avgpx by sym from atrades where 0<deltas0 avgpx
sym | dt                     avgpx
----|  -------------------------------------------
aapl| 2015.01.02 2015.01.03  100.0012 100.0019
goog| 2015.01.01 2015.01.02  599.8873 600.0021
ibm | 2015.01.05 2015.01.07  200.0634 200.0022
```

In order to demonstrate operations on nested columns, we denormalize trades into a keyed table with one row and complex columns for each symbol. We can do this either by grouping without aggregation using select or by using (xgroup). The difference is that (xgroup) does not automatically sort on the result key column.

```
q)dntrades:select dt,tm,qty,px by sym from trades
q)dntrades~`sym xasc `sym xgroup trades
1b
```

We display the first two items of each field to make the structure more evident.

```
q)select 2#dt,2#tm,2#qty,2#px by sym from trades
sym | dt                     tm                              qty        px
----|  -------------------------------------------------------------------------------
    ------
aapl| 2015.01.01 2015.01.01 00:00:00.602 00:00:00.840 540   1260 94.63
92.87
goog| 2015.01.01 2015.01.01 00:00:00.448 00:00:01.039 6940 7260 540.18
560.04
ibm | 2015.01.01 2015.01.01 00:00:00.754 00:00:01.377 3100 5150 194.8
200.96
```

In such a table with compound columns—i.e., lists of simple lists of the same type—you will need adverbs for column operations. Lots of adverbs.

```
q)select sym,cnt:count each dt,avgpx:avg each px from dntrades
sym  cnt     avgpx
-------------------
aapl 3333498 99.99694
goog 3330409 600.02
ibm  3336093 200.0041
```

We can apply our own monadic (favg) function.

```
q)select sym, favgpx:favg each px from dntrades
sym  favgpx
-----------
aapl 49.99748
goog 300.0155
ibm  100.0009
```

To find the volume weighted average price by we use the each-both adverb (') with the dyadic (wavg).

```
q)select sym,vwap:qty wavg' px from dntrades
sym  vwap
-----------
aapl 99.99915
goog 600.0493
ibm  200.0061
```

Note that this adverb generalizes to *n*-adic functions for any *n>1*.

We find the profit of the ideal transaction over the month for each symbol. This is the maximum amount of money that could be made with complete foreknowledge of the market. In other words, find the largest profit obtainable by buying at some traded price and selling at the highest subsequently traded price. To solve this, we reverse the perspective. For each traded price, we look at the minimum of prices that preceded it. The largest such difference is our answer. The maximum draw down is dual.

```
q)select max px-mins px by sym from trades
sym | px
----| ---
aapl| 20
goog| 120
ibm | 40
```

```
q)select min px-maxs px by sym from trades
sym | px
----| ----
aapl| -20
goog| -120
ibm | -40
```

9.13.5 Excursion – Pivot Table

The objective is to pivot a table on a column (or columns) as in Excel. The construct revolves (pun intended) around three columns. The (distinct) values of the *pivot* column become the column names in the result. Each field in the *value* column is placed under the pivot column whose name appears in its original row. The destination row of a value column field is determined by the *key* column field in its original row. This is a pivot in the sense that the original vertical arrangement is transformed to horizontal and rows transform to columns. As usual, an example is worth a thousand words.

We begin with the simple table.

```
q)show t:([]k:1 2 3 2 3; p:`a1`a2`a1`a3`a2; v:100 200 300 400 500)
k p  v
--------
1 a1 100
2 a2 200
3 a1 300
2 a3 400
3 a2 500
```

The desired result pvt is as follows. Observe that this is actually a keyed table but it is simple to unkey it with (xkey).

```
q)pvt
k| a1  a2  a3
-| -----------
1| 100
2|     200 400
3| 300 500
```

We break the solution into multiple steps, beginning with our sample table and then successively generalizing to handle a wider class of use cases.

(1) Collect the unique values of the pivot column p into a list P.

```
q)P:exec distinct p from t
```

(2) Write a query that extracts the key-value pairs for p and v grouped by k.

```
q)exec p!v by k from t
-
```

(3) Enhance the previous query to produce a keyed table by rectangularizing the dictionaries by filling missing values using P#. Magic happens. Observe that we need to name the resulting key column explicitly.

```
q)exec P#p!v by k:k from t
k| a1  a2  a3
-| ----------
1| 100
2|     200 400
3| 300 500
```

(4) Write the query to extract the unique values of the pivot column in functional form.

```
q)P:?[t; (); (); (distinct; `p)]
-
```

(5) Convert the pivot query to functional form.

```
q)?[t;(); (1#`k)!1#`k; (#;`P;(!;`p;`v))]
-
```

(6) Place the previous functional forms in a function that takes the table and the column names as parameters and returns the pivot result.

```
q)dopivot:{[t; kn; pn; vn]
  P:?[t; (); (); (distinct; pn)];
  ?[t;(); (1#kn)!1#kn; (#;`P;(!;pn;vn))]}

q)dopivot[t;`k;`p;`v]
-
```

(7) Write an expression that converts the fields of the pivot column to valid names when they are not—e.g., integers. In general, producing unique, valid names is a non-trivial exercise. Find a solution that (at least) works on tn below.

```
q)tn:([] k:1 2 3 2 3; p:(`a1;2;`a1;3;2); v:100 200 300 400 500)

q:{
  x:(::),x;
  x:1_x:@[x; where not 10h=type each x; string];
   $@[x; where not any x[;0] within/: ("AZ";"az"); "X_",]}

q)dopivot:{[t; kn; pn; vn]
  t:![t; (); 0b; (1#pn)!enlist (`mkNames; pn)];
  P:?[t; (); (); (distinct; pn)];
  ?[t;(); (1#kn)!1#kn; (#; `P;(!;pn;vn))]}

q)dopivot[tn;`k;`p;`v]
_
```

(8) Next, we generalize to the case when there are multiple entries in
v for a single key value. For example, applied to tr below, our current
dopivot misses the 1000 value in v.

```
q)tr:([]k:1 2 3 2 3 1; p:`a1`a2`a1`a3`a2`a1; v:100 200 300 400 500
1000)
q)dopivot[tr;`k;`p;`v]            / misses 1000 value
k| a1  a2  a3
-| ----------
1| 100
2|     200 400
3| 300 500
```

We would like to apply an aggregate function such as sum to obtain,

```
k| a1    a2  a3
-| ------------
1| 1100
2|       200 400
3| 300   500
```

Modify dopivot to take an aggregate function agg and apply it to v as
part of the pivot process. Test it on tr using sum.

```
q)dopivot:{[t; agg; kn; pn; vn]
  t:![t; (); 0b; (1#pn)!enlist (`mkNames; pn)];
  t:?[t; (); (kn,pn)!kn,pn; (1#vn)!enlist (agg;vn)];
  P:?[t; (); (); (distinct; pn)];
  ?[t; (); (1#kn)!1#kn; (#; `P;(!;pn;vn))]}

q)dopivot[tr;sum;`k;`p;`v]
_
```

(9) We would like to handle the case of compound keys—e.g., k1 and
k2 in tk below.

```
q)show tk:([]k1:1 2 3 2 3 1 1;k2:10 20 30 40 50 60 10;
p:`a1`a2`a1`a3`a2`a1`a1;v:100 200 300 400 500 1000 10000)
k1 k2 p  v
-------------
1  10 a1 100
2  20 a2 200
3  30 a1 300
2  40 a3 400
3  50 a2 500
1  60 a1 1000
1  10 a1 10000
```

Modify dopivot to take a list of key column names and test it on tk.

```
q)dopivot:{[t; agg; ks; pn; vn]
  ks,:();
  t:![t; (); 0b; (1#pn)!enlist (`mkNames; pn)];
  t:?[t; (); (ks,pn)!ks,pn; (1#vn)!enlist (agg;vn)];
  P:?[t; (); (); (distinct; pn)];
  ?[t;(); ks!ks; (#;`P;(!;pn;vn))]}

q)dopivot[tk;sum;`k1`k2;`p;`v]
_
```

(10) Modify dopivot to accept a string argument representing a valid where phrase for the input table and use it to constrain the pivot. Test it against tk with the phrase "k1<>2".

```
q)dopivot:{[t; agg; wh; ks; pn; vn]
  ks,:();
  c:enlist parse wh;
  t:?[t; c; 0b; (cols t)!cols t];
  t:![t; (); 0b; (1#pn)!enlist (`mkNames; pn)];
  t:?[t; (); (ks,pn)!ks,pn; (1#vn)!enlist (agg;vn)];
  P:?[t; (); (); (distinct; pn)];
  ?[t; (); ks!ks; (#;`P;(!;pn;vn))]}

q)dopivot[tk;sum;"k1<>2";`k1`k2;`p;`v]
_
```

(11) Finally, modify dopivot to accept an empty list in the aggregate or the where parameters. In the former case, use first as the default aggregate; in the latter, perform no constraint. Test against tk with empty list arguments for both.

```
q)dopivot:{[t; agg; wh; ks; pn; vn]
  ks,:();
  agg:first agg,first;
  c:$[count wh; enlist parse wh; ()];
  t:?[t; c; 0b; (cols t)!cols t];
  t:![t; (); 0b; (1#pn)!enlist (`mkNames; pn)];
  t:?[t; (); (ks,pn)!ks,pn; (1#vn)!enlist (agg;vn)];
  P:?[t; (); (); (distinct; pn)];
  ?[t; (); ks!ks; (#;`P;(!;pn;vn))]}

q)dopivot[tk;();"";`k1`k2;`p;`v]
_
```

We test the efficiency of dopivot by applying it to a modestly large table with a million rows of timeseries data. Take that, Excel!

```
q)t:`date xasc ([] date:2015.01.01+1000000?10;
                   sym:1000000?`aapl`ibm`intc;
                   qty:1+1000000?100)

q)dopivot[t; sum; ""; `date; `sym; `qty]          / ymmv
date      | aapl    ibm     intc
----------| --------------------
2015.01.01| 1688672 1666730 1659389
2015.01.02| 1695257 1688088 1679517
2015.01.03| 1656634 1692806 1688195
2015.01.04| 1686011 1708072 1687046
2015.01.05| 1676870 1683170 1699435
2015.01.06| 1673952 1676820 1687553
2015.01.07| 1683041 1680907 1692974
2015.01.08| 1661363 1688660 1675261
2015.01.09| 1692126 1693217 1690017
2015.01.10| 1698429 1699250 1679042
```

It is an instructive exercise to write unpivot, which takes a pivoted table and reverts the columns back to rows.

10 Execution Control

10.0 Overview

Basic function application in q provides sequential evaluation of a series of expressions. In this chapter we demonstrate how to achieve non-sequential execution in q.

10.1 Control Flow

When writing vector operations in q, the cleanest code and best performance is obtained by avoiding loops and conditional execution. For those times when you simply must write iffy or loopy code, q has versions of the usual constructs.

> **Warning**: Control flow constructs in this section involve branching in the byte code generated by the q interpreter. The offset of the branch destination is limited (currently to 255 byte codes), which means that the sequence of q expressions that can be contained in any part of ($), (?), (if), (do), or (while) must be short. At some point, insertion of one additional statement will break the camel's back, resulting in a 'branch error. This is q's way of rejecting bloated code. In this situation, factor code blocks into separate functions. Better yet, restructure your code.

10.1.1 Basic Conditional Evaluation

Languages of C heritage have a form of in-line *if*, called conditional evaluation, of the form,

$$expr_{cond} \; ? \; expr_{true} \; : \; expr_{false}$$

where $expr_{cond}$ is an expression that evaluates to a Boolean (or int in C and C++). The result of the expression is $expr_{true}$ when $expr_{cond}$ is true (or non-zero) and $expr_{false}$ otherwise.

The same effect can be achieved in q using the triadic overload of ($).

$$\$[expr_{cond}; \; expr_{true}; \; expr_{false}]$$

Here $expr_{cond}$ is an expression that evaluates to a boolean **atom**. Analogous to C, the result of $expr_{cond}$ can be any type whose

316

underlying value is an integer. The result of the conditional is the evaluation of $expr_{true}$ when $expr_{cond}$ is not zero and $expr_{false}$ if it is zero.

```
q)$[1b;42;9*6]
42
q)$[0b;42;9*6]
—
```

> **Tip:** The conditional ($) is a function that always returns a value. It is good practice for $expr_{true}$ and $expr_{cond}$ to have the same type. This is not enforced in q as it is in statically typed functional languages.

The brackets in any q conditional do **not** create lexical scope. This means that variables created within the body exist in the same scope as the conditional. For example, in a fresh q session the variable a in the following is a global that persists outside the conditional.

```
q)a
'a
q)$[1b;a:42;a:43]
42
q)a
42
```

Although evaluation of function arguments in q is eager, evaluation of the expressions in the conditional is short circuited, meaning that only the one selected for return is evaluated. Again in a fresh q session,

```
q)a
'a
q)b
'b
q)$[1b;a:42;b:43]
42
q)a
42
q)b
'b
```

Observe that a test for zero in $expr_{cond}$ is redundant: remove that test and reverse the order of the second and third arguments.

```
q)z:0
q)$[z=0;1.1;-1.1]
1.1
q)$[z;-1.1;1.1]    / equivalent to previous
1.1
```

In contrast with earlier versions of q, some null values are now acceptable for $expr_{cond}$. It is the same as testing for null with the operator (null).

317

```
q)v:0N
q)$[v;`isnull;`notnull]
`isnull
q)$[null v;`isnull;`notnull]
_
```

> **Tip:** Float nulls do not work so the above is probably an accident and you should not count on it

10.1.2 Extended Conditional Evaluation

In languages of C heritage, the *if-else* statement has the form,

```
if (exprcond) {
        statementtrue1;
        .
        .
        .
}
else {
        statementfalse1;
        .
        .
        .
}
```

where $expr_{cond}$ is an expression that evaluates to a Boolean (or int in C and C++). If the expression $expr_{cond}$ is true (i.e., non-zero) the first sequence of statements in braces is executed; otherwise, the second sequence of statements in braces is executed.

A similar effect can be achieved in q using an extended form of conditional evaluation with ($).

$$\$[expr_{cond}; [expr_{true1}; ...]; [expr_{false1}; ...]]$$

where $expr_{cond}$ is an expression as in the basic conditional. When $expr_{cond}$ evaluates to non-zero, the first bracketed sequence of expressions is evaluated in left-to-right order; otherwise, the second bracketed sequence of expressions is evaluated.

```
q)v:42
q)$[v=42; [a:6;b:7;`Everything]; [a:`Life;b:`the;c:`Universe;a,b,c]]
`Everything
q)$[v=43; [a:6;b:7;`everything]; [a:`Life;b:`the;c:`Universe;a,b,c]]
`Life`the`Universe
```

The extended forms of the conditional are still functions with return values. If you are using them strictly for side effects, you are writing imperative, non-vector code and should consider VBA as an alternative.

Languages of C heritage have a cascading form of if-else in which multiple tests can be made,

```
if (expr_cond1) {
    statement_true11;
    .
    .
    .
}
else if (expr_condn) {
    statement_truen1;
    .
    .
    .
}
.
.
.
else {
    statement_false;
    .
    .
    .
}
}
```

In this construction, the $expr_{cond}$ are evaluated consecutively until one is true (non-zero), at which point the associated block of statements is executed and the statement is complete. If none of the expressions passes, the final block of statements, called the *default* case, is executed.

A similar effect can be achieved in q with another extended form of conditional execution.

$$\$[expr_{cond1}; expr_{true1}; \ldots; expr_{condn}; expr_{truen}; expr_{false}]$$

In this form, the conditional expressions are evaluated consecutively until one is non-zero, at which point the associated $expr_{true}$ is evaluated and its result is returned. If none of the conditional expressions evaluates to non-zero, $expr_{false}$ is evaluated and its result is returned. Observe that $expr_{false}$ is the only expression that is not part of a pair, as it has no guarding conditional expression.

> **Tip:** Any condition other than the first is only evaluated if all those prior to it have evaluated to zero. Otherwise put, a condition evaluating to non-zero short-circuits the evaluation of subsequent ones.
>
> ```
> q)a:0
> q)$[a=0;`zero; a>0;`pos; `neg]
> `zero
> q)a:42
> q)$[a=0;`zero; a>0;`pos; `neg]
>
> q)a:-42
> q)$[a=0;`zero; a>0;`pos; `neg]
>
> ```

Finally, the previous extended form of conditional execution can be further extended by substituting a bracketed sequence of expressions for any $expr_{true}$ or $expr_{false}$.

```
$[expr_{cond1}; [expr_{true11}; ...]; ...;
  expr_{condn}; [expr_{truen1}; ...];
  [expr_{false1}; ...]]
```

If you use this, have the decency to align your code properly so that q coders can identify it as bogus q at a glance.

> **Tip:** After a brief Zen meditation, you realize that you can implement "switch" with a dictionary.

10.1.3 Vector Conditional Evaluation

Triadic vector-conditional evaluation (?) has the form,

$$?[v_b; expr_{true}; expr_{false}]$$

where v_b is a simple boolean list and $expr_{true}$ and $expr_{false}$ are of the same type and are either atoms or vectors that conform to v_b. The result conforms to v_b and selects from $expr_{true}$ in positions where v_b is 1b and $expr_{false}$ in positions where v_b has 0b. All arguments of vector-conditional are fully executed. In other words, there is no short circuiting of evaluation.

The following example chooses 42 for items in a list that are multiples of 3.

```
q)L:til 10
q)?[L mod 3; L; 42]
42 1 2 42 4 5 42 7 8 42
```

Vector conditional is especially useful with table columns.

```
q)t:([] c1:1.1 2.2 3.3; c2:10 20 30; c3:100 200 300)
q)update mix:?[c1>2.0; c3; c2] from t
_
```

There are no extended forms of vector conditional. You can get a cascading effect by nesting vector conditional expressions but, like other conditionals, it is subject to the restriction that no internal code jump can exceed 255 byte codes. This limits the degree of nesting that can be used in practice. With t as above,

```
q)update band:?[c2 within 5 15; 1; ?[c2 within 16 25; 2; 3]] from t
_
```

10.1.4 if

The imperative (if) statement conditionally evaluates a sequence of expressions. It is not a function and does not return a value. It has the form,

$$if[expr_{cond}; expr_1; ...; expr_n]$$

The $expr_{cond}$ is evaluated and if it is non-zero the expressions $expr_1$ thru $expr_n$ are evaluated in left-to-right order. As with other conditionals, the brackets do not create lexical scope, so variables defined in the body exist in the same scope as the (if).

> **Tip:** There is no "else" to go with (if). Should you find that this cramps your coding style, please see the previous recommendation about VBA.

Here is an example that creates two global variables and modifies one.

```
q)a:42
q)b:98.6
q)if[a=42;x:6;y:7;b:a*b]
q)x
6
q)y
_
q)b
_
```

> **Tip:** Well-written q code rarely needs (if). One example of legitimate use is pre-checking function arguments to abort execution for bad values.

10.1.5 do

The imperative (do) statement allows repeated execution of a block of statements. It has the form,

$$do[expr_{count}; \ expr_1; \ \ldots; \ expr_n]$$

where $expr_{count}$ must evaluate to an non-negative integer. The expressions $expr_1$ thru $expr_n$ are evaluated $expr_{count}$ times in left-to-right order. Note that (do) is a statement, not a function, and does not have an explicit result.

The following expression is a loopy computation of *n* factorial. It iterates *n* - 1 times, decrementing the factor f on each pass.

```
q)n:5
q)do[-1+f:r:n; r*:f-:1] / do not do this!
q)r
```

> **Tip:** The best recommendation about usage of (do) is: Don't!

The only legitimate use of (do) that the author has encountered is to time the execution of a q expression that runs too quickly for the timer to get an accurate reading, but this has been obviated by the enhanced \t command.

```
q)\t v*v:til 1000000
15
q)\t do[100; v*v:til 1000000]
677
q)\t 100 v*v:til1000000
—
```

10.1.6 while

The imperative (while) statement is an iterator of the form,

$$while[expr_{cond}; \ expr_1; \ \ldots; \ expr_n]$$

where $expr_{cond}$ is evaluated and the expressions $expr_1$ thru $expr_n$ are evaluated repeatedly in left-to-right order as long as $expr_{cond}$ is non-zero. The (while) statement is not a function, does not have an explicit result and does not introduce lexical scope.

> **Tip:** The author has never used (while) in actual code.

Here is loopy factorial redone with (while).

```
q)f:r:n:5
q)while[f-:1;r*:f]        / do not do this either!
q)r
120
```

10.1.7 Return and Signal

Normal function application evaluates each expression in the function body in sequence and terminates after the last one. There are two mechanisms for ending the execution early: one indicates successful completion and the other signals abrupt termination.

To terminate function application immediately and return a normal value, use an empty assignment—that is, (:) with the return value to its right and no variable to its left. For example, in the following instrumented function, application is terminated and the result is returned in the fourth expression. The final expression is never evaluated.

```
q)f:{0N!"Begin"; a:x; b:y; :a*b; "End"}
q)f[6;7]
"Begin"
42
```

To abort function execution immediately with an exception, use *signal*, which is single-quote (') , with an error message to its right. The error message can be provided as a symbol or string.

You too can return pithy error messages. For example, in the following function, execution will be aborted in the fourth expression. The final expression that assigns c is never evaluated.

```
q)g:{0N!"Begin"; a:x; b:y; '"End"; a:b}
q)g[6;7]
"Begin"
'End
```

A function issuing a signal causes the calling routine to fail and this will ripple all the way up the call chain unless protected evaluation is used to trap the exception. See the next section for details on protected evaluation.

A legitimate use of the (if) statement is to terminate execution with an exception. The following snippet would typically reside inside a function body.

```
{
    ...
    if[a<50; '"Bad a"];
    ...
}
```

10.1.8 Protected Evaluation

Languages of C++ heritage have the concept of protected execution using try-catch. The idea is that an unexpected condition arising from any statement enclosed in the try portion does not abort the program. Instead, control transfers to the catch block, where the exception can be handled or passed up to the caller. This mechanism allows the call stack to be unwound gracefully.

Q provides a similar capability using triadic forms of function application. Triadic (@) is used for monadic functions and triadic (.) is used for multivalent functions. The syntax is the same for both.

$$@[f_{mon}; \; a; \; expr_{fail}]$$

$$.[f_{mul}; \; L_{args}; \; expr_{fail}]$$

Here f_{mon} is a monadic function, a is single argument, f_{mul} is a multivalent function, L_{args} is a list of arguments, and $expr_{fail}$ is an expression or function. In both forms, the function is applied to its argument(s). Upon successful application, protected evaluation returns the result of the application. Should an exception arise, $expr_{fail}$ is applied to the resulting error string.

Tip: You can use protected evaluation to log error messages from exceptions that would otherwise crash your program.

Important: If the application of $expr_{fail}$ results in an exception, the protected call itself will fail.

Here is a simple example of using protected evaluation. Suppose a user wishes to enter dynamic q expressions. You could place the expression in a string and pass it to (value) which is essentially the q interpreter. This is a huge security exposure and you should never do this is such a naïve fashion in a production system. Nonetheless, we could do it in a learning environment. The problem is that if the user types an invalid q expression, the generated exception will cause your application to halt. To avoid this, apply (value) with protected evaluation.

```
s:"6*7"
@[value; s; show]
42

q)s:"6*`7"
q)@[value; s; show]
"type"
```

Triadic (.) provides similar protected evaluation for multivalent functions.

```
q)prod:{x*y}
q).[prod; (6;7); show]
42
q).[prod; (6;`7); show]
"type"
```

10.2 Debugging

Debugging in q harkens back to the bad old days, before the advent of debuggers and integrated development environments, when "real men" debugged by inserting `println` in their code. The q gods don't give debugging much consideration because their code always runs correctly the first time. There is no debugger, nor any notion of break points or tracing execution. Things aren't quite as bad as inserting print statements, but we mortals are certainly left to our own devices.

When expression evaluation fails, the console displays a backtick followed by a short and often cryptic error message. This is followed by a dump of the failed operation and the offending values. Many errors manifest as either 'type or 'length, indicating an incompatibility in function arguments somewhere in the bowels of q. The challenge is to discover the root cause of the error.

Since q is interpreted, at any point in the execution of a program the entire runtime environment is accessible. If you think about it, an integrated debugger for a compiled language essentially simulates the interpreter environment. The debugger must go to great lengths to create the environment that is readily available in an interpreter.

Let's get real. Say you want to set a breakpoint in your q program. Easy: just insert a line that you know will fail—use an undefined name.

For example, to pause execution before the last expression in the function f below, insert any undefined name there—"break" is commonly used.

```
q)f:{a:x*x; b:y*y; a+b}

q)f:{a:x*x; b:y*y; break; a+b}
q)f[3;4]
{a:x*x; b:y*y; break; a+b}
'break
q))
```

> **Tip:** Make sure the name you choose is not defined in local or global scope.

In a q session, you can tell that execution has been suspended by the extra parenthesis at the q prompt. At this point, you have the full power of the q console available to inspect the current state of your program.

```
q))x
3
q))y
4
q))a
_
q))b
_
q))a+b
_
```

> **Tip:** Once you have finished your inspection and debugging, you should either return from the function with a value or abort execution using (\). In either case, the extra ")" at the q prompt will disappear.
>
> ```
> q)):abs
> 25
> ```

A slightly more sophisticated technique allows you to continue execution after the break. Here we cause the break one level lower. A forced return entered at the console completes the breakpoint execution and continues execution of f.

```
q)breakpoint:{break}

q)f:{a:x*x; b:y*y; breakpoint[]; a+b}
q)f[3;4]
{break}
'break
q)):0            / arbitrary value is not used
25
```

326

You can accomplish single step tracing after suspended execution by copy/paste of one line at a time into the console. Admittedly this is pretty primitive but if you write well-factored q code there shouldn't be too many lines to copy. This works well enough in practice that it is not a hindrance to finding and correcting bugs.

Tip: You will spend much more time trying to figure out why your q code is not doing what you want than the time spent doing manual debugging.

In a technique passed on by Simon Garland, you can get a useful display of relevant information when a function is suspended. Define a function, say zs, as follows,

```
q)zs:{`d`P`L`G`D!(system"d"),v[1 2 3],enlist last v:value x}
```

This function takes another function as its argument and returns a dictionary with entries for the current directory, function parameters, local variables referenced, global variables referenced and the function definition. We demonstrate with a trivial example.

```
q)b:7
q)f:{a:6; x+a*b}

q)f[`100]    / this is an error
{a:6; x+a*b}
'type
+
`100
42

q))show zs f
d|  `.
P| ,`x
L| ,`a
G| `b
D| "{a:6; x+a*b}"
```

This error dump is actually easy to read. The first line is the definition of the function that has failed. Following that is the error message 'type. The operation that generated the error is (+) and the actual arguments follow. Then our zs gives a nice tabulation of the current context (the root namespace in this case), the parameters of f, the local variables of f, the global variables of f and finally its definition.

A good place to start with zs when you have suspended execution is with the system variable .z.s that holds the suspended function itself.

```
q)zs .z.s
```

10.3 Scripts

A *script* is a q program stored in a text file with an extension of ".q" (or ".k" if you are writing k code). A script can contain any q expressions or commands. The contents of the script are parsed and evaluated sequentially from top to bottom. Global entities created during execution of the script exist in the workspace after the script is loaded and executed.

10.3.1 Creating and Loading a Script

You can create a script in any text editor and save it with a ".q" extension. For example, enter the following script that creates the trades table from Chapter 9.

```
mktrades:{[tickers; sz]
  dt:2015.01.01+sz?31;
  tm:sz?24:00:00.000;
  sym:sz?tickers;
  qty:10*1+sz?1000;
  px:90.0+(sz?2001)%100;
  t:([] dt; tm; sym; qty; px);
  t:`dt`tm xasc t;
  t:update px:6*px from t where sym=`goog;
  t:update px:2*px from t where sym=`ibm;
  t}
```

```
trades:mktrades[`aapl`goog`ibm; 1000000]
```

Now issue the following command to load and execute the script.

```
q)\l /q4m/trades.q
```

Verify that the `trades` table has been created and the records have been inserted.

```
q)count trades
```

A script can be loaded at any time during a session using the (\l) command, called *load*. The load command can be executed programmatically using (system). See Chapter 12 for more on commands.

You can have q load a script on startup by placing its name after the call to the q executable on the operating system command line.

```
$q /q4m/trades.q
KDB+ 3.2 …
q)
q)count trades
1000000
```

10.3.2 Blocks

You can comment out a block of code (i.e., multiple lines) in a script by surrounding it with matching '/' and '\' with each at the beginning of its own line. An unmatched '\' at the beginning of a line exits the script.

Here is a script that demonstrates block comments.

```
a:42
b:0
/
this is a block of
comment text
b:42
and b will not be changed
\
a:43            / this line will be executed
\
nothing from here on will be executed
b:44
```

Immediately after this script is loaded, a will be 43 and b will be 0.

Multi-line expressions are permitted in a script but they have a special form.

- The first line must **not** be indented—i.e., it begins at the left of the line with no initial whitespace.
- Any continuation lines **must** be indented, meaning that there is at least one whitespace character at the beginning of the line.
- In particular, if you put the closing brace to a function definition on its own line, it **must** be indented. Do **not** use the common C style of aligning the closing brace with the function name.
- Empty lines and comment lines (beginning with '/') are permitted anywhere.

329

Table definition and function definition provide nice opportunities for splitting across multiple lines:

- A table can have line breaks after a closing square bracket ']' or after a semicolon separator ';'
- A function can have line breaks after a closing square bracket ']' or after a comma separator ','

10.3.3 Passing Parameters

Parameters are passed to a q script at q startup similarly to argv command line parameters in C. Specifically, the system variable .z.x comprises a list of strings, each containing the character representation of an argument present on the command line that invoked the script. For example, let's modify our trades.q script to pass the number of records to be created as a command line parameter. Note that we parse the passed string to an integer.

```
mktrades:{[tickers; sz]
  dt:2015.01.01+sz?31;
  tm:sz?24:00:00.000;
  sym:sz?tickers;
  qty:10*1+sz?1000;
  px:90.0+(sz?2001)%100;
  t:([] dt; tm; sym; qty; px);
  t:`dt`tm xasc t;
  t:update px:6*px from t where sym=`goog;
  t:update px:2*px from t where sym=`ibm;
  t}

size:"I"$.z.x 0

trades:mktrades[`aapl`goog`ibm; size]
```

Now we invoke the script with the parameter 2000000.

```
>q /q4m/trades.q 2000000
KDB+ 3.2 …
q)count trades
2000000
```

As of this writing (Sep 2015), parameters can be passed when a script is loaded at q startup but **not** when a script is loaded with (\l) or system "l".

Tip: If you put any extra space immediately after \l you will get an error.

---

11 I/O

11.0 Overview

I/O in q is one of the most powerful and succinct features of the language. The names and behavior of the functions are idiosyncratic but the economy of expression is unrivaled.

I/O is realized via *handles*, which are symbolic names of resources such as files or machines on a network. One-and-done operations can be performed directly on the symbolic handle—e.g., you can read a file into memory in a single operation. For continuing operations, you open the symbolic handle to obtain an *open handle*. The open handle is a function that is applied to perform operations. When you have completed the desired operations, you close the open handle to free any allocated resources.

11.1 Binary Data

In q, files come in two flavors: text and binary. Routines to process text data have '0' in their names, whereas routines to process binary data have '1'. A text file is considered to be a list of strings—i.e., a list of char lists—and a binary file is a list of byte lists. While all text files can also be processed as binary data, not all binary data represents text. As mentioned above, file operations use handles.

11.1.1 File Handles

A *file handle* is a symbol that represents the name of a directory or file on persistent storage. A symbolic file handle starts with a colon ':' and has the form,

        `:[path]name

where the bracketed expression represents an optional path and *name* is a file or directory name. The combination should be recognized as valid by the underlying operating system.

> **Tip:** Some q operations require that you append a trailing slash '/' to indicate that you mean a directory. We will point these out.

It is generally easier to work with paths and names as strings so that blanks and other special characters can be handled easily. While (`$) converts a string to a symbol, it can be awkward to include the leading ':' required in the symbolic handle. The operator (hsym), which inserts a leading colon into a symbol, serves this purpose.

```
q)hsym `$"/data/file name.csv"
`:/data/file name.csv
```

Note that q always represents separators in paths by the forward slash '/', even when running on Windows. If you run q on Windows, you can type either '/' or '\' but q will always display '/' in its response.

Tip: To make life easier when you are generating paths dynamically, (hsym) is idempotent, meaning that it will accept its own output and pass it through.

```
q)hsym hsym `$"/data/file name.csv"
```

11.1.2 hcount and hdel

The first one-and-done operation that works directly on a symbolic file handle is (hcount), which returns a long representing the size of the file in bytes as reported the OS.

```
q)hcount `:/data/solong.txt
35
```

The next one-and-done is (hdel), which instructs the OS to remove the file specified its symbolic handle operand.

```
q)hdel `:/data/solong.txt
`:/data/solong.txt
```

Some notes.

- The return value of the symbolic file handle itself indicates that the deletion was successful. It should not be confused with an error message, which starts with a tick rather than a backtick.
- You will get an error message if the file does not exist or if the delete cannot be performed.
- You will not be prompted for confirmation. Back up any files that are important.

11.1.3 Serializing and Deserializing q Entities

Every q entity can be serialized and persisted to storage. Unlike traditional languages, where you must instantiate serializers and writers, things are simple and direct in q. This is because q data is self-describing, so that its internal representation can be written out as a sequence of bytes and then read directly back into memory. This is as close to the Star Trek transporter as we are likely to get.

The magic is done by (an overload of) the dyadic (set), whose left operand is a file handle and right operand is the entity to be written. The result is the symbolic handle of the written file. The file is automatically closed once the write is complete.

```
q)`:/data/a set 42
`:/data/a
q)`:/data/L set 10 20 30

q)`:/data/t set ([] c1:`a`b`c; c2:10 20 30)
```

> **Note:** The behavior of (set) is to create the file if it does not exist and overwrite it if it does. It will also create the directory path if it does not exist.

A serialized q data file can be read using (an overload of) the monadic (get), whose argument is a symbolic file handle and whose result is the q entity contained in the data file.

```
q)get `:/data/a
42
q)get `:/data/L

q)get `:/data/t
```

An equivalent way to read a data file is with (an overload of) (value).

```
q)value `:/data/t
```

Alternatively, you can use the command (\l) to load a data file into memory and assign it to a variable with the same name as the file. Here you do **not** use a file handle; rather, specify the path to the file without any decoration. In a fresh q session,

```
q)t
't
q)\l /data/t
't
q)t
_
```

11.1.4 Binary Data Files

As with traditional languages, for continuing operations on a q data file, you open the file, perform the operation(s) and then close it. Unlike traditional languages, opening a symbolic handle returns a function, called an open handle, that is used to perform operations.

As mentioned previously, q files come in two flavors, binary and text. Serialized q data persisted with (set) is written in binary form with a header at the beginning of the file. You can read it as raw binary data to inspect its internals.

Open a data file handle with (hopen), whose result is a function called the *open handle*. This function should be stored in a variable, traditionally h, which is functionally applied to data to write it to the file. We will explain the result of applying the open handle shortly. We begin with a file containing serialized q data and show how to append to it.

```
q)`:/data/L set 10 20 30
`:/data/L

q)h:hopen `:/data/L
q)h[42]
3i
q)h 100 200
3i
```

> **Tip:** Always apply (hclose) to the open handle to close it and flush any data that might be buffered. Failure to do so may cause your program to run out of file handles unnecessarily.

We verify that the appends have been made.

```
q)hclose h

q)get `:/data/L
10 20 30 42 100 200
```

We can also create a new file and write raw binary data to it.

334

```
q)h:hopen `:/data/raw
q)h[42]
3i
q)h 10 20 30
3i
q)hclose h
```

Now, what is the deal with the 3i return value of applying the open handle?

```
q)h:hopen `:/data/raw
q)h 43
3i
```

In fact, the return value is the value of the open handle itself.

```
q)h
3i
```

Surely, you say, we can't use an int as a function to write data. But you would be wrong.

```
q)h:hopen `:/data/new
q)h
3i
q)3i[100 200 300]
3i
q)hclose 3i
q)get `:/data/new
_
```

> **Tip:** Apparently q assigns an int to each open file and keeps track of which int values are valid handles. This accounts for the cryptic error message when you attempt to use variables with simple list notation.
>
> ```
> q)a:42
> q)b:43
> q)a b
> ': Bad file descriptor
> ```

11.1.5 Writing and Reading Binary

Apply (read1) on a file handle to read **any** file into q as a list of bytes. For example, we can read the previously serialized value L as bytes.

```
q)read1 `:/data/L set 10 20 30
0xfe200700000000000300000000000000a0000000000000014000000000000001e..
```

This shows the internal representation of the serialized q entity. How cool is that?

If you want to write raw binary data, as opposed to the internal representation of a q entity containing the data, use the infelicitously named (1:). It takes a symbolic file handle as its left argument and a simple byte list as its right argument. Bytes in the right operand are essentially streamed to the file.

```
q)`:/data/answer.bin 1:  0x06072a
`:/data/answer.bin
q)read1 `:/data/answer.bin
0x06072a
```

11.1.6 Using Dot Amend

Fundamentalists can use dot amend in place of (set) to serialize q entities to files. To write the file, or overwrite an existing file, use assign (:).

```
q).[`:/data/raw; (); :; 1001 1002 1003]
`:/data/raw
q)get `:/data/raw
1001 1002 1003
```

To append to an existing file use (,).

```
q).[`:/data/raw; (); ,; 42]
`:/data/raw
q)get `:/data/raw
1001 1002 1003 42
```

11.2 Save and Load on Tables

We have already seen that it is easy to write and read tables to/from persistent storage.

```
q)`:/data/t set ([] c1:`a`b`c; c2:10 20 30; c3:1.1 2.2 3.3)
`:/data/t
q)get `:/data/t
```

The (save) and (load) functions make this even easier.

In its simplest form, (save) serializes a table in a **global** variable to a binary file having the same name as the variable. It overwrites an existing file.

```
q)t:([] c1:`a`b`c; c2:10 20 30; c3:1.1 2.2 3.3)
q)save `:/data/t
`:/data/t
q)get `:/data/t
_
```

This is equivalent to using (set) above with the table name as file name.

As you might expect, (load) is the inverse of (save) meaning that it reads a serialized table from a file into a variable with the same name as the file. It creates the variable in the workspace or overwrites it if it already exists.

In a fresh q session after t has been saved as above,

```
q)t          / t doesn't exist
't
q)load `:/data/t
`t
q)t          / now it does
_
```

You can also use (save) to write a table to a text file. You determine the format of the text with the file extension in the file handle.

Tip: All the following versions of (save) can also be performed with the more general (0:)—see §11.5.

Save the table with ".txt" extension to obtain tab-delimited records. There is no corresponding (load) but you can parse the text file—see §11.5.1.

```
q)save `:data/t.txt
`:data/t.txt
```

The resulting file is,

```
c1\tc2\tc3
a\t10\t1.1
b\t20\t2.2
c\t30\t3.3
```

Save the table with ".csv" extension to obtain comma-separated values. There is no corresponding (load) but you can parse the csv file—see §11.5.2.

```
q)save `:data/t.csv
`:data/t.csv
```

The resulting file is,

```
c1,c2,c3
a,10,1.1
b,20,2.2
c,30,3.3
```

Save the table with ".xml" extension obtain xml records. There is no direct way to read xml into q although libraries have been contributed—see code.kx.com.

```
q)save `:data/t.xml
`:data/t.xml
```

The resulting file is,

```
<R>
<r><c1>a</c1><c2>10</c2><c3>1.1</c3></r>
<r><c1>b</c1><c2>20</c2><c3>2.2</c3></r>
<r><c1>c</c1><c2>30</c2><c3>3.3</c3></r>
</R>
```

Save the table with ".xls" extension obtain an Excel spreadsheet. This file can be loaded by Excel work-alikes.

```
q)save `:data/t.xls
`:data/t.xls
```

11.3 Splayed Tables

We have already seen how to persist a table to a file using (set). There are no restrictions on the types of columns in the table or the file name in this scenario.

```
q)`:/data/t set ([] c1:`a`b`c; c2:10 20 30; c3:1.1 2.2 3.3)
`:/data/t
q)get `:/data/t
```

This creates a single file, as the OS verifies.

```
>ls -l /data/t
-rw-r--r--  1 jeffry  wheel  98 Mar  6 08:22 /data/t
```

For larger tables that may not fit into memory on all machines, you can ask q to serialize each column of the table to its own file in a specified directory. A table persisted in this form is called a *splayed* table. The advantage is that when querying a splayed table, only the columns referred to in the query will be loaded into memory. This is a substantial memory win for a table having many columns.

338

> **Tip**: It is worthwhile looking up the origin of the English word "splay". Also, please don't spay your tables.

To splay a table, use (set) and specify a directory as the target location indicated by a trailing slash '/' in the left operand.

```
q)`:/data/tsplay/ set ([] c1:10 20 30; c2:1.1 2.2 3.3)
`:/data/tsplay/
```

List the directory in the OS and you will see a directory `tsplay` that contains three files, one file for each column in the original table, as well as a hidden .d file.

```
>ls -l -d /data/tsplay
drwxr-xr-x  5 jeffry  wheel  170 Mar  6 08:36 /data/tsplay

>ls -l -a  /data/tsplay
total 24
drwxr-xr-x  5 jeffry  wheel  170 Mar  6 08:36 .
drwxr-xr-x  9 jeffry  wheel  306 Mar  6 08:36 ..
-rw-r--r--  1 jeffry  wheel   14 Mar  6 08:36 .d
-rw-r--r--  1 jeffry  wheel   40 Mar  6 08:36 c1
-rw-r--r--  1 jeffry  wheel   40 Mar  6 08:36 c2
```

Nearly all the metadata regarding the splayed table can be read from the file system—i.e., the name of table from directory and names of the columns from the files. The one missing bit is the order of the columns, which is stored as a serialized list in the hidden .d file.

```
q)get hsym `$"/data/tsplay/.d"
`c1`c2
```

> **Important:** There are restrictions on tables that can be splayed.
>
> - All columns must be simple or *compound* lists. The latter means a list of simple lists of uniform type. An arbitrary general list column cannot be splayed.
>
> - Symbol columns must be enumerated.

Thus the following succeed.

```
q)`:/data/tok/ set ([] c1:2000.01.01+til 3; c2:1 2 3)
`:/data/tok/

q)`:/data/tok/ set ([] c1:1 2 3; c2:(1.1 2.2; enlist 3.3; 4.4 5.5))
`:/data/tok/
```

And the following fail.

```
q)`:/data/toops/ set ([] c1:1 2 3; c2:(1;`1;"a"))
k){$[@x;.[x;();::;y];-19!((,y),x)]}
'type

q)`:/data/toops/ set ([] c1:`a`b`c; c2:10 20 30)
k){$[@x;.[x;();::;y];-19!((,y),x)]}
'type
```

The convention for enumerating symbols in splayed tables is to enumerate all symbol columns in all tables over the domain sym and store the resulting sym list in the root directory—i.e., one level above the directory holding the splayed table. You can do this manually but practically no one does.

```
q)`:/db/tsplay/ set ([] `sym?c1:`a`b`c; c2:10 20 30)
`:/db/tsplay/
q)sym
`a`b`c
q)`:/db/sym set sym
`:/db/sym
```

Normally folks use one of the .Q utilities, in spite of the official Kx admonition not to use them. For example, here we use (.Q.en).

```
q)`:/db/tsplay/ set .Q.en[`:/db; ([] c1:`a`b`c; c2:10 20 30)]
`:/db/tsplay/
```

Only unofficially documented, (.Q.en) prepares a qualified table for splaying by enumerating all its symbol columns. The first argument is the symbolic file handle of the root directory for the persistent residence of the enumeration domain sym (no choice in the name). The second argument is a table. See §14.5.2 for more detail on its behavior.

11.4 Text Data

We have seen that q views a record in a binary data file as a list of bytes. Similarly, a record in a text file is viewed as a list of char—i.e., a string. Thus reading a text file results in a list of strings and you pass a list of strings to write to a text file.

11.4.1 Reading and Writing Text Files

Read a text file with the monadic (read0) that takes a symbolic file handle argument. The result is a list of strings, one for each line in the file. For the file /data/solong.txt with content,

```
So long
and thanks
for all the fish
```

we find,

```
q)read0 `:/data/solong.txt
"So long"
"and thanks"
"for all the fish"
```

You can see the underlying binary values of the text by using (read1) or casting the result of (read0) to char.

```
q)read1 `:/data/solong.txt
_
q)"x"$read0 `:/data/solong.txt
0x4c696665
0x54686520556e6976657273650
0x416e6420457665727974686696e67
```

Or you can read the data as binary and cast the result to char. Observe that the data is a simple list of char so the newline character does not cause line breaks in the console display.

```
q)"c"$read1 `:/data/solong.txt
"Life\nThe Universe\nAnd Everything\n"
```

To write string as text use the (infelicitously named) dyadic (0:), which takes a file handle in the left operand and a list of strings in the right operand. It creates the directory path if necessary and overwrites the file if it already exists.

```
q)`:/data/solong.txt 0: ("Life"; "The Universe"; "And Everything")
`:/data/solong.txt
q)read0 `:/data/solong.txt
_
```

11.4.2 Using hopen and hclose

Just as with a binary data file, a symbolic text file handle can be opened with (hopen). The result is again an int that is conventionally stored in the variable h and is used with function application syntax to write data. The difference is that instead of using plain h to write binary data, you use neg[h] to write strings as text. Seriously.

341

```
q)h:hopen `:/data/new.txt
q)neg[h] enlist "This"
-3i
q)neg[h] ("and"; "that")
-3i
q)hclose h
q)read0 `:/data/new.txt
_
```

Tip: Observe that you apply (hclose) to h, not to neg[h].

If the file already exists, opening with (hopen) and applying the open handle will append rather than overwrite.

```
q)h:hopen `:/data/new.txt
q)neg[h] ("and"; "more")
-3i
q)hclose h
q)read0 `:/data/new.txt
_
```

11.4.3 Preparing Text

We saw the built-in functions for saving tables as text files in §11.2. When you need to control the filename, you can write the table yourself with (0:), but then you must prepare the table columns as formatted text. A separate overload of (0:) is available for this purpose. A confusing naming convention, to say the least.

In this use, (0:) has left operand a char delimiter and right operand a table or list of columns. Observe the use of the pre-defined constant csv, which is simply ",".

```
q)t:([] c1:`a`b`c; c2:1 2 3)
q)"\t" 0: t
"c1\tc2"
"a\t1"
"b\t2"
"c\t3"
q)"|" 0: t
_
q)csv
","
q)csv 0: t
_
q)`:/data/t.csv 0: csv 0: t
_
```

In the last snippet we applied (0:) with two different meanings: to prepare and then write text. We hope you've grown fond of this name, since §11.5 will introduce yet another version of (0:) for parsing text records.

342

11.5 Parsing Records

Dyadic forms of (0:) and (1:) parse individual fields according to data type from text or binary records. Field parsing is based on the following field types.

0	1	Type	Width(1)	Format(0)
B	b	boolean	1	[1tTyY]
X	x	byte	1	
H	h	short	2	[0-9a-fA-F][0-9a-fA-F]
I	i	int	4	
J	j	long	8	
E	e	real	4	
F	f	float	8	
C	c	char	1	
	s	symbol	n	
S				
P	p	timestamp	8	date?timespan
M	m	month	4	[yy]yy[?]mm
D	d	date	4	[yy]yy[?]mm[?]dd [m]m/[d]d/[yy]yy
Z	z	datetime	8	date?time hh[:]mm[:]ss[[.]ddddddddd
N	n	timespan	8	
U	u	minute	4	hh[:]mm
V	v	second	4	hh[:]mm[:]ss
T	t	time	4	hh[:]mm[:]ss[[.]ddd]
blank	skip			
*				literal chars

The column labeled '0' contains the (upper case) field type char for text data. The (lower case) char in column '1' is for binary data. The column labeled 'Width(1)' contains the number of bytes that will be parsed for a binary read. The column labeled 'Format(0)' displays the format(s) that are accepted in a text read.

343

> **Tip:** The parsed records are returned in column form rather than row form to make it easy to associate a list of symbol names with (!) and then flip into a table.

11.5.1 Fixed Width Records

The dyadic form of (0:) and (1:) for reading fixed length files is,

$$(L_t; L_w) \; 0: \; f$$

$$(L_t; L_w) \; 1: \; f$$

The left operand is a nested list containing two items: L_t is a simple list of char containing one letter per field; L_w is a simple list of int containing one integer width per field. The sum of the field widths in L_w should equal the width of the record. The result of the function is a list of lists, one list arising from each field.

We demonstrate (0:) here since it is more commonly used; (1:) works analogously. The simplest form of the right operand f is a symbolic file handle. For example, suppose we have a file with records of the form,

```
1001   98.000ABCDEF1234Garbage2015.01.01
1002   42.001GHUJKL0123Garbage2015.01.02
1003   44.123nopqrs9876Garbage2015.01.03
```

We could parse the records of the file with,

```
q)("JFS D";4 8 10 7 10) 0: `:/data/Fixed.txt
1001       1002       1003
98         42.001     44.123
ABCDEF1234 GHUJKL0123 nopqrs9876
2015.01.01 2015.01.02 2015.01.03
```

This reads a text file containing fixed length records of width 39. The first field is a long occupying 4 positions; the second field is a float occupying 8 positions; the third field consists of a symbol occupying 10 positions; the fourth slot of 6 positions is ignored; the fifth field is a date occupying 10 positions.

You might think that the widths are superfluous, but they are not. The actual data width can be narrower than the normal size due to small values, as in our case of the long field. Or you may need to specify a width larger than that required by the corresponding data type due to whitespace in the fields, as in the case of our float field.

Observe how easy it is to make a table from the result.

```
q)flip `c1`c2`c3`c4!("JFS D";4 8 10 7 10) 0: `:/data/Fixed.txt
c1   c2      c3         c4
-----------------------------------
1001 98      ABCDEF1234 2015.01.01
1002 42.001  GHUJKL0123 2015.01.02
1003 44.123  nopqrs9876 2015.01.03
```

Also note that it is possible to parse a list of strings using the same format, since they represent text records in memory.

```
q)fixed: read0 `:/data/Fixed.txt
q)("JFS D";4 8 10 7 10) 0: fixed
_
```

The more general form for the right operand f is,

$$(h_{file}; i; n)$$

where h_{file} is a symbolic file handle, i is the offset into the file to begin reading and n is the number of bytes to read. This is useful for sampling a file or for large files that cannot be read into memory in a single gulp.

> **Tip:** A read operation should begin and end on record boundaries or you will get meaningless results.

In our trivial example, the following reads just the second and third records,

```
q)("JFS D";4 8 10 7 10) 0: (`:/data/Fixed.txt; 40; 80)
_
```

11.5.2 Variable Length Records

The dyadic form of (0:) and (1:) for reading variable length, delimited files is,

$$(L_t; D) \ 0: \ f$$

$$(L_t; D) \ 1: \ f$$

The left operand is a list comprising two lists. L_t is a simple list of char containing one type letter per corresponding field. The right operand D is either a char representing the delimiting character or an enlisted char.

Specify *D* as a delimiter char when the first record of the file does **not** contain column names. In this case, the result of the parse is a list of **column** lists, each of which contains items of type specified by L_t. The simplest form of the right operand *f* is a symbolic file handle.

For example, say we have a comma-separated file /data/Simple.csv having records,

```
1001,DBT12345678,98.6
1002,EQT98765432,24.75
1004,CCR00000001,121.23
```

Parsing with a delimiter char "," results in a list of column lists. As with parsing fixed format recodes, it is easy to make the result into a table.

```
q)("JSF"; ",") 0: read0 `:/data/Simple.csv
1001        1002        1004
DBT12345678 EQT98765432 CCR00000001
98.6        24.7        121.23
q)flip `c1`c2`c3!("JSF"; ",") 0: read0 `:/data/Simple.csv
```

Observe that it is possible to retrieve the second field as a string instead of a symbol using "*" as the data type specifier,

```
q)("J*F"; ",") 0: read0 `:/data/Simple.csv
1001          1002          1004
"DBT12345678" "EQT98765432" "CCR00000001"
98.6          24.7          121.23
```

Specify *D* as an enlisted char when the first record contains a separated list of names. Subsequent records are read as data specified by the types in L_t. The result is a table in which the column names are taken from the first record.

Say we have a comma-separated file /data/Titles.csv having records,

```
id,ticker,price
1001,DBT12345678,98.6
1002,EQT98765432,24.7
1004,CCR00000001,121.23
```

Reading with an enlisted "," delimiter results in a table.

```
q)("JSF"; enlist ",") 0: `:/data/Titles.csv
id   ticker     price
----------------------
1001 DBT12345678 98.6
1002 EQT98765432 24.7
1004 CCR00000001 121.23
```

11.5.3 Key-Value Records

The operator (0:) can also be used to process text representing key-value pairs. In this situation, the left operand is a three-character string P_f that specifies the pair format. The first char of P_f can be "S" to indicate the key is a string or "I" to indicate the key is an integer. The second char indicates the key-value separator. The third char indicates the pair delimiter.

The following examples illustrate various combinations in P_f.

```
q)"S=;" 0: "one=1;two=2;three=3"
one  two  three
,"1" ,"2" ,"3"

q)"S:/" 0: "one:1/two:2/three:3"
—

q)"I=;" 0: "1=one;2=two;3=three"
—
```

Again it is easy to make the result into a table.

```
q)flip `k`v!"I=;" 0: "1=one;2=two;3=three"
k v
---------
1 "one"
2 "two"
3 "three"
```

11.6 Interprocess Communication

The ease with which a q process can communicate with another q process residing on the network is one of the most impressive features of q. We shall cover all the basics of interprocess communication (IPC) so that you can follow the section on callbacks in Chapter 1- *Q Shock and Awe*.

We shall use the following terminology. The process that initiates the communication is called the *client*, while the process receiving and processing requests is the *server*. The server process can be on the same machine, the same network, a different network or on the Internet, so long as it is accessible. The communication can be *synchronous* (wait for a result to be returned) or *asynchronous* (don't wait and no result returned).

The only way to learn IPC is to do it, and the easiest way to do this is to set up two processes on the same machine. We recommend you use the machine running your q sessions for this tutorial, provided it will allow a port to be opened. In what follows, we shall assume that a server q process has been started on a machine with an open port.

```
>q -p 5042
q)
```

The client process is a separate q process running on the same machine.

```
>q
q)
```

11.6.1 Communication Handle

Symbolic communication handles look similar to file handles but they specify resources on the network. A communication handle has the form,

`` `:[server]:port ``

Here the bracketed expression represents an optional server machine identifier and *port* is a port number. An omitted server specification, or one of the form "localhost", refers to the machine on which the originating q session lives. The following both refer to port 5042 on the same machine as the q session in which they are entered.

```
q)`::5042

q)`:localhost:5042
```

You can refer to a machine on the network by name. For example, on the author's laptop the following is equivalent to the two previous network handles.

```
q)`:aerowing:5042
```

You can use the IP address of a machine.

```
q)`:198.162.0.2:5042
_
```

Finally, you can also use a url.

```
q)`:www.myurl.com:5042
_
```

11.6.2 Opening a Connection Handle

As with a file handle, apply (hopen) to a communication handle to obtain an open *connection handle* that is used as a function. As before, the value is an int that is traditionally stored in the variable h. Also as with file I/O, the behavior of this function differs between using the original positive handle or its negation.

Let's see how this works with our two sessions. (You did start them, didn't you?). Remember, the session that opened port 5042 is the server; the other session is the client. In the **client** session, open a handle to the server and store it in h, then apply h to the string as shown. Finally close the connection handle.

```
q)h:hopen `::5042
q)h "a:6*7"
q)h "a"
42
q)hclose h
```

> ***Tip:*** Whitespace between h and the quoted string is optional, as this is simply function juxtaposition. We include it for readability.

As you have no doubt realized, the application of h sent the string to the server to be evaluated. On the server, we see,

```
q)a
42
```

How cool is that?

11.6.3 Remote Execution

We have seen that when you open a connection to a q process, you have the full capability of that process available remotely. Apply the connection handle to any q expression in a string and it will be evaluated on the server. As you contemplate the IPC Zen, a dark cloud passes over your tranquility. You realize that, by default, the server is wide open.

> **Important:** Allowing quoted q strings to be executed on a server makes the server susceptible to all manner of breaches. Good practice does not permit this on a production server. You can mitigate this by having your server process accept only requests whose first item is a symbol (see below), which you should verify is the name of a function you have decided to expose.

An alternate format for remote execution is to apply the connection handler to a list of the form,

$$(f; arg_1; arg_2; \ldots)$$

Here f is a client-side expression that evaluates to a map that will be applied on the server. It can be:

- The value of, or variable associated to, a map on the **client**
- The symbolic name of a map on the **server**.

We use the term map here to be any q expression that can be evaluated as function application—e.g., a list on an index, a dictionary on a key or a function on an argument. Most commonly f is a function

The remaining items arg_1, arg_2, ... are optional values sent along to the server for the evaluation. These are arguments when f is a function, indices when it is a list, or keys when it is a dictionary.

Application of the connection handle to such a list sends the list to the server where it is evaluated. Any result is sent back to the client, where it is presented as the result of the connection handle application. By simply applying the naked handle, this sequence of steps is **synchronous**, meaning that execution of the q session on the client blocks until the result of the server evaluation is returned.

Our examples will cover the case when f is of function type since that is most common. We first consider the first case when f is a map on the client side. In this situation the function (list, dictionary, etc.) is actually transported to the server along with the supplied arguments, where it is applied.

On the client in our two-session setup:

```
q)h:hopen`::5042                          / client
q)h ({x*y}; 6; 7)
42
q)f:{x*y}
q)h (f; 6; 7)
42
```

Before you get too enamored of this form, we point out the limitations that disqualify it from production use. First, global variables referred to in the transported function will need to be present remotely in the exact contexts in effect when the function was defined. This can be avoided by restricting f to be a pure function that does not refer to any global entities. More damning is:

> **Important:** Allowing a function to be sent to the server for remote execution is as dangerous as sending quoted q strings. The function can access resources on the server and instigate an attack. Good practice does not permit this in production environments.

The remaining format for remote execution can be made safe for production environments. The function to be executed remotely must already be defined on the server and you pass its name and arguments via the connection handle.

On the server,

```
q)g:{x*y}                                 / server
```

On the client,

```
q)h (`g; 6; 7)                            / client
42
```

Now consider the case when the remote function performs an operation on a table and returns the result. This is the q analogue of a remote stored procedure. For example, suppose t and f are defined on the server as,

```
q)t:([] c1:`a`b`c; c2:1 2 3)              / server
q)f:{[x] select c2 from t where c1=x}
```

Now "call" the function f remotely from the client.

```
q)h (`f; `b)                              / client
c2
--
2
```

The difference from SQL stored procedures is that the remote procedure can be **any** q function on the server, making the full power of q available remotely.

11.6.4 Synchronous and Asynchronous Messages

The IPC in the previous sections was **synchronous**, meaning that upon application of the connection handle, the client process blocks, waiting for a result from the server before proceeding. The value returned from the server becomes the return value of the open handle application.

Under the covers, IPC is implemented as messages passed over an open connection between q processes. When the **positive** open handle is applied to an argument, the message passing is **synchronous**, meaning that the following steps occur in sequence.

- The client sends a message containing the argument(s) of the handle application to the server and waits for a return message.
- The server receives the message, interprets it as the appropriate function application and obtains the result.
- The server sends a message containing the result back to the client.
- The client receives the result and resumes execution from the point it left off.

When a client sends multiple messages to a server in synchronous message passing, the next message is not sent until the result of the previous message is received. Consequently the messages always arrive at the server in the order in which they are sent. Also, the results from the server arrive back at the client in the order in which the original messages were sent.

It is also possible to perform asynchronous IPC in q. In this case the message is sent to the server and execution on the client continues immediately. In particular, there is no return value from the server. This is useful to initiate a task on the server when you don't care about the result. For example, you could initiate a long running operation, or you could send a message that the server will route to other processes.

Use the negation of the open connection handle to send an **asynchronous** message to the server. Let's define an instrumented function on the server to demonstrate what is happening.

```
q)sq:{0N!x*x}                          / server
```

Now invoke sq asynchronously from the client

```
q)neg[h] (`sq; 5)                      / client
q)
```

You will observe 25 displayed on the server console. Also, the client session returns immediately with no return value. The expression on the console actually has a nil value :: that is suppressed by the console display.

Important: When sending asynchronous messages, always send an empty "chaser" message immediately before applying (hclose) to the open handle. If you do not do this, buffered messages may not be sent when the connection is closed.

In order to convince ourselves that the client actually does return immediately without waiting for a return from the server, we wrap the client expression in a function. Observe that the client continues with the next statement.

```
q){neg[h] (`sq.; 5); 42}[]             / client
42
```

Because a q session is single threaded by default, the server will process messages in the order in which they are received. However, in asynchronous messaging there is no guarantee that the messages arrive at the server in the order in which they are sent. It can be difficult to observe indeterminancy in simple examples, but you must assume that it will occur in practice.

11.6.5 Processing Messages

Assuming that you have passed the server either a function from the client side or the name of a function on the server side, the appropriate function is evaluated on the server. During evaluation, the communication handle of the remote process is available in the system variable .z.w ("who" called). For an asynchronous call, this can be used to send messages back to the server during the function application on the server.

> ***Tip:*** Both the client and the server have connection handles when a connection between them is opened. However, these handles are assigned independently and their int values are not equal in general.

Here is a simple example showing how to use .z.w to send a message back to the client. On the server, we define a function that displays its received parameter and then asynchronously calls mycallback with the passed argument incremented.

```
q)f:{show "Received ",string x; neg[.z.w] (`mycallback; x+1)}
```

On the client we define mycallback to display its parameter on the console. Then we make an asynchronous call to the function f on the server with an argument of 42.

```
q)mycallback:{show "Returned ",string x;}

q)neg[h] (`f; 42)
q)"Returned 43"
```

The result is that "Received 42" is displayed on the server console and "Returned 43" is displayed on the client console. Congratulations! We have just invented callbacks in q.

> ***Tip:*** When performing asynchronous messaging, always use neg[.z.w] to ensure that all messages are asynchronous. Otherwise you will get a deadlock as each process waits for the other.

You can override the default behavior of message processing in q by assigning your own handler(s) to the appropriate system variables. Assign your function to the variable .z.pg to trap and process synchronous messages and to .z.ps for asynchronous messages. The names end in 'g' and 's' because synchronous processing has "get" semantics and asynchronous processing has "set" semantics.

In the following we set the asynchronous handler to a trivial function, essentially ignoring asynchronous calls.

On the server,

```
q).z.ps:{show "ignore"}              / server
```

On the client send an **asynchronous** message.

```
q)neg[h] "6*7"                       / client
```

354

This results in "ignore" being displayed on the server console.

Now we set the synchronous handler to a function that only accepts "safe" remote calls by function name. It then performs a protected evaluation on the function with the arguments passed, thus ensuring that a failed application does not hang the server.

On the server,

```
q).z.pg:{$[-11h=type first x; .[value first x; 1_x; ::]; `unsupported]}
```

Now send **synchronous** messages from the client.

```
q)h (`sq; 5)                          / client
25
q)h (`sq; `5)
"type"

q)h "6*7"
 unsupported
q)h ({x*y};6;7)
 unsupported
```

You can also specify handlers to be called upon connection open and close by assigning functions to the system variables .z.po and .z.pc, respectively. The connection handle of the sending process is passed as the lone argument to the functions assigned to .z.po and to .z.pc.

Here is a simple example that tracks connections and allows client processes to register callbacks with the server. Start a fresh q session on the server and open port 5042. Create a keyed table called Registry and define a function that can be invoked remotely to register a callback. Attach a handler to .z.po that initializes a dummy entry in Registry for the connection being opened and attach a handler to .z.pc to remove the record when a connection is closed.

```
q)Registry:([zw:`int$()] callback:`symbol$())

q)register:{[cb] `Registry upsert (.z.w; cb);}

q).z.po:{`Registry upsert (x; `unregistered);}
q .z.pc:{delete from `Registry where zw=x;}
```

Start a fresh q session on the client and connect to the server.

```
q)h:hopen`::5042  / client
```

We check that an item has been entered into Registry on the server.

```
q)Registry                                     / server
zw| callback
--| -----------
6 | unregistered
```

Next we register the name of a callback function from the client. Note the asynchronous message.

```
q)neg[h] (`register; `mycallback)            / client
```

Again we check Registry on the server and observe that our callback name has indeed been registered.

```
q)Registry                                   / server
zw| callback
--| ----------
6 | mycallback
```

Finally, we close the connection on the client.

```
q)hclose h                                   / client
```

And observe that the client has been automatically unregistered.

```
q).z.pg:{show x 0; show x 1; ; string value 1_x 0}
zw| callback
--| --------
```

11.6.6 Remote Queries

In this section, we demonstrate how to execute q-sql queries against a remote server. First, we splay a table to stand for a time series database. We use the mktrades script that we created in §9.3.1 to create a trades table with 1,000,000 rows and then splay it to disk.

```
q)trade:mktrades[`aapl`goog`ibm; 1000000]
q)(`:/db/trade/) set .Q.en[`:/db;]
_
```

Now start a fresh server process (the server), open a port, say 5042, and map the splayed trade table into memory. Check that the mapping succeeded by running a query.

```
q)\p 5042                                    / server
q)\l /db

q)select from trade where dt=2015.01.01,sym=`ibm
dt         tm           sym qty  px
-------------------------------------------------
2015.01.01 00:00:01.796 ibm 7080 218.74
2015.01.01 00:00:10.581 ibm 3250 206.88
..
```

Leave the server process running and start another fresh process (the client), open a connection to the server and send the same query to the server for remote execution.

```
q)h:hopen `::5042                            / client
q)h "select from trade where dt=2015.01.01,sym=`ibm"
dt         tm           sym qty  px
-------------------------------------------------
2015.01.01 00:00:01.796 ibm 7080 218.74
2015.01.01 00:00:10.581 ibm 3250 206.88
..
```

We have already pointed out that allowing remote execution of arbitrary strings is bad practice because it exposes the server to injection attack. So here is a simplistic example of a "safe" function that can be used as a stored procedure. It takes a symbolic table name, a list of symbolic column names for the result and a date range for the where phrase. Enter on the server:

```
q)extract:{[tn;cnms;dtrng] ?[tn;enlist (within;`dt;
dtrng);0b;cnms!cnms]}
```

Now on the client we (synchronously) call the stored procedure by name with appropriate arguments.

```
q)h (`extract;`trade;`dt`tm`sym`qty`px;2015.01.01 2015.01.02)
dt         tm           sym  qty  px
-------------------------------------------------
2015.01.01 00:00:01.194 aapl 6770 94.62
2015.01.01 00:00:01.796 ibm  7080 218.74
..
```

> *Tip:* In an actual application you would validate the input parameters and wrap the core evaluation in protected evaluation to trap unanticipated errors. You would also want to implement an entitlements system based on LDAP.

11.7 HTTP and Web sockets

11.7.1 Http Connections

When you open a port in a q session, by default that session serves http requests. To demonstrate this, start a q session and open a port, say 5042. Then bring up a relatively recent browser on the same machine (the author uses Chrome) and enter the following url,

```
http://localhost:5042/?6*7
```

You should see 42 in the browser page display.

You can trap HTTP GET and POST traffic by assigning functions to the system variables .z.ph and .z.pp respectively. The default handler for .z.ph is to evaluate the content of the first item of the passed argument.

> *Tip:* There is no default handler for .z.pp.

Here is a simple example that duplicates the default GET processing and shows the two items of its list argument. Define the following handler on the server process opened previously. It displays the two items of the input list then executes the first after removing the leading `` `?' `` and then returns the result as a string.

```
q).z.ph:{show x 0; show x 1; ; string value 1_x 0}    / server
```

Now enter the following from a browser on the same machine.

```
http://localhost:5042/?6*7
```

The server will display,

```
q)"?6*7"
Host          | "localhost:5042"
Connection    | "keep-alive"
Cache-Control | "max-age=0"
Accept        |
"text/html,application/xhtml+xml,application/xml;q=0.9,image/webp,*/*;q
=0.8"
User-Agent    | "Mozilla/5.0 (Macintosh; Intel Mac OS X 10_9_5)
AppleWebKit/537.36 (KHTML, like Gecko) Chrome/41.0.2272.89
Safari/537.36"
Accept-Encoding| "gzip, deflate, sdch"
Accept-Language| "en-US,en;q=0.8"
```

And the browser page displays "42".

11.7.2 Basic WebSockets

WebSockets is a network protocol that upgrades an initial HTTP handshake into a TCP/IP socket connection. It was initially used to enhance communication capability between browsers and web servers but it can be used for general client-server applications. Once the WebSocket connection is established, either the client or server can message the other; in particular, this provides the capability for the server to push data to the client.

> **Important:** As of this writing (Sep 2015) q implements only asynchronous messaging in WebSockets.

In this section we show the basic mechanism for establishing a websocket connection between a browser and a q process acting as the server. We use Chrome for the examples but recent versions of Internet Explorer are now WebSockets capable and should work similarly.

> **Note:** In the examples of this section we assume basic familiarity with HTML5 and Javascript.

We begin with an extremely simple HTML page with a button that, when clicked, displays the answer to life, the universe and everything. Save the following as a text file sample0.html in a location accessible to your browser.

```
<!doctype html>
<html>
<head>
<script>
    function sayN(n) {
        document.getElementById('answer').textContent = n;
    }
</script>
</head>
```

359

```
<body>
  <h1 style='font-size:200px' id='answer'></h1>
  <button onclick='sayN(42)'>get the answer</button>
</body>
</html>
```

In our case we saved the file to /pages/sample0.html on the local drive, so we enter the following url in the browser:

```
file:///pages/sample0.html
```

You should see a page with a single button labeled "get the answer". Click the button and you will see the answer in a very large font.

Now we enhance this basic page to connect to a q process via WebSockets and retrieve the answer from q. Save the following script as sample1.html. We explain it below.

> **Note:** For simplicity in the example, we have placed a copy of c.js in the pages directory. You should modify this to reflect its location in your installation.

```
<!doctype html>
<html>
<head>
<script src="c.js"></script>
<script>
 var serverurl = "//localhost:5042/",
     c = connect(),
     ws;

   function connect() {
     if ("WebSocket" in window) {
       ws = new WebSocket("ws:" + serverurl);
       ws.binaryType="arraybuffer";
       ws.onopen=function(e){
         ws.send(serialize({ payload: "What is the meaning of life?" }));
       };
       ws.onclose=function(e){
       };
       ws.onmessage=function(e){
         sayN(deserialize(e.data));
       };
       ws.onerror=function(e) {window.alert("WS Error") };
     } else alert("WebSockets not supported on your browser.");
   }


   function sayN(n) {
        document.getElementById('answer').textContent = n;
   }
</script>
```

This script first declares the script c.js, which is required for using q websockets.

The script then defines Javascript variables

- `serverurl` to hold the url of our q service
- `c` to hold the connection object returned by the connect function
- `ws` to hold a websocket object.

The function `connect()` is where the websocket action happens.

- It first tests to see if "WebSocket" is in the window, meaning that the browser supports websockets. If so, it makes the connection to the server; otherwise it displays an error alert.
- The first step in the connection is to create a websocket object by connecting to the specified server url, and storing the result in `ws`.
- Then set the `binaryType` field in `ws` to the value needed by the q sockets code.

Now we assign handlers for the main websockets events.

- The open handler serializes (into q form) a Javascript object with a 'payload' field and then sends it to the server. Consequently when a connection is opened, we immediately ask the server the meaning of life.
- The close handler is empty.
- The message handler deserializes the data field of the parameter `e` and applies the `sayN` function to display the result on the page.
- The error handler displays an alert page with the error message.

The `sayN` function locates the 'answer' field on the page and places the text of its argument there. Finally, the script defines a simple html element `answer`.

In contrast, the server side q code is blissfully short. Start a fresh q session, open port 5042 and set the WebSockets handler `.z.ws` to a function that will be invoked to handle WebSockets messages.

```
q)\p 5042
q).z.ws:{0N!-9!x; neg[.z.w] -8!42}
```

The handler first deserializes its parameter and displays it to the console for debugging, at which point we have no further use for it in this example. Then it serializes the answer to the question asked by the browser and **asynchronously** sends it back to the browser. That's all there is to it!

Now point the browser to,

```
file:///pages/sample1.html
```

and you will see the answer displayed on the page. At this point you are equipped to follow §1.19 in *Q Shock and Awe*.

11.7.3 Pushing Data to the Browser

In ordinary web applications, the browser initiates interaction with the server. It sends an
 request to a specific url on the server and the server replies with the requested page or data. Each such interaction is self-contained and is synchronous in that the browser waits for the server response.

In WebSockets the browser initiates the connection, but once the WebSocket request for protocol upgrade is successful, the browser—i.e., client—and the server are on equal footing. Either side can send messages. Moreover, in the current q implementation of WebSockets all interaction is asynchronous. Given that most current browsers and the default q session are both single-threaded, you don't have to worry about races and deadlocks but you do have to set up callbacks.

In this section we demonstrate how the q server can push data to the browser, beginning with the browser script. Actually this script is a simplification of sample1.html in that we remove the initial call to the server upon open; everything else remains the same. The key point is that the onmessage handler will be called every time data is received, resulting in the data being displayed on the screen. Save the following as sample2.html.

```
<!doctype html>
<html>
<head>
<script src="c.js"></script>
<script>
 var serverurl = "//localhost:4242/",
     c = connect(),
     ws;

   function connect() {
     if ("WebSocket" in window) {
       ws = new WebSocket("ws:" + serverurl);
       ws.binaryType="arraybuffer";
       ws.onopen=function(e){
       };
       ws.onclose=function(e){
       };
       ws.onmessage=function(e){
         sayN(deserialize(e.data));
       };
       ws.onerror=function(e) {window.alert("WS Error") };
     } else alert("WebSockets not supported on your browser.");
   }
   function toQ(x) { ws.send(serialize({ payload: x })); }

   function sayN(n) {
       document.getElementById('answer').textContent = n;
   }
</script>
</head>
<body>
  <h1 style='font-size:200px' id='answer'></h1>
</body>
</html>
```

And now for the q side. You can enter the following in the console of a fresh q session; or you can save it as a script and load it with \l.

```
q)\p 5042
q)answer:42
q).z.po:{`requestor set x; system "t 1000";}
q).z.ts:{neg[requestor] -8!answer;; answer+:1;}
```

Here is what's happening in the q code.

- First we open the port and initialize the answer variable.
- Then we set the connection open handler to store the client .z.w value of its parameter into the global requestor and start the system timer firing every 1000 milliseconds. Note that this only happens **after** the browser initiates a connection.
- Finally, we set the timer handler to send an asynchronous message containing the serialized value of answer and then increment answer.

Now point the browser to

```
file:///pages/sample2.html
```

and you will see the answer ticking every second on the page

12 Workspace Organization

12.0 Overview

The collection of all q entities that have been created in a q session comprises the workspace. This includes not only explicitly created variables but also ancillary items such as enumerations, open handlers, tables mapped from storage and other internal structures.

Like any programming environment of reasonable complexity, q has the potential for name clashes—e.g., when two different scripts define variables of the same name. Because q does not have lexical scoping and local variables are strictly scoped to the function in which they are defined, name clashes between locals is not a problem. But global variables are exposed. To illustrate, suppose you load a script that creates a global foobar. Then you load another script that also creates foobar. The result is that the second script overwrites the value assigned in the first script.

This is the simplest example of a condition in which two portions of a program contend for the same resource. Things get more complicated when concurrency is introduced, in which case the contention can lead to what is called a *race condition*. There is a school of programming that says mutable shared state is the root of all evil in distributed programming. Fortunately q is single-threaded by default and the implementation of threads (wisely) does not support mutating global variables. Nonetheless, simple name clashes are still a real problem.

12.1 Namespaces

A partial solution to name clashes is *namespaces*, which is the idea of placing a (usually hierarchical) structure on names. This is customarily done by specifying a separator character, which is distinct from other valid name characters. You are familiar with this construct from the file system used by most operating systems. The Unix file system uses the separator '/' and the Windows file system uses '\'.

The idea is that a compound name with embedded separators represents a nested series of containers. For example, in the Unix file system, the path /mydir/myfile represents a directory (container) mydir that holds a file myfile. Or /d1/d2/fn represents a directory d1

365

that contains a directory d2 that contains the file fn. The root container, designated / in Unix, holds all other entities.

Namespaces in many programming languages work similarly, using '.' as the separator. In q the containers are called *contexts*. For example, .jab.x represents a variable x contained in the jab context. The context jab has the symbolic name `.jab and the fully qualified name of its variable is `.jab.x.

A notable difference between q namespacing and most others is the way the root is handled. Naming for entities in the root context does not work as you might expect based on the file system analogy. The syntactic form .name does **not** refer to the global variable name in the root context; rather, it refers to the context name in the root. The fully qualified name for an entity x in the root is simply x.

This has the following consequence that causes grief to qbies.

Namespaces Fact of Life #1: There is no syntactic way inside a function to distinguish between a local variable x and the global x in the root namespace.

If you follow the Namespacing conventions at the end of this chapter, you can minimize potential discomfort. However, based on real-world experience, we point out the following.

Tip: Inside a function you can not access the global variable foo in the root context as .foo. Instead, .foo refers to the dictionary that holds all entities of the foo context. If you assign a value to .foo you wipe out the entire foo context.

12.2 Contexts

Namespacing in q is implemented with dictionaries. A context is a dictionary whose keys are the symbolic names of the variables in the corresponding namespace. The context dictionary associates each variable name with its currently assigned value.

The name of a context has the same restrictions as q variable names except that '.' is allowable. The following are all valid names of contexts in the root.

```
.a
.q
.cat
.an_ugly_context_name
```

Thus `.cat.bubba` represents the entity bubba in the `.cat` context.

With that out of the way, we can nest contexts.

```
.cat.bengal.nuba
.cat.abyssinian.orion
```

Here we have the entity nuba in the bengal context in the cat context; or the orion entity in the abyssinian context in the cat context.

Astute readers already have a question. How do we distinguish between the first case, in which `.cat.bubba` is the variable bubba in the cat context, and the second case where `.cat.bengal` is a context? For example, can we emulate the file system, which appends the separator '/' to indicate a directory (container). The answer is:

> ***Namespacing Fact of Life #2***: The interpretation of a fully qualified name depends on its underlying value. If it is a properly constructed dictionary, it is a context. If it is anything else, it is a variable.

Kx reserves all root namespaces of a single letter, as well `.kx`, for its own use. It is worth noting that most q built-in functions that are not written in C live in the `.q` namespace. As of this writing (Sep 2015) the namespaces that are actively used by Kx include `.h`, `.j`, `.o`, `.q`, `.u`, `.z` and `.Q`.

> **_Tip:_** Although q prohibits you from re-assigning its own functions during program execution, some programmers think it is clever to override their definitions in the q.k file. This is bad practice bordering on malfeasance. It courts disaster should Kx change the internal implementation of those routines in a future release.

12.3 Creating Contexts

When you start a fresh q session, all global variables you create live in the root context. All previous examples in this tutorial have created global variable variables in the root simply because we did not indicate otherwise—i.e., we used only unqualified variable names.

Start a fresh q session and create some global variables, beginning in the root.

```
q)answer:42
q)calculate:{(x*x)+(-1*x)+1}
```

To use namespacing, there is no equivalent to mkdir that creates a context before it can be used. Simply specify a qualified name and the context will be created if it does not exist.

```
q).foo.a:42          / context foo created
q).foo.double:{2*x}  / existing context foo used
```

Now suppose a separate script uses the bar namespace with different definitions for a and double.

```
q).bar.a:43          / context bar created
q).bar.double:{2*x}  / existing context bar used
```

We can now load that script without clobbering our root variables, so we have solved the original problem posed in the introduction to this chapter.

> **_Tip:_** Be very careful about placing globals in the root. As the author's father would say, "You're cruisin' for a bruisin'".

When working with contexts, apply an overload of the key operator to list the names of all contexts in the root.

```
q)key `
`q`Q`h`j`o`foo`bar
```

There is no need to stop at one level of namespace. You can nest as deeply as you like and all the intermediate contexts will be created as needed. Suppose we work for a company Adiabatic Programming Laboratory. We might structure our library of computation routines something like the following.

```
q).apl.core.calc.array.fill0:{0.0^x}
```

This single assignment causes the nested series of contexts apl, core, calc and array to be created and a function fill0 to be placed in the innermost context array.

12.4 Context as Dictionary

As mentioned previously, a context is a specially formatted q dictionary. Its keys are the symbolic names of the variables it contains; each is associated with the current value of the corresponding variable.

The context dictionaries are dictionaries that live in the workspace along with ordinary variables, which have special meaning to q. We can perform operations on them just as with our own dictionaries.

When we start a fresh q session, the root dictionary is empty. As with any variable, we can reveal the root context by applying get (or value) to its name and then applying the utility -3! to display its internal form since it is empty.

```
q)-3! get `.
"(`symbol$())!()"
```

Here we see an empty key list of symbols and a general empty list of values. After defining variables in the root, an ordinary dictionary emerges.

```
q)get `.
a     | 42
double| {2*x}
```

> **Tip:** The entries in a context dictionary are sorted by name.

Things get more interesting when we use namespacing and create a context.

```
q).jab.wrong:43

q)get `.
a     | 42
double| {2*x}

q)get `.jab
      | ::
wrong | 43
```

Observe that the newly created context dictionary for .jab is **not** physically in the root directory; it is a separate dictionary.

> ***Advanced***: You might wonder about the significance of the (::) in the first entry of the .jab context dictionary. It is there to prevent the value list of the context dictionary from collapsing to a simple list in case all the variables should have values of the same scalar type. This would then prevent subsequent definition of variables of other types in that context.

As they say in certain quarters, q eats its own dog food, meaning all ordinary operations can be performed on a context dictionary. For example, we can look up the values associated with `a in the root and with `wrong in the .jab context.

```
q)`.[`a]
42
q)`.jab[`wrong]
43
```

In fact you can use this to access an obscured global inside a function.

```
q)a
42
q){a:43; `.[`a]}[]
42
```

While this sort of thing makes for cute parlor tricks, we do not advise using it in real code.

> ***Recommendation***: Use (get) and (set) to retrieve and store global variables by name, especially inside functions.
>
> ```
> q){`a set 1+ get `a}[]
> `a
> q)43
> 43
> ```

12.5 Expunging from a Context

We have seen that a context is a directory that maps a context's entity names to their values. This means that in order to expunge an entity from a context, we could directly remove it from the dictionary. But this is bad practice since it uses the underlying implementation and the actual expression is prone to typing error.

Instead, q provides a special overload of the delete template explicitly for this purpose.

```
q)a:42
q).jab.wrong:43
q)delete a from `.
.
q)a
'a
q)delete wrong from `.jab
.jab
q)\v
`symbol$()
q)\v .jab
`symbol$()
```

Indeed, we issue the \v command to display the names of variables in a context (current context if none is specified) to verify that the variables are gone.

12.6 Saving and Loading Contexts

Since a context is a dictionary, you can persist it—and all its contents—as a serialized q object using (set).

For example, to write out the root context, retrieve it by name and set it into a file.

```
q)`:/data/root set get `.
`:/data/root
```

Conversely, you can read the serialized object back into memory using (get) on the file and then overwrite the current root context using (set)

```
q)`. set get `:/data/root
```

> ***Tip:*** If you organize your globals carefully, this makes check pointing the state of your application very simple. Overlaying the root context replaces all its entries. As the saying goes, "Be careful what you ask for."

12.7 Working in a Context

We return to the analogy of paths in the file system. The operating system keeps track of the current working directory for each program. This is merely a bit of state that points to a logical location in the file system. The main feature is it allows paths for items at or below the current working directory to be specified in *relative* form.

For example, if we start with the current working directory as the root and we wish to access a file /db/2015.03.01/trades.dat, then we must use the full path. However, if we issue the OS command,

    cd /db

then /db becomes the current working directory and we can specify the path of the file as simply 2015.03.01/trades.dat. Note the lack of the leading '/', which signifies a relative path as opposed to an absolute one. This provides significant simplification for deeply nested directory structures, which often arises in large development environments.

A q session has a similar concept. At any point in the session there is a *current working context*. At the beginning of a fresh q session, the current working context is the root context and you use absolute names for all global variables. We can change the working context with the \d command (for "directory" by analogy to the fie system). After you change the current working context, you can use relative names for global variables. Here we create two globals in the root context and then switch the current working context to show relative names.

```
q).jab.util.counter:0
q).jab.util.incrctr:{[] `.jab.util.counter set 1+get
 .jab.util.counter}
q).jab.util.incrctr[]
 .jab.util.counter

q)\d .jab
q.jab)util.incrctr[]
 .jab.util.counter
q.jab)util.counter
2
```

Notice that the q prompt changes to let you know the current working context.

There is a subtle point about how globals are bound during function definition that we must point out. To illustrate, start a fresh q session and do the following.

```
q)state:`NY
q).jab.f1:{[] state}

q)\d .jab
q.jab)state:0N
q.jab)f2:{[] state}

q.jab)\d .
q).jab.f1[]
`NY
q).jab.f2[]
0N

q).jab.f1
{[] state}
q).jab.f2
{[] state}
```

We began by defining a variable state in the root context to hold a two-character code for one of the 50 Unites States of America. Also from the root context, we define a function f1 in the .jab context that returns the value of state from the root context. Next we switch to the .jab context and define a variable state that holds the integer value of a state machine, along with a function f2 that returns the value of this global.

We return to the root context, apply each function using an absolute path name and observe the expected values. Namespacing has done its job by avoiding a clash between the disparate state variables, so what's the issue? Look closely at the display of the two function bodies. They are identical! How does q know which state variable to access at runtime?

373

> **Namespacing Fact of Life #3**: Any unqualified global reference in a function is bound to the current working context in effect at the point of the function **definition**. That context is not explicitly displayed in the function body.

This has the undesirable consequence of requiring a potential user of the function to know the circumstances of its definition.

But wait, there's more. Let's redo the initial example of this section in a fresh q session, but change the current working context two levels down instead of one.

```
q).jab.util.counter:0
q).jab.util.incrctr:{[] `.jab.util.counter set 1+get
`.jab.util.counter}

q)\d .jab.util
'.jab.util
```

You can't do it!

> **Namespacing Fact of Life #4**: You can only set the current working context one level down from the root. This is truly unfortunate.

You might be tempted to abandon namespacing altogether, but don't. If you adhere to the following recommendations, you will avoid the issues mentioned above and namespacing will work effectively.

Recommendations for Namespacing:

- Use namespacing at arbitrary depth to create hierarchical organization of global variables, both data and functions.
- Keep related functions and any globals they require together in an appropriate context in the hierarchy with a descriptive name.
- By convention, q namespaces are all lower case.
- Define all global entities from the root context using fully qualified names.
- Always refer to global entities using fully qualified names.

Essentially the last two recommendations amount to avoiding all use of \d to switch the current working context. Here is one way to define the functions f1 and f2 above in a fresh q session so that everything is explicit.

```
q).jab.geog.state:`NY
q).jab.geog.f1:{[] .jab.geog.state}
q).jab.machine.state:ON
q).jab.machine.f2:{[] .jab.machine.state}
q).jab.geog.f1
{[] .jab.geog.state}
q).jab.machine.f2
{[] .jab.machine.state}
```

13 Commands and System Variables

13.1 Command Format

Commands control aspects of the q run-time environment. A command begins with a back-slash '\' followed by the command name. Many commands have optional parameter(s) separated from the command name by a blank (multiple blanks or other whitespace characters are not permitted). Case is significant in the command name.

Notes on optional parameters:

- Commands whose optional parameter sets an environmental value will display the current value when the parameter is omitted
- Commands whose parameter refers to a namespace apply to the current working context if the parameter is omitted.

You could execute a command programmatically by placing it in a string as an argument to (value). Observe that you must escape the '\' in the string.

```
q)value "Error! Hyperlink reference not valid."        / bad
practice!
```

> **Tip:** Never do this in production—it exposes your system to all manner of attacks!

Instead use the built-in (system) that at least checks for a valid command. Note that it also eliminates the backslash and hence the need to escape it.

```
q)system "p 5042"
```

13.1.1 List Tables (\a)

The command \a [*namespace*], where *namespace* is an optional namespace, returns a sorted list of symbolic names of all tables in a context. When used without a parameter, it returns the tables in the current working context. For example, in a fresh q session,

```
q)\a
`symbol$()
q)t:([] c1:`a`b`c; c2:10 20 30)
q)\a
,`t
q).jab.t:([] c1:`a`b`c; c2:10 20 30)
q)\a .jab
,`t
```

13.1.2 Views/Aliases (\b)

The command \b [*namespace*] returns a sorted list of the symbolic names of the aliases (a.k.a. views, dependencies) in a context. In a fresh q session,

```
q)\b
`symbol$()
q)a:42
q)b::a+1
q)c::b*b
q)\b
`s#`b`c
```

See §13.3.3 for the related .z.b.

13.1.3 Pending Views/Aliases (\B)

The command \B [*namespace*] (note upper case) returns a sorted list of the symbolic names of the aliases (a.k.a. views, dependencies) in a context that are stale—i.e., there is a pending update that will be realized on the next reference. In a fresh q session,

```
q)x:42
q)a::x+1
q)\B
,`a
q)a
43
q)\B
`symbol$()
```

See §13.3.3 for the related .z.b.

13.1.4 Console (\c)

The command \c [h w] displays (no arguments) or sets (pair of height and width as integers) the size of the virtual q console display. The default is 25 80i. In a fresh q session,

```
q)\c
25 80i
q)\c 10 20
q)2#enlist "abcdefghijkmlnopqrstuvwxyz"
"abcdefghijkmlnop..
"abcdefghijkmlnop..
```

13.1.5 Web Console (\C)

The command \C [h w] (note upper case) displays (no arguments) or sets (pair of height and width as integers) the size of the virtual q console display for HTTP requests. The default is 25 80i. In a fresh q session, open port 5042 and point the browser to

   http://localhost:5042/?10 cut til 20

The browser page will display,

```
 0  1  2  3  4  5  6  7  8  9
10 11 12 13 14 15 16 17 18 19
```

Now issue the q command,

```
q)\C 10 20
```

and refresh the browser page. The page will now display,

```
 0  1  2  3  4  5 ..
10 11 12 13 14 15 ..
```

13.1.6 Change OS Directory (\cd)

The \cd [*path*] command is passed directly through to the OS. To display the current directory, issue \cd with no argument.

```
q)\cd
"/Users/jeffry"
```

To change the current working directory, issue \cd followed by the path of the desired directory. If the specified directory does not exist, q displays the error message from the OS.

The \cd command creates the directory if it does not exist. For example, the directory /data is initially empty.

379

```
q)\ls /data
q)\cd /data/new
q)\ls /data
"new"
```

13.1.7 Context (\d)

The \d [*namespace*] command displays or changes the current context (a.k.a. directory in early versions of k). To determine the current context, issue \d with no parameter. In a fresh q session this will be the root. To change the current working context, include its namespace with the \d command. If the specified context does not exist, it will be created.

```
q)\d
.
q)\d .jab
q.jab)\d .
q)\d .jab
q.jab)\d
.jab
q.jab)\d .
q)\d
.
```

> **Important:** See our recommendations against using \d in §12.7.

13.1.8 Error Trap (\e)

The \e [0|1] command displays or changes the behavior of a q process when an exception occurs during processing a client (i.e., remote) IPC request.

In a fresh q session the default is 0, meaning that when an exception occurs the stack of the failing function is cleared and execution continues. This is the desired behavior for a production server, as you do not want wayward client requests to disable the process.

In a development or testing scenario you can set this value to 1 to enable the familiar stack trace from the interactive console.

13.1.9 Functions (\f)

The \f [*namespace*] command displays a sorted list of symbolic names of functions in the current, or specified, working context. In a fresh q session,

```
q)\f
`symbol$()
q)f:{x*x}
q)g:{x*x*x}
q)\f
`s#`f`g
q).jab.f:{[] 42}
q)\f .jab
,`f
```

13.1.10 Garbage Collection (\g)

Following is a description of q/kdb+ memory management provided by Charles Skelton, the Kx CTO.

- Q/Kdb+ manages its own thread local heap.
- Vectors always have a capacity and a used size (the count).
- There is no garbage since q/kdb+ uses reference counting. As soon as there are no references to an object, its memory is returned to the heap.
- During that return of memory, q/kdb+ checks if the capacity of the object is >=64MB. If it is and \g is 1, the memory is returned immediately to the OS; otherwise, the memory is returned to the thread local heap for reuse.
- Executing .Q.gc[] additionally attempts to coalesce pieces of the heap into their original allocation units and returns any units >=64MB to the OS.
- Beginning with 3.3 2015.08.23—Linux only—unused pages in the heap are dropped from RSS during .Q.gc[].
- When q/kdb+ is denied additional address space from the OS, it will invoke .Q.gc[] and retry the request to the OS. Should that fail, it will exit with 'wsfull.
- When slave threads are configured and .Q.gc[] is invoked in the main thread it will automatically invoke .Q.gc[] in each slave thread. If the call is instigated in a slave thread—i.e., not the main thread—it will affect that thread's local heap only.

See §13.2.5 for the related command line parameter -g.

13.1.11 Load (\l)

The \l *path* command loads a q resource from persistent storage—here "load" is used in a generic sense. The *path* parameter can be a directory or a file. Loosely speaking, the rules for loading are,

- When something is recognized as a q resource, the loading routine does what is appropriate to make that resource available in the workspace.
- When something is not a recognized q resource, it fails.

The loading process recognizes two types of files:

- An file can be a q (or k) script, which is executed as if the individual lines were entered from the console
- A file can be a serialized q entity—e.g., the sym file for a splayed or partitioned table. In this case, the entity is deserialized into memory into a variable having the name of the file.

The situation for a directory is more complicated.

- The directory of a splayed table is mapped into memory with the name of the directory as the table name. None of the actual table data is actually loaded into memory at this time.
- For a directory name that is the value of one of the permitted partition types, the most recent partition directory is inspected for splayed directories and each such directory is mapped into memory with the name of the splayed directory.
- The root of a kdb+ database can contain: serialized q entities (e.g., the sym file), scripts (e.g., a start-up script), splayed table directories, partition directories or a par.txt file. In this case, the loading routine simply "does" each entity that it finds, as outlined above. The scripts are executed last.

For example, to load the distribution script sp.q from the /mypath directory,

```
q)\l /mypath/sp.q
```

To map a database whose root is /mypath/db,

```
q)\l /mypath/db
```

When a directory is mapped, the current working directory in the OS is set to that directory. This allows relative paths to subordinate items in the database and also helps to avoid wayward operations.

> **Tip:** Once you have mapped a database into memory, you can issue the command \1 . to remap the data without executing any start-up script(s) in the root.

13.1.12 GMT Offset (\o)

The \o [offset] command displays or changes the offset from GMT for q date/time values in the current q session. When the absolute value of the integer offset is strictly less than 24 it is interpreted as hours; if it is 24 or greater it is interpreted as minutes.

In a fresh q session, the value is 0Ni, meaning that the underlying OS time zone offset is used.

```
q).z.t                    / GMT
15:20:10.892
q).z.T                    / I live in NY
11:20:07.700
q)\o                      / Using OS offset
0Ni
q).z.t-.z.T               / No daylight savings in UK yet
04:00:00.000
q)\o -10                  / Think about moving to Hawaii
q).z.T                    / Much better
05:21:23.155
q).z.t-.z.T               / Hawaii doesn't use daylight saving
10:00:00.000
```

See §13.2.7 for the related command line parameter -o.

13.1.13 Port (\p)

The \p [port] command displays or changes the port on which the q process is listening. In a fresh q session the value is 0i, meaning that no port is open and connection attempts are rejected. To close the open port, use 0i as port. In a fresh q session,

```
q)\p
0i
q)\p 5042
q)\p
5042i
q)\p 0
```

When you issue the \p command, q attempts to open the port but the security settings of your machine must allow it.

> **Important**: Once you open a port, that q session is wide open to all connections, including to HTTP traffic. We strongly recommend that you implement appropriate security around any process with an open port in a production environment.

See §13.2.8 for the related command line parameter -p.

13.1.14 Display Precision (\P)

The command \P [*precision*] (note upper case) shows or sets the display precision for floating point numbers—i.e., float and real types—to the specified number of digits.

> **Note:** Only the display of the floating point values is affected. The internal representation remains unchanged.

The permissible values are 0-17, with 0 meaning maximum. The default precision is 7, meaning that the display of float or real values is rounded to the seventh significant digit. In a fresh q session,

```
q)\P
7i
q)1%3
0.3333333
q)2%3
0.6666667
q)\P 0
q)1%3
0.33333333333333331
q)2%3
0.66666666666666663
```

Notice the schmutz in the 17th significant digit. This is part of the dark mystery of binary floating point that is not mentioned in polite company.

You can use the semi-official functions .Q.f and .Q.fmt for controlled formatting of floating point values as strings.

See §13.2.10 for the related command line parameter -P.

13.1.15 Replication (\r)

The replication command \r is reserved for system use when using replicating servers. Do **not** use manually.

See §13.2.12 for the related command line parameter –r.

13.1.16 Slaves (\s)

The \s command displays the number of slaves available to the current q process. Read only. See §13.2.13 for setting this value with the command line parameter –s.

13.1.17 Seed (\S)

The \S [*seed*] command (note upper case) displays or sets the initial seed for pseudo-random number generation to the integer value *seed*. This is useful for obtaining repeatable results from randomized testing. The default value is -314159.

In a simple q session without slaves and multi-threaded input, the behavior is simple. Resetting the seed to the default value allows the pseudo-random values to be reproduced.

```
q)\S
-314159i
q)5?10
8 1 9 5 4
q)5?10
6 6 1 8 5
q)\S -314159i
q)5?10
8 1 9 5 4
```

When the q process is not started in single-threaded mode, things are more complicated.

- When the q process is started with a positive number of slaves, each slave gets its own seed (set internally) based on the slave number.
- When the process is started in multi-threaded input mode, each thread gets a seed based on the socket descriptor.
- When the process is started with negative slaves, each process on a specified range of ports gets its own seed based on the port number.

13.1.18 Set Timer (\t)

The \t command has two interpretations, depending the type of its parameter. When \t [*millis*] is issued with a positive integer argument, it sets the number of milliseconds between timer ticks. The default value is 0i, meaning that the timer does not fire. Setting to a non-zero value starts the timer, which will fire after the specified number of milliseconds Reset to 0i to turn it off.

```
q).z.ts:{show .z.P}
q)\t 2000
q).z.ts:{show .z.P}
q)2015.03.24D10:59:34.993826000
2015.03.24D10:59:36.993888000
2015.03.24D10:59:38.992911000
\t 0
q)
```

> **Note:** The actual timer tick frequency is determined by the timing granularity supported by the underling operating system. This can be considerably different from a millisecond.

See §13.2.14 for the related command line parameter -t.

13.1.19 Elapsed Time (\t *expr*)

When \t *expr* is issued with a valid q expression, the expression is evaluated and the execution duration in milliseconds is reported. This can be used to profile code execution when tuning an application.

Some expressions execute so quickly in q that the result is less than the timer granularity. Fortunately \t:*x* obviates what was formerly the only valid use of do in q—namely, repeating the expression evaluation to raise its execution time above the timer floor.

```
q)\t sum til 100000
0
q)\t:1000 sum til 100000
453
```

We conclude that adding the first 100,000 integers once requires approximately .45 milliseconds.

> **Tip:** Of course you would never evaluate this exact expression in practice; instead, use the insight of the young Gauss.

13.1.20 Elapsed Time and Space (\ts *expr*)

The \ts *expr* command is an enhancement of the version of \t that times an expression. It provides both the time and the number of bytes used in evaluating the expression.

```
q)\ts log til 100000
4 3145856
```

You can also specify the number of repetitions, as with \t.

```
q)\ts:100 log til 100000
248 3145824
```

13.1.21 Timeout (\T)

The \T *secs* command (note upper case) sets the number of **seconds** a remotely initiated execution will run before timing out. The default value is 0, meaning that such execution will not timeout. This is useful to protect against runaway client calls when the q process is acting as a server.

See §13.2.15 for the related command line parameter -T.

13.1.22 User Password (\u)

When the q process has been started with the –u command to load a password file, the \u command reloads the password file. This allows the password to be changed while the process is running.

See §13.2.17 for the related command line parameter -u.

13.1.23 Variables (\v)

The \v [*namespace*] command displays a sorted list of symbolic names of all variables in the specified context when the *namespace* parameter is present, or the current working context if it is not. In a fresh q session,

```
q)\v
`symbol$()
q)a:b:c:42
q)\v
`a`b`c
q)\v .
`a`b`c

q).jab.a:43
q)\v .jab
,`a
```

13.1.24 Workspace (\w)

The workspace command \w [0] displays information about resource utilization in the current q session. When the parameter is not present, it returns a list of six integers:

- Number of bytes allocated
- Number bytes available in heap
- Maximum heap size used heretofore in session
- Maximum bytes available as specified at startup in -w
- Number of bytes for mapped entities
- Number of bytes of physical (i.e. machine) memory

For example, in a fresh q session on the author's laptop:

```
q)\w
118256 67108864 67108864 0 0 17179869184
q)bigdata:til 200000000
q)\w
2147601952 2214592512 2214592512 0 0 17179869184
```

When the parameter is present, \w 0 returns a list with two items relating to symbol usage: the number of symbols and the corresponding number of bytes of memory used. For example, in a fresh q session on the author's laptop:

```
q)\w 0
566 18470
q)lottasyms:1000000?`5
q)\w
4312768 67108864 67108864 0 0 17179869184
```

13.1.25 Week Offset (\W)

The week offset command \W [offset] (note upper case) displays or sets the week offset. An offset of 0 corresponds to Saturday. The default is 2, which is Monday. This is useful in controlling weekends when aggregating weekly data. In a fresh q session,

```
q)\w
2i
q)group `week$2015.01.01+til 10
2014.12.29| 0 1 2 3
2015.01.05| 4 5 6 7 8 9
q)\w 0
q)group `week$2015.01.01+til 10
2014.12.27| 0 1
2015.01.03| 2 3 4 5 6 7 8
2015.01.10| ,9
q)\w 1
q)group `week$2015.01.01+til 10
_
```

13.1.26 Expunge Handler (\x)

The expunge handler command \x *handler* un-assigns a user specified event handler for one of the .z.* event handlers and restores the default system behavior. For example, here is how you can customize the console response and then restore the original behavior.

```
q).z.pi:{"==>",.Q.s value x}
q)42
==>42
q)43
==>43
q)\x .z.pi
==>q)43
43
q)44
44
```

> **Note:** There is no default handler for .z.ph so expunge does not work there.

13.1.27 Date Format (\z)

The date parsing format command \z [0|1] displays or specifies the format for date parsing. A value of 0 corresponds to month-then-day—as in *mm/dd/yyyy*—and a value of 1 corresponds to day-then month—as in *dd/mm/yyyy*. The default value is 0i. In a fresh q session,

```
q)\z
0i
q)"D"$"12/31/2015"
2015.12.31
q)"D"$"31/12/2015"
0Nd
q)\z 1
q)"D"$"12/31/2015"
0Nd
q)"D"$"31/12/2015"
2015.12.31
```

See §13.2.21 for the related command line parameter -z.

13.1.28 Lock Script (_)

The _ command with no parameter checks to see if client write access is blocked. See the description of –b in §13.2.1.

The _ *script.q* command transforms the specified script file into an equivalent one in script.q_ that can be loaded and executed with \l but whose contents are scrambled for human eyes. The resulting file cannot be viewed, serialized or modified.

For example, suppose we have saved the following script as /scripts/sensitive.q.

```
secret:42
reveal:{[] 42}
```

Then we can lock it as follows.

```
q)\_ sensitive.q
`sensitive.q_
q)\l sensitive.q_
q)secret
q)reveal[]
42
q)reveal                  / ignored
q)-8!reveal               / ignored
q)read1`:sensitive.q_     / scrambled
_
```

13.1.29 Redirect (\1 and \2)

These commands \1 and \2 allow you to redirect the OS stdout and stderr from within a q session. Follow the command with a file name for the redirected output. In a fresh q session,

390

```
q)\1 /data/out.txt
q)1+2*til 5
q)\2 /data/err.txt
6*`7
\\
```

```
>cat /data/out.txt
1 3 5 7 9
>cat /data/err.txt
q)'type
```

13.1.30 Operating System (\text)

The command \oscmd, in which oscmd is any text not recognized as a q command, is assumed to be an operating system command and is passed to the OS for execution. Any output to stdout will be returned to q as strings. This is handy to avoid having to exit the q session and can be done programmatically with the (system) function. For example, on the author's laptop,

```
q)\pwd
"/q4m"
q)\ls /pages
"c.js"
"sample0.html"
"sample1.html"
"sample2.html"
"ws101.html"
"ws101.q"
q)pages:system "ls /pages"
q)pages
_
```

Tip: If oscmd results in an operating system error, an exception will be thrown in q. For safe programmatic execution, you can trap the exception by executing oscmd with system wrapped in protected evaluation.

13.1.31 Interrupt (ctrl-c and ctrl-z)

You can interrupt a long-running q function with ctrl-c. Note that some q functions are so tight that the interrupt may not be registered. You can terminate any q console session with extreme prejudice using ctrl-z, which will result in all contents of the workspace being lost.

13.1.32 Terminate (\)

Use \ to terminate one level of suspended execution arrived at via an exception.

```
q)f:{x*y}
q)f[2;`3]
{x*y}
'type
*
2
`3

q))\
q)□
```

Tip: Do not have an itchy trigger finger when exiting multiple levels of suspended evaluation, as \\ will exit the q session immediately.

If you are adventuresome, you can also issue \ at the normal q console prompt to toggle between the q interpreter and the k interpreter.

```
q)\
  a:42
  -a
-42
  \
q)-a
'-_
```

13.1.33 Exit (\\)

To exit the q process, enter a double backslash \\ at any console prompt.

```
q)\\
$
```

Important: There is no confirmation prompt for \\. The q session is terminated with extreme prejudice.

Tip: For programmatic q shutdown, use (exit) with a return value, which can be piped into other processes.

13.2 Command Line Parameters

When you start q from the command line, you can optionally follow the q executable immediately with a file or directory to be "loaded" upon startup. This is effectively the same as issuing the \l command with that file or directory as the first action in the q session.

Following the q executable and the file name, you can include one or more command line options. Each is prefaced with '-' and followed by whitespace and an optional parameter value. Many of the command line parameters have equivalent q commands that can be issued within the session.

13.2.1 Block Database Modification (-b)

The –b command line parameter disallows connected clients to modify data. This includes setting global variables or modifying files.

> **Tip:** This behavior is only in effect for operations initiated via remote (i.e., client) connection, so you will not see the effects in a console seesion on the server process.

13.2.2 Console Size (-c)

The –c *r c* parameter specifies a pair of integers for the size of the q virtual console display as rows and columns. The default size is 25 80i.

13.2.3 HTTP Console (-C)

The –C *r c* parameter (note upper case) specifies a pair of integers for the size of the HTTP virtual console display as rows and columns. The default setting is 36 by 2000.

13.2.4 Client Error Trapping (-e)

The -e 0|1 parameter enables or disables trapping exceptions arising during processing IPC requests. The default is 0.

13.2.5 Garbage Collection (-g)

The -g 0|1 parameter sets the garbage collection behavior. See §13.1.8 for an explanation.

13.2.6 Logging (-l and -L)

The –l parameter starts q with logging of remote requests enabled. Following is a brief description of how logging works; see the Kx site for more information. The -L parameter (note upper case) forces disk write on each remote execution.

A logging server uses files with .log and .qdb extensions and name specified immediately after the q executable on the command line that starts q. For example, starting q with

```
$q /data/logdemo -l
```

will use files /data/logdemo.log and /data/logdemo.qdb.

The idea of logging is that each time a remote request is executed, it is logged. Periodically the application issues the \l command to checkpoint the current state of the workspace (more specifically, to serialize and persist the root context) and clear the log.

Should a logging process terminate abruptly, restarting it with the same -l command causes the most recently persisted state to be restored. Specifically, the serialized root context is restored from the .qdb file and requests that were processed after the state was persisted are replayed from the .log file.

Note that although only remote requests are logged, the process can ensure that its own activity is logged by sending requests to itself with the reserved handle 0.

Here is a simple session that demonstrates the logging scenario using local activity. Remote activity works the same.

```
>q /data/logdemo -l
q)0 "a:42"
q)0 "b:43"
q)\l
q)\\
```

```
>q /data/logdemo -l
q)a
42
q)b
4
```

13.2.7 Offset (-o)

The -o *offset* parameter specifies the offset from GMT for q time values. See §13.1.10 for an explanation.

13.2.8 Port (-p)

The –p *portnum* parameter opens *portnum* for TCP/IP and HTTP traffic. The default is 0 meaning that no port is open.

> **Tip:** Only one port can be open in a given q session.

13.2.9 Multithreaded Session (-p)

The –p *-portnum* parameter starts the q session in multithreaded mode. See the Kx site for information on how this works.

13.2.10 Display Precision (-P)

The –P *digits* parameter (note upper case) specifies the number of digits for floating point display. See §13.1.12 for an explanation.

13.2.11 Quiet (-q)

The –q parameter starts q quietly, meaning that no start-up banner is displayed and there is no q prompt at the console.

13.2.12 Replicate (-r)

The –r parameter starts a replicating q server. See the Kx web site for information on replication.

13.2.13 Slaves (-s)

The –s *N* parameter starts the q process with *N* slaves for concurrent execution. See the Kx web site for information on slaves.

13.2.14 Timer (-t)

The –t *millis* command specifies the number of milliseconds between timer ticks. See §13.1.17 for an explanation.

13.2.15 Timeout (-T)

The –T *secs* parameter specifies the number of seconds for timeout of remote requests. See §13.1.20 for an explanation.

13.2.16 Exit (-u)

The –u 1 parameter disables calling out to the OS via (system).

13.2.17 User Validation (-u)

The –u *filename* parameter starts a q session with a file of user names and passwords that will be checked when a remote connection requests is received. The remote connection has **no access** outside the database root directory.

13.2.18 User Validation (-U)

The –U *filename* parameter (note upper case) starts a q session with a file of user names and passwords that will be checked when a remote connection requests is received. **No restriction** is placed on file system access by remote connections.

13.2.19 Workspace Size (-w)

The –w *bytes* parameter specifies the maximum virtual size of the workspace in bytes. Any attempt to allocate more than this amount of memory will result in a 'wsfull exception and immediate termination of the q process. The default is twice the amount of physical machine memory.

13.2.20 Week Offset (-W)

The –W *offset* parameter (note upper case) sets the offset of the beginning of the week relative to Saturday. See §13.1.24 for the related w command.

13.2.21 Date Parsing Format (-z)

The –z 0|1 parameter specifies the date parsing format. See §13.1.26 for details in the related w command.

13.3 System Variables

Variables in the .z namespace reflect q environmental information and behavior.

13.3.1 IP Address (.z.a)

The system variable .z.a is an encoded int representing the IP address of the current running q instance. To see the usual four-integer IP address, decode the int using base 256. For example, on the author's laptop,

```
q).z.a
-1407972861i
q)`int$0x0 vs .z.a
172 20 10 3i
```

13.3.2 Access Control (.z.ac)

Assign a function to the system variable .z.ac to process Single Sign On (SSO) token cookies from the HTTP header. Your handler is passed a two-item list comprising the request text and a dictionary containing the elements of the request header. Your custom code should process the `Authorization value of the dictionary and should return a list in one of the following forms:

- (0; "") to indicate 401 page not found
- (1; "*username*") to indicate that *username* has been validated and to assign this value to .z.u
- (2; "*raw text*") to send raw response text to the client

Note that .z.ac supersedes .z.pw when defined.

13.3.3 Dependencies (.z.b)

The system variable .z.b is a dictionary that represents the (direct) dependencies of all aliases. The keys are symbolic names of entities in the workspace and the associated values are lists of symbolic names of entities that depend directly on the entity named by the key.

In a fresh q session,

```
q)a::x+y
q)b::x*x
q)c::a+b
q).z.b
x| `a`b
y| ,`a
a| ,`c
b| ,`c
```

It is a nice exercise to write a q expression that recursively finds all dependencies, not just direct ones. Another nice exercise is to invert

397

the dictionary to relate the name of an entity to everything it depends on.

13.3.4 Cores (.z.c)

The system variable .z.c represents the number of cores on the physical machine hosting the q process. Hardware with hyper threading reports the number of virtual cores.

13.3.5 Exit Routine (.z.exit)

The system variable .z.exit specifies a handler to be called just before the q process exits in order to clean up resources.

> ***Important:*** The handler cannot cancel the exit.

The parameter passed to the handler is 0i if the exit was invoked manually with \\ or it is the argument to the (exit) function when that was called programmatically.

In a fresh q session,

```
q).z.exit:{show x}
q)\\
0i
```

Or in another fresh q session,

```
q).z.exit:{show x}
q)exit 43
43i
```

Note that if the handler itself throws an exception—deliberate or otherwise—the session will be suspended at that error.

```
q).z.exit:{'bad}
q)exit 0
{'bad}
'bad
q))
```

> **Tip:** The default exit behavior can be restored by expunging with \x.

13.3.6 Global Date (.z.d)

The system variable .z.d retrieves the date component of Greenwich Mean Time (GMT) and is equivalent to `date$.z.p.

13.3.7 Local Date (.z.D)

The system variable .z.D retrieves the local date component according to the time zone offset from GMT and is equivalent to `date$.z.P.

13.3.8 Startup File (.z.f)

The system variable .z.f is a symbol representing the file parameter entered on the q start-up command line. For example,

```
$ q /scripts/answer.q
q).z.f
`/scripts/answer.q
```

13.3.9 Host (.z.h)

The variable .z.h is a symbol representing the network name of the host running the q instance, which is the same as the OS command hostname on Unix. For example, on the author's laptop,

```
q).z.h
`aerowing.local
```

13.3.10 Process ID (.z.i)

The variable .z.i is an int representing the process id of the running q instance. For example, on the author's laptop,

```
q).z.i
4903i
```

> **Note:** As of this writing (Sep 2015), .z.i is not implemented on Windows.

13.3.11 Release Date (.z.k)

The system variable .z.k is a date value representing the release date of the running q instance. For example, on the author's laptop,

```
q).z.k
2014.11.01
```

13.3.12 Release Version (.z.K)

The system variable .z.K is a float value representing the major version of the running q instance. For example, on the author's laptop,

```
q).z.K
3.2
```

13.3.13 License Information (.z.l)

The system variable .z.l is a list of strings containing information about the license of the running kdb+ instance. The most useful are the items in positions 1 and 2, which represent the expiry date and update date, respectively. For example, on a system long, long ago,

```
q).z.l
("";"2007.07.01";"2007.07.01";,"1";,"1";,"0";,"0")
```

> **Tip:** The value of .z.l is () for 32–bit non-production versions of q.

13.3.14 GMT Timespan (.z.n)

The system variable .z.n retrieves the timespan component of Greenwich Mean Time (GMT) and is equivalent to `timespan$.z.p.

13.3.15 Local Timespan (.z.N)

The system variable .z.N retrieves the local timespan component according to the time zone offset from GMT and is equivalent to `timespan$.z.P.

13.3.16 OS (.z.o)

The system variable .z.o is a symbol representing the operating system hosting the current q process. For example, this text is being written on a 32-bit Mac system.

```
q).z.o
`m32
```

13.3.17 GMT Timestamp (.z.p)

The system variable .z.p retrieves the current Greenwich Mean Time (GMT) with nanosecond resolution. It is the basis for all other date and time values in the .z namepsace.

For example, at the exact time of this writing we find,

```
q).z.p
2015.03.26D17:40:21.997067000
```

13.3.18 Local Timestamp (.z.P)

The system variable .z.P displays the current local nanosecond resolution from .z.p according to the time zone offset.

For example, at the exact time of this writing in the Hawaii time zone we find,

```
q).z.P
2015.03.26D07:41:11.269534000
```

13.3.19 On Close (.z.pc)

Assign a q function to the system variable .z.pc to be invoked **after** a connection is closed—a.k.a. "process close." At the point your handler is invoked, the other variables associated with the connection—e.g., .z.w—have already been wiped. The handle of the connection that has just been closed is passed as the lone parameter to your handler so that you can clean up any resources associated with it in your application.

To reset to the default setting, expunge the handler with \x .z.pc.

13.3.20 Peach Distribution (.z.pd)

Assign an int list or q function representing an event handler to the system variable .z.pd for use by (peach) for a q process that has been started with the –s command line parameter with a negative value. Your handler supplies a list of ints representing open handles to other processes and will be called by (peach) when it distributes work to those processes. These handles must not be used for other processing as (peach) will close any handle the presents data it is not excepting. See §A.68.2 on distributed processing with (peach).

> ***Important:*** The int return list of your handler must have the `` `u# ``
> attribute applied.

Here is a simple example that opens and returns five handles on the local machine starting at port 20000. It assumes that worker processes have already been started with these ports open. See the Kx site for more comprehensive examples

```
q).z.pd:{`u#hopen each 20000+til 5}
```

13.3.21 On Synchronous Message (.z.pg)

Assign a function to the system variable .z.pg to be invoked whenever a remote client q process makes a synchronous call over an open connection—a.k.a. "process get." The name derives from the fact that a synchronous call has get semantics. The default behavior applies (value) to the incoming massage.

To reset to the default setting, expunge the handler with \x .z.pg.

13.3.22 On HTTP Get (.z.ph)

Assign a function to the system variable .z.ph to be evaluated whenever a synchronous HTTP request is routed to the current q process—a.k.a. "process http." See §11.7.1 for a discussion.

To reset to the default setting, expunge the handler with \x .z.ph.

13.3.23 On Input (.z.pi)

Assign a function to the system variable .z.pi to be evaluated when q echoes the result of user input to the console—a.k.a. "process input."

For example, the following mimics the console display of pre-2.4 q versions.

```
q).z.pi:{-1 .Q.s1 value x}
```

To reset to the default behavior, expunge the handler with \x .z.pi.

13.3.24 HTTP Options method (.z.pm)

Assign a function to the system variable .z.pm to receive HTTP OPTIONS as,

```
(`OPTIONS;requestText;requestHeaderDict)
```

13.3.25 On Open (.z.po)

Assign a function to the system variable .z.po to be evaluated after a connection to the current q process has been successfully opened—a.k.a. "process open." See §11.6 for a discussion. The local handle of the connecting process is passed in the second parameter.

To reset to the default setting, expunge the handler with \x .z.po.

13.3.26 On HTTP Post (.z.pp)

Assign a function to the system variable .z.pp to be evaluated whenever an HTTP post is routed to the current q process—a.k.a. "process post." See §11.7 for a discussion of .z.pg, whose parameters are the same.

To reset the .z.pp to the default setting, expunge the handler with \x .z.pp.

13.3.27 On Set (.z.ps)

Assign a function to the system variable .z.ps to be evaluated whenever a client process sends an asynchronous message to the current q process—a.k.a. "process set." The name derives from the fact that an asynchronous call has set semantics. The parameter passed to your handler is the message content. The default behavior is to invoke (value).

To reset the to the default setting, expunge the handler with \x .z.ps.

13.3.28 On Password (.z.pw)

Assign a function to the system variable .z.pw to be evaluated after the command line −u and −U checks but before the .z.po handler—a.k.a. "**p**ass**w**ord." This can be used to implement authorization—i.e., who is allowed to do what. Your handler should accept two parameters: a symbolic user name and a password string. It should return a boolean pass/fail indicator.

To reset to the default setting, expunge the handler with \x .z.pw.

13.3.29 Quiet Mode (.z.q)

The system variable .z.q is a read-only boolean indicating whether q was started in quiet mode using the −q 1 command line parameter.

13.3.30 Self (.z.s)

The system variable .z.s represents the current function during function evaluation. This can be useful when writing recursive functions but there is often a better way to do this using adverbs. For example, here is a stack-eating recursive factorial.

```
q){$[x=1;x;x*.z.s x-1]} 10
3628800
```

13.3.31 GMT Date (.z.t)

The system variable .z.t retrieves the time component of Greenwich Mean Time (GMT) and is equivalent to `time$.z.p.

13.3.32 Local Date (.z.T)

The system variable .z.T retrieves the local date component according to the time zone offset from GMT and is equivalent to `time$.z.P.

13.3.33 On Timer (.z.ts)

Assign a function to the system variable .z.ts to be evaluated on every timer tick—see §13.1.18 for the command \t to start/stop the timer. For example, the following assigns a handler to display local time to the console, turns on the timer to fire (approximately) every two seconds and turns it off after a few ticks.

```
q).z.ts:{show .z.P}
q)\t 2000
q)2015.03.26D12:48:24.487145000
2015.03.26D12:48:26.488286000
2015.03.26D12:48:28.488237000
2015.03.26D12:48:30.488372000
q)2015.03.26D12:48:32.488206000
2015.03.26D12:48:34.488370000
\t 0
q)
```

To restore the default behavior, expunge the handler with \x .z.ts.

13.3.34 User (.z.u)

The system variable .z.u is a symbol that represents the user id of the q session.

> **Tip:** Inside the processing of a remote message on a server, .z.u represents the user id of the remote session.

13.3.35 On Value Set (.z.vs)

Assign a function to the system variable .z.vs to be evaluated **after** a global variable in the root context is set. The parameters for your handler are the symbolic name of the global being set and the subdomain of the assignment. For example, in a fresh q session,

```
q)a:42
q)m:(1 2; 3 4)
q).z.vs:{0N!(x;y;value x)}
q)a:43
(`a;();43)
q)m[0;0]:42
(`m;0 0;(42 2;3 4))
```

To restore the default behavior, expunge the handler with \x .z.vs.

13.3.36 Who (.z.w)

The system variable .z.w represents the handle of "who" is in communication during the current remote call. At the console prompt, the value is 0i, representing the interactive user. In the midst of processing a remote message, it is the (local) open handle associated with that remote client on this process.

13.3.37 Handle Queues (.z.W)

The system variable .z.W (note upper case) returns a list of dictionaries whose keys are open handles and whose values are lists of bytes in the corresponding output queue. See the Kx site for more details.

13.3.38 On WebSocket Close (.z.wc)

Introduced in q3.3, the system variable .z.wc can be assigned a handler that is called when a websocket connection is closed. Prior to q3.3 this was handled in .z.pc.

Your handler is executed immediately **after** a websocket connection has been closed. Since the connection has been closed by the time the handler is called, there are no valid remote values for .z.a, .z.u or .z.w. Consequently the local values are returned.

> **Tip:** This is useful to cleanup things like a table of users keyed by handle, in which case you use the just-closed handle that is passed as a parameter to .z.wc.

13.3.39 On WebSocket Open (.z.wo)

Introduced in q3.3, the system variable .z.wo can be assigned a handler that is called when a websocket conection is opened. Prior to q3.3 this was handled in .z.po.

Your handler is executed just **after** a websocket connection to a kdb+ session has been initialized—i.e., once it has been validated against a –u/–U file (if specified) and .z.pw checks. The argument is the just-opened handle.

> **Tip:** This handler is typically used to build a dictionary of handles associated with session information such as .z.a or .z.u.

13.3.40 On WebSocket Message (.z.ws)

Assign a function to the system variable .z.ws to be evaluated whenever a message arrives over a WebSocket. See §11.7 for examples.

13.3.41 Command Line Parameters (.z.x)

The system variable .z.x is a list of strings representing the command line parameters provided after the name of the file or directory on the command line invocation of the q process. For example, if q is invoked from the OS console with,

```
q convertargs.q 42 forty 2.0
```

we find,

```
q).z.f
 convertargs.q
q).z.x
("42";"forty";"2.0")
```

13.3.42 Raw Command Line (.z.X)

The system variable .z.X was introduced in q3.3. It is a string representing the unprocessed command line that invoked the q process, beginning with the invocation of q. For example,

```
$rlwrap m32/q trade.q -p 12345 -u 1 -b -MyParam foo
KDB+ 3.3 2015.09.02 Copyright (C) 1993-2015 Kx Systems
...
q).z.X
"m32/q"
"trade.q"
"-p"
"12345"
"-u"
"1"
"-b"
"-MyParam"
"foo"

q).z.x
"-MyParam"
"foo"
```

13.3.43 GMT Datetime (.z.z)

The system variable .z.z retrieves the GMT date component and is equivalent to `datetime$.z.p.

Note: This is deprecated in favor of .z.p.

13.3.44 Local Datetime (.z.Z)

The system variable `.z.Z` retrieves the local date component according to the time zone offset from GMT and is equivalent to `` `datetime$.z.P``.

Note: This is deprecated in favor of .z.P.

13.3.45 Zip Defaults (.z.zd)

The system variable `.z.zp` displays or sets a list of parameters for data compression: logical block size, compression algorithm and compression level. For example, the following are reasonable settings.

```
q).z.zd:17 2 6
```

See the Kx site for more details on the implementation of data compression.

14 Introduction to Kdb+

14.0 Overview

In this chapter we provide an introduction to kdb+, which is the database offering from Kx. Roughly speaking, kdb+ is what happens when q tables are persisted and then mapped back into memory for operations. Of course, things are more complicated than that.

> **Important**: Many examples in this chapter use directories that are parented directly to the root. This is done for pedagogical reasons and also to make paths short enough to fit on a page without wrapping. Unless you are creating kdb+ databases on a machine over which you have complete control, you will **not** be able to create directories in the root. When emulating the examples here, you should change the paths to relative paths that live under a directory that you control. You can usually do this by removing the leading '/' in the path.

14.1 Tables in Memory and Serialization

It is possible to maintain a table entirely in memory, provided you have enough physical memory to hold it. There is one problem with this from a database perspective:

- An in-memory table is ephemeral—meaning that all modifications are lost if the q process dies.

One solution is to serialize the table to persistent storage using (set) or similar mechanisms. In this section we recapitulate material from previous chapters from this perspective.

14.1.1 Tables and Keyed Tables

A table is the (flip) of a column dictionary, in which address slots are reversed but no data is moved during the transpose. For example, here is a table with two simple list columns.

```
q)flip `s`v!(`a`b`c;100 200 300)
```

Table definition syntax permits tables to be defined in more readable format.

```
q)([] s:`a`b`c; v:100 200 300)
```

The schema of a table has the same form but with empty columns—i.e., no rows.

```
q)([] s:`symbol$(); v:`int$())
q)t:([] s:`a`b; v:10 20)
```

It is good practice to prototype the empty lists in a schema; unfortunately, this is not possible if the corresponding columns are not simple lists.

The type of any table is 98h and the function (meta) summarizes the column names, types and attributes in a result keyed table.

```
q)meta ([] s:`symbol$(); v:`int$())
```

A keyed table is a dictionary that establishes positional correspondence between a table of (presumably unique) keys and a table of values.

```
q)([] id:1001 1002 1003)!([] s:`a`b`c; v:100 200 300)
id  | s v
----| -----
1001| a 100
1002| b 200
1003| c 300
```

Table definition syntax is more compact.

```
q)([id:1001 1002 1003]  s:`a`b`c; v:100 200 300)
```

The type of any keyed table is 99h, since it is a dictionary and (meta) applies exactly as with tables.

14.1.2 Foreign Keys and Link Columns

A foreign key is one or more table columns that are enumerated over the key component of a keyed table. For example, the column id in the table below is a foreign key over kt. Note that the foreign key column is identified by the name of its target table in the result of (meta).

```
q)kt:([id:1001 1002 100]  s:`a`b`c; v:100 200 300)
q)t:([]; id:`kt$1002 1001 1003 1001; q:100 101 102 103)
q)meta t
c | t f  a
--| ------
id| j kt
q | j
```

A query on a table having a foreign key can access columns in the keyed table via dot notation.

```
q)select id.v, q from t
v   q
-------
200 100
100 101
300 102
100 103
```

A link column is similar to a foreign key, in that its entries are indices of rows in a table, but you must perform the lookup manually. The advantages of link columns are:

- The target can be a table or keyed table.
- The target can be the table containing the link column.
- Link columns can be splayed or partitioned, whereas foreign keys cannot.

Here is the previous foreign key example redone with a link column against a table.

```
q)tk:([] id:1001 1002 100; s:`a`b`c; v:100 200 300)
q)t:([]; id:`tk!(exec id from tk)?1002 1001 1003 1001; q:100 101 102
103)
q)meta t
c | t f  a
--| ------
id| i tk
q | j
```

Important: As of this writing (Sep 2015) integers are 64-bit in q3+, enumerations are 32-bit. In particular, the integers stored in a link column are truncated to 32 bits by the (!) operator. Observe that type of the link column id in the previous example is I even thought the result of the (?) operation is of type j. One consequence is that you cannot use links columns with tables of more than 2^{32} records.

Here is an example that uses a link column to implement a hierarchical structure in a table. The column pid is a link column that relates a row to its parent row.

```
q)tree:([] id:0 1 2 3 4; pid:`tree!0N 0 0 1 1; v:100 200 300 400 500)
q)select from tree where pid=0      / find children of root
_
```

14.1.3 Serializing Tables

It is possible to persist any table (or keyed table) using the general q serialization/deserialization capability of (set) and (get). There is no restriction on table or column types.

```
q)`:/data/t set ([] s:`a`b`c; v:100 200 300)
`:/data/t
q)\\
```

```
>q
q)t:get `:/data/t
q)t
_
```

You can serialize foreign keys and link columns and bring them back into memory.

```
q)kt:([id:1001 1002 1003] s:`a`b`c; v:100 200 300)
q)tk:([] id:1001 1002 100; s:`a`b`c; v:100 200 300)
q)`:/data/kt set kt
`:/data/kt
q)`:/data/tk set tk
`:/data/tk
q)`:/data/t1 set ([]; id:`kt$1002 1001 1003 1001; q:100 101 102 103)
`:/data/t1
q)`:/data/t2 set ([]; id:`kt!(exec id from tk)?1002 1001 1003 1001;
q:100 101 102 103)
`:/data/t2
q)\\
```

```
>q
q)kt:get `:/data/kt
q)tk:get `:/data/tk
q)t1:get `:/data/t1
q)t2:get `:/data/t2
```

14.1.4 Operating on Serialized Tables

You operate on a serialized table by loading it into memory with (get) or \l.

```
q)`:/data/t set ([] s:`a`b`c; v:100 200 300)
`:/data/t
q)\l /data/t
`t
q)select from t

q)t1: get `:/data/t
q)select from t1
```

Alternatively, you can perform a query on a serialized table by specifying its file handle as the table name.

```
q)`:/data/t set ([] s:`a`b`c; v:100 200 300)
`:/data/t
q)select from `:/data/t where s in `a`c
s v
-----
a 100
c 300
q)`:/data/t upsert (`x;42)
`:/data/t
q).[`:/data/t;();,;([] s:`y`z; v:400 500)]
`:/data/t
q)select from `:/data/t where s in `x`y`z
```

Similar operations are available on keyed tables.

```
q)`:/data/kt set ([k:`a`b`c] v:10 20 30)
`:/data/kt
q)`:/data/kt upsert (`b;200)
`:/data/kt
q)`:/data/kt upsert (`x;42)
`:/data/kt
q)select from `:/data/kt
k| v
-| ---
a| 10
b| 200
c| 30
x| 42
```

> **Note:** The limitation to using a serialized table or keyed table is that, behind the scenes, the operations load it into memory and write it back out. Amongst other things, this means that anyone wanting to work with it must be able to fit it into memory in its entirety.

14.1.5 The Database View

Persisting a table via serialization creates a single file in the OS file system. Let's raise our perspective to the 50,000-foot level. From this height, we see the table as a single point.

Big Picture (0): We think of a serialized table as a zero-dimensional persisted form since it is stored in a single file and is not decomposed.

```
                file
table           ▪
```

Here the ▪ represents the contents of the table as an opaque entity. This contrasts with higher-dimensional forms we shall encounter later.

14.2 Splayed Tables

In the previous section, we saw that it is possible to persist tables using serialization. From a database perspective there are (at least) two issues with operating on serialized tables due to the fact that the entire table is loaded into memory.

- The entire table must fit into memory on each user's machine.
- Operations against the persisted table will be slow due to reloading the entire table each time.

14.2.0 Splaying a Table

When a table is too large to fit into memory as a single entity, we can persist its components into a directory. This is called *splaying* the table because the table is pulled apart into its constituent columns (it is an interesting exercise to look up the derivation of this word in English). Splaying solves the memory/reload issue because a splayed table is mapped into memory; columns are loaded on demand then memory is released when no longer needed. Tables with many columns especially benefit from splaying since most queries refer to only a handful of columns and only those columns will actually be loaded.

A splayed table corresponds to a directory whose name **is** the table name. Each column list of the table is serialized into a file whose name **is** the column name.

Tip: You don't have any choice in the names.

A list of the symbolic column names is serialized to the hidden file .d in the directory to record column order. This is the **only** metadata stored by kdb+; all other metadata is read from directory and file names.

414

Customarily the splayed directory is created one level down from a directory that serves as the root of the database.

```
/root
  /tablename              <- splayed table directory
   .d                     <- file with column names
   column1name            <- column data file
   column2name            <- column data file
   ...
```

From the 50,000-foot level, we see the following on the file system.

Big Picture (1): We think of a splayed table as a persisted form that is cut vertically along columns.

	column1	column2	column3	...
table	▪	▪	▪	...

Geometrically, the persisted table is 1-dimensional—there is a point for each column in the persisted image of the table.

14.2.1 Creating Splayed Tables

We start with a very simple example of creating a splayed table. Make sure you include the trailing '/' in the file handle; otherwise, you will serialize the table into a single file.

```
q)`:/db/t/ set ([] v1:10 20 30; v2:1.1 2.2 3.3)
`:/data/t/
q)\ls -a /db/t
"."
".."
".d"
"v1"
"v2"
```

It is also possible to create a splayed table with (upsert), or with the equivalent generalized application, using the file handle as the table name. When the file does not exist, these act like (set).

```
q)`:/db/t2/ upsert ([] v1:10 20 30; v2:1.1 2.2 3.3)
```

```
q).[`:/db/t3/; (); ,; ([] v1:10 20 30; v2:1.1 2.2 3.3)]
```

Reading the constituents of the splayed directory with (get) demonstrates that they are simply serialized q entities.

```
q)get `:/db/t/v1
10 20 30
q)get `:/db/t/v2

q)get `:/db/t/.d
`v1`v2
```

Of course, if your notion of fashion is a hair shirt, you can splay your table manually. In a fresh /db directory,

```
q)t:([] v1:10 20 30; v2:1.1 2.2 3.3)
q)cs:cols t
q){[cname] (hsym `$"/db/",string cname) set t cname} each cs

q)`:/db/.d set cs
```

There are serious restrictions on what can be splayed.

    (1)   Tables can be splayed. Keyed tables **cannot**.

           This might seem to preclude relational capabilities since it eliminates persisting a foreign key relation. But the day is saved by link columns, which can be persisted. See §14.1.2.

    (2)   Only columns that are simple lists or compound lists can be splayed. By *compound* list we mean a list of simple lists of uniform type.

           The isn't too limiting in practice since data often comes in a uniform format that can be readily put into simple or compound lists. Incidentally, the reason for this restriction is that working with mapped general lists would be much slower than working with simple or compound lists, especially for very large data sets. See §14.2.4for more on nested columns.

    (3)   All symbol columns must be enumerated.

           This restriction might seem to complicate life but there are conventions and utilities that eliminate most of the pain. See §14.2.2

14.2.2 Splayed Tables with Symbol Columns

The convention for symbol columns in splayed (and partitioned) tables is that **all** symbol columns in **all** tables are enumerated over the list sym, which is serialized into the root directory.

The author prefers to use a projected from of the utility .Q.en for enumerating symbols. Its first parameter is the file handle of the root directory (the location of the sym file) and its second parameter is the table whose symbol columns you wish enumerated. Here is a simple example.

```
q)`:/db/t/ set .Q.en[`:/db;] ([] s1:`a`b`c; v:10 20 30; s2:`x`y`z)
`:/db/t/
q)\ls /db
"sym"
,"t"
q)\\
```

```
>q
q)\l /db
q)sym
`a`b`c`x`y`z
q)select from t
_
```

We offer several observations on the action of .Q.en this example.

- If there is a sym list in memory, it is overwritten
- If there is a sym list on disk it is locked and then loaded into memory
- If no sym list exists in memory or on disk and empty one is created.
- All symbols in all symbol columns of the table are conditionally enumerated over the sym list in memory.
- Once the enumeration is complete the sym list in memory is serialized to the root and the file is unlocked.

Once again, you could don your hair shirt and do symbol enumeration manually.

```
q)t:([] s1:`a`b`c; v:10 20 30; s2:`x`y`z)
q)sym:()
q)`:/db/t/ set @[t;exec c from meta t where "s"=t; `sym?]
_
q)sym
_
\\
```

```
>q
q)\l /db
q)select from t
_
```

14.2.3 Splayed Tables with Nested Columns

The only nested columns that can be splayed are what we call
compound lists—i.e., lists of simple lists of uniform type. The most
common example is a list of strings, which is a list of lists of char. A
compound column is indicated by an upper case letter in the result of
(meta). For example, here is a table having two compound columns,
which can be splayed in a fresh directory db.

```
q)meta ([] ci:(1 2 3; enlist 4; 5 6); cstr:("abc";enlist"d";"ef"))
c   | t f a
----| -----
x   | J
cstr| C
q)`:/db/tcomp2/ set ([] ci:(1 2 3; enlist 4; 5 6);
cstr:("abc";enlist"d";"ef"))
_
```

By contrast, the following table cannot be splayed and results in an
error.

```
q)meta ([] c:(1;1,1;`1))
c| t f a
-| -----
c|
q)`:/db/tcomp2/ set ([] c:(1;1,1;`1))
k){$[@x;.[x;();:;y];-19!((,y),x)]}
'type
q.q))
```

> **Tip:** You might reasonably think that you can use the result of (meta)
> to determine whether your table can be splayed by checking for a
> blank in the t column. You would be wrong since (meta) only
> examines the initial item of a column list and improperly reports some
> mixed columns as compound.

```
q)meta ([] c:(1 2 3 ;1,1;`1))
c| t f a
-| -----
c| J
q)`:/db/tbad/ set  ([] c:(1 2 3 ;1,1;`1))
k){$[@x;.[x;();:;y];-19!((,y),x)]}
'type
q.q))
```

The following function will tell you which columns of a table cannot be
splayed.

```
{where {(ts~1#0h)|1<count ts:distinct (type each)x} each flip x}
```

When you splay a table with compound columns, q creates not one but two files for each compound column. For example, in a fresh directory /db, we splay a table with a single string column and then inspect the splayed directory.

```
q)`:/db/tstr/ set ([] c:("abc";enlist "d";"ef"))
q)system "ls -a /db/tstr"
,"."
".."
".d"
,"c"
"c#"
```

Observe that there are two files associated with the compound column —namely, c and c#. If you examine these files you will discover that the "sharp" file contains the binary data of the original list in flattened form and the non-sharp file is a serialized q list of integers representing the lengths of each sublist of the original list.

```
q)"c"$read1 hsym `$"/db/tstr/c#"
"abcdef"
q)read1 hsym `$"/db/tstr/c"
0xfe205700000000000300000000000000030000000000000004000000000000006000
00000000000
```

Interestingly, (get) reconstitutes the list from the non-sharp file.

```
q)get  hsym `$"/db/tstr/c"
"abc"
,"d"
"ef"
```

The purpose of writing compound columns as two files is to speed up operations against them when the splayed table is mapped into memory. Of course, the processing won't be as fast as for a simple column, but it is still plenty fast for most purposes.

One question that always arises when designing a kdb+ database is whether to store text data as symbols or strings. The advantage of symbols is that they have atomic semantics and, since they are integers under the covers once they are enumerated, processing is quite fast. The main issue with symbols is that if you make all text into symbols, your sym list gets enormous and the advantages of enumeration disappear.

In contrast, strings do not pollute the sym list with one-off instances and are reasonably fast. The disadvantage is that they are not first class and you must revert to teenage years by using (like) to match them.

Recommendation: Only make text columns into symbols when the fields will be drawn from a small, reasonably stable domain and there is significant repetition in their use. When in doubt, start with a string column. It is much easier to convert a string column to symbols that it is to remove symbols from the sym list.

A text column that is drawn from a fixed list or a lookup table is an ideal candidate. So are invariant keys, provided the key domain is small and will not grow unreasonably. On the other hand, fields such as comments or notes should always be strings.

14.2.4 Basic Operations on Splayed Tables

Let us create a splayed table in a fresh /db.

```
q)`:/db/t/ set .Q.en[`:/db;] ([] s1:`a`b`c; v:10 20 30; s2:`x`y`z)
```

To operate on a splayed table you can map it into memory in one of two ways.

Tip: Note the lack of a trailing '/' in both techniques of mapping the table below.

You can specify a splayed table on the q startup command immediately after the q executable.

```
$q /db/t
q)select from t
```

Alternatively, you can use \l to map the table.

Tip: Confusingly, folks say they are "loading" the table, even though none of the table data is actually brought into memory in this step.

```
q)\l /db/t
`t
q)select from t
```

The illusion that the table is actually in memory after it is mapped is convincing. Many fundamental table operations work on splayed tables.

```
q)\a
, t
q)meta t
c | t f a
--| -----
s1| s
v | j
s2| s
q)cols t
`s1`v`s2
q)type t
98h
q)count t
3
```

You can index records.

```
q)t[0]
s1| `sym$`a
v | 10
s2| `sym$`x
```

You **cannot** use dot notation to extract columns from a splayed table but you **can** extract a column with symbol indexing.

```
q)t.s1
'type
q)t `s1
`sym$`a`b`c
```

You can use both `select` and `exec` templates on a splayed table.

```
q)select v from t where s1=`c
```

```
q)exec s1 from t
```

Tip: This contrasts with partitioned tables where you can only use `select`.

14.2.5 Operations on a Splayed Directory

As of this writing (Sep 2015), the table operations available against the file handle of a splayed table are: `select`, `exec`, `upsert`, `xasc`, `` `attr# `` (apply an attribute).

With t splayed as above,

```
q)select from `:/db/t

q)exec v  from `:/db/t

q)`v xdesc `:/db/t

q)@[`:/db/t;`s1;`p#]

q)\l /db
q)meta t
_
```

We point out a source of confusion to qbies. Specifically, the behavior of update on a splayed table that has been mapped into memory. Starting with a fresh directory /db, create a splayed table, map it into memory and then update it.

```
q)`:/db/t/ set .Q.en[`:/db;] ([] s1:`a`b`c; v:10 20 30; s2:`x`y`z)

q)\l /db
q)update v:300 from `t where s1=`c
`t
q)select from t
s1 v   s2
---------
a  10  x
b  20  y
c  300 z
```

But a rude surprise awaits when we remap the table.

```
q)\l /db
q)select from t
s1 v  s2
--------
a  10 x
b  20 y
c  30 z
```

> **Note:** Updates applied to a mapped table are only visible in the workspace and are not reflected on disk. There may be scenarios where this is useful but we advise avoiding it.

And now we arrive at a fundamental limitation of kdb+.

> **Really Important:** It is not possible to use built-in operations to update data in persisted splayed tables.

You read that correctly. Kdb+ is intended to store data that is not updated or deleted once it has been written. We shall see in the next section how to append to a splayed table, which makes it possible to process updates and deletes in a bitemporal fashion, but this capability is not available out of the box.

14.2.6 Appending to a Splayed Table

Since upsert acts as insert on regular (non-keyed) tables and only non-keyed tables can be splayed, we use upsert with the splayed directory name in order to append records to a splayed table on disk. This is a good thing, since (insert) doesn't work on splayed tables. Also, because symbol columns must be enumerated for splayed tables, it is best to make rows into tables.

In a fresh /db,

```
q)`:/db/t/ set .Q.en[`:/db;] ([] s1:`a`b`c; v:10 20 30; s2:`x`y`z)

q)`:/db/t/ upsert .Q.en[`:/db;] ([] s1:`d`e; v:40 50; s2:`u`v)

q)`:/db/t upsert .Q.en[`:/db;] enlist `s1`v`s2!(`f;60;`t)

q)`:/db/t upsert .Q.en[`:/db;] flip `s1`v`s2!flip
((`g;70;`r);(`h;80;`s))

q)\l / db
q)select from t
```

You can use upsert in this fashion to build large splayed tables incrementally. The following example can be enhanced to create a splayed table step-by-step as batches of new records arrive. In a fresh /db,

```
q)batch:{[rt;tn;recs] hsym[`$rt,"/",tn,"/"] upsert .Q.en[hsym `$rt;]
recs}
q)dayrecs:{([] dt:x; ti:asc 100?24:00:00; sym:100?`ibm`aapl;
qty:100*1+100?1000)}
q)appday:batch["/db";"t";]

q)appday dayrecs 2015.01.01

q)appday dayrecs 2015.01.02

q)appday dayrecs 2015.01.03

q)\l /db
q)select from t
```

14.2.7 Manual Operations on a Splayed Directory

Although there are no built-in operations to update splayed tables on disk, you can perform such operations by manipulating the serialized files.

> **Important:** The examples shown here should be used with caution, as none of the operations are atomic; they are simply file system manipulation. Even read-only users could see inconsistent data, so things are best done when no other users are accessing the database.

Here is an example of how to simulate an (update .. where) on a single column. In a fresh /db,

```
q)`:/db/t/ set ([] ti:09:30:00 09:31:00; p:101.5 33.5)
q)`:/db/t/p set .[get `:/db/t/p; where 09:31:00=get `:/db/t/ti; :;42.0]
q)\l /db/t
q)select from t
```

To add a new column of nulls to an existing splayed table, we first get the row count form any column file. Then we revise the .d file with the new column name. This example is easily modified to place arbitrary data in the new column.

```
q)`:/db/t/s set (count get `:/db/t/ti)#`
q)`:/db/t/.d set get[`:/db/t/.d] union `s
```

To delete a column, remove its file and revise the .d file to reflect its absence.

```
q)system "rm /db/t/s"
q)`:/db/t/.d set get[`:/db/t/.d] except `s

q)\l /db
q)select from t
```

While you can sort a splayed table on disk, suppose you want to implement your own custom sort. We shoe how to create the standard sort. First create the appropriate sort index with (iasc) or (idesc) and then use this to re-index all the column files. Here we perform a descending sort by the ti column.

```
q)cs:system "ls /db/t"
q)I:idesc `:/db/t/ti
q){pth set get[pth:hsym `$"/db/t/",x] I} each cs
`:/db/t/ix`:/db/t/p`:/db/t/ti
q)\l /db
q)select from t
_
```

14.2.8 Working with sym Files

On occasion you may need to perform operations involving the sym files. For example, you may want to move a table from one database to another. Or you may find that your sym domain has become polluted due to symbol columns that should have been strings. Or you may have unwisely chosen to have many different enumeration domains and you wish to consolidate them into one. All these situations can be resolved by careful operations on the sym file(s).

> **Tip:** Updating sym files is delicate and should be done with great care, only after you have made a complete backup of the root directory. Corrupting the sym file will almost certainly render your database useless.

In our first example we show how to merge a table from one database into another. Suppose we have root directories /db1 and /db2, both with the standard sym file in the root and with splayed tables t1 and t2, respectively. In fresh directories /db1 and /db2,

```
q)`:/db1/t1/ set .Q.en[`:/db1;] ([] s:`a`b`c; v:10 20 30)
_
q)`:/db2/t2/ set .Q.en[`:/db2;] ([] s:`c`d`e; v:300 400 500)
_
q)get `:/db1/sym
`a`b`c
q)get `:/db2/sym
`c`d`e
```

In order to copy table t2 to the /db1 root, we un-enumerate all its symbol columns and then re-enumerate them in the target database.

```
q)symcols2:exec c from meta `:/db2/t2 where t="s"
q)t2noenum:@[select from `:/db2/t2;symcols2;value]
q)`:/db1/t2/ set .Q.en[`:/db1] t2noenum
_
q)get `:/db1/sym
`a`b`c`d`e
```

In another example, suppose that we mistakenly made a comment column into symbols instead of strings, with the result being a pollution of the sym domain with many single use items. In a fresh

/db, we save t1 with a valid symbol column and then screwup on the comment field in t2.

```
q)`:/db/t1/ set .Q.en[`:/db;] ([] s:`a`b`c; v:10 20 30)
q)`:/db/t2/ set .Q.en[`:/db;] ([] c:1 2 3; comment:`$("abc";"de";"fg"))
q)get `:/db/sym
`a`b`c`abc`de`fg
```

First we load the database and remove the offending comments from the sym list.

```
q)\l /db
q)sym:sym except exec comment from t2
q)sym
```

Next we re-enumerate the re-typed culprit table over the clean sym list and re-splay it. Note that we use (`sym?) for the enumeration since it is possible that some of the comments actually overlapped with symbols from other tables.

```
q)reenum:{@[x;exec c from meta x where t="s";`sym?]}
q)`:/db/t2/ set reenum ([] s:`a`b`c; comment:("abc";"de";"fg"))
```

Next we un-enumerate, re-enumerate and re-splay the remaining tables.

```
q)ts:system["a"] except `t2
q)unenum:{@[select from x; exec c from meta x where t="s";value]}
q){(hsym `$"/db/",string[x],"/") set reenum unenum x} each ts
```

Finally we overwrite the sym file with the correct sym list that is now in memory and reload the database to check our handiwork.

```
q)`:/db/sym set sym
q)\l /db
q)meta t1

q)meta t2
```

14.2.9 Splayed Tables with Link Columns

We previously pointed out that you cannot splay a keyed table, and therefore cannot have a foreign key relation between splayed tables. However, you can splay a link column and then use dot notation just as you would with a foreign key. You must do the work of creating the index yourself, just as with link columns with tables in memory.

In our first example, we create the link at the same time as we splay the tables. This is the same as creating the link on in-memory tables and then splaying them. In a fresh /db,

```
q)t1:([] c1:`c`b`a; c2: 10 20 30)
q)t2:([] c3:`a`b`a`c; c4: 1. 2. 3. 4.)
q)update t1lnk:`t1!t1[`c1]?t2[`c3] from `t2

q)`:/db/t1/ set `.Q.en[`:/db;] t1

q)`:/db/t2/ set `.Q.en[`:/db;] t2

q)\\
```

```
$q
q)\l /db
q)meta t2
c     | t f a
------| ------
c3    | s
c4    | f
t1lnk | i t1
q)select c3,t1lnk.c2,c4 from t2
```

Now we redo this example, assuming that the tables have already been splayed. You could map the database into memory but let's work directly with the files. We have the additional step of appending the link columns to the .d file for t2.

```
q)`:/db/t1/ set .Q.en[`:/db;] ([] c1:`c`b`a; c2: 10 20 30)

q)`:/db/t2/ set .Q.en[`:/db;] ([] c3:`a`b`a`c; c4: 1. 2. 3. 4.)

q)`:/db/t2/t1link set `t1!(get `:/db/t1/c1)?get `:/db/t2/c3

q).[`:/db/t2/.d;();,;`t1link]

q)\l /db
q)meta t2
```

14.2.10 Query Execution on Splayed Tables

As we noted in the introduction of the chapter, splayed tables are a memory win, in that the table is mapped into memory and columns are actually loaded only as needed. Since a typical query requires only a handful of columns, this can greatly reduce the amount of memory required to process a table with many columns.

In addition to the memory win, if the same columns are referenced again soon, there is a good chance that their data is cached, either in memory or by the storage controller. This can be a significant performance win.

There is also a more subtle performance win in how the where phrase is implemented. As mentioned in Chapter 11, each where subphrase produces a boolean vector that acts as mask, on which positions will be examined in the subsequent grouping and aggregation. When the table is mapped, this can also significantly reduce the amount of data that is loaded into memory.

14.3 Partitioned Tables

To recap the previous section, a splayed table has been split vertically along its columns and is subsequently mapped into memory. When a query is executed against the mapped table, column data is loaded as needed and is presumably cached for subsequent access. This reduces the table's memory footprint, especially for tables with many columns.

Some timeseries data is so large that even the individual columns may not fit into memory—for example, daily trades and quotes for an entire exchange. In this case, we can further decompose the table by slicing horizontally—called *partitioning* in kdb+. For example, the solution for trades and quotes is to slice into daily portions. The result is a collection of daily splayed directories, one for each day for which data exists.

> *Tip:* All partitioned tables are splayed but not all splayed tables are partitioned.

14.3.1 Partitions

A *partitioned* table is a splayed table that is further decomposed by grouping records having common values along a column of special type. The allowable special column types have the property that the underlying value is an integer: date, month, year and long.

The slice of records having a given value is splayed into a directory, called a *partition*, whose name **is** that common value. In the canonical Finance example, historical trades (or quotes) are stored in daily partition directories—remember a q date is an integer under the covers.

Big Picture (2): We think of a partitioned table as a two-dimensional persisted form since it is cut in two directions: vertically by splaying along columns and horizontally by slicing into partitions.

	column1	column2	column3	...
partition1	▪	▪	▪	...
partition2	▪	▪	▪	...
...	...	...	...	...

Here each ▪ represents a (partial) column of a partition slice as an opaque entity.

As with splaying, kdb+ implements partitioning using the OS directory structure. Each partition must be stored in a directory immediately under the database root directory. The directory name **is** the common column value for all the rows in the partition. Each partition directory in turn contains a subdirectory holding a splayed table with the records for that slice. The two-dimensional decomposition is reflected in two levels of nested directories under the root.

Since each splayed table subdirectory name **is** the name of the table, these names must be consistent across all partitions. Likewise, as portions of a single table, all splayed slices should have identical schemas. This means that each slice directory contains column files with the same names and internal data types, as well as identical .d files.

```
/root
   /partitionvalue1
      /tablename
         .d
         column1name
         column2name
         ...
   /partitionvalue2
      /tablename
         .d
         column1name
         column2name
         ...
   ...
```

> ***Important:*** Since a partition directory name factors out the common value for all records in its slice, do not include the partition column when you splay a partition slice—e.g., do not include a date column for a daily partitioned table. Instead, kdb+ infers the name, value and type from the partition directory name and creates a virtual column from this information. The name of the virtual column is set by q and cannot be controlled.

14.3.2 Partition Domain

We call the type of the virtual column for the partition the *partition domain*. As noted previously, the partition domain must have an underlying integral value.

> ***Tip:*** You cannot use a symbol column as a partition domain, even if the symbols are enumerated.

For example, suppose we have daily timeseries data. A daily partitioning could look as follows.

```
2015.01.01, 2015.01.02, …
```

The virtual column is date in this case. Under each partition directory, there is a subdirectory t with that day's slice of records.

```
/db
    /2015.01.01
       /t              <- trade records for 2015.01.01
    /2015.01.02
       /t              <- trade records for 2015.01.02        …
```

> ***Important:*** A kdb+ database can only have a single partition domain. This means that you must create separate databases if you need partitions of different granularity. For example, you cannot have daily and monthly partitions in one database.

There is no requirement that there be entries for every value in the partition domain. For example, there may be no trades for holidays.

```
/db
    /2014.12.31
       /t
    /2015.01.02
       /t
    …
```

If we partition by month,

    2015.01m, 2015.02m, …

the virtual column name is month.

For daily data that requires frequent multi-year queries, partitioning by year may be better.

    2010, 2011, …

In this case, the virtual column is year even though there is no year type in q. The values are recognized as valid q years if they are less than 10,000.

You can also partition by an arbitrary int such as a bin number.

    0, 1, …

This results in a virtual column int.

14.3.3 Creating Partitioned Tables

For simplicity, our first example has no symbols. In a fresh /db,

```
q)`:/db/2015.01.01/t/ set ([] ti:09:30:00 09:31:00; p:101 102f)

q)`:/db/2015.01.02/t/ set ([] ti:09:30:00 09:31:00; p:101.5 102.5)

q)\l /db
q)t             / never do this at home!
date       ti       p
-----------------------------
2015.01.01 09:30:00 101
2015.01.01 09:31:00 102
2015.01.02 09:30:00 101.5
2015.01.02 09:31:00 102.5
```

The table appears to be in the workspace, along with the virtual date columns, but this is an illusion. It is actually mapped into memory. The request to display t forces all columns for all days to be loaded into memory.

> **Important:** Always qualify the partition column in the first where subphrase in any query against a partitioned table. If you do not, you will cause all partitions to be loaded into memory and will probably live-lock the server. Well before this completes, your colleagues will be at your desk with pitchforks and burning torches.

A more responsible way to create the previous display is,

```
q)select from t where date within 2015.01.01 2015.01.02
```

Here we partition tables with symbols in a fresh /db. Note that we wrap the line in our display.

```
q)`:/db/2015.01.01/t/ set
   .Q.en[`:/db;] ([] ti:09:30:00 09:31:00; s:`ibm`msft; p:101 33f)

q)`:/db/2015.01.02/t/ set
   .Q.en[`:/db;] ([] ti:09:30:00 09:31:00; s:`ibm`msft; p:101.5 33.5)

q)\l /db
q)select from t where date within 2015.01.01 2015.01.02
```

14.3.4 Working with Partitioned Tables

Continuing with the last example of the previous section, we can apply some basic operations on a partitioned table that has been mapped. Observe that the virtual partition column is included in the results of (meta) and (cols).

```
q)count t

q)meta t
c    | t f a
-----| -----
date | d
ti   | v
s    | s
p    | f
q)cols t
`date`ti`s`p
q)type t
98h
```

However, none of the following work on partitioned tables, even thought they work on splayed tables.

```
t[0j]
t[;`p]
0#t
exec from t
select[1] from t
```

```
`p xasc t
```

> **Tip:** The fact that exec doesn't work on partitioned tables is annoying but the workaround is,
>
> ```
> exec … from select … from …
> ```

The select template, or the equivalent functional form, is **the** way to access data for a partitioned table. We have already seen how to retrieve the records for consecutive days. Here is the query to retrieve a day's slice.

```
q)select from t where date=2015.01.01
```

Here is how to retrieve the first or last day without hardcoding the date.

```
q)select from t where date=first date

q)select from t where date=max date
```

Always place the partition column constraint first.

```
q)select from t where date=2015.01.01, ti<09:30:30
```

You can group by the partition column. Note we have wrapped the line for display.

```
q)select hi:max p, lo:min p by date from t
  where date within 2015.01.01 2015.01.02
```

14.3.5 The Virtual Column i in Partitioned Tables

In a partitioned table, the virtual column i does **not** refer to absolute row number as it does with in-memory and splayed tables. Instead, it refers to the relative row number within a partition. Thus, a constraint on i alone would apply across all partitions and the result will contain that row in each partition slice—probably not what you want and almost certainly a bad idea (colleagues with pitchforks again).

Continuing with the previous example, the following query retrieves the initial record from each of the specified partitions.

```
q)select from t where date in 2015.01.01 2015.01.02, i=0
```

The following queries retrieve the first and last records in the table, respectively.

```
q) select from t where date=first date, i=0
q) select from t where date=max date, i=max i
```

See §14.4.5 for using .Q.ind to index **across** partitions.

14.3.6 Query Execution on Partitioned Tables

Query execution against a partitioned table is more complex than execution against a splayed table. Understanding how it works is necessary to achieve good design and performance with kdb+ databases.

Recall that the motivation for partitions was to avoid loading entire columns into memory. Behind the scenes, kdb+ achieves this as follows.

- Analyze the where phrase to determine which partition slices are targeted by the query
- Process the remaining where sub-phrases to determine the column sub-domains that must be loaded.
- Process the query separately against the requisite partition slices to obtain partial results.
- Combine the partial results to obtain the final result.

Reading only partial column slices of a table having many partitions is clearly a big memory and performance win. But things are even more interesting with regard to the third point above. If you have started q without slaves, the query is executed sequentially against the partitions and the time to complete is (roughly) the sum of the time against each of the partition slices.

By contrast, if you have started q with slaves, the query will be executed concurrently, once slice per slave. Thus, you can see significant speedup provided the query is compute-bound and the slaves are running on separate cores. On the other hand, if the query is I/O bound and you have only a single I/O channel to the data, you may see no speedup.

Next we discuss how kdb+ executes some types of queries concurrently.

14.3.7 Map-Reduce

We start with a brief introduction to map-reduce. Suppose we want to compute some aggregation—say the sum or the average—of a large list of numbers and have at our disposal a crop of interns armed with smartphones. Our strategy is to decompose the overall task into two stages. In the first stage, we split the list into roughly (but not exactly) equal size sublists, distributing one to each intern along with instructions on what to compute. In the second step, we collect the (partial) results from each intern and combine them to get the overall result. This is what good managers do, after all.

Think about how to do this for sum before continuing. For the sum, you could instruct each intern to compute the sum of her list and then compute the sum of the individual sums. The same simple approach works for count or maximum.

For average, things aren't quite so simple. If you simply have each intern compute an average of her list, you will need to weight each partial average by the size of the sublist to get the final average. Thus you need the count too. You quickly realize that you can distribute the average computation more effectively. Instead of asking each intern to return the average and count for her list, ask her to compute the sum and the count. In the reduction step, you obtain the overall average as the sum of the partial sums divided by the sum of the partial counts.

More generally, map-reduce decomposes an operation on a (presumably large) list into two suboperations, op_{map} and op_{reduce}. In the first step, called 'map', op_{map} is performed on each sublist to obtain a list of partial results. In the second step, called "reduce", the partial result lists are combined with op_{reduce} to obtain the final result. A good exercise (and interview question) is to express sorting a list using map-reduce. In greater generality, map-reduce may apply the two steps recursively—i.e., the reduce step may itself involve a map-reduce, etc.

It is easy to see how map-reduce applies to a query against a partitioned table, since the table is a list of records sliced into sub-lists by the partitioning. The challenge is to decompose the query into a map step and a reduce step. The solution depends on whether the query involves aggregation.

If there is no aggregation, the result of the query on each partition is simply the computed columns for the list of the records in the partition slice matching the constraint. In other words, produce a partial result table by computing the columns of the query across partitions. Because all the partial result tables conform, union the partial result tables in order of their virtual partition column values. In summary: fan the query across the partitions and union the ordered results.

Things are more interesting when the query contains aggregation. For aggregates that kdb+ recognizes as map-reducible, it applies the map operation across partition slices to obtain partial results. It then applies the reduce operation across the partial result tables to obtain the final result table.

At the time of this writing (Sep 2015), the aggregates that kdb+ can decompose with map-reduce are: (avg), (cor), (count), (cov), (dev), (distinct), (first), (last), (max), (med), (min), (prd), (sum), (var), (wavg), (wsum).

To make this more concrete, we re-examine computing an average against a daily partitioned trades table.

```
select avg size from trade where date within ...
```

Because kdb+ recognizes (avg) as an aggregate it can decompose with map-reduce, it performs the calculation in two steps. Specifically, op_{map} computes the sum and record count for each date, while op_{reduce} divides the sum of the daily sums by the sum of the daily counts to give the average. The user gets the expected result and is none the wiser unless q was started with slaves, in which case the result maybe faster than linear.

14.3.8 Multiple Partitioned Tables

Recall that there can be only one partition domain in a given kdb+ root—i.e., daily, monthly, yearly or long. However, multiple tables can share this partitioning.

For example, quotes and trades can coexist in a daily partition. That layout would look something like,

```
/db
    /2015.01.01
      /trade
      /quote
    /2015.01.02
      /trade
      /quote
```

> **Important:** Although not all potential partition values need be populated, any value that is populated must contain slices for all tables.
>
> The following layout is in error.
>
> ```
> /db
>     /2015.01.01        <- this is a bad partition!
>       /quote
>     /2015.01.02
>       /trade
>
>       /quote
> ```

We demonstrate how to create a simplified database with tables standing for trades and quotes in a fresh db directory. Notice that we wrap the lines that do not fit within this page margin.

```
q)`:/db/2015.01.01/t/ set .Queen[`:/db;]
  ([] ti:09:30:00 09:31:00; sym:`ibm`msft;p:101 33f)

q)`:/db/2015.01.02/t/ set .Q.en[`:/db;]
  ([] ti:09:30:00 09:31:00; sym:`ibm`msft;p:101.5 33.5)


q)`:/db/2015.01.01/q/ set .Q.en[`:/db;]
  ([] ti:09:30:00 09:31:00; sym:`ibm`msft;b:100.75 32.75; a:101.25
33.25f)

q)`:/db/2015.01.02/q/ set .Q.en[`:/db;]
  ([] ti:09:30:00 09:30:00; sym:`ibm`msft;b:101.25 33.25; a:101.75
33.75)
```

Mapping the root, we now find both are available.

```
q)select from t where date within 2015.01.01 2015.01.02

q)select from q where date within 2015.01.01 2015.01.02
```

Next we add a historical slice for q on 2014.12.31 but negelct to add the corresponding slice for t. Things seem fine when we map the root and query q on the newly added date.

```
q)`:/db/2014.12.31/q/ set .Q.en[`:/db;] ([] ti:09:30:00 09:31:00;
sym:`ibm`msft; b:101. 33.; a:101.5 33.5f)
`:/db/2014.12.31/q/
q)\l /db
q)select from q where date=2014.12.31
_
```

But we get a nasty surprise when we query t on the missing date.

```
q)select from t where date=2014.12.31
k){0!(?).@[x;0;p1[;y;z]]}
'./2014.12.31/t/ti: No such file or directory
.
?
(+`ti`sym`p!`:./2014.12.31/t;();0b;())
q.Q))
```

We could remedy this by splaying an empty copy of t on that date. Instead we use the utility .Q.chk that fills all missing slices with empty tables from the most recent partition. We remap and find things are fine.

```
q).Q.chk `:/db
_
q)\l /db
q)select from t where date=2014.12.31
_
```

> **Tip:** If you neglect to place a table slice in the most recent partition, the table will effectively disappear from your database since kdb+ inspects only that partition to determine which tables are present.

Continuing with our previous (repaired) example we add a trade slice for 2015.01.03 but neglect to add a quotes slice. When we remap, the table q is nowhere to be found.

```
q)`:/db/2015.01.03/t/ set .Queen[`:/db;]
  ([] ti:09:30:00 09:31:00; sym:`ibm`msft;p:101 33f)
_
q)\l /db
q)\a
,`t
```

Here is one way to fill will an empty slice.

```
q)`:/db/2015.01.03/q/ set  0#select from `:/db/2015.01.02/q
q)\l /db
q)\a
`q`t
```

14.3.9 Examples of Other Partition Domain Types

We present simple examples of partitions with the other permissible types. For simplicity, we do not include symbol columns; to do so, merely add the call to .Q.en as in previous examples.

Yearly partitioning can be a good solution when you regularly need to retrieve multiple years of daily data. Note that we explicitly include the date column but not the year column, which is virtual. In a fresh /db,

```
q)`:/db/2015/t/ set ([] date:2015.01.01 2015.01.02; p:101 102f)
`:/db/2015/t/
q)`:/db/2014/t/ set ([] date:2014.01.01 2014.01.02; p:101.5 102.5)
`:/db/2014/t/
q)\l /db
q)select from t where year within 2014 2015
```

Monthly partitioning can be a good compromise between daily and yearly when you have both single day and year-to-date queries. We explicitly include the date column but not the month column, which is virtual.

> **Tip:** Do **not** include a trailing '/' in the partition directory name but **do** include it in the queries.

In a fresh /db,

```
q)`:/db/2015.01/t/ set ([] date:2015.01.01 2015.01.02; p:101 102f)
`:/db/2015.01/t/
q)`:/db/2015.02/t/ set ([] date:2015.02.01 2015.02.02; p:101.5 102.5)
`:/db/2015.02/t/
q)\l /db
q)select from t where month within 2015.01m 2015.02m
```

You can partition by a long to slice into arbitrary bins. The data need not be daily. In a fresh /db,

```
q)`:/db/1/t/ set ([] ti:09:30:00 09:31:00; p:101 102f)

q)`:/db/2/t/ set ([] ti:09:30:00 09:31:00; p:101.5 102.5)

q)\l /db
q)select from t where in within 1 2
```

14.3.10 Partitioned Tables with Links

You can create links between tables in the same partitioned database with the following restriction.

> **Note:** A link column in the slice of a partitioned table must be intra-partition—i.e., it must refer to another table in the same slice. In particular, you cannot link across days in a daily partitioned database.

Since the daily slices are splayed tables, the mechanics of creating links for partitioned tables are the same as for splayed tables. We first demonstrate how to create a link as the slices are created in memory and splayed. Again we avoid symbols for simplicity; to include them, add a call to .Q.en as in previous examples.

We create two days of linked tables in a fresh db.

```
q)t1:([] id:101 102 103; v:1.1 2.2 3.3)
q)`:/db/2015.01.01/t1/ set t1

q)`:/db/2015.01.01/t2/ set ([] id:`t1!t1[`id]?103 101 101 102; n:10 20
30 40)

q)`:/db/2015.01.02/t/ set t1

q)`:/db/2015.01.02/t2/ set ([] id:`t1!t1[`id]?105 104 104; n:50 60 70)
```

Now we map the root and use dot notation on the link column.

```
q)\l /db
q)select date,n,id.v from t2 where date in 2015.01.01 2015.01.02
```

Adding a link column to persisted partitions is only a bit more complicated. Here we create a link on (enumerated) symbol columns. In a fresh /db we first create the partitioned tables without the link.

```
q)`:/db/2015.01.01/t1/ set .Q.en[`:/db;] ([] id:`c`b`a; c1: 10 20 30)
q)`:/db/2015.01.02/t1/ set .Q.en[`:/db;] ([] id:`x`a; c1: 40 50)
q)`:/db/2015.01.01/t2/ set .Q.en[`:/db;] ([]id:`a`b`a`c; c2: 1 2 3 4.)
q)`:/db/2015.01.02/t2/ set .Q.en[`:/db;] ([] id:`x`a`x; c2:5 6 7.)
```

Presumably at a later time, we add the link column to t2 in each partition, making sure to update the .d files.

```
q)`:/db/2015.01.01/t2/t1lnk set
   `t1!get[`:/db/2015.01.01/t1/id]?get[`:/db/2015.01.01/t2/id]

q)`:/db/2015.01.01/t2/.d set get[`:/db/2015.01.01/t2/.d],`t1lnk

q)`:/db/2015.01.02/t2/t1lnk set
   `t1!get[`:/db/2015.01.02/t1/id]?get[`:/db/2015.01.02/t2/id]

q)`:/db/2015.01.02/t2/.d set get[`:/db/2015.01.02/t2/.d],`t1lnk
```

Now we can map the root and use dot notation.

```
q)select date,id,t1lnk.c1,c2 from t2 where date<=2015.01.02
```

14.4 Segmented Tables

We saw in the previous section that queries against partitioned tables execute separately across the partitions. When q is started without slaves this is a memory win but not a performance win, except for the reduced amount of data manipulation required. When q is started with slaves this can offer significant performance enhancement for compute-bound queries.

In large timeseries databases, the queries are often I/O-bound. In this case, the multiple slaves for a partitioned query will mostly be waiting on I/O (or Godot). The solution requires multiple I/O channels so that data retrieval and processing can occur in parallel. Kdb+ provides another level of data decomposition to enable parallel processing in this scenario.

Traditional kdb+ parlance did not distinguish between this level and the basic partitioning we encountered in the last section. We find this confusing and, at the suggestion of Simon Garland of Kx, have introduced the terminology of *segmentation*.

14.4.1 Segments

Segmentation is an additional level of structure on top of partitioning. *Segmentation* spreads a partitioned table's records across multiple directories that have the same structure as the root directory in a partitioned database. Each pseudo-root, called a *segment*, is thus a directory that contains a collection of partition directories. The segment directories are presumably on independent I/O channels so that data retrieval can occur in parallel.

You can use any criteria to decompose partition slices, as long as the results are conforming record subsets that are disjoint and complete—i.e., they reconstitute the original table with no omissions or duplication. The decomposition can be along rows, along partitions or by some combination thereof, but it cannot occur only along columns since all records must conform across the decomposition.

> *Important:* You must ensure that the segments conform and are complete and disjoint, since kdb+ will not check this when you write the data files. In particular, overlapping segments will result in duplicate records in query results and an incomplete decomposition will result in dropped records.

Big Picture (3): .We view a segmented table as a three-dimensional persisted form: the table is cut vertically by splaying, sliced horizontally by partitions and is additionally segmented across physical locations. The primary purpose of the third dimension is to allow operations against the tables to take advantage of parallel I/O and concurrent processing. Following is an abstract representation of segmentation:

segment1

	column1	column2	...
partition*	▪	▪	...
partition*	▪	▪	...
...	...	...	...

segment2

	column1	column2	...
partition*	▪	▪	...
partition*	▪	▪	...
...	...	...	...

...

Here each ▪ represents a (partial) column of a partition slice as an opaque entity.

In contrast to the partitioned table layout in which partitions reside under the root, the segment directories must **not** reside under the root. The only portion of a segmented table (other than the sym file for enumerated symbol columns) that lives in the root is a file called par.txt containing the paths of the physical locations of the segments, one segment path per line.

Here is how the abstract segmentation discussed above would be laid out on the file system.

```
/db
     [sym]
     par.txt
 ================     <- channel 1
 /segment1
     /partition*
          /table*
          /table*
          ...
     /partition*
          /table*
          /table*
          ...
 ================     <- channel 2
 /segment2
     /partition*
          /table*
          /table*
          ...
     /partition*
          /table*
          /table*
          ...
 ================ ...
```

To make this more concrete, we demonstrate how to segment daily trades (and eventually quotes) in several useful ways. To begin, we create segments by bucketing trades into alternating days of the week.

```
/1                      <- drive 1
    /2015.01.01
        /t              <- day's trades
    /2015.01.03
        /t              <- day's trades
    ...
=============
/2                      <- drive 2
    /2015.01.02
        /t              <- day's trades
    /2015.01.04
        /t              <- day's trades
    ...
```

This segmentation represents grouping of partitions, so it is orthogonal to the partitioning. It is clearly complete and disjoint and is easily generalizable to round-robining every *n* business days.

We could alternatively create segments by splitting the daily slices into records with symbols starting with a-m and those starting with n-z. Here we are decomposing based on the values in a symbol column, which we could not do with simple partitioning.

```
/am                     <- drive 1
    /2015.01.01
        /t              <- day's trades for syms a-m
    /2015.01.02
        /t              <- day's trades for syms a-m
    ...
=============
/nz                     <- drive 2
    /2015.01.01
        /t              <- day's trades for syms n-z
    /2015.01.02
        /t              <- day's trades for syms n-z
    ...
```

This segmentation clearly results in complete, disjoint subsets. It is not orthogonal to the partitioning because a single day's trades span multiple segments. It is easily generalizable to *n* segments by splitting the alphabet into *n* roughly equal portions.

Alternately, we can create segments by splitting the daily slices into trades from NYSE and trades from NASDAQ.

```
/nyse                   <- drive 1
    /2015.01.01
        /t              <- day's trades for nyse
    /2015.01.02
        /t              <- day's trades for nyse
    ...
=============
/nasd                   <- drive 2
    /2015.01.01
        /t              <- day's trades for nasd
```

```
/2015.01.02
    /t                    <- day's trades for nasd      …
```

The segmentation is also not orthogonal to the partitioning since a single day's trades span multiple segments. It is clearly complete and disjoint and is easily generalizable to multiple exchanges—e.g., all Asian exchanges.

Finally, we provide an example of a non-uniform segmentation, in which some partitions span segments and others do not. The *A* segment contains trades from the beginning of day 1 until lunchtime of day 2. The *B* segment contains the trades from lunchtime of day 2 through the end of day 3. The *C* segment contains all trades from day 4. We rely on our understanding of the business logic to know that segmentation is disjoint and complete.

```
/seg A                    <- drive 1
    /2015.01.01
        /t                    <- entire day's trades
    /2015.01.02
        /t                    <- morning trades
=============
/seg B                    <- drive 2
    /2015.01.02
        /t                    <- afternoon trades
    /2015.01.03
        /t                    <- entire day's trades
=============
/seg C                    <- drive 3
    /2015.01.04
        /t                    <- entire day's trades
```

This sort of segmentation can be useful if your query patterns are not uniform across days.

14.4.2 Segmentation vs. Partitions

We collect the following into tabular form so that you can use it for meditation.

445

	Partitioned Table	Segmented Table
Record location	All partitions (and hence all records) reside under the root directory.	None of the segments (and hence no records) reside under the root.
I/O channels	All partitions (and hence all records) reside on a single I/O channel.	The segments (and hence the records) should reside on multiple I/O channels.
Processing	Partitions loaded and processed sequentially in aggregation queries.	Given appropriate slaves and cores, aggregate queries load segments in parallel and process them concurrently.
Decomposition	Partition by grouping rows on the values of a virtual column of underlying integral type.	Segment by any criteria yielding disjoint and complete decomposition.
Symbols	Cannot partition on a symbol column	Can segment along a symbol column
Virtual Column	Partition column not stored. Virtual column values inferred from directory names	No special column associated with segmentation (virtual column from underlying partition still present)

14.4.3 Creating Segmented Tables

There is no one-size-fits-all utility to create segments. Instead, you write a q program that places a subset of each partition slice into a segment. You can create segments and partitions at the same time by including logic in your data load script to extract slice subsets and place them in the appropriate directory on the appropriate drive.

Along with creating the partitions, you must also specify the locations of the segments in an ASCII text file par.txt located in the root. Each line of par.txt contains the path of one segment directory; symlinks are acceptable.

> **Important:** The segment paths must not be under the root. Qbies who make this mistake will prefer Vogon poetry.

We illustrate the process by creating segmented tables for each example in §14.4.1. Our intent is to demonstrate how to create the segments and observe how execution of the query pieces the segment results back together. Initially we create the segments without concern for placing them on multiple drives and running multiple slaves, as we are not (yet) considering performance. That comes shortly.

We begin with the example in which daily slices are segmented alternately across two bins. This will result in roughly even access and will give good performance assuming the queries are uniformly distributed across days. The storage layout looks like,

```
/1
    /2015.01.01
        /t
    /2015.01.03
        /t
  /2
    /2015.01.02
        /t
    /2015.01.04
        /t
```

The corresponding par.txt file is,

```
/1
/2
```

In a fresh directories /1, /2 and /db we construct the segments and write the par.txt file.

```
q)`:/1/2015.01.01/t/ set .Q.en[`:/db;]
  ([] ti:09:30:00 09:31:00; s:`ibm`t; p:101 17f)

q)`:/2/2015.01.02/t/ set .Q.en[`:/db;]
  ([] ti:09:30:00 09:31:00; s:`ibm`t; p:101.5 17.5)

q)`:/1/2015.01.03/t/ set .Q.en[`:/db;]
  ([] ti:09:30:00 09:31:00; s:`ibm`t; p:103 16.5f)
`:/1/2015.01.03/t/
q)`:/2/2015.01.04/t/ set .Q.en[`:/db;]
  ([] ti:09:30:00 09:31:00; s:`ibm`t; p:102 17f)


q)`:/db/par.txt 0: ("/1"; "/2")


q)\l /db
q)select from t where date within 2015.01.01 2015.01.04
```

Next we segment trades by symbol range. The storage layout looks like,

```
/am
      /2015.01.01
      /2015.01.02
/nz
      /2015.01.01
      /2015.01.02
```

The corresponding par.txt file is,

```
/am
/nz
```

We begin with fresh directories /am, /an, and /db and a utility function to extract records for symbols within a range. Then we create the segments and write out the par.txt file.

```
q)extr:{[t;r] select from t where (`$1#'string sym) within r}

q)t1:.Q.en[`:/db;] ([] ti:09:30:00 09:31:00; sym:`ibm`t; p:101 17f)
q)`:/am/2015.01.01/t/ set extr[t1;`a`m]

q)`:/nz/2015.01.01/t/ set extr[t1;`n`z]


q)t2:.Q.en[`:/db;] ([] ti:09:30:00 09:31:00; sym:`ibm`t; p:101.5 17.5)
q)`:/am/2015.01.02/t/ set extr[t2;`a`m]

q) `:/nz/2015.01.02/t/ set extr[t2;`n`z]


q)`:/db/par.txt 0: ("/am"; "/nz")
`:/db/par.txt

q)\l /db
q)select from t where date within 2015.01.01 2015.01.02
```

Next we segment trades by exchange. The storage layout looks like,

```
/nyse
      /2015.01.01
           /t
      /2015.01.02
           /t
/nasd
      /2015.01.01
           /t
      /2015.01.02
           /t
```

The corresponding par.txt file is,

```
/nyse
/nasd
```

Segment construction is completely analogous to that of the previous example. We begin with fresh directories /nyse, /nasd, /db and a utility to extract records by exchange.

```
q)extr:{[t;e] select from t where ex=e}
q)t1:.Q.en[`:/db;] ([] ti:09:30:00 09:31:00; s:`ibm`aapl; p:101
17f;ex:`n`o)
q)`:/nyse/2015.01.01/t/ set extr[t1;`n]

q)`:/nasd/2015.01.01/t/ set extr[t1;`o]

q)t2:.Q.en[`:/db;] ([] ti:09:30:00 09:31:00; s:`aapl`ibm; p:143 102f;
ex:`o`n)
q)`:/nyse/2015.01.02/t/ set extr[t2;`n]

q)`:/nasd/2015.01.02/t/ set extr[t2;`o]


q)`:/db/par.txt 0: ("/nyse"; "/nasd")


q)\l /db
q)select from t where date within 2015.01.01 2015.01.02
```

Finally we show how to distribute a day across segments. The storage
layout looks like,

```
/seg A
     /2015.01.01
     /2015.01.02
/seg B
     /2015.01.02
     /2015.01.03
/seg C
     /2015.01.04
```

The corresponding par.txt file is,

```
/A
/B
/C
```

In fresh directories /A, /B, /C and /db,

```
q) t1:.Q.en[`:/db;] ([] ti:09:30:00 12:31:00; s:`ibm`t; p:101 17f)
q) `:/A/2015.01.01/t/ set t1
_
q)t2:.Q.en[`:/db;] ([] ti:09:31:00 12:32:00; s:`ibm`t; p:102 18f)
q) `:/A/2015.01.02/t/ set select from t2 where ti<=12:00:00
_
q) `:/B/2015.01.02/t/ set select from t2 where ti>12:00:00
_
q)t3:.Q.en[`:/db;] ([] ti:09:33:00 12:33:00; s:`ibm`t; p:103 19f)
q) `:/B/2015.01.03/t/ set t3
_
q)t4:.Q.en[`:/db;] ([] ti:09:34:00 12:35:00; s:`ibm`t; p:104 20f)
q) `:/C/2015.01.04/t/ set t4
_

q) `:/db/par.txt 0: ("/A";"/B";"/C")
_

q)\l /db
q)select from t where date within 2015.01.01 2015.01.04
_
```

14.4.4 Multiple Segmented Tables

Multiple tables that share a partition can also be segmented. While there is no requirement that the tables be distributed similarly across the segmentation, they should do so if you expect to use links or joins between them. In this section, we create (vastly simplified) trades and quotes that share a segmentation in order to do joins.

Our actual segmentation layout is designed to allow parallel retrieval for (aj). We first observe that it performs an equijoin on the sym and date columns, while it performs a non-equijoin on the time column. Thus we want all the time values for a given symbol and date in one segment. Consequently, segmentation by symbol range will allow parallelization of (aj) across symbols.

Here is a simple version of this scheme.

```
/a_m                      <- segment for first portion of alphabet
    /2015.01.01           <- the specific day
        /t                <- that day's trades for symbols a-m
        /q                <- that day's quotes for symbols a-m
    /2015.01.02           <- the specific day
        /t                <- that day's trades for symbols a-m
        /q                <- that day's quotes for symbols a-m
==================
/n_z                      <- segment for second portion of alphabet
    /2015.01.01           <- the specific day
        /t                <- that day's trades for symbols n-z
        /q                <- that day's quotes for symbols n-z
    /2015.01.02           <- the specific day
        /t                <- that day's trades for symbols n-z
        /q                <- that day's quotes for symbols n-z
==================
```

451

The corresponding par.txt file is,

```
/a_m
/n_z
```

Setting up the segments and partitions is a matter of getting the details right. In our simplified example, we pretend that the directories /am and /nz reside on different drives. In fresh directories /am, /nz and /db,

```
q)extr:{[t;r] select from t where (`$1#'string sym) within r}
q)/ day 1
q)t:.Q.en[`:/db;] ([] ti:09:30:00 09:31:00; sym:`ibm`t; p:101 17f)
q)q:.Q.en[`:/db;] ([] ti:09:29:59 09:29:59 09:30:00; sym:`ibm`t`ibm;
p:100.5 17 101)
q)`:/am/2015.01.01/t/ set extr[t;`a`m]

q)`:/nz/2015.01.01/t/ set extr[t;`n`z]

q)`:/am/2015.01.01/q/ set extr[q;`a`m]
)
q)`:/nz/2015.01.01/q/ set extr[q;`n`z]

```

```
q)/ day 2
q)t:.Q.en[`:/db;] ([] ti:09:30:00 09:31:00; sym:`t`ibm; p:17.1 100.9)
q)q:.Q.en[`:/db;] ([] ti:09:29:59 09:29:59 09:30:00; sym:`t`ibm`t;p:17
100.8 17.1)
q)`:/am/2015.01.02/t/ set extr[t;`a`m]

q)`:/nz/2015.01.02/t/ set extr[t;`n`z]

q)`:/am/2015.01.02/q/ set extr[q;`a`m]

q)`:/nz/2015.01.02/q/ set extr[q;`n`z]

q)`:/db/par.txt 0: ("/am"; "/nz")

```

```
q)\l /db

q)dr:2015.01.01 2015.01.02
q)select from t where date within dr

q)select from q where date within dr

```

Now let's do the (aj). We could be naïve and pull all requisite data into the workspace, but this would be inefficient in memory and slow, assuming it would fit.

```
q)aj[`date`sym`ti;select from t where date within dr;
    select from q where date within dr]

```

Instead we start q with slaves and use (peach) to run things in parallel across the segmentation.

```
$q -s 2
  KDB+ ...
q)aj1:{aj[`sym`ti;select from t where date=d; select from q where
date=d]}
q)raze aj1 peach 2015.01.01 2015.01.02
q)raze aj1 peach 2015.01.01 2015.01.02
_
```

14.4.5 Query Execution against Segmented Tables

The performance goal is to scale out by taking advantage of parallel I/O and concurrent processing. We would ideally like to achieve 100% saturation of the I/O channels and 100% utilization of each core. How do we approach these levels on a kdb+ server? The key insight in kdb+ design and tuning is that a vector calculation on in-memory data is much faster than retrieving data from storage. This suggests our first two design principles.

    (1)   Maximize the number of independent I/O channels to retrieve data in parallel.

    (2)   Maximize server memory in order to allocate each slave thread as much memory as it needs.

Suppose we can satisfy these two objectives by having storage devices attached to the kdb+ server over n independent I/O channels—for example, the author's laptop has SSD storage that appears as multiple independent I/O channels. In this scenario, we are led to our next observation.

    (3)   Create n segments to spread data retrieval across the n channels in order to maximize I/O parallelization.

To ensure that data can be processed from all n channels simultaneously and that no two threads contend for data, we are led to our final objective.

    (4)   Have (at least) n slave threads

The precise form of segmentation and number of slaves will depend on the actual data and queries.

Now assuming we have such an environment, does kdb+ execute a query against a segmented table in our scenario of n segments and n slaves.? Essentially, it decomposes a qualifying query into two steps via map-reduce:

- Map: a revised form of the original query that executes on each segment
- Reduce: aggregate the segment results

The use of map-reduce allows kdb+ to perform preliminary calculations as close to the data as possible and to perform aggregation centrally at the last step.

To begin, kdb+ compares the query's requisite partitions to the segment layout in par.txt and determines the footprint of the target partitions on each segment. The result is a nested list, each item being the partition list for one segment.

To execute the map step, kdb+ creates a revised query containing the map sub-operation from the original query, which it dispatches to all *n* slaves via (peach). Each slave is provided the partition list for one segment and computes the revised query for its segment. For example, the revised query for (avg) is:

- Compute the sum and count of the sublist

With this knowledge, we examine execution **within** one slave, where the revised query is applied against a segment's partition footprint. Here kdb+ **sequentially** applies the map sub-operations of the original query across the targeted partitions to obtain partition result tables that it then collects into a list representing one segment result.

Now we stand back and examine execution **across** the slaves by squinting to make partition detail disappear. At this level, the original query's map step has *n* slaves retrieving segment data **in parallel** and calculating segment results. Once all slaves complete, the nested list of segment results is flattened and reordered by partition value.

Finally, kdb+ employs the original query reduce step to combine the full list of ordered partition results into the query result table. Whew!

> **Note:** Kdb+ treats a vanilla partitioned table –i.e., without a `par.txt`– as having a single segment. The astute reader will realize that the description in §14.3.3 is actually the degenerate case of this section.

14.4.5 Balancing Slaves and Cores

In our quest to reach 100% saturation of I/O and CPU, we consider how to optimize the use of slaves and cores. As seen in the previous section, the query via map-reduce provides good progress toward our original objective of I/O saturation. The slaves can load data from all n channels in parallel without contention.

We now investigate channel and core utilization. Since kdb+ will only use as many slaves to process a query as there are segments in the query footprint, we consider two cases.

I/O-bound: Assuming that the query has light calculation compared to data retrieval (common in kdb+), having n slaves on n cores is close to optimal: most of the time, all n slaves will be waiting for data. When a partition load completes, there will be a brief burst of computation, followed by another long load. So we conclude for this scenario:

n channels => n segments => n slaves => n cores

Balanced I/O-compute: Consider the scenario in which both the I/O and calculation are intensive. While one slave is waiting on data, another slave on the same core could be crunching; conversely, while one slave is crunching another slave on that core could be loading data. Thus to maximize channel and core utilization, we actually want *2n* slaves on *n* cores. We conclude that in this scenario we should have *2n* segments, two per channel. On average, there will be one slave per core loading data and one slave per core crunching the data it has just loaded.

n channels => 2n segments => 2n slaves => n cores

These conclusions rely on many implicit assumptions that we have glossed over. In practice, you should view them as guidelines, with the goal of feeding data to kdb+ as fast as possible. The optimum configuration for your situation will depend on your particular query mix. For example, queries that do VWAP calculations are closer to the first scenario, whereas queries doing regression analysis are closer to the second.

A good strategy is to construct your initial configuration using one of the above scenarios. Then load a good approximation of your anticipated data and query mix, and simulate a realistic user load. Observe the I/O saturation and CPU utilization and adjust the number of slaves and cores allocated to the q process accordingly.

14.4.6 Sample Performance Data

Our examples are based on simulated trade data randomly generated to match one month of US equity data spanning August and September 2014. The data is in the table trade, whose most significant columns time, sym, tp and ts represent respectively arrival time, instrument symbol, trade price and trade size columns. The trade data is partitioned by date.

The following output is generated from a version of kdb+ that has been instrumented to show the intermediate steps during query execution. The first example query shows how the simple aggregate avg tp is decomposed into the pair sum and count in the map step, followed by division of the sums of sums by the sum of counts for the reduce step. Here the data is not segmented—i.e., there is no par.txt file.

The added instrumentation exposes 3 stages of execution of a query.

1. Analyze query:
   - Decompose query into map and reduce components (if appropriate)
   - Determine and apply partition constraints
   - Map query onto segments and partitions (query plan)
2. Execute map step, if appropriate
3. Compute final result (reduce step)

```
q)select avg tp from trade where date in -3#date
"---   map/reduce:   input   aggregates,   map   query,   reduce   query   ---"
(,`tp)!,(avg;`tp)
`0`1!((sum;($["f"];`tp));(#:;`i))
(,`tp)!,(%;(sum;`0);(sum;`1))

"---           query           plan:         segments/partitions          ---"
(`trade;();()!();`0`1!((sum;($["f"];`tp));(#:;`i)))
2014.09.24 2014.09.25 2014.09.28
```

```
"---    partition   query:   query,   segment,   partition,   result   ---"
(`trade;();()!();`0`1!((sum;($["f"];`tp));(#:;`i)))
`:.
2014.09.24
+`0`1!(,1.419538e+10;,27914938)


"---    partition   query:   query,   segment,   partition,   result   ---"
(`trade;();()!();`0`1!((sum;($["f"];`tp));(#:;`i)))
`:. 2014.09.25 +`0`1!(,1.419318e+10;,24485503)


"---    partition   query:   query,   segment,   partition,   result   ---"
(`trade;();()!();`0`1!((sum;($["f"];`tp));(#:;`i)))
`:. 2014.09.28 +`0`1!(,1.388645e+10;,20162485)


"---            query           plan           result          ---"
(+`0`1!(,1.419538e+10;,27914938);+`0`1!(,1.419318e+10;,24485503);
+`0`1!(,1.388645e+10;,20162485))


"--- final result ---" tp -------- 582.5979
```

First note that `0 and `1 are used as intermediate columns. Observe that avg tp is decomposed into a map step.

```
`1:sum "f"$tp and `0:count i
```

and a reduce step

```
tp:(sum `0)%sum `1.
```

Also observe that expressions are displayed in their parse tree format and that count is expressed as its k equivalent: the monadic form of (#).

The next example uses par.txt to segment the data into four segments: (/d/d1/data, /d/d2/data, /d/d3/data, /d/d4/data). It also uses a by date clause to sidestep the need to break up the query into map and reduce components (our data is partitioned by date). For clarity, we execute the query only on the last 16 partitions as well as on a subset of symbols. Observe that the "query plan" contains more information than that of the previous example: the query, a list of all partitions, a list of all segments, and a nested list of partitions belonging to segments.

```
q)select avg tp by date from trade where date in -16#date,sym in syms

"---          query          plan:          segments/partitions          ---"
(`trade;,(in;`sym;`syms);(`symbol$())!`symbol$();(,`tp)!,(avg;`tp))
2014.08.18   2014.08.19   2014.08.20   2014.08.21   2014.08.24   2014.08.25
2014.08.26   2014.08.27   2014.08.28   2014.08.31   2014.09.01   2014.09.02
2014.09.03          2014.09.04          2014.09.08          2014.09.09
`:/d/d1/data`:/d/d2/data`:/d/d3/data`:/d/d4/data   ((`:/d/d1/data;2014.08.21
2014.08.25   2014.09.02);  (`:/d/d2/data;2014.08.18   2014.08.26   2014.09.03);
(`:/d/d3/data;2014.08.19   2014.08.27   2014.08.31   2014.09.04   2014.09.08);
(`:/d/d4/data;2014.08.20 2014.08.24 2014.08.28 2014.09.01 2014.09.09))

"---   partition   query:   query,   segment,   partition,   result   ---"
(`trade;,(in;`sym;`syms);(`symbol$())!`symbol$();(,`tp)!,(avg;`tp))
`:/d/d1/data
2014.08.21 +(,`tp)!,,15.42632

"---   partition   query:   query,   segment,   partition,   result   ---"
(`trade;,(in;`sym;`syms);(`symbol$())!`symbol$();(,`tp)!,(avg;`tp))
`:/d/d1/data
2014.08.25
+(,`tp)!,,15.04996

"---   partition   query:   query,   segment,   partition,   result   ---"
(`trade;,(in;`sym;`syms);(`symbol$())!`symbol$();(,`tp)!,(avg;`tp))
`:/d/d1/data
2014.09.02
+(,`tp)!,,14.16648

"---   partition   query:   query,   segment,   partition,   result   ---"
(`trade;,(in;`sym;`syms);(`symbol$())!`symbol$();(,`tp)!,(avg;`tp))
`:/d/d2/data 2014.08.18
+(,`tp)!,,14.16883
... (some output removed for brevity) ...

"---   partition   query:   query,   segment,   partition,   result   ---"
(`trade;,(in;`sym;`syms);(`symbol$())!`symbol$();(,`tp)!,(avg;`tp))
`:/d/d3/data
2014.09.08
+(,`tp)!,,15.59198

"---   partition   query:   query,   segment,   partition,   result   ---"
(`trade;,(in;`sym;`syms);(`symbol$())!`symbol$();(,`tp)!,(avg;`tp))
`:/d/d4/data 2014.08.20
+(,`tp)!,,15.2657
```

```
"---    partition   query:   query,   segment,   partition,   result   ---"
(`trade;,(in;`sym;`syms);(`symbol$())!`symbol$();(,`tp)!,(avg;`tp))
`:/d/d4/data
2014.08.24 +(,`tp)!,,14.75603


"---    partition   query:   query,   segment,   partition,   result   ---"
(`trade;,(in;`sym;`syms);(`symbol$())!`symbol$();(,`tp)!,(avg;`tp))
`:/d/d4/data 2014.08.28
+(,`tp)!,,14.37194


"---    partition   query:   query,   segment,   partition,   result   ---"
(`trade;,(in;`sym;`syms);(`symbol$())!`symbol$();(,`tp)!,(avg;`tp))
`:/d/d4/data 2014.09.01
+(,`tp)!,,13.25797


"---    partition   query:   query,   segment,   partition,   result   ---"
(`trade;,(in;`sym;`syms);(`symbol$())!`symbol$();(,`tp)!,(avg;`tp))
`:/d/d4/data 2014.09.09
+(,`tp)!,,14.98316


"---            query           plan            result            ---"
(+(,`tp)!,,14.16883;+(,`tp)!,,15.05272;+(,`tp)!,,15.2657;+(,`tp)!,,15.42632;
+(,`tp)!,,14.75603;+(,`tp)!,,15.04996;+(,`tp)!,,15.69218;+(,`tp)!,,15.53095;
+(,`tp)!,,14.37194;+(,`tp)!,,14.32488;+(,`tp)!,,13.25797;+(,`tp)!,,14.16648;
+(,`tp)!,,15.58938;+(,`tp)!,,16.1427;+(,`tp)!,,15.59198;+(,`tp)!,,14.98316)


"--- final result ---"
date       | tp
-----------| --------
2014.08.18| 14.16883
2014.08.19| 15.05272
2014.08.20| 15.2657
2014.08.21| 15.42632
2014.08.24| 14.75603
2014.08.25| 15.04996
2014.08.26| 15.69218
2014.08.27| 15.53095
2014.08.28| 14.37194
2014.08.31| 14.32488
2014.09.01| 13.25797
2014.09.02| 14.16648
2014.09.03| 15.58938
2014.09.04| 16.1427
2014.09.08| 15.59198
2014.09.09| 14.98316
```

The previous example was run with no slaves—i.e., on a single-threaded q process. Consequently, the queries run sequentially across segments and partitions.

Now observe what happens when we match the number of slaves to the number of segments in our database by invoking q with -s 4.

```
q)select avg tp by date from trade where date in -16#date,sym in syms

"---          query          plan:       segments/partitions          ---"
(`trade;,(in;`sym;`syms);(`symbol$())!`symbol$();(,`tp)!,(avg;`tp))
2014.08.18    2014.08.19    2014.08.20    2014.08.21    2014.08.24    2014.08.25
2014.08.26    2014.08.27    2014.08.28    2014.08.31    2014.09.01    2014.09.02
2014.09.03          2014.09.04          2014.09.08          2014.09.09
`:/d/d1/data`:/d/d2/data`:/d/d3/data`:/d/d4/data    ((`:/d/d1/data;2014.08.21
2014.08.25  2014.09.02);  (`:/d/d2/data;2014.08.18  2014.08.26  2014.09.03);
(`:/d/d3/data;2014.08.19  2014.08.27  2014.08.31  2014.09.04  2014.09.08);
(`:/d/d4/data;2014.08.20 2014.08.24 2014.08.28 2014.09.01 2014.09.09))

"--- partition query: query, segment, partition, result ---"
"--- partition query: query, segment, partition, result ---"
"--- partition query: query, segment, partition, result ---"

(`trade;,(in;`sym;`syms);(`symbol$())!`symbol$();(,`tp)!,(avg;`tp))
`:/d/d1/data
2014.08.21

"---    partition    query:    query,    segment,    partition,    result    ---"
(`trade;,(in;`sym;`syms);(`symbol$())!`symbol$();(,`tp)!,(avg;`tp))
`:/d/d4/data
2014.08.20
(`trade;,(in;`sym;`syms);(`symbol$())!`symbol$();(,`tp)!,(avg;`tp))
`:/d/d3/data
2014.08.19
(`trade;,(in;`sym;`syms);(`symbol$())!`symbol$();(,`tp)!,(avg;`tp))
`:/d/d2/data
2014.08.18
+(,`tp)!,,15.55121

"---    partition    query:    query,    segment,    partition,    result    ---"
(`trade;,(in;`sym;`syms);(`symbol$())!`symbol$();(,`tp)!,(avg;`tp))
`:/d/d3/data
2014.08.27
+(,`tp)!,,15.47055 +(,`tp)!,,15.21819

"--- partition query: query, segment, partition, result ---"
```

```
"---    partition    query:   query,   segment,   partition,   result    ---"
(`trade;,(in;`sym;`syms);(`symbol$())!`symbol$();(,`tp)!,(avg;`tp))
`:/d/d2/data
2014.08.26
(`trade;,(in;`sym;`syms);(`symbol$())!`symbol$();(,`tp)!,(avg;`tp))
`:/d/d4/data
2014.08.24
+(,`tp)!,,14.81711

"---    partition    query:   query,   segment,   partition,   result    ---"
(`trade;,(in;`sym;`syms);(`symbol$())!`symbol$();(,`tp)!,(avg;`tp))
`:/d/d1/data
2014.08.25
+(,`tp)!,,14.92875

"---    partition    query:   query,   segment,   partition,   result    ---"
+(,`tp)!,,16.07275

"---    partition    query:   query,   segment,   partition,   result    ---"
(`trade;,(in;`sym;`syms);(`symbol$())!`symbol$();(,`tp)!,(avg;`tp))
`:/d/d3/data
2014.08.31
+(,`tp)!,,15.55499
(`trade;,(in;`sym;`syms);(`symbol$())!`symbol$();(,`tp)!,(avg;`tp))
`:/d/d4/data
2014.08.28

"---    partition    query:   query,   segment,   partition,   result    ---"
(`trade;,(in;`sym;`syms);(`symbol$())!`symbol$();(,`tp)!,(avg;`tp))
`:/d/d2/data
2014.09.03
+(,`tp)!,,13.43061 +(,`tp)!,,15.29159 +(,`tp)!,,12.64993

"--- partition query: query, segment, partition, result ---"
"--- partition query: query, segment, partition, result ---"
"---    partition    query:   query,   segment,   partition,   result    ---"
(`trade;,(in;`sym;`syms);(`symbol$())!`symbol$();(,`tp)!,(avg;`tp))
(`trade;,(in;`sym;`syms);(`symbol$())!`symbol$();(,`tp)!,(avg;`tp))
(`trade;,(in;`sym;`syms);(`symbol$())!`symbol$();(,`tp)!,(avg;`tp))
`:/d/d3/data
`:/d/d4/data
2014.09.04
2014.09.01
+(,`tp)!,,176.6311
`:/d/d1/data
2014.09.02
+(,`tp)!,,151.7784
+(,`tp)!,,13.67089
```

461

```
"---   partition   query:   query,   segment,   partition,   result   ---"
(`trade;,(in;`sym;`syms);(`symbol$()))!`symbol$();(,`tp)!,(avg;`tp))
`:/d/d4/data
2014.09.09
+(,`tp)!,,179.799

"---   partition   query:   query,   segment,   partition,   result   ---"
(`trade;,(in;`sym;`syms);(`symbol$()))!`symbol$();(,`tp)!,(avg;`tp))
`:/d/d3/data
2014.09.08
+(,`tp)!,,193.7031
+(,`tp)!,,48.75286

"---            query           plan           result            ---"
(+(,`tp)!,,15.47055;+(,`tp)!,,15.55121;+(,`tp)!,,15.21819;+(,`tp)!,,14.81711;
+(,`tp)!,,16.07275;+(,`tp)!,,15.29159;+(,`tp)!,,15.55499;+(,`tp)!,,14.92875;
+(,`tp)!,,12.64993;+(,`tp)!,,13.43061;+(,`tp)!,,13.67089;+(,`tp)!,,151.7784;
+(,`tp)!,,176.6311;+(,`tp)!,,179.799;+(,`tp)!,,193.7031;+(,`tp)!,,48.75286)

"--- final result ---"
date      | tp
----------| --------
2014.08.18| 15.47055
2014.08.19| 15.55121
2014.08.20| 15.21819
2014.08.21| 14.81711
2014.08.24| 16.07275
2014.08.25| 15.29159
2014.08.26| 15.55499
2014.08.27| 14.92875
2014.08.28| 12.64993
2014.08.31| 13.43061
2014.09.01| 13.67089
2014.09.02| 151.7784
2014.09.03| 176.6311
2014.09.04| 179.799
2014.09.08| 193.7031
2014.09.09| 48.75286
```

Here the output from four slaves running concurrently is interleaved. One slave executes for each segment, with each slave executing the query on its segment sequentially across its partitions. We see how an appropriately configured server can take advantage of available I/O bandwidth to speed up query execution using segments and slaves.

14.5 Utilities for Splaying an Partitioning

The .Q namespace contains useful functions for creating and maintaining splayed and partitioned tables. Although Kx disclaims support for customer use, nearly everyone uses them and they have become de facto standard. In this section, we describe the more commonly used entries and demonstrate their use.

14.5.1 .Q.qp

The monadic .Q.qp asks the residency of its table argument. It returns 1b if its argument is a partitioned table mapped into memory, 0b if it is splayed and 0 for anything else. In a fresh /db,

```
q)`:/db/tser set ([] c1:1 2 3; c2:1.1 2.2 3.3)
q)`:/db/tsplay/ set ([] c1:1 2 3; c2:1.1 2.2 3.3)
q)`:/db/2015.01.01/tpart/ set ([] c1:1 2 3; c2:1.1 2.2 3.3)
q)\l /db
q).Q.qp tser
0
q).Q.qp tsplay
0b
q).Q.qp tpart
1b
```

14.5.2 .Q.en

The dyadic .Q.en takes a symbolic file handle of a root directory as its first argument and a table as its second argument. As a side effect, it creates a list sym comprising the unique items across all symbol columns and writes it to an eponymous file in the specified directory. It returns a table obtained from the original table by enumerating its symbol column(s) over sym.

In a fresh /db,

```
q)sym
'sym
q).Q.en[`:/db;] ([] s:`a`b`v;v:10 20 30)
s v
----
a 10
b 20
v 30
q)sym
`a`b`v
q)get `:/db/sym
`a`b`v
```

Here is more detail on the actual sequence of operations for .Q.en.

- The variable sym is created (in memory) by loading the file sym from the specified root, should such exist, or as the empty symbol list if not. An existing sym variable in the workspace is **overwritten** in this step.
- All symbol columns of (a copy of) the table are conditionally enumerated over the sym list.
- The sym variable is serialized to the specified root directory.
- The enumerated table is returned from the function application.

14.5.3 .Q.pv

The variable .Q.pv is a list containing the values of the partition domain—i.e., the values corresponding to the slice directories actually found in the root. This is useful if you need to iterate over all the partitions.

In a fresh /db,

```
q)`:/db/2015.01.01/t/ set ([] c1:1 2 3; c2:1.1 2.2 3.3)

q)`:/db/2015.01.03/t/ set ([] c1:4 5; 4.4 5.5)

q)\l /db
q).Q.pv
2015.01.01 2015.01.03
```

14.5.4 .Q.ind

As we saw in §14.3, the virtual column i reflects the **relative** row number in a partitioned table. That is, the value of i is the offset of the records within the partition slice. How to retrieve records by absolute within a partition or segmented?

A masochist might use a q expression to determine the partition and relative row for the absolute row number. It is less painful to use the dyadic .Q.ind, whose first argument is a partitioned table and whose second argument is a **list** of long values representing absolute row numbers. The result is a table in memory. You must enlist a single index value.

In a fresh /db,

```
q)`:/db/2015.01.01/t/ set ([] c1:1 2 3; c2:1.1 2.2 3.3)
q)`:/db/2015.01.03/t/ set ([] c1:4 5; c2:4.4 5.5)
q)\l /db
q)select from t where date within 2015.01.01 2015.01.03

q).Q.ind[t;1 3]
date       c1 c2
----------------
2015.01.01 2  2.2
2015.01.03 4  4.4
q).Q.ind[t;enlist 2]
```

14.5.5 .Q.dpft

The utility .Q.dpft assists in creating partitioned and segmented tables by incorporating the functionality of .Q.en at a slightly higher level. It is convenient when partitions are loaded and written out iteratively.

The first parameter is the symbolic file handle of the database root directory. The second parameter is the q data value that will become the name of the partition subdirectory. The third parameter is the name of the field to which the `p# attribute is applied (usually `sym for trades and quotes). The last parameter is the table name.

The .Q.dpft function rearranges (a copy of) the named table so that the partition column is first and the parted column is second, and then splays it into the specified partition in the specified directory. When appropriate, it enumerates all symbol columns over sym and saves a sym list in the root. The result is the table name if the operation is successful.

Notes:

* Because the final parameter is a table name, this function cannot be applied to a local variable.
* The table columns must be simple or compound lists.
* The source table cannot be a keyed table.

We recycle our favorite example, using .Q.dpft to write it as a partitioned table into a fresh /db.

```
q)t:([] ti:09:30:00 09:31:00; sym:`ibm`msft; p:101.5 33.5)
q).Q.dpft[`:/db;2015.01.01;`sym;`t]

q)t:([] ti:09:31:00 09:32:00; sym:`ibm`msft; p:101 33f)
q).Q.dpft[`:/db;2015.01.02;`sym;`t]

q)\l /db
q)select from t where date in 2015.01.01 2015.01.02
```

14.5.6 .Q.fs

In many cases, splayed tables (as well as partitioned or segmented slices) are too large to fit into memory. Thus, we face the dilemma of how to create such tables, since splaying requires the table to be in memory. The utility .Q.fs comes to the rescue by allowing us to process text files in "chunks."

Note: The chunk size used by .Q.fs is hard-coded. If this does not provide adequate performance may wish to use .Q.fsn, which exposes the chunk size as an additional parameter. The optimal chunk size will vary for each application.

Loosely speaking, .Q.fs applies a function to the records of a text file in "chunks" instead of processing the entire file in one gulp. It iterates the function over a number of bite-sized record lists. As a trivial warm-up, we create a text file containing the first 100000 non-negative integers, one per line and we chunk the calculation of their squares. (The call to 0N! enables us to see the result of each chunk as it is processed.)

```
q)`:/data/L 0: string til 100000

q).Q.fs[{0N!x*x};`:/data/L]
0 1 4 9 16 25 36 49 64 81 100 121 144 169 196 225 256 289 324 361 400
441 484..
560979225 561026596 561073969 561121344 561168721 561216100 561263481
5613108..
2071888324 2071979361 2072070400 2072161441 2072252484 2072343529
2072434576 ..
4536157201 4536291904 4536426609 4536561316 4536696025 4536830736
4536965449 ..
7953785856 7953964225 7954142596 7954320969 7954499344 7954677721
7954856100 ..
588890
```

While chunking provides no material benefit in this trivial example, it is easily adaptable to larger problems. Assume we have a csv file containing one day's pseudo-trade records (here we manufacture a one).

```
q)ct:00:00:00.000+(10*(til 100000))mod `int$24:00:00.000
q)ix:100000?til 2
q)cs:(`ibm`ms) ix
q)cp:(115 25@ix)+-1.+100000?1.
q)trade:([] ti:ct; sym:cs; px:cp)
q)save `:/data/trade.csv

q) read0 `:/data/trade.csv
"ti,sym,px"
"00:00:00.000,ibm,114.767"
"00:00:00.010,ibm,114.7566"
"00:00:00.020,ibm,114.1825"
...
```

We intend to save this data into a kdb+ daily partition slice, but suppose that loading it all at once results in a WSFULL error because our q process has insufficient memory. We demonstrate how to read the csv file and write out to the partition slice in chunks. For convenience, we wrap the read and symbol enumeration into a function ldchunk. Then we use .Q.fs to iterate ldchunk over the chunks, upserting each result to the partition directory. Again we instrument with 0N! to see each chunk result.

```
q)ldchunk:{.Q.en[`:/db] flip `time`sym`price!("TSF";",") 0: x}
q).Q.fs[{0N!.[`:/db/2015.01.01/t/;();,;ldchunk x]}] `:/data/trade.csv
`:/db/2015.01.01/t/
`:/db/2015.01.01/t/
`:/db/2015.01.01/t/
...
2638673j
```

We verify that the partition is properly written.

```
q)\l /db
q)select from t where date=2015.01.01
```

When performance matters in the real world, we would proceed to sort the completed partition slice by time within sym and apply the `p# attribute to the sym column.

```
q)`sym`time xasc `:/db/2015.01.01/t

q)@[`:/db/2015.01.01/t; `sym; `p#]

q)\l /db
q)meta t
c    | t f a
-----| -----
date | d
time | t
sym  | s   p
price| f
```

14.5.7 .Q.chk

The utility .Q.chk is a monadic function whose argument is the symbolic file handle of a root directory. It examines each partition subdirectory in the root and writes an empty splayed slice of the appropriate form wherever a table is missing in a partition.

We reconstruct our trades and quotes example, this time using .Q.dpft. In a fresh /db,

```
q)t:([] ti:09:30:00 09:31:00; sym:`ibm`msft; p:101 33f)
q).Q.dpft[`:/db;2015.01.01;`sym;`t]

q)t:([] ti:09:30:00 09:31:00; sym:`ibm`msft; p:101.5 33.5)
q).Q.dpft[`:/db;2015.01.02;`sym;`t]

q)q:([] ti:09:30:00 09:31:00; sym:`ibm`msft;b:100.75 32.75; a:101.25 33.25f)
q).Q.dpft[`:/db;2015.01.01;`sym;`q]

q)q:([] ti:09:30:00 09:31:00; sym:`ibm`msft;b:101.25 33.25; a:101.75 33.75)
q).Q.dpft[`:/db;2015.01.02;`sym;`q]
```

Now we introduce two new partitions, each containing a slice for just one table.

```
q)q:([] ti:09:30:00 09:31:00; sym:`ibm`msft;b:101. 33.; a:101.5 34f)
q).Q.dpft[`:/db;2009.01.03;`sym;`q]

q) t:([] ti:09:30:00 09:31:00; sym:`ibm`msft; p:102 34f)
q).Q.dpft[`:/db;2009.01.04;`sym;`t]
```

This will make the table q disappear since it is not in the most recent partition; also a query for t fail on 2015.01.03. We use .Q.chk to fix things.

```
q).Q.chk `:/db
()
()
,`:/db/2009.01.04
,`:/db/2009.01.03

q)select from t where date=2015.01.03
ti sym p
--------

q)select from q where date=2015.01.04
ti sym b a
----------
```

Notice that .Q.chk tells you which partitions it is fixing but not which tables.

14.5.8 .Q.view

The monadic .Q.view is handy when you are executing queries against partitioned or segmented tables. Recall that multiple tables can share the partitioning. The argument of .Q.view is a list of partition values that acts as a filter for all queries against any partitioned table in the database. Otherwise put, the practical effect of applying .Q.view is to add its argument as a constraint in the first sub-phrase of the where clause of every query. This can guard against run-away queries that ask for all historical data, for example.

In the following example, we create a daily partitioned table with three days of data in a fresh /db. By using .Q.view to restrict the view, we reign in the unqualified query.

```
q)`:/db/2015.01.01/t/ set ([] ti:09:30:00 09:31:00; p:101 102f)
`:/db/2015.01.01/t/
q)`:/db/2015.01.02/t/ set ([] ti:09:30:00 09:31:00; p:100 100f)
`:/db/2015.01.02/t/
q)`:/db/2015.01.03/t/ set ([] ti:09:30:00 09:31:00; p:103 104f)
`:/db/2015.01.03/t/

q)\l /db
q).Q.view 2015.01.02 2015.01.03
q)select from t      / normally dangerous!
date       ti       p
---------------------
2015.01.02 09:30:00 100
2015.01.02 09:31:00 100
2015.01.03 09:30:00 103
2015.01.03 09:31:00 104
```

This is especially useful when you are testing or when you expose large historical databases to users who are prone to forget that they must qualify their queries by date. To reset the default view to all partitions, invoke .Q.view niladically.

```
q).Q.view[]
q)select from t  / once again gets everthing!
date       ti      p
---------------------
2015.01.01 09:30:00 101
2015.01.01 09:31:00 102
2015.01.02 09:30:00 100
2015.01.02 09:31:00 100
2015.01.03 09:30:00 103
2015.01.03 09:31:00 104
```

You can use the partition value variable .Q.pv in the argument to .Q.view.

```
q).Q.view[]
q).Q.pv
2015.01.01 2015.01.02 2015.01.03
q).Q.view -2#.Q.pv
q)select from t         / <- normally dangerous
date       ti      p
---------------------
2015.01.02 09:30:00 100
2015.01.02 09:31:00 100
2015.01.03 09:30:00 103
2015.01.03 09:31:00 104
```

14.6 Kdb Database

Many kdb+ newcomers find the notion of a kdb+ database shrouded in mystery. In this section, we answer common qbie questions.

- What is a kdb+ database?
- How is it different from an RDBMS?
- How do I create a kdb+ database?
- How do I startup a kdb+ database?
- What happens at startup?

14.6.1 Comparing kdb+ to an RDBMS

While q-sql makes certain aspects of a kdb+ database seem familiar to a SQL programmer, the two are quite different under the covers. Folks coming into the world of q and kdb+ from a traditional RDBMS environment may feel as if they have entered the Matrix after taking the red pill from Morpheus. The fundamental differences are:

1. Kdb+ is based on lists, which are ordered collections allowing duplicates, whereas SQL is based on sets, which are unordered collections of distinct elements.

2. Kdb+ stores data as contiguous items in column lists, whereas an RDMS stores data as fields within non-contiguous rows. Neo in kdb+ says, "There are no rows."
3. Kdb+ table operations are vector operations on columns, whereas SQL operates on individual fields and rows.

We summarize the major differences between an RDBMS and kdb+ in the following chart.

	Traditional RDBMS	Kdb+ Database
Table Creation	Tables defined declaratively using DDL and created on disk.	Tables created functionally in the q language.
Data Persistence	Tables and related metadata held in an opaque repository. Tables are stored by row.	Serialized q entities stored in the O/S file system. No separate table metadata. Tables are stored by column.
Data Access	Access to stored information is via DDL for metadata and SQL for data. Must retrieve via a query into program.	Data directly accessible in q. q-sql provides query forms for table manipulation.
Memory Residency	Tables reside on disk; query result sets reside in program memory.	Tables live in memory but can be persisted to disk. Column subsets are page faulted into memory for mapped tables.
Data Format	Based on sets, which are unordered collection of distinct items. Data is stored in fields within rows, which are not contiguous.	Based on lists, which are ordered collections allowing duplicates. Data is stored as contiguous items in column lists.
Data Modification	Persisted table modifiable via SQL (INSERT, UPDATE, etc.)	Memory resident tables modifiable via q and q-sql. Persisted table modifiable only with append (upsert)
Data Programming	SQL is declarative relational. Programs, called stored procedures, written in proprietary procedural language.	Programs written in integrated vector functional language q. Tables are first class entities in q.
Transactions	Support for transactions via COMMIT and ROLLBACK.	No built-in transaction support.

14.6.2 The Physical Layout of a kdb+ Database

Here is a Zen koan: What is a kdb+ database? At the most basic level, a kdb+ database is a file system directory (and subdirectories) holding q entities. This directory is the *root* of the database. All constituents of the database are simply q entities saved in files. Database entities either reside at some level under the root or are pointed to from par.txt under the root.

We describe the various kdb+ database components in this section and show examples in the following section. In our descriptions we use /db as our root, but this is arbitrary.

14.6.2.1 The sym File

The sym file is an optional serialized q data file containing a list of unique symbols used as the domain for symbol enumeration. Placing the sym file in the root guarantees that it will be loaded into memory at q startup.

```
/db
    sym     ...
```

There is no strict requirement that there be only one enumeration domain, but conventionally all symbol columns from all tables are enumerated over a single domain sym. The .Q utilities that handle symbol enumeration assume this. If you choose to have multiple enumeration domains, be aware that symbols in the resulting enumerated values will act as expected under (=) but not with (~) since they have different types. You can resolve the enumerations with (value) if this is a problem.

> **Important:** Pay very careful attention to the sym file, as it is a single point of failure. Corrupting or losing it will result in all your symbol columns being irresolvable. Good practice is to use conditional enumeration—e.g., `:/db/sym?—when you enumerate symbols manually or use .Q utilities that do this for you. Always back up your database before operating on the sym file.

The sym file will not normally be a choke point when loading historical data from an external source into a kdb+ because conditional enumeration (and the .Q utilities) use file locking to mediate concurrent updates. Alternately, if the symbol domain is known in advance, you can load the sym list into memory and use nonconditional enumeration—i.e., `sym$. For example, one approach is to create a preprocessing utility in Perl to extract all symbols from the source data, import this as a list in q and place the distinct items in sym. Then create the historical partitions running concurrent processes that use unconditional enumerations. Be mindful that unconditional enumeration fails for a symbol not in the domain.

14.6.2.2 Other Serialized Files in Root

While it is seldom done in practice (perhaps because few kdb+ programmers are aware of the possibility), it is possible to place any serialized q entity into the root and have it loaded into an eponymous file. This can be a more efficient than using a script to initialize variables in the workspace.

> **Tip:** If you use this, don't go overboard. Also, it might break .Q.en.

```
/db
      [sym]
      var1
      var2
      ...
```

One type of serialized file that can be initialized in this fashion is a reference table (or keyed table) of modest size (up to millions of rows). Such a table will be loaded into memory in its entirety, so lookups or joins on it will be quite fast.

It is possible to (re)load the entire state of the root context automatically by serializing that directory and loading it in this fashion.

14.6.2.3 Scripts

A script in the root can hold arbitrary q code that will be loaded upon startup. In particular, functions defined in such a script can be viewed as stored procedures for the database. While it is possible to have multiple q scripts in the root, you probably want precise control over the order in which the scripts are executed. Good practice is to keep in the root one startup script that loads scripts residing in libraries elsewhere.

```
/db

    ...

    init.q
```

14.6.2.4 Splayed Tables

Reference tables of intermediate size (up to tens of millions of rows) can be splayed under the root. Splayed table directories must be immediately under the root.

```
/db
 [sym]

   ...

 /splay1
 /splay2

   ...
```

Because splayed tables are mapped and columns are page-faulted into memory as needed, no more than a few columns will be simultaneously resident in the workspace. Assuming that the server has adequate memory available to kdb+, q should expect to find recently accessed columns cached by the OS. In this scenario, performance of lookups against splayed tables can be close to that of in-memory tables.

14.6.2.5 Partitioned Tables

The partition directories of non-segmented tables must be immediately under the root. Every partition directory contains a subdirectory for each table sharing the partition; in each subdirectory is the splayed slice for that table's partition value. For example, for daily partitioned trades and quotes, a day's directory would contain a splayed directory for that day's trades and another splayed directory for that day's quotes.

```
/db
    [sym]
    ...
    /part1
        /trade
        /quote
    /part2
        /trade
        /quote      ...
```

There need not be a directory for every partition value but the partition directories must have a uniform structure. That is, a partition value having **any** entry must contain splayed directories for **all** tables in the partition. Splay an empty schema for a table having no records for a partition value.

14.6.2.6 Segmented Tables

In contrast to normal partitioned tables (i.e., non-segmented tables) in which all records live under the root, no records of a segmented table can reside under the root. Instead, the root contains a text file par.txt having one entry per line. Each entry represents an OS path for a segment directory containing the data in that segment; symlinks are permissible.

Each segment directory contains partition directories whose structure is completely analogous to that of a regular partitioned table. There is one directory per partition value and beneath that, one subdirectory per table. Note that depending on the nature of the segmentation, multiple segment directories may contain directories for the same partition value. The previous restriction about consistency across partition directories applies to segments.

```
/db
    [sym]
    …
    par.txt
    …
  == drive 1 =============
 /seg1
    /part1
    /part2
    …
  == drive 2 =============
 /seg2
    /parta
    /partb
    …
  == … =============
```

14.6.3 Creating and Populating a kdb+ Database

Here we demonstrate how to create and populate various kdb+ database configurations. Although the examples are simplistic, they cover most common situations.

There are no wizards for laying out and populating a kdb+ database. Instead, you must write each component in the correct form to the correct location. There are utilities to help with the process but it is your responsibility to ensure that everything is valid. Improperly structured directories or incorrectly written data files will generate run-time errors the first time q code attempts to access them.

Once you have created a kdb+ database, start a q process pointing at the root directory of the database to attach it to the session. Alternately, in a running q instance you can issue \l on the root directory.

14.6.3.1 What Happens at Startup?

This question has a deceptively simple answer. When you point q at a directory or file, it applies a single rule:

Whatever it recognizes as its own, it does.

Thus, a serialized q entity is loaded; a splayed, partitioned or segmented table is mapped; a script is executed.

> **Important:** Almost anything that q does not recognize causes it to abort that portion of startup. In particular, if q discovers foreign or undecipherable files in splayed, partitioned or segmented directories, it will not map the tables contained there. Even unexpected hidden files (e.g., those written by the Mac OS Finder) will abort the map.

When you point q startup at a directory, that directory becomes the root directory for the kdb+ database and also the current working directory for the OS. We shall refer to this scenario as *kdb+ startup* to distinguish it from an arbitrary q session. We shall cover the items that Kdb+ startup finds in the order that it handles them.

1. Serialized q entities
2. Splayed tables
3. Partitioned or segmented tables
4. Scripts

> **Tip:** File handles that are not fully qualified—i.e., relative paths—are interpreted relative to the q home directory.

14.6.3.2 Serialized q Entities

When kdb+ startup recognizes a serialized q data file, it loads that data into an eponymous variable. The canonical example is the sym file in the root, containing the serialized list of (unique) symbols in the enumeration domain for (all) symbol columns. Multiple serialized entities are loaded in the order in which the OS file system lists them.

In our first example, we manually write out a sym file, exit q and then start kdb+ pointing at the root.

```
q)`:/db/sym set `a`b`c`z`x`y
`:/db/sym
q)\\
```

```
$q /db
q)sym
`a`b`c`z`x`y
```

Starting with a fresh /db, we place a defined "constant," a utility function and a serialized keyed table in the root.

```
q) `:/db/LIFE set 42
`:/db/LIFE
q)`:/db/f set {x*y}
`:/db/f
q)`:/db/lookup set ([s:`a`b`c] v:1 2 3)
`:/db/lookup
q)\\
```

```
$q /db
q)LIFE
```

```
q)f
```

```
q)lookup
```

As of this writing (Sep 2015), q will not look for serialized data in directories other than the root. Nor will it automatically load serialized data whose file names have extensions. However, you can load such data files manually using \l or get.

14.6.3.3 Splayed Tables

When kdb+ startup finds a subdirectory immediately beneath the root that it recognizes as a splayed table, it maps the table into memory. All symbol columns must be enumerated for a table to be splayed. Ensure that the sym file is in the root directory if you do not use a built-in utility.

Starting with a fresh /db, we splay two tables under the root. The first does not have symbol columns; the second does.

```
q)`:/db/tref/ set ([] c1:1 2 3; c2:1.1 2.2 3.3)
```

```
q)`:/db/cust/ set .Q.en[`:/db;] ([] sym:`ibm`msft`goog;
name:`oracle`microsoft`google)
```

```
q)\\
```

```
$q /db
q)select from tref
c1 c2
```

```
q)select from cust
```

14.6.3.4 Partitioned Tables

If kdb+ startup finds subdirectories immediately beneath the root whose names constitute valid partition values, it examines them for splayed tables comprising partition slices. Valid partitioned tables are mapped. The presence of partitioned tables is independent of the presence of (plain) splayed tables. Partitioned tables and segmented tables are mutually exclusive.

> **Note:** All symbol columns in every partition slice must be enumerated, customarily over a file sym in the root. Ensure that the sym file is in the root directory if you do not use the built-in utilities.

We recreate the previous example in which multiple tables share a daily partition in a fresh /db.

```
q) `:/db/2015.01.01/t/ set .Q.en[`:/db;]
  ([] ti:09:30:00 09:31:00; sym:`ibm`msft; p:101 33f)

q)`:/db/2015.01.02/t/ set .Q.en[`:/db;]
  ([] ti:09:30:00 09:31:00;sym:`ibm`msft; p:101.5 33.5)

q)`:/db/2015.01.01/q/ set .Q.en[`:/db;]
  ([] ti:09:30:00 09:31:00;sym`ibm`msft; b:100.75 32.75; a:101.25
33.25f)

q)`:/db/2015.01.02/q/ set .Q.en[`:/db;]
  ([] ti:09:30:00 09:30:00;sym:`ibm`msft; b:101.25 33.25; a:101.75
33.75)

q)\\
```

```
$ q /db
q)\l /db
q
q)select from t where date within 2015.01.01 2015.01.02

q)select from q where date within 2015.01.01 2015.01.02
```

14.6.3.5 Segmented Tables

When kdb+ startup finds a par.txt file in the root, it interprets each line as a segment location and it examines the locations for valid segments of partitioned tables. Valid tables are mapped.

> **Important:** Ensure that the segment directories are not located under the root; otherwise you will relive the table scene in the first Alien movie.

The presence of segmented tables is independent of the presence of plain splayed tables. Segmented tables and partitioned tables are mutually exclusive. All symbol columns in every segment must be enumerated. Ensure that the (common) sym file is in the root directory.

We recreate the previous example from §14.4 in which multiple tables share segmentation by symbol range. In fresh directories /am, /nz and /db,

```
q)extr:{[t;r] select from t where (`$1#'string sym) within r}
q)t:.Q.en[`:/db;] ([] ti:09:30:00 09:31:00; sym:`ibm`t; p:101 17f)
q)q:.Q.en[`:/db;] ([] ti:09:29:59 09:29:59 09:30:00;
                        sym:`ibm`t`ibm; b:100.75 16.9 100.8;a:101.25 17.1
101.1)
q)`:/am/2015.01.01/t/ set extr[t;`a`m]

q)`:/nz/2015.01.01/t/ set extr[t;`n`z]

q)`:/am/2015.01.01/q/ set extr[q;`a`m]

q)`:/nz/2015.01.01/q/ set extr[q;`n`z]

q)t:.Q.en[`:/db;] ([] ti:09:30:00 09:31:00; sym:`t`ibm; p:17.1 100.9)
q)q:.Q.en[`:/db;] ([] ti:09:29:59 09:29:59 09:30:00;
                        sym:`t`ibm`t;b:17 100.7 17.1;a:17.2 101.25 17.25)
q)`:/am/2015.01.02/t/ set extr[t;`a`m]

q)`:/nz/2015.01.02/t/ set extr[t;`n`z]

q)`:/am/2015.01.02/q/ set extr[q;`a`m]

q)`:/nz/2015.01.02/q/ set extr[q;`n`z]

q)`:/db/par.txt 0: ("/am"; "/nz")
`:/db/par.txt
q)\\
```

```
$q
q)\l /db
q)select from t where date within 2015.01.01 2015.01.02

q)select from q where date within 2015.01.01 2015.01.02
```

14.6.3.6 Scripts

Files with extension .q are interpreted as q scripts; those with extension .k as k scripts. Scripts found in the root are loaded and executed in alphabetical order. You will probably want better control over the order of execution, so it is best to have in the root a single script that loads other scripts in the desired sequence.

> **Note:** An invalid expression in a script causes the entire script load to abort. Locating the invalid entry can be non-trivial since by default console display is suppressed during load. Judicious use of (0N!) can be helpful. Sometimes using binary search using block comments is an effective approach to locating the offending line. Bottom line: keep scripts short!

In our first example, we initialize the workspace using a startup script /db/init.q that we create from q (because we can). You could do it in any text editor.

```
q)`:/db/init.q 0: ("LIFE:42";"f:{x*y}";"lookup:([s:`a`b`c] v:1 2 3)")
`:/db/init.q
q)\\
```

```
$q /db
q)LIFE

q)f

q)lookup

```

Since scripts are loaded as the last step in kdb+ startup, any loaded script can rely on startup, serialized variables and mapped tables bring present. For example, in a fresh /db we create a splayed table and a startup script from within q and then run the script at startup.

```
q)`:/db/cust/ set .Q.en[`:/db;] ([]
sym:`ibm`msft`goog;name:`oracle`microsoft`google)

q)`:/db/init.q 0: ("sym"; "show select from cust")

q)\\
```

```
$q /db
`ibm`msft`goog`oracle`microsoft`google
sym   name
-------------
ibm   oracle
msft  microsoft
goog  google
q)
```

Now we demonstrate a script that loads other scripts. Start with a fresh /db. We write out a script having a library function (you could do it in a text editor) and then load that script from init.q at startup.

```
q)`:/scripts/expr.q 0: enlist ".jab.lib.expr.subst:{x@y}"

q)`:/db/init.q 0: enlist "\\l /scripts/expr.q"

q)\\
```

482

```
$q /db
q).jab.lib.expr.subst
{x@y}
```

14.7 Putting It All Together

In this section, we combine the various constituents of a kdb+ database demonstrated in the previous sections to give two archetypal examples. The first has partitioned tables; the second has segmented tables.

14.7.1 Partitioned Database

To construct our partitioned database, we combine the steps in previous sections to obtain the following meta-script. (We assume that the scripts in /lib already exist.)

```
/ create serialized variables
`:/db/LIFE set 42
`:/db/f set {x*y}
`:/db/lookup set ([s:`a`b`c] v:1 2 3)

/ create splayed tables
`:/db/tref/ set ([] c1:1 2 3; c2:1.1 2.2 3.3)
`:/db/cust/ set .Q.en[`:/db;] ([] sym:`ibm`msft`goog;
   name:`:/db/sym?`oracle`microsoft`google)
/create partitioned tables
`:/db/2015.01.01/t/ set .Q.en[`:/db;] ([] ti:09:30:00 09:31:00;
   sym:`ibm`msft; p:101 33f)
`:/db/2015.01.02/t/ set .Q.en[`:/db;] ([] ti:09:30:00 09:31:00;
   sym:`ibm`msft; p:101.5 33.5)
`:/db/2015.01.01/q/ set  .Q>en[`:/db;] ([] ti:09:30:00 09:31:00;
   sym:`ibm`msft; b:100.75 32.75; a:101.25 33.25f)
`:/db/20015.01.02/q/ set   .Q.en[`:/db;] ([] ti:09:30:00 09:30:00;
   sym:`ibm`msft; b:101.25 33.25; a:101.75 33.75)

/ create load script
`:/db/init.q 0: ("TheUniverse:42";"\\l /lib/math.q";
                  "\\l /lib/expr.q")
```

Now execute this script to create the database. The resulting partitioned database has the following layout.

```
/db
    sym
    LIFE
    F
    Lookup
    /tref
        .d
        c1
        c2
    /cust
        .d
        sym
        name
```

```
/2009.01.01
    /t
        .d
        ti
        sym
        p
    /q
        .d
        ti
        sym
        b
        a
/2009.01.02
    /t
        .d
        ti
        sym
        p
    /q
        .d
        ti
        sym
        b
        a
init.q
```

14.7.2 Segmented Database

To construct a segmented database, we combine previous steps to obtain the following meta-script. (We again assume that the scripts in /lib already exist.)

```
/ create serialized variables
`:/db/LIFE set 42
`:/db/f set {x*y}
`:/db/lookup set ([s:`a`b`c] v:1 2 3)

/ create splayed tables
`:/db/tref/ set ([] c1:1 2 3; c2:1.1 2.2 3.3)
`:/db/cust/ set .Q.en[`:/db;] ([] sym:`ibm`msft`goog;
    name:`oracle`microsoft`google)

/ create segmented tables
extr:{[t;r] select from t where (`$1#'string sym) within r}
t:.Q.en[`:/db;] ([] ti:09:30:00 09:31:00; sym:`ibm`t; p:101 17f)
q:.Q.en[`:/db;] ([] ti:09:29:59 09:29:59 09:30:00;
  sym:`ibm`t`ibm; b:100.75 16.9 100.8;a:101.25 17.1 101.1)
`:/am/2015.01.01/t/ set extr[t; `a`m]
`:/nz/2015.01.01/t/ set extr[t; `n`z]
`:/am/2015.01.01/q/ set extr[q; `a`m]
`:/nz/20015.01.01/q/ set extr[q; `n`z]
t:.Q.en[`:/db;] ([] ti:09:30:00 09:31:00; sym:`t`ibm; p:17.1 100.9)
q:.Q.en[`:/db;] ([] ti:09:29:59 09:29:59 09:30:00;
  sym:`t`ibm`t; b:17 100.7 17.1;a:17.2 101.25 17.25)
`:/am/2015.01.02/t/ set extr[t; `a`m]
`:/nz/2015.01.02/t/ set extr[t; `n`z]
`:/am/2015.01.02/q/ set extr[q; `a`m]
`:/nz/2015.01.02/q/ set extr[q; `n`z]

`:/db/par.txt 0: ("/am"; "/nz")

/ create load script
```

```
`:/db/init.q 0: ("TheUniverse:6*7";"\\l /lib/math.q";"\\l /lib/expr.q")
```

Now execute this script to create the database. The resulting partitioned database has the following layout.

```
/db
     sym
     LIFE
     F
     Lookup
     /tref
          .d
          c1
          c2
     /cust
          .d
          sym
          name
     par.txt
     init.q
 == drive 1 ==
/am
     /2009.01.01
          /t
               .d
               ti
               sym
               p
          /q
               .d
               ti
               sym
               b
               a
     /2009.01.02
          /t
               .d
               ti
               sym
               p
          /q
               .d
               ti
               sym
               b
               a
 == drive 2 ==
/nz
     /2009.01.01
          /t
               .d
               ti
               sym
               p
          /q
               .d
               ti
               sym
               b
               a
     /2009.01.02
          /t
               .d
```

```
          ti
          sym
          p
    /q
          .d
          ti
          sym
          b
          a
```

14.8 There's No Place Like QHOME

We discuss how kdb+ interacts with the OS environment when it looks for files.

14.8.1 The Environment Variables

Three environment variables QHOME, QLIC and QINIT are used by kdb+ at startup.

The environment variable QHOME specifies the directory where kdb+ expects to find the bootstrap file q.k. By default, it also looks there for the license file k4.lic. If QHOME is not defined, kdb+ falls back to $HOME/q for Unix-based systems and c:\q for Windows.

The environment variable QLIC overrides the default location for the license file. If QLIC is not defined, kdb+ falls back to QHOME (or its fallback).

The environment variable QINIT specifies the name of the file that is executed immediately after the load of q.k. If QINIT is not defined, kdb+ attempts to load the file q.q from QHOME. If QHOME is not defined or q.q is not found, no error is reported.

> **Note:** The file in QINIT is executed in the root context (i.e., \d .).

14.8.2 q in da hood

Upon startup, the current directory is the directory from which the q session was started.

After startup, an easy way to see where in the file system the q executable resides is to use a function such as the niladic whereami below. Recall that the command \cd acts like the OS cd command by returning the current working directory.

```
whereami:{-1 "cd ~ ",system "cd";}
```

Loading a script that resides elsewhere does not in itself change the current directory; of course, if that script executes a \cd then the current directory may change. In particular, the current directory is not temporarily changed to the location of the target script.

Loading a database, either as part of the startup invocation or via a \l command, changes the current directory to the database root. All subsequent relative access is based from there. This is important when starting q with -u as it determines the file hierarchy visibility.

When asked to load a file whose name is not fully qualified, q first searches the current directory. If the file is not found, it then searches QHOME if it is defined and $HOME otherwise.

A   Built-in Functions

A.0 Overview

The collection of built-in functions in q is rich and powerful. We include here a user guide for those built-ins that were not covered in the main text. For more details, see the Reference section at code.kx.com.

A.1 acos

The atomic (acos) is the mathematical inverse of (cos). For a float argument between -1 and 1, (acos) returns the float between 0 and π whose cosine is the argument.

```
q)acos 1
0f
```

```
q)acos 1.414213562373095
0n
```

```
q)acos -1
3.141593
```

```
q)acos 0
1.570796
```

A.2 all

The aggregate (all) is (&/), which applies (&) cumulatively across a numeric list and returns the boolean result.

```
q)all 100100b
0b
q)all 10 20 30
1b
```

A.3 and

The function (and) is the same as (&) for people who like typing extra characters.

```
q)1b and 0b
0b
```

```
q)42 and 43
42
```

A.4 any

The aggregate (any) is (|\), which applies (|) cumulatively across a numeric list and returns the boolean result.

```
q)any 100100b
1b
```

```
q)any null til 10
0b
```

A.5 asc

The uniform function (asc) returns its argument list of comparables sorted in ascending order with the `s# attribute applied. When evaluated on a dictionary, it reorders the key-value pairs (on a copy) so that the values are sorted.

```
q)asc 3 7 2 8 1 9
`s#1 2 3 7 8 9
```

```
q)asc `b`c`a!3 2 1
a| 1
c| 2
b| 3
```

A.6 asin

The atomic (asin) is the mathematical inverse of (sin). For a float argument between -1 and 1, (asin) returns the float between $-\pi/2$ and $\pi/2$ whose sine is the argument.

```
q)asin 0
0f
```

```
q)asin 1.414213562373095%2
0.7853982
```

```
q)asin 1
1.570796
```

```
q)asin -1
-1.570796
```

A.7 atan

The atomic (atan) is the mathematical inverse of (tan). For a float argument, (atan) returns the float between –π/2 and π/2 whose tangent is the argument.

```
q)atan 0
0f
```

```
q)atan 1.414213562373095
0.9553166
```

```
q)atan 1
0.7853982
```

A.8 attr

The function (attr) returns any attribute of its argument as a symbol. No attributes is the empty symbol

```
q)attr til 5
```

```
q)attr asc 30 20 40 10
`s
```

A.9 avg

The aggregate (avg) returns the float average of a numeric list.

```
q)avg 1+til 1000
500.5
```

The function (avg) is equivalent to

```
{sum[x]%count x}
```

It is possible to apply (avg) to a nested list provided the sublists conform. In this context, the result conforms to the sublists and the average is calculated recursively on the sublists.

```
q)avg (1 2;100 200;1000 2000)
367 734f
```

A.10 avgs

The uniform (avgs) is (avg\), which computes the running averages of a numeric list.

```
q)avgs 1+til 10
1 1.5 2 2.5 3 3.5 4 4.5 5 5.5
```

A.11 bin

The dyadic (bin) takes a simple list of items (*target*) sorted in strictly increasing order as its first parameter. It is atomic in its second parameter (*source*). Loosely speaking, the result of (bin) is the position at which *source* would fall in *target*, looking from the left. The type of *source* must **strictly** match the type of *target*; no type promotion is performed.

Note: While the items of the first argument (bin) should be in strictly increasing order for the result to meaningful, this condition is not enforced. The result of (bin) when the first argument is not strictly increasing is essentially undefined.

More precisely, the result is –1 if *source* is less than the first item in *target*. Otherwise, the result is the index of the last item of *target* that is less than or equal to *source*; this is the found index if *source* is in *target*. If *source* is greater than the last item in *target*, the result is the last index of *target*

Tip: For large sorted lists, the binary search performed by (bin) can be much faster than the linear search performed by (?).

Here are some examples.

```
q)L:1.0+til 50000000
q)L bin 25000000.
24999999
q)L?25000000.
24999999
q)\t L bin 25000000.
0
q)\t L?25000000.
33
```

```
q)L bin 25000000.5
24999999
62
q)L?25000000.5
50000000
q)\t L bin 25000000.5
0
q)\t L?25000000.5
63
```

```
q)L bin 50000000.5
49999999
q)L?50000000.5
50000000
```

A.12 binr

The dyadic (binr) is closely related to (bin). Whereas (bin) looks from the left, (binr) looks from the right. The result is the index of the first item of the first parameter that is greater than or equal to the second parameter.

```
q)L:1.0+til 50000000
q)L bin 25000000.5
24999999
q)L binr 25000000.5
25000000
```

A.13 choose (?)

The dyadic function choose is a form of (?) that generates pseudo-random results.

In the case where the first parameter is a non-negative long and the second parameter is a non-negative numeric value (*bound*), (?) returns a list of pseudo-random numbers **with replacement** between 0 and *bound*, not including *bound*.

```
q)5?10
2 4 5 4 2
q)5?10
7 8 5 6 4
q)10?100.0
10.24432 86.71096 72.78528 16.27662 68.84756 81.77547 75.20102 10.86824
95.98..
q)10?100.0
64.30982 67.08738 67.89082 41.2317 98.77844 38.67353 72.6781 40.46546
83.5506..
```

In the case where the first parameter is a negative long and the second parameter is a non-negative long (*bound*), (?) returns a list of pseudo-random numbers **without replacement** between 0 and *bound*, not including *bound*.

```
q)-5?10
1 8 5 7 0
q)5?10
2 4 5 4 2
```

> **Zen Moment**: The expression −*n*?*n* returns a random permutation of til n.

In case the second parameter is a list (*source*) and the first parameter is a long (*count*), (?) returns a list of *count* items randomly drawn from *source*, with replacement for positive *count* and without replacement for negative *count*.

```
q)5?`a`b`c`d`e`f
`b`c`f`f`b
q)5?`a`b`c`d`e`f
`e`e`a`e`e
```

```
q)-5?`a`b`c`d`e`f
`c`a`d`f`e
q)-5?`a`b`c`d`e`f
`f`a`e`d`c
```

In case the first parameter is a positive long (*count*) and the second argument is a symbol of the form `*n* where *n* is a positive integer no greater than eight, the result is a random list of *count* symbols, each comprising exactly *n* characters. The symbols are distinct when *count* is negative.

```
q)10?`1
`c`d`o`m`h`m`n`e`m`m
q)-10?`1
`h`p`j`n`e`o`a`k`l`i
q)-10?`3
`emb`agl`mho`ndm`gmj`egi`gek`hcc`mmb`kbh
```

A.14 Conditionally Enumerate (?)

Conditional enumerate (?) has first parameter the symbolic name of a (presumably unique) list of symbols (*target*). It is atomic in the second parameter, which is a symbol (*source*). The result is the enumeration of *source* over *target*, where *source* is appended to *target* if it is not already contained therein. As a side effect of the function, symbols from *source* not in *target* are appended to *target*.

```
q)sym:`a`b`c
q)`sym?`a`x`b`y`z
`sym$`a`x`b`y`z
q)sym
`a`b`c`x`y`z
```

A.15 cor

The dyadic (cor) takes two numeric lists of the same count and returns the mathematical correlation between the items of the two lists as a float.

```
q)23 -11 35 0 cor 42  21 73 39
0.9070229
```

The function (cor) is equivalent to

```
{cov[x;y]%dev[x]*dev y}
```

A.16 count

The aggregate (count) returns a long representing the number of items in its atom or list parameter. As with any function defined on lists, it also applies to the value list of a dictionary and hence to tables and keyed tables.

```
q)count 42
1
```

```
q)count til 100
100
```

```
q)count `a`b`c`d!10 20 30 40
4
```

```
q)count ([] c1:10 20 30; c2:1.1 2.2 3.3)
3
```

```
q)count ([k:10 20] c:`one`two)
2
```

> **Tip:** You cannot use (count) to determine whether an entity is an atom or list since atoms and singletons both have count 1. Instead test the sign of the type.

```
q)0>signum type 42
1b
```

```
q)0>signum type enlist 42
0b
```

> **Tip:** Do you know why they call it count? Because it loves to count! Nyah, ha, ha, ha, ha. Vun, and two, and tree, and ...

A.17 cov

The dyadic (cov) takes two numeric lists of the same length and returns a float equal to the mathematical covariance between the items of the two lists. If both arguments are lists, they must have the same count; atoms return 0f.

```
q)23 -11 35 0 cov 42  21 73 39
411.25
```

The function (cov) is equivalent to,

> avg[x*y]-avg[x]*avg y}

A.18 cross

The dyadic (cross) takes atoms or lists as arguments and returns their Cartesian product—that is, the set of all pairs drawn from the two arguments.

```
q)1 2 cross `a`b`c
1 `a
1 `b
1 `c
2 `a
2 `b
2 `c
```

> **Tip:** You can also apply (cross) to dictionaries and tables.

The function (cross) is equivalent to,

> {raze x,\:/:y}

A.19 cut

The dyadic function (cut) can take a list of long (*indices*) as its first parameter and a list (*source*) as it right parameter. It returns the list obtained by splitting *source* at the positions in *indices*.

> **Tip:** If the initial item of indices is not 0, the first sublist split out is dropped.

```
q)L:10 20 30 40 50 60 70 80 90 100
q)0 2 5 7 cut L
10 20
30 40 50
60 70
80 90 100
```

```
q)2 5 7 cut L
30 40 50
60 70
80 90 100
```

When the first parameter is a non-negative integral atom (*width*), *source* is split at indices that are multiples of *width*.

```
q)2 cut L
10 20
30 40
50 60
70 80
90 100
```

```
q)3 cut L
10 20 30
40 50 60
70 80 90
,100
```

A.20 cut (_)

The dyadic function (_) has several forms, depending on the types of its parameters. See also (drop) and (cut).

Tip: When (_) is used infix, surrounding it with whitespace will avoid it getting mixed up with variable names, since '_' is a valid q name character.

When the first parameter is an integral atom (*count*) and the second parameters is a list (*source*), the result is *source* with *count* items dropped from the head *if* count is positive and from the tail when *count* is negative.

```
q)2 _ 10 20 30 40 50 60 70 80 90 100
30 40 50 60 70 80 90 100
```

```
q)-2 _ 10 20 30 40 50 60 70 80 90 100
10 20 30 40 50 60 70 80
```

When the first parameter of (_) is a list of long (*indices*) and the second parameter as a list (*source*) , it returns the list obtained by splitting *source* at the positions in *indices*. This is the same behavior as (cut) for this signature.

> *Tip:* If the initial item of indices is not 0, the first sublist split out is dropped.

```
q)L:10 20 30 40 50 60 70 80 90 100
q)0 2 5 7 _ L
10 20
30 40 50
60 70
80 90 100
```

```
q)2 5 7 _ L
30 40 50
60 70
80 90 100
```

When the second parameter of (_) is a dictionary (*source*) and the first parameter is a list of key values whose type matches *source*, the result is a dictionary obtained by removing the specified key-value pairs from the target. Since tables and keyed tables are dictionaries, (_) applies to them by extension.

```
q)`a`c _ `a`b`c!10 20 30
b| 20
```

```
q)`c1`c2 _ ([] c1:`a`b; c2:10 20; c3:1.1 2.2)
c3
---
1.1
2.2
```

```
q)([] k:`a`c) _ ([k:`a`b`c] v:10 20 30)
k| v
-| --
b| 20
```

> *Tip:* The first parameter must be a list, so a single value for the first parameter in this form must be enlisted.

```
q)(enlist `b) _ `a`b`c!10 20 30
a| 10
c| 30
```

When the first parameter of (_) is a list or a dictionary (*source*) and the second parameter is an atom representing an index or key, the result is obtained by deleting the specified item from (a copy of) *source*.

```
q)101 102 103 104 105 _ 2
101 102 104 105
```

```
q)(`a`b`c!10 20 30) _ `b
a| 10
c| 30
```

```
q)([] c1:`a`b; c2:10 20; c3:1.1 2.2) _ 1
c1 c2 c3
--------
a  10 1.1
```

```
q)([k:101 102 103] c:`one`two`three) _ 102
k  | c
---| -----
101| one
103| three
```

A.21 deltas

The uniform (deltas) is (-':), which returns the difference of each item in a numeric list with its predecessor.

```
q)deltas 1 2 3 4 5
1 1 1 1 1
```

```
q)deltas 96.25 93.25 58.25 73.25 89.50 84.00 84.25
96.25 -3 -35 15 16.25 -5.5 0.25
```

If you are looking to bound the absolute difference between successive elements, the second example shows that the initial item of the result will be troublesome. In this case, you can use,

```
deltas0:{first[x] -': x}
```

In our example above,

```
q)deltas0 96.25 93.25 58.25 73.25 89.50 84.00 84.25
0 -3 -35 15 16.25 -5.5 0.25
```

A.22 desc

The uniform (desc) returns (a copy of) its argument list of comparables sorted in descending order. When evaluated on a dictionary, it reorders the key-value pairs (on a copy) so that the values are sorted.

```
q)desc 3 7 2 8 1 9
9 8 7 3 2 1
```

```
q)desc `b`c`a!2 3 1
c| 3
b| 2
a| 1
```

A.23 dev

The aggregate (dev) returns the float standard deviation of a numeric list.

```
q)dev 1000?100.
29.40271
```

The function (dev) is equivalent to,

```
{sqrt var x}
```

A.24 differ

The uniform (differ) is

```
not (~':)
```

It asks if each item in a list is not identical to its predecessor. The item at index 0 in the result is always 1b.

```
q)differ 0 1 1 2 3 2 2 2 4 1 1 3 4 4 4 4 5
11011100110110001b
```

```
q)differ "mississippi"
```

```
q)differ (1 2; 1 2; 3 4 5)
101b
```

One use of (differ) is to locate runs of repeated items in a list.

```
q)L:0 1 1 2 3 2 2 2 4 1 1 3 4 4 4 4 5
q)nd|next nd:not differ L
01100111011011110b
```

A.25 distinct

The function (distinct) returns the unique items in its list argument, in order of first occurrence. Note that it does **not** apply the `u# attribute.

```
q)distinct 1 2 3 2 3 4 6 4 3 5 6
1 2 3 4 6 5
```

> ***Tip:*** Following is a test for existence of duplicates.
>
> ```
> {count[x]=count distinct x}
> ```

Since a table is a list of records, (distinct) effectively removes duplicate rows. All fields' records must be identical for them to be considered identical.

```
q)distinct ([]a:1 2 3 2 1;
b:`washington`adams`jefferson`adams`washington)
a b
------------
1 washington
2 adams
3 jefferson
q)distinct ([]a:1 2 3 2 1;
b:`washington`adams`jefferson`adams`wasington)
_
```

A.26 enlist

The function (enlist) returns a list whose items comprise its arguments. The most common use is to create a singleton list from a single argument.

Unlike user-defined functions, the number of arguments to (enlist) is not restricted to eight.

```
q)enlist 42
,42
```

```
q)count enlist 10 20 30
1
```

```
q)enlist[1;2;3;4;5;6;7;8;9;10]
1 2 3 4 5 6 7 8 9 10
```

A.27 eval

The monadic (eval) evaluates a list that is a valid q parse tree; it is the same code used in the q interpreter. Such a list can be produced using (parse) on a string containing a valid q expression, or by hand—if you know what you're doing. A full discussion of parse trees is beyond the scope of this tutorial.

```
q)eval parse "a:6*7"
42
```

```
q)a
42
```

```
q)eval (+;1;(*;6;7))
43
```

A.28 except

The dyadic (except) takes a list (or dictionary) as its first parameter (*target*) and an atom or list of items (or keys) of the same type as *target* for its second parameter (*source*) and returns those items in *target* that are not specified in *source*. The returned items are in the order of their first occurrence in *target*.

```
q)1 2 3 4 3 2 except 2
1 3 4 3
```

```
q)string[2015.01.01] except "."
"20150101"
```

```
q)(`a`b`c`d!10 20 30 40) except `a`d!10 40
20 30
```

```
q)([] c1:`a`b`c`d; c2:10 20 30 40) except ([] c1:`a`d; c2:10 40)
c1 c2
-----
b  20
c  30
```

> *Tip:* The result of (except) is always a list.

A.29 exit

The monadic (exit) takes a long as its parameter (*retval*) and causes the q process to exit, returning *retval* to the OS.

> *Important:* There is no prompt for confirmation.

A.30 fill (^)

The dyadic fill (^) takes a list as its second parameter (*target*) and an atom of the same type as its first parameter (*fillval*). It returns (a copy of) *target* with null values filled with *fillval*.

```
q)42^1 2 3 0N 5 0N
1 2 3 42 5 42
```

```
q)"_"^"Now is the time"
"Now_is_the_time"
```

```
q)`NA^`First`Second``Fourth
`First`Second`NA`Fourth
```

Fill is atomic in the second parameter.

```
q)42^(1;0N;(100;200 0N))
1
42
(100;200 42)
```

Like all functions, fill operates on the values of a dictionary.

```
q)42^`a`b`c`d!100 0N 200 0
a| 100
b| 42
c| 200
d| 0
```

```
q)0^([]c1:1.0 2.0 0n; c2:0N 2 0N)
c1 c2
-----
1  0
2  2
0  0
```

A.31 find (?)

The form of dyadic (?) called "find" takes a list (*target*) as its first parameter and an atom of the same type (*source*) as its second parameter. It returns the index of the first occurrence of *source* in *target* or the count of *target* if it is not found. It is atomic in the second parameter.

The simplest case is when *source* is an atom.

```
q)100 99 98 87 96 98?98
2
```

```
q)`one`two`three?`four
3
```

```
q)"Now is the time"?"the"
7 8 9
```

> **Tip:** The first example demonstrates that find returns only the index of the first occurrence of source. To find the indices of all occurrences you could use,

```
q){where x=y}[100 99 98 87 96 98;98]
2 5
```

Find also works on general lists, although if you need this you should probably consider redesigning your program.

```
q)(1 2; 3 4; `a`b)?`a`b
2
```

```
q)((0;1 2);3 4;5 6)?5 6
2
```

Find can also take a dictionary as its first parameter (*target*) and a dictionary value as its second parameter (*value*). It returns the first key that maps to *value*. It is atomic in the second parameter.

```
q)(`a`b`c`d!10 20 30 10)?10
`a
q)(`a`b`c`d!10 20 30 10)?10 30
`a`c
```

By extension, find applies to tables and keyed tables.

```
q)([] c1:`a`b`c; c2:10 20 30)?`c1`c2!(`b;20)
1
```

```
q)([] c1:`a`b`c; c2:10 20 30)?(`b;20)
1
```

```
q)([k:1 2 3] c:100 101 102)?101
k| 2
```

> ***Zen Moment***: Viewing a list or dictionary as a mapping, find is the inverse mapping.

A.32 fills

The uniform (fills) is (^\), which fills forward, meaning that non-null items are filled over succeeding null items.

```
q)fills 1 0N 3 0N 0N 5
1 1 3 3 3 5
```

```
q)fills `x``y```z
`x`x`y`y`y`z
```

```
q)update fills c2 from ([] `a`b`c`d`e`f; c2:1 0N 3 0N 0N 5)
x c2
----
a 1
b 1
c 3
d 3
e 3
f 5
```

If you need to fill initial nulls, use the dyadic form of (^\).

```
q)fills 0N 0N 3 0N 5
0N 0N 3 3 5
```

```
q)0 ^\ 0N 0N 3 0N 5
0 0 3 3 5
```

A.33 flip

The monadic function (flip) transposes a rectangular list, column dictionary or table (*source*).

When *source* is a rectangular list, the items are rearranged, effectively reversing the first two indices in indexing. For example,

```
q)show m:(1 2 3;10 20 30)
1  2  3
10 20 30
```

```
q)flip m
1 10
2 20
3 30
```

When (flip) converts a column dictionary to a table and vice versa, no data is actually rearranged. Only column indexing is reversed.

```
q)dc:`c1`c2!(`a`b`c;10 20 30)
q)t:([] c1:`a`b`c; c2:10 20 30)
q)dc[`c1;2]~t[2;`c1]
```

A.34 getenv

The monadic function (getenv) takes a symbol argument representing the name of an OS environment variable and returns the value (if any) of that environment variable as a string.

```
q)getenv `SHELL
"/bin/bash"
```

A.35 group

The monadic function (group) takes a list (*source*) and returns a dictionary in which each distinct item in *source* is mapped to the indices of its occurrences in *source*. The keys of the result are in the order of their first appearance in *source*.

```
q)group "i miss mississippi"
i| 0 3 8 11 14 17
 | 1 6
m| 2 7
s| 4 5 9 10 12 13
p| 15 16
```

A.36 gtime

The atomic (gtime) converts local time to UTC time.

```
q).z.P
2015.04.12D12:10:20.685653000
q)gtime .z.P
2015.04.12D22:10:24.861692000
q).z.p
2015.04.12D22:10:28.597654000
```

A.37 iasc

The uniform (iasc) takes a list or a dictionary (*source*). Considering *source* as a mapping, the result of (iasc) is a list of the indices/keys of source in the order that would sort it ascending. Otherwise put, composing *source* with the result of (iasc) sorts in ascending order.

```
q)L:30 70 20 80 10 90
q)iasc L
4 2 0 1 3 5
q)L iasc L
10 20 30 70 80 90
```

```
q)d:`c`a`b!30 10 20
q)iasc d
`a`b`c
q)d iasc d
10 20 30
```

This is useful when you want to use one list to control the order of others—e.g., manual sort on the serialized columns of a splayed table (see §14.3).

> **Zen Moment**: The composite iasc iasc provides the list of indices that transforms the sorted entity back to the original.

A.38 identity

The monadic function denoted (::) is the identity function—i.e., it returns its argument.

506

```
q)::[42]
42
```

```
q)(::) `Zaphod
`Zaphod
```

The identity function **cannot** be used naked with juxtaposition or (@). You must either enclose it in parentheses or enclose its argument in square brackets.

A.39 idesc

The monadic function (idesc) takes a list or a dictionary (*source*). Considering *source* as a mapping, the result of (idesc) is a list of the indices/keys of source in the order that would sort it descending. Otherwise put, composing *source* with the result of (idesc) sorts in descending order.

```
q)L:30 70 20 80 10 90
q)idesc L
5 3 1 0 2 4
q)L idesc L
90 80 70 30 20 10
```

```
q)d:`c`a`b!30 10 20
q)idesc d
`c`b`a
q)d idesc d
30 20 10
```

This is useful when you want to use one list to control the order of others—e.g., manual sort on the serialized columns of a splayed table (see §14.2).

> **Zen Moment**: The composite idesc idesc provides the list of indices that transforms the sorted entity back to the original.

A.40 in

The dyadic function (in) is atomic in its first parameter (*source*) and takes an atom or list second parameter (*target*). It returns a boolean indicating whether *source* appears in *target*. The comparison is strict with regard to type.

```
q)42 in 0 6 7 42 98
1b
```

```
q)4 in 42
0b
```

```
q)"4" in "42"
1b
```

```
q)"cat" in "abcdefg"
110b
```

A.41 inter

The dyadic (inter) returns the items in its first list parameter that occur in its second list parameter.

```
q)1 2 3 4 inter 3 4 5
3 4
```

Lists differ from sets in that they are ordered and allow duplicates, so (inter) is not commutative in general.

```
q)1 2 3 1 inter 4 1
1 1
q)4 1 inter 1 2 3 1
,1
```

```
q)1 2 3 inter 4 3 2
2 3
q)4 3 2 inter 1 2 3
3 2
```

You can use (inter) to find common records in tables having identical schemas.

```
q)t1:([] c1:`a`b`c; c2:10 20 30)
q)t2:([] c1:`c`d; c2:30 40)
q)t1 inter t2
c1 c2
-----
c  30
```

A.42 inv

The monadic (inv) returns the inverse of a float matrix.

```
q)m:(1.1 2.1 3.1; 2.3 3.4 4.5; 5.6 7.8 9.8)
q)inv m
-8.165138 16.51376  -5
12.20183  -30.18349 10
-5.045872 14.58716  -5
```

An integer matrix must be cast to float.

508

A.43 join (,)

The dyadic join (,) appends its second parameter to the first. When both operands are either lists or atoms, the result concatenates the second parameter to the first .

```
q)1,2 3 4
1 2 3 4
```

```
q)1 2 3,4
1 2 3 4
```

```
q)1 2,3 4
1 2 3 4
```

The result is a general list unless all items are of homogeneous type.

```
q)1 2 3,4.0
1
2
3
4f
```

When both parameters are dictionaries, the result is the merge of the second parameter into the first using upsert semantics. Otherwise put, assignments in the second parameter prevail over those in the first.

```
q)(`a`b`c!10 20 30),`c`d!300 400
a| 10
b| 20
c| 300
d| 400
```

By extension, you can use (,) on tables and keyed tables with identical schemas.

A.44 key

The (key) operator vies for the title of most overloaded q operator. Its eponymous action is to return the key of a dictionary, including the special case of the key table portion of a keyed table. It can be applied by value or name.

```
q)key `a`b`c!10 20 30
```

```
q)kt:([k:`a`b`c] v:10 20 30)
q)key kt
```

```
q)key `kt
```

A context—i.e. the content of a namespace—is a dictionary, so (key) applied to the symbolic name will return the names of its constituents. Observe that contexts below the root all have an initial null name.

```
q)key `.
_
q).jab.a:42
q)key `.jab
_
```

To list all contexts, apply (key) to the null symbol.

```
q)key `
`q`Q`h`j`o`jab
```

Given a **simple** list, (key) returns the symbolic name of its type.

```
q)key 10 20 30
`long
q)key "so long"
_
```

Given an enumerated entity, (key) returns the name of its enumeration domain. This applies to foreign key columns, where it returns the name of the target keyed table.

```
q)sym:`c`b`a
q)key `sym$`a`b`a`c`a
_

q)kt:([k:`a`b`c] v:10 20 30)
q)t:([] k:`kt$`a`b`a`b`a; v: 10 20 30 49 59)
q)key t `k
_
```

Given an I/O handle corresponding to a directory, (key) returns a list of the symbolic names of entities in that directory, including hidden files.

```
q)\ls q
"README.txt"
"m32"
"q.k"
"q.q"
"s.k"
"sp.q"
"trade.q"
```

```
q)key `:q
`.DS_Store`README.txt`m32`q.k`q.q`s.k`sp.q`trade.q
```

> **Tip:** An empty directory returns an empty list of type symbol whereas a non-existent directory returns an empty general list.

This provides a simple test for the existence of a directory.

```
q)\ls q/jab
ls: q/jab: No such file or directory
'os
q)()~key `:q/jab
1b
q)\mkdir q/jab
q)key `:q/jab
`symbol$()
```

Given an I/O handle corresponding to a file, (key) returns the symbolic file name if the file exists and the general empty list () if it does not. As above, this provides a test for existence of the file.

```
q)key `:q/trade.q
`:q/trade.q
q)()~key `:q/quote.q
1b
```

Last, but not least, (key) also acts as a synonym of (til).

```
q)key 10
_
```

A.45 like

The dyadic (like) performs pattern matching on its first string parameter (*source*) according to the pattern in its string second parameter (*pattern*). It returns a boolean result indicating whether *pattern* is matched. The pattern is expressed as a mix of regular characters and special formatting characters. The special chars are '?', '*', the pair '[' and ']', and a '^' that is enclosed in square brackets.

The special char '?' represents an arbitrary single character in the pattern.

```
q)"fan" like "f?n"
1b
```

```
q)"fun" like "f?n"
1b
```

```
q)"foP" like "f?p"
0b
```

The special char '*' represents an arbitrary sequence of characters in the pattern.

As of this writing (Sep 2015), only a single occurrence of '*'is allowed in the pattern, except that a '*' can occur at both the beginning and end of the pattern.

```
q)"how" like "h*"
1b
```

```
q)"hercules" like "h*"
1b
```

```
q)"wealth" like "*h"
1b
```

```
q)"flight" like "*h*"
1b
```

```
q)"Jones" like "J?ne*"
```

```
q)"Joynes" like "J*ne*"
'nyi
```

The special character pair '[' and ']' encloses a sequence of alternatives for a single character match.

```
q)"flap" like "fl[ao]p"
1b
```

```
q)"flip" like "fl[ao]p"
0b
```

```
q)"459-0609" like "[0-9][0-9][0-9]-0[0-9][0-9][0-9]"
1b
```

```
q)"459-0609" like "[0-9][0-9][0-9]-1[0-9][0-9][0-9]"
0b
```

The special character '^' is used in conjunction with '[' and ']' to indicate that the enclosed sequence of characters is disallowed. For example, to test whether a string ends in a numeric character,

```
q)"M26d" like "*[^0-9]"
1b
```

```
q)"Joe999" like "*[^0-9]"
0b
```

Enclose a special char in square brackets to escape it as a normal char.

```
q)"a_c" like "a[*]"
0b
```

```
q)"a*c" like "a[*]c"
1b
```

A.46 lower

The atomic (lower) takes a char, string or symbol argument and returns the result of converting all alpha text to lower case.

```
q)lower `A
`a
```

```
q)lower "a Bc42De"
"a bc42de"
```

A.47 lsq

The dyadic matrix function (lsq) takes float matrix parameters A and B and returns the matrix X that solves the following matrix equation, where · is matrix multiplication.

$$A = X \cdot B$$

For example,

```
q)A:(1.1 2.2 3.3;4.4 5.5 6.6;7.7 8.8 9.9)
q)B:(1.1 2.1 3.1; 2.3 3.4 4.5; 5.6 7.8 9.8)
q)A lsq B
1.211009   -0.1009174 2.993439e-12
-2.119266 2.926606   -3.996803e-12
-5.449541 5.954128   -1.758593e-11
```

Observe that (lsq) is equivalent to,

```
q)A mmu inv B
1.211009   -0.1009174 1.77991e-12
-2.119266 2.926606   -5.81224e-12
-5.449541 5.954128   -1.337952e-11
```

Integer matrices must be cast to float.

A.48 ltime

The atomic (ltime) converts UTC time to local time.

```
q).z.P
2015.04.12D12:12:42.475837000
```

```
q)ltime .z.P
2015.04.12D02:12:45.987860000
```

```
q).z.p
2015.04.12D22:12:47.859567000
```

A.49 ltrim

The monadic (ltrim) takes a string parameter and returns the result of removing leading blanks.

```
q)ltrim "   abc   "
"abc   "
q)ltrim "   "
""
```

You can also apply (ltrim) to a non-blank char but it fails for a blank char.

```
q)ltrim "a"
"a"
q)ltrim " "
k){$[~t&77h>t:@x;.z.s'x;" "=*x;(+/&\" "=x)_x;x]}
'type
 __
 1b
" "
```

A.50 mavg

The dyadic (mavg) takes first parameter a long (*length*) and returns the *length*-wise moving average of its numeric list second parameter (*source*). At each position in *source*, it computes the average of the *length* preceding items, or as many as are available up to *length*, ignoring internal nulls. It is uniform in its second argument.

In the following example, the first item in the result is the average of itself only; the second result item is the average of the first two source items; all other items reflect the average of the item at the position along with its two predecessors.

```
q)3 mavg 10 20 30 40 50
10 15 20 30 40f
```

```
q)3 mavg 0N 10 20 30 40 50
0n 10 15 20 30 40
```

> **Tip:** For length 1, the result is the source converted to float.

A.51 max

The aggregate (max) is (|/), which applies (|) cumulatively across a list of items of underlying numeric type and returns the final result. It is the same as (any) on a boolean list.

```
q)max 100100b
1b
```

```
q)max 10?2015.01.01
2013.09.09
```

A.52 maxs

The uniform (maxs) is (|\), which applies (|) across a list of comparable items and returns the intermediate results.

```
q)maxs 1 2 5 4 10
1 2 5 5 10
```

```
q)maxs "Beeblebrox"
"Beeelllrrx"
```

A.53 mcount

The uniform dyadic (mcount) takes first parameter a long (*length*) and returns an long equal to the *length*-wise moving count of its list second parameter (*source*). At each position in *source*, it counts the number of non-null preceding items up to *length*. This function is useful in computing other moving quantities, such as moving average, since it correctly reports the number of predecessors at the head of the list and also ignores internal nulls.

```
q)3 mcount 10 20 30 40 50
1 2 3 3 3i
```

```
q)3 mcount 10 20 0N 40 50 60 0N
1 2 2 2 2 3 2i
```

A.54 md5

The monadic function (md5) computes the MD5 (Message Digest Algorithm 5) hash of a string as a list of 16 bytes.

515

```
q)md5 "Life the Universe and Everything"
0x0e9a5631e4db880d43808504d05348df
```

A.55 mdev

The uniform dyadic (mdev) takes first parameter a long (*length*) and returns the *length*-wise moving standard deviation of its numeric list second parameter (*source*). At each position in *source*, it computes the standard deviation of the *length* preceding items, or as many as are available at that position up to *length*. It excludes internal nulls from the calculation.

```
q)3 mdev 10 20 30 40 50
0 5 8.164966 8.164966 8.164966
```

```
q)3 mdev 10 20 30 0N 50
0 5 8.164966 5 10
```

A.56 med

The aggregate (med) returns the float median of a numeric list.

For lists and dictionaries, the result is a float.

```
q)med 1000?1000.
499.1908
```

The function (med) is equivalent to,

```
{avg x (iasc x)@floor .5*-1 0+count x,:()}
```

A.57 min

The aggregate (min) is (&/), which applies (&) cumulatively across a list of underlying numeric type and returns the final result. It is the same as (and) for a boolean list.

```
q)min 100?100
2
```

```
q)min 100100b
0b
```

A.58 mins

The uniform (mins) is (&\), which computes the cumulative minimums of a list of comparables and returns the intermediate results.

```
q)mins 10 4 5 1 2
10 4 4 1 1
```

```
q)mins "the cat"
"theecaa"
```

A.59 mmax

The uniform dyadic (mmax) takes first parameter a long (*length*) and returns the *length*-wise moving maximum of its second parameter list of comparables (*source*). At each position in *source*, it computes the maximum of the *length* preceding items, or as many as are available at that position up to *length*.

In the following example, the first item in the result is the max of itself only; the second result item is the max of the first two source items; all other items reflect the max of the item at the position along with its two predecessors.

```
q)3 mmax 20 10 30 50 40
20 20 30 50 50
```

```
q)3 mmax 20 10 30 0N 40
20 20 30 30 40
```

A.60 mmin

The uniform dyadic (mmin) takes first parameter a long (*length*) and returns the *length*-wise moving minimum of its second parameter list of comparables (*source*). At each position in *source*, it computes the minimum of the *length* preceding items, or as many as are available at that position up to *length*.

In the following example, the first item in the result is the min of itself only; the second result item is the min of the first two source items; all other items reflect the min of the item at the position along with its two predecessors.

```
q)3 mmin 20 10 30 50 40
20 10 10 10 30
```

For *length* less than or equal to 0 the result is *source*.

A.61 mmu

The dyadic matrix multiplication (mmu) returns the matrix product of its two float vector or matrix parameters, which must be of the correct shape. It reduces to dot product on vectors. Integer matrices must be cast to float.

```
q)m1:(1.1 2.2 3.3;4.4 5.5 6.6;7.7 8.8 9.9)
q)m1 mmu flip m1
16.94 38.72  60.5
38.72 93.17  147.62
60.5  147.62 234.74
```

```
q)m2:`float$(0 0 1; 0 1 0; 1 0 0)
q)m2 mmu m2
1 0 0
0 1 0
0 0 1
```

```
q)1 2 3f mmu 1 2 3f
14f
```

The ($) operator is overloaded to yield matrix multiplication when its parameters are float vectors or matrices.

```
q)m2 $ m2
1 0 0
0 1 0
0 0 1
```

A.62 msum

The uniform dyadic (msum) takes first parameter a long (*length*) and returns the *length*-wise moving sum of its numeric list second parameter (*source*). At each position in *source*, it computes the sum of the *length* preceding items, or as many as are available at that position up to *length*. It excludes internal nulls from the sum.

In the following example, the first item in the result is the sum of itself only; the second result item is the sum of the first two source items; all other items reflect the sum of the item at the position along with its two predecessors.

```
q)3 msum 10 20 30 40 50
10 30 60 90 120
```

A.63 next

The uniform (next) returns its list parameter shifted one position to the left with a null (or empty) in the last item. Otherwise put, each item in the original is replaced with its successor.

```
q)next 1 2 3 4 5
2 3 4 5 0N
```

```
q)next (1 2; 3 4 5; 6 7)
3 4 5
6 7
`long$()
```

A.64 null

The atomic function (null) tests its argument for null value. It is preferred to testing for equality as it works for all types.

```
q)null 42
0b
```

```
q)null 0n
1b
```

```
q)null "Now is the time"
000100100010000b
```

A common idiom combines (where) with (null) to obtain the positions of the null items in a list.

```
q)where null 1 2 3 0N 5 0N
3 5
```

Because (null) is atomic, it picks out null values in all fields.

```
q)null ([] c1:`a``b; c2:0N 20 30)
c1 c2
-----
0  1
1  0
0  0
```

This can be used to identify null columns.

```
q)where all null ([] c1:`a`b`c; c2:0n 0n 0n; c3:10 0N 30)
,`c2
```

A.65 or

The function (or) is the same as (|) for people who like typing extra characters.

```
q)1b or 0b
1b
```

```
q)42 or 43
43
```

A.66 over

The function (over) is a convenience function that renames the monadic form of (/) for those allergic to k.

```
q){x+2*y} over 2 3 5 7
32
```

```
q)(+) over 2 3 5 7
17
```

A.67 parse

The monadic (parse) returns the q parse tree for a string representing a q expression. Applying (eval) to the result of (parse) effectively evaluates the expression. The composition of (eval) after (parse) is essentially the q interpreter. A discussion of q parse trees is beyond the scope of this tutorial.

```
q)parse "7*4+2"
*
7
(+;4;2)
q)eval parse "7*4+2"
42
```

It is useful to apply (parse) to a string containing a query template for the purpose of expressing the query in functional form. The result will often include k code but it is usually recognizable and you can use it in functional form.

> **Tip:** The constraint portion of the resulting parse tree will contain an extra level of nesting displayed in the k form (,,).

You must remove one level for the functional form.

```
q)t:([]c1:`a`b`c; c2:10 20 30)
q)parse "select c2:2*c2 from t where c1=`c"
?
`t
,,(=;`c1;,`c)
0b
(,`c2)!,(*;2;`c2)

q)?[`t; enlist (=;`c1;enlist `c); 0b; (enlist `c2)!enlist (*;2;`c2)]
c2
--
60
```

A.68 peach

A full discussion of how q handles concurrency and distributed processing is beyond the scope of this text. We provide a description of the essential features in q3.2 as of this writing (Sep 2015) and refer the reader to the Kx site for up-to-date details.

Concurrency in q uses two basic constructs: (peach) and slaves. Slaves can be either threads spawned by the main q process or independent q processes. How many and which type of slaves are declared to the q process at startup. The function (peach) is a "parallel" version of (each) that applies a function over a list by distributing the items of the list across slaves. This is q's implementation of the "map" portion of the distributed map-reduce paradigm, which is much-ballyhooed in other environments.

> **Tip:** If q is not started with slaves, (peach) reverts to (each), meaning function application across the list occurs sequentially in the main q thread.

Use the command line parameter –s to start a slave-enabled q session. In classic Arthurian fashion, the interpretation of –s depends on the sign of the integer that follows it. A **positive** integer *n* indicates that the q process should start with *n* slave **threads** to be used by (peach). A **negative** integer *–n* means that you will provide *n* independent slave q **processes** for (peach) to use. The physical implementation of work distribution is different in these two cases, but the logical result is the same.

A.68.1 Threads

When q is started with –s *n*, the q process automatically spawns *n* slave threads in addition to the main thread at startup. When you subsequently use (peach) to apply a function—i.e., map it—across a list, the application is automatically distributed across the slave threads for you. The result of the application is the same as if you had used (each) but if q is running on a machine with multiple cores, you should expect a speedup, depending on what the function does, how slave threads are allocated to cores and the load on your machine. For example, on the author's laptop that has 4 cores and hyperthreading, we find that the benefit of multiple slaves for evaluating a compute-intensive calculation on a list of 8 items plateaus at 4 slaves.

```
$ rlwrap q/m32/q -s 2
q)\t {sum exp x?1.0} each 8#1000000
134
q)\t {sum exp x?1.0} peach 8#1000000
72

$ rlwrap q/m32/q -s 4
q)\t {sum exp x?1.0} each 8#1000000
136
q)\t {sum exp x?1.0} peach 8#1000000
46

$ rlwrap q/m32/q -s 8
q)\t {sum exp x?1.0} each 8#1000000
135
q)\t {sum exp x?1.0} peach 8#1000000
43
```

In order to maintain consistency during concurrent application, the following restriction is placed on function evaluation within slave threads. Code executed in a slave thread **cannot** update global variables—i.e., a function can only update local variables.

> **Tip:** If you use a timer on the main thread or other tricks to update globals that are read by slave threads, you are cruising for a bruising. While these updates are locked, there is no notion of a transaction with attendant rollback. It is unlikely that your function executing on the timer is atomic at the hardware level. Should it fail mid-flight, you should expect the workspace would be in an inconsistent state with no built-in recovery mechanism.

Now we describe how the slave thread execution is implemented. The items in the list are pre-assigned to slaves in a round-robin fashion. For example, if you (peach) a function on a list with 9 items in a session with 4 slaves: items 0, 4 and 8 will be executed sequentially on slave 0; items 1, 5 and 9 will be executed sequentially on slave 1; items 2 and 6 will be executed sequentially on slave 2; and items 3 and 7 will be executed sequentially on slave 3. The sequential execution within slaves occurs concurrently across slaves.

The slaves use thread-local heaps and the (partial) results of application within each slave are serialized and copied to the main thread where they are deserialized and assembled into the final result. Since there is overhead associated with serialization/deserialization, we have:

> **Tip:** A function applied with (peach) should do enough computation to outweigh the serialization overhead. You can estimate the serialization time an space of a q entity with,
>
> ```
> \ts:100 -9!-8!entity
> ```

We collect here observations on execution within a slave. See the Kx site for more details.

(1) If the list has a **single** item, (peach) application occurs in the **main** q thread only.

(2) If the function applied with (peach) performs grouping on a symbol list—e.g., a select that groups on a ticker symbol—this will be significantly slower in the slave because the optimized algorithm used in the main thread is not available in the slave.

(3) In q3.*, a socket can be used from the main thread only. As there is no locking around a socket descriptor, a communication handle shared between threads would result in garbage due to message interleaving.

(4) Each slave thread has its own heap, a minimum of 64MB. Executing .Q.gc[] in the main thread triggers garbage collection in the slave threads too. Automatic garbage collection within each thread is only executed for that particular thread, not across all threads.

(5) Symbols are internalized in a single memory area accessible to all threads.

A.68.2 Distributed peach

Starting q with −s −n indicates:

(1) In addition to the main q process, you will instantiate *n* workers, where a worker is an independent q process with an open port

(2) You will connect the master q process to each worker

(3)   You will provide the master process a unique'd list of open handles to the workers

The list of handles to the workers is obtained from the system variable .z.pd upon each invocation of (peach). You can set .z.pd either to an integer list of open handles with the `u# attribute applied, or a function that returns the same.

> **Tip:** You must apply the `u# attribute or you will get the error:
>
>   '.z.pd - expected unique vector of int handles

In contrast to the situation with slave threads, where the threads are created for you automatically, with distributed (peach) it is your responsibility to instantiate the separate worker processes and make them available to the main q process. In production environments this may entail meeting security requirements—e.g., Kerberos. You can start the workers externally to your main process or you can start them from within the process using (system).

The workers can be on the same machine as the master process or on any machine on a network so long as it is accessible from the master process. Since they are independent q processes that share no data with the main process, the distributed function is not restricted as to what it can do on the worker. This provides a very flexible framework for distributed computing.

Once you have started the worker processes, you must open a connection to each one, keeping track of the open handles.

> **Tip:** You cannot use these handles for other messaging, as (peach) will close any handle that presents a message not in its expected format.

You can assign the unique'd list of the open connections to .z.pd or you can return such a list from a function that you assign to .z.pd. In contrast to the slave thread implementation, where the assignment to slaves is determined in advance, individual computations are automatically distributed to workers that become free. Thus we get a simple form of dynamic load balancing.

Following is an example that starts four external workers on the same machine from within the master process, wires the workers directly into .z.pd and then uses (peach) to distribute work to them.

```
~$q -s -4
..
q){system "q -q -p ",string[x]," &"} each 20000+til 4

q).z.pd:`u#hopen each `$"::",/:string 20000+til 4
q)\t {sum exp x?1.0} each 8#1000000
134
q)\t {sum exp x?1.0} peach 8#1000000
46
```

You can also assign to .z.pd a function that manages the connections. The code below monitors closing connections via .z.pc, which removes the handle of any closed connection from its self-maintained list of active handles. The function assigned to .z.pd checks to see if all expected handles are open and, if not, closes any open handles and then reopens all the specified handles.

```
q)handles:`u#`int$()
q).z.pd:{
  if[0>=n:neg system "s";
   '"must start q with -s -n"];
  if[n<>count handles; hclose each handles;
    handles set `u#hopen each 20000+til n];
  handles}
q).z.pc:{`handles set `u#handles except x;}
```

A.69 prd

The aggregate (prd) is (*/), which applies (*) cumulatively across a numeric list and returns the final result.

> **Tip:** Note the missing 'o' in the name.

```
q)prd 1+til 5
```

```
q)prd 1+til 5
120
```

```
q)prd 10?100.
2.667807e+13
```

It is possible to apply (prd) to a nested list provided the sublists conform. In this case, the result conforms to the sublists and the product is calculated recursively on the sublists.

```
q)prd (1 2; 100 200; 1000 2000)
100000 800000
```

A.70 prds

The uniform (prds) is (*\), which applies (*) cumulatively across a list of numeric type and returns the intermediate results.

> *Tip:* Note the missing 'o' in the name.

```
q)prds 1+til 5
1 2 6 24 120
```

A.71 prev

The uniform (prev) returns a list argument shifted one position to the right with a null (or empty) in the first item. Otherwise put, each item in the original is replaced with its predecessor.

```
q)prev 1 2 3 4 5
0N 1 2 3 4
```

```
q)prev (1 2; 3 4 5; 6 7)
`long$()
1 2
3 4 5
```

A.72 prior

The function (prior) is a convenience function that renames the monadic form of (':) for those allergic to k.

```
q)(-) prior 10 11 12 13 14
10 1 1 1 1
```

A.73 rank

The uniform (rank) returns the sort order of each item in a list of comparables.

```
q)rank 50 20 30 10 40
4 1 2 0 3
```

```
q)rank `x`a`b`z`c
3 0 1 4 2
```

A.74 ratios

The uniform (ratios) is (%':), which applies (%) across a list of numeric type and returns the intermediate results. That is, it returns the ratio of each item with its predecessor. The initial item in the result is 1.0.

```
q)ratios 10 20 30 40 50
10 2 1.5 1.333333 1.25
```

> **Tip:** If you are looking to bound the relative difference between successive elements, this example shows that the initial item of the result will be troublesome.

In this case, you can use,

```
ratios1:{first[x] %': x}
```

For our example above,

```
q)ratios1 10 20 30 40 50
1 2 1.5 1.333333 1.25
```

A.75 raze

The monadic (raze) is (,/). It effectively eliminates the top-most level of nesting from a list by concatenating across it.

```
q)raze (1 2 3;3; 4 5)
1 2 3 3 4 5
```

Observe that (raze) only removes the top-most level of nesting but you can use (each) to reach deeper levels.

```
q)raze ((1 2;3 4);(5;(6 7;8 9)))
1 2
3 4
5
(6 7;8 9)
q)raze each  ((1 2;3 4);(5;(6 7;8 9)))
1 2 3 4
(5;6 7;8 9)a
```

A.76 reval

Introduced in q3.3, (reval) is a version of (eval) that behaves as if the command line option -b had been set. This means that all updates on the server are blocked for the duration of the evaluation. See §A.27 and §13.2.1.

A.77 reverse

The uniform function (reverse) inverts the item order of its list argument.

```
q)reverse 1 2 3 4 5
5 4 3 2 1
```

```
q)reverse `a`b`c!10 20 30
c| 30
b| 20
a| 10
```

```
q)reverse ([] c1:`a`b`c; c2:10 20 30)
c1 c2
-----
c  30
b  20
a  10
```

```
q)reverse ([k:`a`b`c] v:10 20 30)
k| v
-| --
c| 30
b| 20
a| 10
```

For nested entities, the reversal takes place only at the topmost level but you can use (each) to reach lower levels.

```
q)reverse (1 2 3;"abc";`Four`Score`and`Seven)
`Four`Score`and`Seven
"abc"
1 2 3
```

```
q)reverse each (1 2 3;"abc";`Four`Score`and`Seven)
3 2 1
"cba"
`Seven`and`Score`Four
```

A.78 rload

The function (rload) is a convenience function that loads a splayed table into a variable with the same name as the splayed directory. The usual way to do this is with (get), whose result can be assigned to an arbitrary variable.

```
q)`:db/t/ set ([] c1:10 20 30; c2:1.2 2.2 3.3)
`:db/t/
q)rload `:db/t
`t
q)count t
3
```

```
q)t1:get `:db/t
q)count t1
3
```

A.79 rotate

The uniform dyadic (rotate) takes as its first parameter a long (*length*) and returns the result of rotating its second parameter by *length* positions. The rotation is to the left for positive *length* and to the right for negative *length*. For *length* 0, it returns the source.

```
q)2 rotate 1 2 3 4 5
3 4 5 1 2
```

```
q)22 rotate 1 2 3 4 5
3 4 5 1 2
```

A.80 rsave

The function (rsave) is a convenience function that splays a table variable to a directory with the same name. The preferred way to do this is with (set), which allows the directory name to be specified.

```
q)t:([] c1:10 20 30; c2:1.2 2.2 3.3)
q)rsave `:db/t
 :db/t/
q)`:db/t1/ set t
 :db/t1/
```

A.81 rtrim

The monadic (rtrim) takes a string argument and returns the result of removing trailing blanks.

```
q)rtrim "   abc   "
"   abc"
q)rtrim "   "
""
```

You can apply (rtrim) to a non-blank char but it fails for a blank char.

```
q)rtrim "a"
"a"
q)rtrim " "
k){$[~t&77h>t:@x;.z.s'x;" "=*x;(+/&\" "=x)_x;x]}
'type
-
1b
" "
```

A.82 scan

The function (scan) is a convenience function that renames the monadic form of (\) for those allergic to k.

```
q){x+2*y} scan 2 3 5 7
2 8 18 32
```

```
q)(+) scan  2 3 5 7
2 5 10 17
```

A.83 scov

The dyadic (scov) returns the statistical covariance of its numeric list arguments of the same length.

```
q)2 3 5 7 scov 4 3 0 2
-2.416667
```

It is equivalent to,

```
{cov[x;y]*count[x]%-1+count x}
```

A.84 sdev

The monadic (sdev) returns the statistical standard deviation of its numeric list argument.

```
q)sdev 10 343 232 55
155.1322
```

It is equivalent to,

```
{sqrt var[x]*count[x]%-1+count x}
```

A.85 setenv

The dyadic (setenv) takes a symbol first parameter representing the name of an OS environment variable and a string second parameter.

It calls the underlying OS to set the named environment variable to the specified string value.

```
q) `FOO setenv "test"
q)getenv `FOO
_
```

A.86 sin

The atomic (sin) takes a float and returns its mathematical sine.

```
q)sin 0f
0f
```

```
q)pi:3.141592653589793
q)sin pi
1.224647e-16
```

```
q)pi%2
1.570796
```

```
q)sin pi%4
0.7071068
```

A.87 ss

The dyadic (ss), for "string search", performs similar pattern matching as (like) against its first string parameter (*source*), looking for matches to its string second parameter (*pattern*). However, the result of (ss) is a list containing the position(s) of the matches of the pattern in *source*.

```
q)ss["Now is the time for all good men to come to";"me"]
13 29 38
```

```
q)"fun" ss "f?n"
,0
```

If no matches are found, an empty list of long is returned.

```
q)ss["ab";"z"]
`long$()
```

> **Note:** You cannot use * to match with (ss).

```
q)"fun" ss "f*n"
'length
```

A.88 ssr

The triadic (ssr), for "string search and replace", extends the capability of (ss) with replacement. The result is a string based on the first string parameter (*source*) in which all occurrences of the second string parameter (*pattern*) are replaced with the third string argument.

```
q)ssr["suffering succotash";"s";"th"]
"thuffering thuccotathh"
```

> **Note:** You cannot use * to match with (ssr).

You can use the over adverb with (ssr) to replace multiple items.

```
q)(ssr/)["results_%div_%dept.csv"; ("%div";"%dept"); ("banking";"m&a")]
"results_banking_m&a.csv"
```

A.89 string

The monadic (string) can be applied to any q entity to produce a textual representation. For atoms, lists and functions, the result of (string) is a list of char that does not contain any q formatting characters. Following are some examples.

```
q)string 42
"42"
```

```
q)string 6*7
"42"
```

```
q)string 424224242i
"424224242"
```

```
q)string `Zaphod
"Zaphod"
```

```
q)string {[a] a*a}
"{[a] a*a}"
```

The first example demonstrates that (string) is **not** atomic, because the result of applying it to an atom is a *list* of char.

Although (string) is not atomic, it is pseudo-atomic, in that it recurses through a list.

```
q)string 42 98
"42"
"98"
q)("42";"98")
"42"
"98"
```

This accounts for the un-intuitive behavior of (string) on an actual string.

```
q)string "Beeblebrox"
,"B"
,"e"
,"e"
,"b"
,"l"
,"e"
,"b"
,"r"
,"o"
```

Considering a list as a mapping, (string) acts on the range of the mapping. Viewing a dictionary as a generalized list, we conclude that the action of (string) on a dictionary should also apply to its range.

```
q)string 1 2 3!100 101 102
1| "100"
2| "101"
3| "102"
```

A table is the flip of a column dictionary, so we expect (string) to operate on the range of the column dictionary.

```
q)string ([] a:1 2 3; b:`a`b`c)
a     b
--------
,"1" ,"a"
,"2" ,"b"
,"3" ,"c"
```

Finally, a keyed table is a dictionary, so we expect (string) to operate on the value table.

```
q)string ([k:1 2 3] c:100 101 102)
k| c
-| -----
1| "100"
2| "101"
3| "102"
```

A.90 sublist

The dyadic (sublist) retrieves a sub-list of contiguous items from a list. The first parameter is a simple list of two non-negative integers:

the first item is the starting index (*start*); the second item is the number of items to retrieve (*count*). The second parameter (*target*) is a list or dictionary.

```
q)0 3 sublist 10 20 30 40 50
10 20 30
```

```
q)0 10 sublist "abcdef"
"abcdef"
```

```
q)0 2 sublist `a`b`c!10 20 30
a| 10
b| 20
```

> **Tip:** The construct (0 n sublist ...) is preferred to (n# ...) for extracting the first n items from a list since the latter will repeat the initial items if necessary to reach the specified count. This is ignored surprisingly often in practice.

A.91 sum

The aggregate (sum) is (+/), which applies (+) cumulatively across a numeric list and returns the final result.

```
q)sum 1+til 100
5050
```

```
q)sum 100?100.
5387.56
```

It is possible to apply (sum) to a nested list provided the sublists conform. In this case, the result conforms to the sublists and the sum is calculated recursively on the sublists.

```
q)sum (1 2;100 200;1000 2000)
1101 2202
```

A.92 sums

The uniform (sums) is (+\), which applies (+) cumulatively across a list of numeric type and returns the intermediate results.

```
q)sums 1+til 10
1 3 6 10 15 21 28 36 45 55
```

A.93 sv

The dyadic (sv)—"scalar from vector"—has several forms. It is usually written infix since that is easier to read.

The first form takes a char as its first parameter and a list of strings (*source*) as its second. It returns a string that is the concatenation of the strings in *source*, separated by the specified char.

```
q)"," sv ("Now";"is";"the";"time";"")
"Now,is,the,time,"
```

When (sv) is used with an empty symbol as its first parameter and a list of symbols as its second (*source*), the result is a symbol in which the items in *source* are concatenated with a separating dot. This is useful for q context names.

```
q)` sv `qalib`stat
`qalib.stat
```

When (sv) is used with an empty symbol as its first parameter and a symbol second parameter (*source*) whose first item is a file handle, the result is a symbol in which the items in *source* are concatenated with a separating '/'. This is useful for fully qualified path names.

```
q)` sv `:`q`tutorial`draft`3
`:/q/tutorial/draft/3
```

When (sv) is used with an empty symbol as its first parameter and a list of strings as the second parameter, it concatenates the strings, inserting a new line character after each.

```
q)` sv ("abc";"de")
"abc\nde\n"
```

When (sv) is used with a long first parameter (*base*) that is greater than 1, together with a second parameter of a simple list of place values expressed in *base*, the result is a long representing the converted base 10 value.

```
q)2 sv 101010b
42
```

```
q)10 sv 1 2 3 4 2
12342
```

```
q)256 sv 0x001092
4242
```

More precisely, the last version of (sv) evaluates the polynomial,

$$(d[n-1]*b \text{ exp } n-1) + \ldots +d[0]$$

where d is the list of digits, n is the count of d, and b is the base.

Thus, we find,

```
q)10 sv 1 2 3 11 2
12412
```

```
q)-10 sv 2 1 5
195
```

A.94 svar

The monadic (svar) returns the statistical standard variance of its numeric list argument.

```
q)svar 2 3 5 7
4.916667
```

It is equivalent to,

```
{var[x]*count[x]%-1+count x}
```

> **_Warning_**: The (svar) function was added in version 3.2 meaning that Finance apps can no longer use a variable name "svar" for stress value at risk in this and later versions.

A.95 system

The monadic (system) takes a string argument and executes it is a q command, if recognized, or an OS command otherwise. This is convenient to execute q commands programmatically. The normal result of the command becomes the return value of the evaluation.

Do **not** include the initial '\' as you would when executing the command from the q session prompt.

```
q)system "c"
25 80i
q)system "c 40 400"
q)system "c"
40 400i
```

```
q)system "cd /data"
q)system "pwd"
"/data"
```

A.96 take/reshape (#)

The dyadic function (#) has several forms.

When the first parameter of (#) is an integer atom (*count*), it returns *count* items from the atom or list second parameter (*source*). The items are extracted from the head when *source* is positive and from the tail when count is *negative*. When *count* is zero, the result is an empty list of the same type as the first item in *source*. When *count* is greater than the count of *source*, items are repeatedly drawn from *source* as described until *count* items are obtained.

> **Tip:** The result of take is always a list.

```
q)2#10 20 30 40 50
10 20
```

```
q)-3#10 20 30 40 50
30 40 50
```

```
q)0#10 20 30 40 5
`long$()
```

```
q)3#42
42 42 42
```

```
q)10#10 20 30 40 5
10 20 30 40 5 10 20 30 40 5
```

The idiom 0#atom is a common way to create an empty list of the type of atom.

```
q)meta ([] a:0#0; b:0#`)
c| t f a
-| -----
a| j
b| s
```

Since a dictionary is ordered, take also applies to dictionaries and, by extension, to tables and keyed tables.

```
q)2#`a`b`c!10 20 30
a| 10
b| 20
```

```
q)-2#([] c1:`a`b`c; c2:10 20 30)
c1 c2
-----
b  20
c  30
```

```
q)2#([k:`a`b`c] v:10 20 30)
k| v
-| --
a| 10
b| 20
```

Another form of take has first parameter a list of keys and the second parameter a dictionary. The result is the sub-dictionary for these keys.

```
q)`a`c#`a`b`c!10 20 30
a| 10
c| 30
```

Since a table is a column dictionary this form also applies to a table with a list of column names.

```
q)`c1`c2#([] c1:`a`b`c; c2:10 20 30; c3:1.1 2.2 3.3)
c1 c2
-----
a  10
b  20
c  30
```

Using an anonymous table is a nifty way to generate a list of keys for takes with a keyed table.

```
q)([] k:`a`c)#([k:`a`b`c] v:10 20 30)
k| v
-| --
a| 10
c| 30
```

Another form of take has first parameter a list $(r; c)$ of two non-negative integers and second parameter a list or atom (*source*). The result is a nested list with r items, each having c items, drawn sequentially from the beginning of *source*, repeatedly if necessary. Otherwise put, the result is an r by c array obtained by reshaping *source*.

```
q)2 3#10 20 30 40 50
10 20 30
40 50 10
```

If in the previous form either r or c is null, the result is a nested list obtained by reshaping the second parameter into the specified number of rows or columns. This is generally a ragged array.

```
q)2 0N#10 20 30 40 50
10 20 30
40 50
q)0N 3#10 20 30 40 50
10 20 30
40 5
```

A.97 tan

The atomic (tan) takes a float and returns its mathematical tangent.

```
q)tan 0
0f
```

```
q)pi:3.141592653589793
q)tan pi
-1.224647e-16
```

```
q)tan pi%2
1.633124e+16
```

```
q)tan pi%4
1f
```

```
q)tan pi%8
0.4142136
```

The function (tan) is equivalent to

```
(sin x)%cos x
```

A.98 til

The monadic (til) takes a non-negative long parameter (*n*) and returns a list of *n* consecutive longs starting with 0.

> **Tip:** The argument is not including in the result.

```
q)til 4
0 1 2 3
```

```
q)count til 1000000
1000000
```

The result of (til) is always a list.

```
q)til 0
`long$()
```

```
q)til 1
,0
```

To generate other regular numeric sequences, perform vector operations on the result of (til).

```
q)1+til 10
1 2 3 4 5 6 7 8 9 10
```

```
q)2*til 10
0 2 4 6 8 10 12 14 16 18
```

```
q)1+2*til 10
1 3 5 7 9 11 13 15 17 19
```

```
q).5*til 10
0 0.5 1 1.5 2 2.5 3 3.5 4 4.5
```

```
q)2015.01.01+til 5
2015.01.01 2015.01.02 2015.01.03 2015.01.04 2015.01.05
```

A.99 trim

The monadic (trim) takes a string argument and returns the result of removing leading and trailing blanks.

```
q)trim "   abc   "
"abc"
```

The function (trim) is equivalent to,

```
{ltrim rtrim x}.
```

A.100 ungroup

The monadic (ungroup) flattens tables with nested columns that are the result of a select query that groups without aggregation, or of (xgroup). Of course you can also apply it to tables with nested columns of the same form that are otherwise generated.

The action of (ungroup) expands each key group, resulting in one row for each item in the nested columns. The fields in a result row are drawn from corresponding positions across the nested columns.

We use the distribution example.

```
q)\l sp.q
+`p`city!(`p$`p1`p2`p3`p4`p5`p6`p1`p2;`london`london`london`london`lond
on`lon..
(`s#+(,`color)!,`s#`blue`green`red)!+(,`qty)!,900 1000 1200
+`s`p`qty!(`s$`s1`s1`s1`s2`s3`s4; `p$`p1`p4`p6`p2`p2`p4;300 200 100 400
200 300)
```

```
q)sp
s  p  qty
---------
s1 p1 300
s1 p2 200
s1 p3 400
s1 p4 200
s4 p5 100
s1 p6 100
s2 p1 300
s2 p2 400
s3 p2 200
```

```
q)select s, qty by p from sp
p | s               qty
--| -------------------------------
p1| `s$`s1`s2        300 300
p2| `s$`s1`s2`s3`s4  200 400 200 200
p3| `s$,`s1          ,400
p4| `s$`s1`s4        200 300
p5| `s$`s4`s1        100 400
p6| `s$,`s1          ,100
```

```
q)ungroup select s, qty by p from sp
p  s  qty
---------
p1 s1 300
p1 s2 300
p2 s1 200
p2 s2 400
p2 s3 200
p2 s4 200
p3 s1 400
p4 s1 200
p4 s4 300
p5 s4 100
p5 s1 400
p6 s1 100
```

```
q)`p xgroup sp
p | s               qty
--| -------------------------------
p1| `s$`s1`s2        300 300
p2| `s$`s1`s2`s3`s4  200 400 200 200
p3| `s$,`s1          ,400
p4| `s$`s1`s4        200 300
p5| `s$`s4`s1        100 400
p6| `s$,`s1          ,100
```

```
q)ungroup `p xgroup sp
p  s  qty
---------
p1 s1 300
p1 s2 300
p2 s1 200
p2 s2 400
p2 s3 200
p2 s4 200
p3 s1 400
p4 s1 200
p4 s4 300
p5 s4 100
p5 s1 400
p6 s1 100
```

> **Tip:** Observe that (ungroup) is not quite the inverse of a grouping operation. Since grouping sorts on the keys, a subsequent (ungroup) returns the original records sorted by the grouped column(s).

A.101 union

The dyadic (union) returns the set theoretic union of its two list parameters. The result has the distinct items of the two parameters in order of their first appearance.

```
q)1 1 2 3 union 2 2 3 4
1 2 3 4
q)"a good time" union "was had by all"
"a godtimewshbyl"
```

Since a table is a list of records, (union) can be used to perform the analogue of SQL UNION for tables having the same schemas.

```
q)([] c1:`a`b`c; c2:10 20 30) union ([] c1:`c`d; c2:300 400)
c1 c2
------
a  10
b  20
c  30
c  300
d  400
```

> **Tip:** Use (uj) for tables that do not have matching schemas—see §9.9.7.

A.102 upper

The atomic (upper) takes a char, string or symbol argument and returns the result of converting any alpha characters to upper case.

```
q)upper `a
`A
```

```
q)upper `a`b
`A`B
```

```
q)upper "a Bc42De"
"A BC42DE"
```

A.103 value

The function (value) also vies for the title as the most overloaded q operator.

> **Tip:** The functions (value) and (get) are identical. Conventionally (get) is used with file I/O.

When (value) is applied to a symbolic variable name, it returns the associated value.

```
q)a:42
q)value `a
42
```

When applied to a dictionary, (value) returns the keys of the dictionary. This includes the special case of the value table of a keyed table.

```
q)value `a`b`c!10 20 30
10 20 30
```

```
q)kt:([k:`a`b`c] v:10 20 30)
q)value kt
_
```

A common idiom uses (value) to extract the columns lists from a table.

```
q)value flip ([] c1:`a`b`c; c2:10 20 30)
a b c
10 20 30
```

When (value) is applied to an enumerated value, it de-enumerates it. This is handy when switching between kdb+ databases having different sym domains.

```
q)sym:()
q)ev:`sym?`a`x`b`y`a`c`b
q)ev
`sym$`a`x`b`y`a`c`b
q)value ev
`a`x`b`y`a`c`b
```

Given a function, (value) returns the following list,

```
(bytecode;parms;locals;(context;globals);constants[0];...;constants[n];defn)
```

```
q)f:{[a;b]d::neg c:a*b+42;c+e}
q)value f
0xa0794178430316220b048100028276410004
`a`b
,`c
`.`d`e
42
"{[a;b]d::neg c:a*b+42;c+e}"q)sym:()
```

Given an alias (aka "view"), (value) returns the list

```
(cached value;parse tree;dependencies;definition)
```

When the evaluation of the expression in the alias is as yet deferred, the cached value is ::.

```
q)a:42
q)b::a+1             / evaluation is deferred
q)value `.[`b]       / inspect global context
::
(+;`a;1)
,`a
"a+1"

q)b                  / force evaluation
43
q)value `.[`b]
43
(+;`a;1)
,`a
"a+1"
```

Given a projection, (value) returns a list containing the function body followed by the supplied arguments.

```
q)f:{x+y+z}
q)value f[2;3;]
{x+y+z}
2
3
::

q)value +[2]
_
```

Given a function that is the result of applying a k adverb, (value) returns the argument to the adverb, viewing the latter as a higher order function.

```
q)value (+/)
+
q)value (+')
+
q)f:{x+y}
q)value (f')
{x+y}
```

The final and most powerful form of (value) is that it is the q interpreter itself. It will evaluate a string as if it had been typed at the console.

```
q)value "6*7"
42
q)value "{x*x} til 10"
0 1 4 9 16 25 36 49 64 81
```

It will also evaluate a parse tree—i.e., a (potentially) nested list of functions followed by arguments. If the function is specified by name, that name is resolved first.

```
q)value (*; 6; 7)
42
q)f:{x*y}
q)value (`f; 6; 7)
42
```

Important: This use of the (value) function is a powerful feature that allows q code to be written and executed on the fly. This can expose your program to potential attack unless done very carefully. If abused, it can quickly lead to unmaintainable code. (The spellchecker suggests "unmentionable" instead of "unmaintainable." How did it know?)

A.104 var

The aggregate (var) takes a numeric list and returns the mathematical variance of the items as a float.

```
q)var 42 45 37 38
13.66667
```

The function (var) is equivalent to

```
{(avg[x*x]) - (avg[x])*(avg[x])}
```

A.105 vs

The dyadic (vs)—"vector from scalar"—has several versions.   It is usually written infix for ease of reading.

The first form takes a char as its first parameter and a string (*source*) as its second parameter. It returns a list of strings containing the tokens of *source* as delimited by the specified char.

```
q)" " vs "Now is the time "
"Now"
"is"
"the"
"time"
""
```

Tip: You probably want to trim the input in the above example.

When (vs) is used with an empty symbol as its first parameter and a symbol second parameter (*source*) containing dots, it returns a simple symbol list obtained by splitting *source* along the dots.

```
q)` vs `qalib.stat
`qalib`stat
```

When (vs) is used with an empty symbol as its first parameter and a symbol representing a fully qualified file name as the second parameter, it returns a simple list of symbols in which the first item is the path and the second item is the file name. Note that in this usage, (vs) is not quite the inverse of (sv).

```
q)` vs `qalib.stat
`qalib`stat
```

When (vs) is used with a null of binary type as the first parameter and an value of integer type as the second parameter (*source*), it returns a simple list whose items comprise the digits of the corresponding binary representation of *source*.

```
q)0x00 vs 4242
0x0000000000001092
```

```
q)10h$0x00 vs 8151631268726338926j
"q is fun"
```

```
q)0b vs 42
0000000000000000000000000000000000000000000000000000000000101010b
```

The 0b version can be used to display the internal representation of special values.

```
q)0b vs 0w
0111111111111111111111111111111111111111111111111111111111111111b
q)0b vs -0w
1000000000000000000000000000000000000000000000000000000000000001b
```

A.106 wavg

The dyadic (wavg) takes two numeric lists of the same count and returns the float average of the items in the second parameter, weighted by the items of the first.

```
q)1 2 3 4 wavg 500 400 300 200
300f
```

The function (wavg) is equivalent to,

```
{(sum x*y)%sum x}
```

It is possible to apply (wavg) to a nested list provided all sublists of both parameters conform. In this context, the result conforms to the sublists and the weighted average is calculated recursively across the sublists.

```
q)(1 2;3 4) wavg (500 400; 300 200)
350 266.6667
```

A.107 where

The monadic (where) has two forms.

The first form returns the indices of 1b in a boolean list, or the keys associated to 1b in a dictionary with boolean values.

```
q)where 101010b
0 2 4
q)where `a`b`c`d`e`f!101010b
`a`c`e
```

This is useful when the boolean mapping is the result of a predicate.

```
q)where ","="First, second, third"
5 13
```

```
q)@[L; where L=","; :; "\t"]
"First\t second\t third"
```

```
q)where null `a`b`c`d`e`f!1 0n 3 4 0n 6
`b`e
```

When the argument of (where) is a list of non-negative long (c), the result is a list obtained by catenating c[i] copies of i, for each item in c.

```
q)where 2 1 3
0 0 1 2 2 2
q)where 2 1 0 3 2
0 0 1 3 3 3 4 4
q)where 4#1
0 1 2 3
```

> **Zen Moment**: The second form of (where) generalizes the form on a boolean list.

A.108 within

The dyadic (within) is atomic in its first parameter (*source*) and takes a second parameter that is a list (b;e) that are comparable. It returns a boolean representing whether *source* is greater than or equal to b and less than or equal to e. It will do type promotion on arguments.

```
q)3 within 2 5
1b
```

```
q)(til 7)within 2 5
0011110b
```

```
q)"c" within "az"
1b
```

```
q)2015.03.14 within 2015.02.01 2015
1b
```

```
q)`ab within `a`b
1b
```

```
q)100 within "aj"
1b
```

> **Tip:** Ensure the items in the second argument are in increasing order or you will get no matches.

A.109 wsum

The dyadic (wsum) takes two numeric lists of the same count and returns the float sum of the items of second parameter weighted by the items of the first.

```
q)1 2 3 4 wsum 500 400 300 200
3000f
```

The function (wsum) is equivalent to,

```
{sum x*y}
```

It is possible to apply (wsum) to a nested list provided all sublists of both arguments conform. In this case, the result conforms to the sublists and the weighted sum is calculated recursively across the sublists.

```
q)(1 2;3 4) wsum (500 400;300 200)
1400 1600
```

A.110 xbar

The uniform dyadic (xbar) takes first parameter a non-negative numeric atom (*width*) and returns the smallest integral multiple of *width* that is less than or equal to its second parameter. Visually, the result is the left endpoint of the band of width *width* that contains the second parameter. Since (xbar) is atomic in the second parameter, this is an effective way to bin the items in a numeric list.

```
q)1 xbar 0 .5 1 1.5 2 2.5 3 3.5
0 0 1 1 2 2 3 3f
```

```
q)1.5 xbar 0 .5 1 1.5 2 2.5 3 3.5
0 0 0 1.5 1.5 1.5 3 3
```

```
q)2 xbar 0 .5 1 1.5 2 2.5 3 3.5
0 0 0 0 2 2 2 2f
```

Since a q month is actually the count of months since the millennium, you can use (xbar) to determine quarters. Recall that a month is equal to the first day of the month.

```
q)`date$3 xbar `month$2015.11.19      / beginning of that quarter
2015.10.01
q)`date$3+3 xbar `month$2015.11.19    / beginning of next quarter

q)-1+`date$3+3 xbar `month$2015.11.19  / end of that quarter

```

A.111 xprev

The dyadic (xprev) takes a long as its first parameter (*shift*) and shifts the list in its second parameter by *shift* positions. When *shift* is 0 or

549

positive, the shift is forward; otherwise it is backward. The beginning—respectively end—of the list is filled with *shift* null (or empty) items.

```
q)2 xprev 10 20 30 40 50
0N 0N 10 20 30
```

```
q)-2 xprev 10 20 30 40 50
30 40 50 0N 0N
```

```
q)2 xprev (1 2 3; 4 5; enlist 6; 7 8)
`long$()
`long$()
1 2 3
4 5
```

A.112 xrank

The dyadic (xrank) has first parameter a positive long (*n*) and is uniform in its second parameter (*source*). It returns a list of long containing the *n*-quantile into which each item of *source* falls, considering *source* as a distribution. For example, choosing *n* to be 4 returns quartiles and 100 yields percentiles.

```
q)4 xrank 30 10 40 20 90
1 0 2 0 3
```

```
q)100 xrank 200?1000.
35 14 30 96 19 68 39 21 91 73 27 79 30 66 27 79 75 8 99 84 84 77 ..
```

B Error Messages

B.1 Runtime Errors

Error	Example	Description
Access		Attempt to read files above directory, run system commands or failed usr/pwd
Assign	cos:12	Attempt to reuse a reserved word
Conn		Too many incoming connections (1022 max)
Domain	til -1	Argument out of domain
Fail	`s#3 2	Invalid attribute setting
Glim		As of q3.2 there is no limit on number of `g# attrbutes
Length	(til 2)+til 3	Incompatible list lengths
limit		Attempt to create list longer than allowable maximum (2 billion in q2.*) or trying to serialize an object > 2GB in any version.
loop	a::b::a	Circular reference loop
mismatch		Columns cannot be aligned for operation
mlim		More than 999 nested columns in splayed table
nyi		Not yet implemented
os		Operating system error
pl		peach can't handle parallel lambda's (2.3 only)
Q7		Unimplemented op on file nested array
rank	+[2;3;4]	Invalid rank or valence
splay		Unimplimented op on splayed table
stack		Exhausted stack space
stop		User interrupt(ctrl-c) or time limit (-T)
stype	'42	Invalid type used to signal
type	til 4.2	Wrong type
value		Missing value
vdl		Attempted multithread update
wsfull		malloc failed. ran out of swap (or addressability on 32bit). or hit -w limit
xxx	'xxx	*xxx* undefined

551

B.2 Parse Errors

Error	Example	Description

(
)
[
]
{
}
"
		Unpaired item

branch		A branch (if;do;while;$[.;.;.]) more than 255 byte codes away
char		Invalid character
constants		Too many constants (max 96)
globals		Too many global variables (255 max)
locals		Too many local variables (24 max)
params		Too many parameters (8 max)

B.3 System Errors

Error	Example	Description

xxx:yyy		*xxx* is a kdb+ message
		yyy is the OS message
		
		xxx can be
		  addr
		  close
		  conn
		  p (from –p)
		  snd
		  rcv
		  filename (invalid)

B.4 License Errors

Error	Example	Description
cpu		Exceeded number of licensed cpu's
exp		Expiry date passed
host		Unlicensed host
k4.lic		k4.lic file not found, check QHOME/QLIC
os		Unlicensed OS
srv		Attempt to use client-only license in server mod
upd		Attempt to use version of kdb+ more recent than update date
user		Unlicensed user
wha		Invalid system date

Index

564

End

```
q)\\
```

Made in the USA
San Bernardino, CA
15 October 2016